MOMOGUMI PLUS SENKI

Volume 2

Created by Eri SAKONDO

HAMBURG // LONDON // LOS ANGELES // TOKYO

Momogumi Plus Senki Volume 2
Created by Eri SAKONDO

Translation - Aimi Tokutake
English Adaptation - Rachel Brown
Retouch and Lettering - Star Print Brokers
Production Artist - Rui Kyo
Graphic Designer - Al-Insan Lashley

Editor - Cindy Suzuki
Print Production Manager - Lucas Rivera
Managing Editor - Vy Nguyen
Senior Designer - Louis Csontos
Art Director - Al-Insan Lashley
Associate Publisher - Marco F. Pavia
President and C.O.O. - John Parker
C.E.O. and Chief Creative Officer - Stu Levy

A  Manga

TOKYOPOP and are trademarks or registered trademarks of TOKYOPOP Inc.

TOKYOPOP Inc.
5900 Wilshire Blvd. Suite 2000
Los Angeles, CA 90036

E-mail: info@TOKYOPOP.com
Come visit us online at www.TOKYOPOP.com

MOMOGUMI PLUS SENKI Volume 2 © Eri SAKONDO 2006
First published in Japan in 2006 by KADOKAWA SHOTEN
PUBLISHING CO., LTD., Tokyo. English translation rights
arranged with KADOKAWA SHOTEN PUBLISHING
CO., LTD., Tokyo through TUTTLE–MORI AGENCY, INC., Tokyo.
English text copyright © 2009 TOKYOPOP Inc.

ISBN: 978-1-4278-1563-7

First TOKYOPOP printing: January 2010
10 9 8 7 6 5 4 3 2 1
Printed in the USA

MOMOGUMI PLUS SENKI

ERI SAKONDO

Volume 2

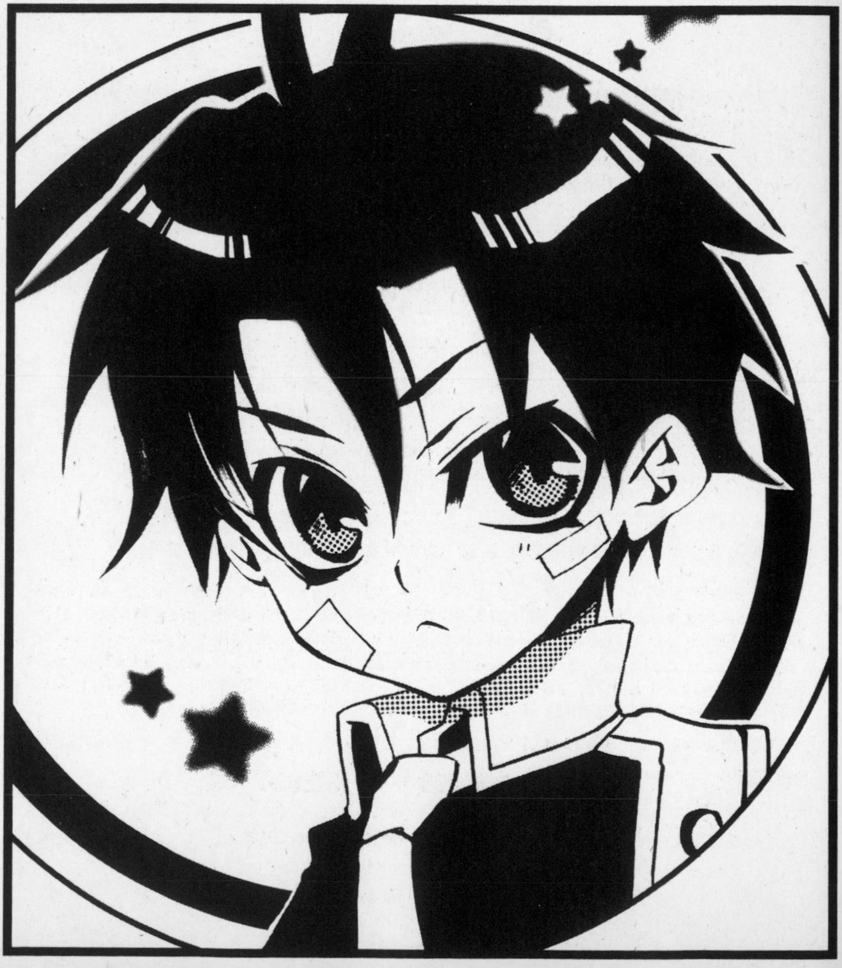

Characters & Story So Far

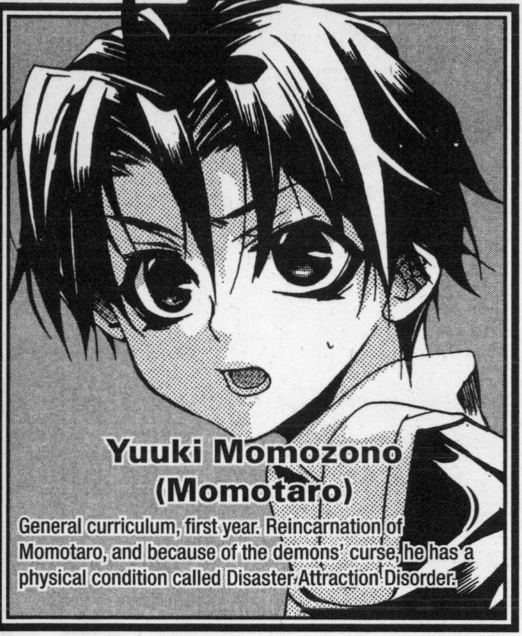
Yuuki Momozono
(Momotaro)
General curriculum, first year. Reincarnation of Momotaro, and because of the demons' curse, he has a physical condition called Disaster Attraction Disorder.

Yuuki's Disaster Attraction Disorder keeps him from making any friends because he's so dangerous to be around. After transferring into Aitan Gakuen, the gigantic, mysterious school, he immediately finds out that that he's the reincarnation of a demon hunter who was the basis for the Japanese folktale "Momotaro." It turns out that he has Disaster Attraction Disorder because he was cursed by demons—and that if he doesn't break the curse by the time he's 18, he's going to die! Yuuki, along with his companions the pheasant, monkey and dog who join forces with him, swears to defeat the demons and take back his happiness.

After defeating the friendly Red Demon, he obtains the Kibi Dango, the legendary weapon. After that, Yuuki manages to beat the Green Demon. The demons' locations or how many there are left to defeat, is still unknown. In the midst of haunting anxiety, time continues to pass by, minute by minute. What enemies will Yuuki and his friends have to face?

Jyuki

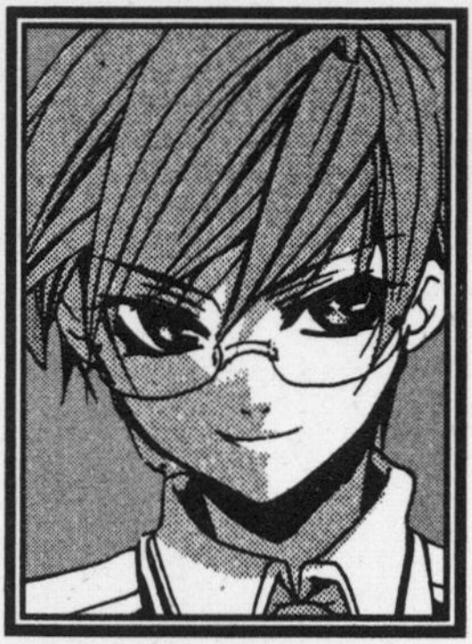

Masahiko Inukai

(Dog)

Math and science curriculum, first year. Always gets picked on.

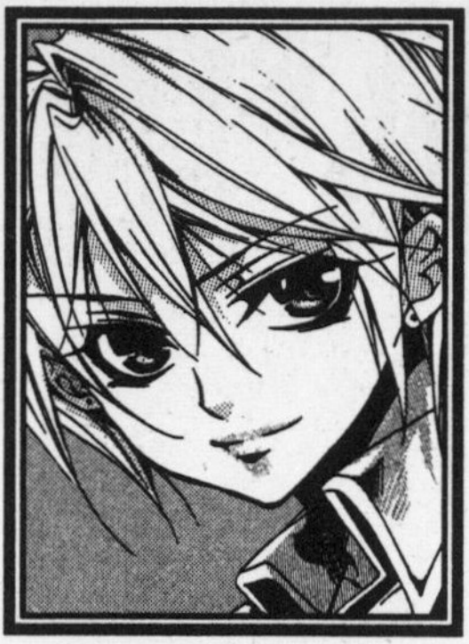

Sawa Koenji

(Monkey)

Physical education curriculum, first year. His personality gets him into a lot of fights.

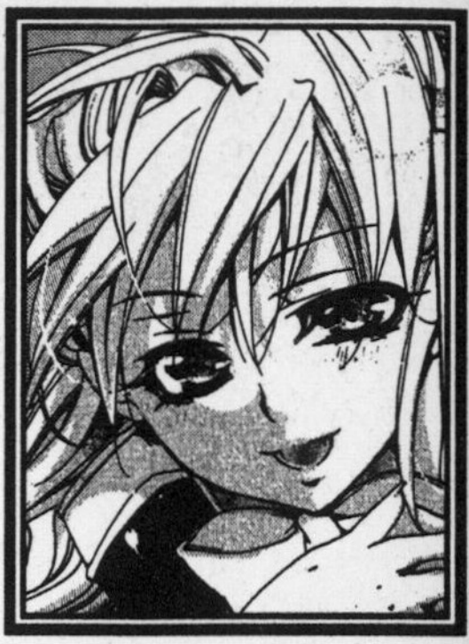

Yukishiro Kijinogi

(Pheasant)

Literature curriculum, first year. A beautiful girl but she tends to get nosebleeds.

The Reincarnates

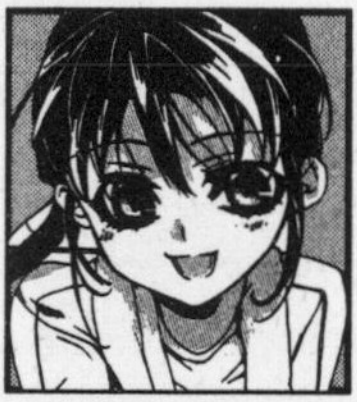

Kiyoko Shibaura

(Grandpa)

Agriculture curriculum, second year. Very macho despite her looks.

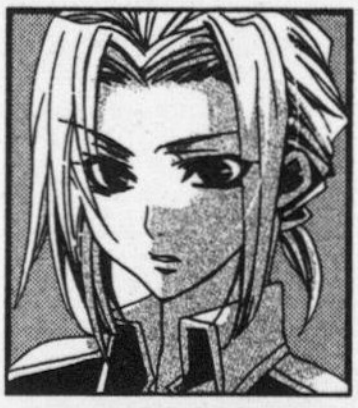

Ryoichi Kawahara

(Grandma)

Home economics curriculum, second year. A sewing expert.

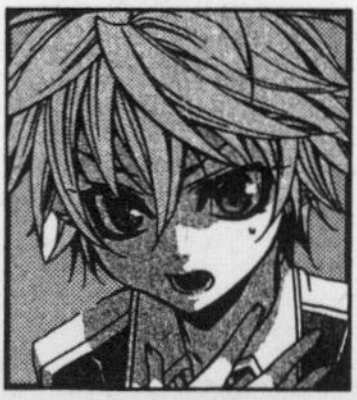

Shinya Wanno

(Issun Boushi)

Literature curriculum, first year. Demons cursed him, and he can't grow any taller.

Demons

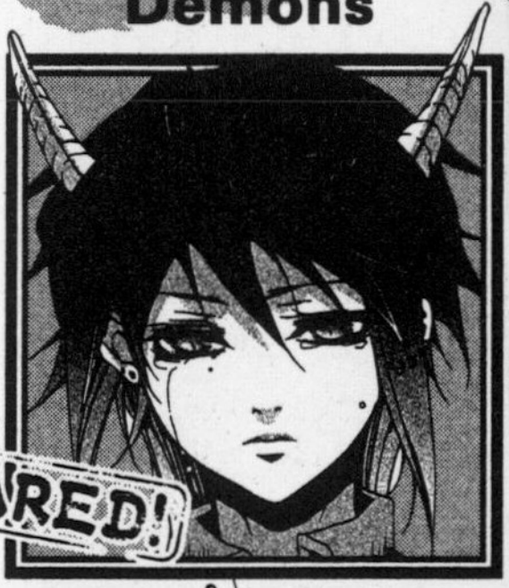
CLEARED!

Ko Kureuchi

(Red Demon)

Talent and entertainment curriculum, first year. A popular model, and now Yuuki's friend.

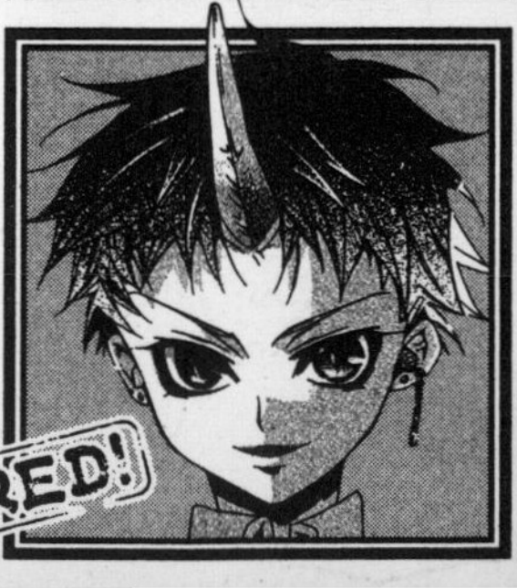
CLEARED!

Uraha Yanagi

(Green Demon)

Vocal performance curriculum, first year. A boy soprano soloist.

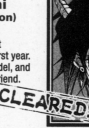

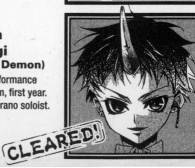

MOMOGUMI PLUS SENKI

CONTENTS

Chapter 6

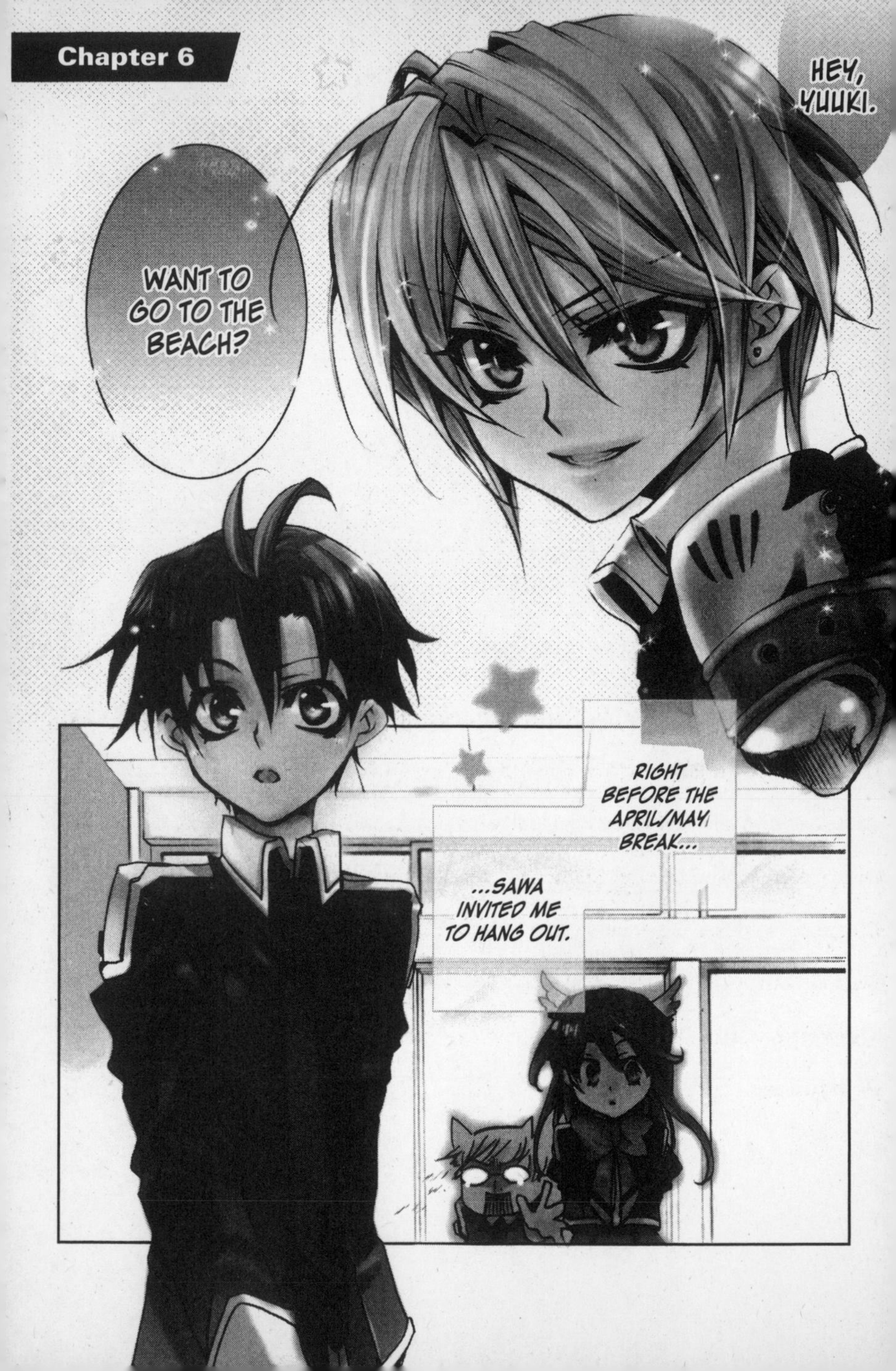
HEY, YUUKI.
WANT TO GO TO THE BEACH?
RIGHT BEFORE THE APRIL/MAY BREAK...
...SAWA INVITED ME TO HANG OUT.

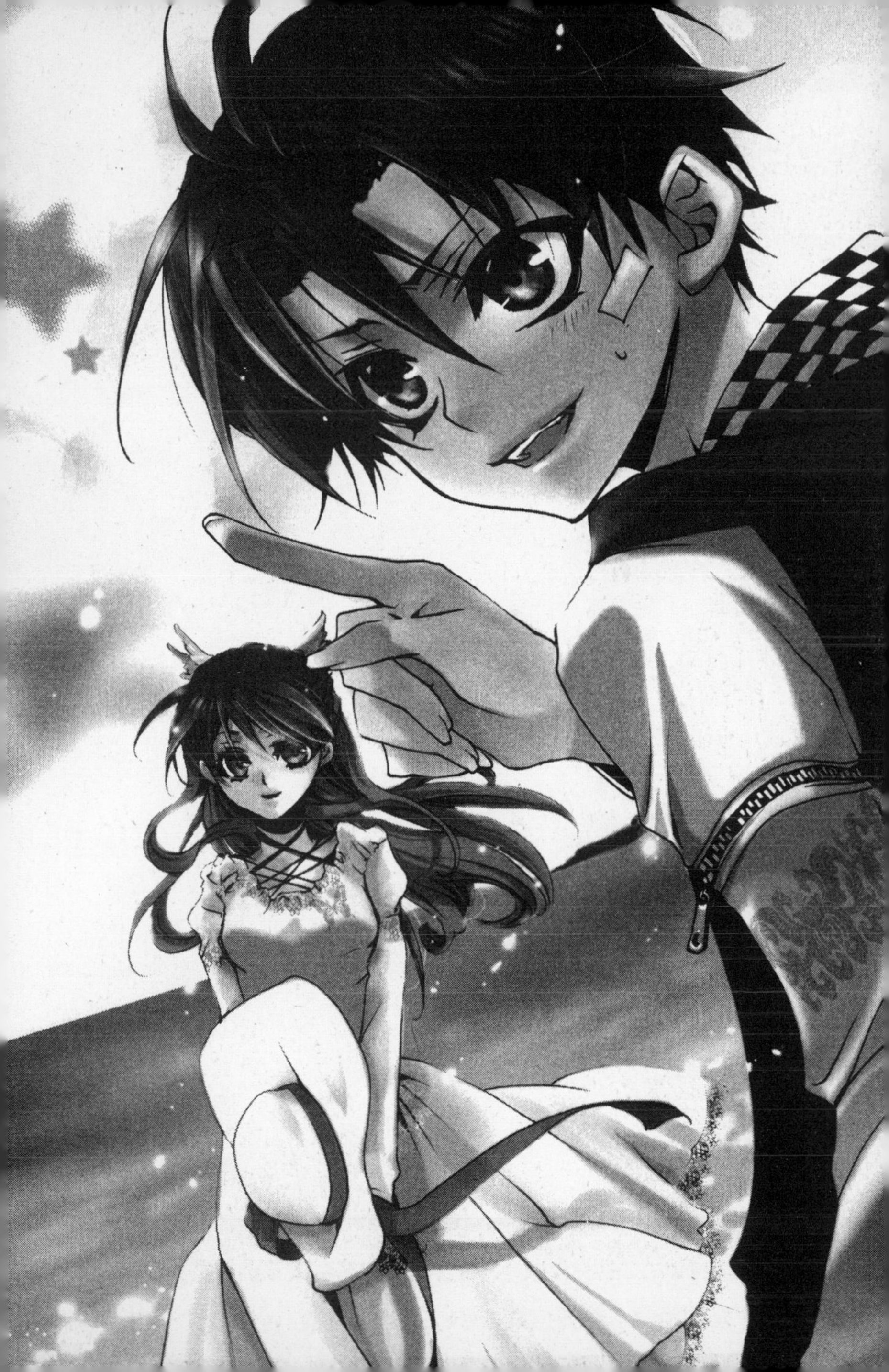

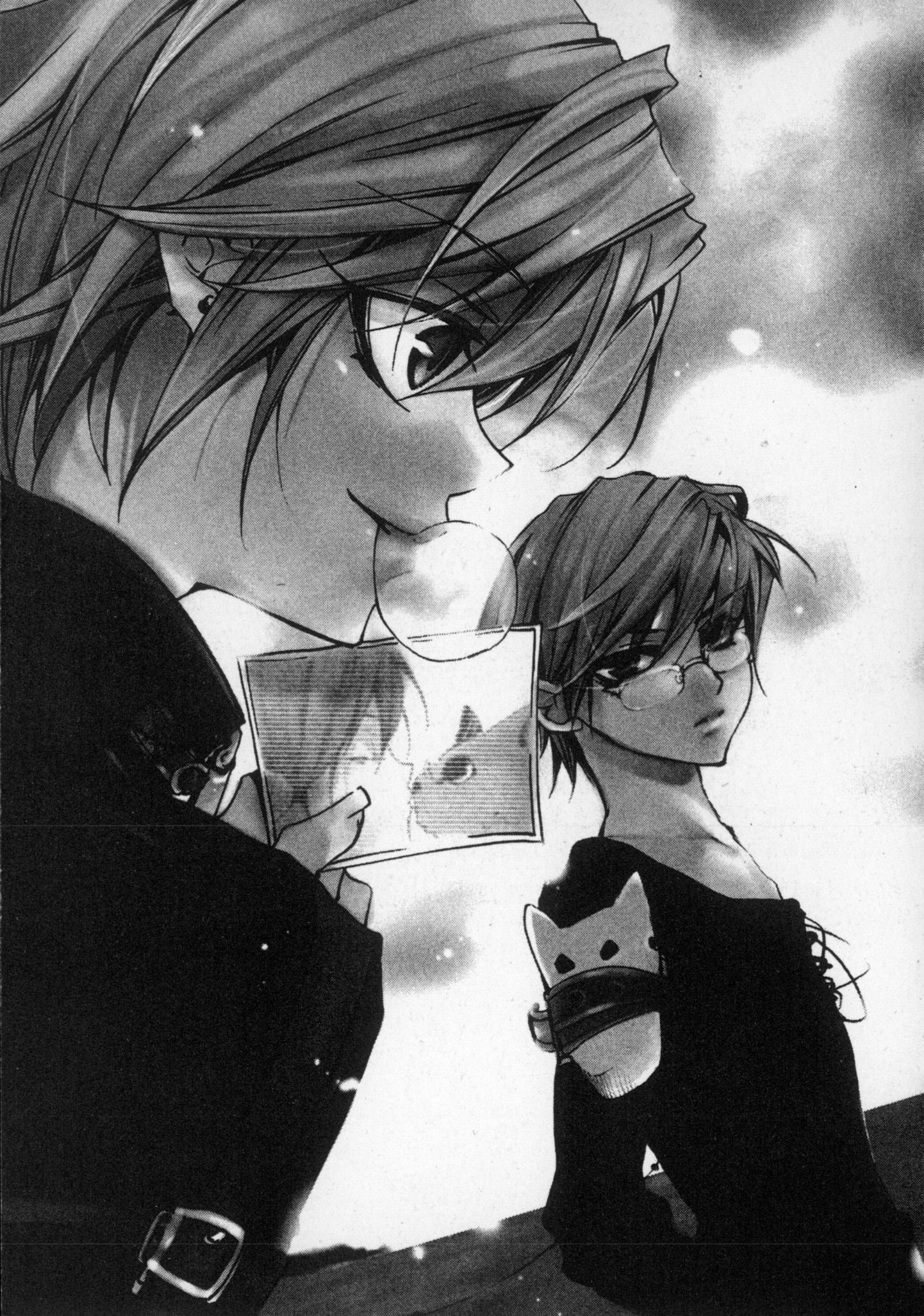

Chapter 6: The Beasts' Secret Gathering in May, Part 1

桃組+戦記

プラス

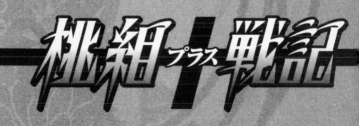

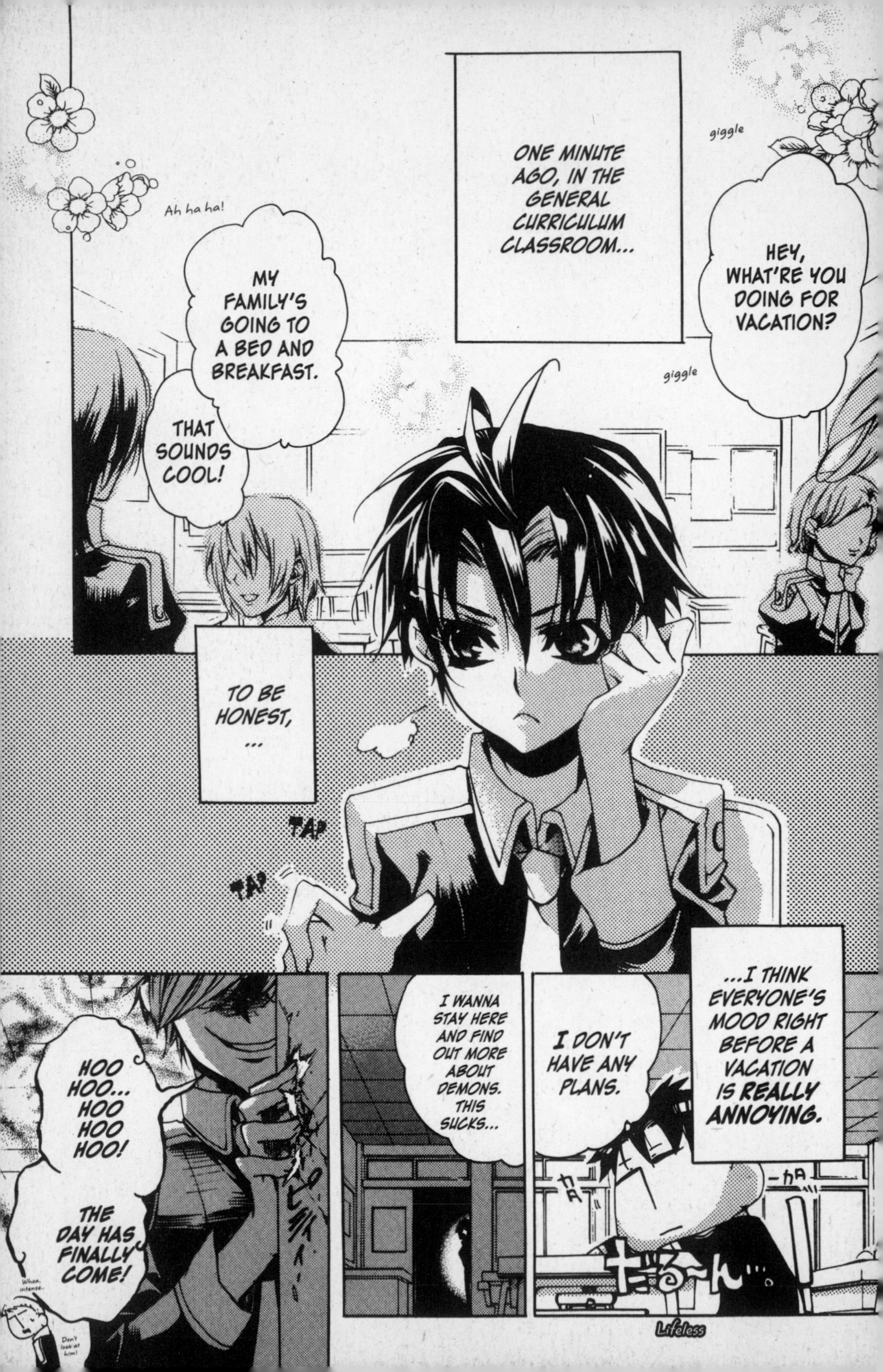
ONE MINUTE AGO, IN THE GENERAL CURRICULUM CLASSROOM...
giggle
HEY, WHAT'RE YOU DOING FOR VACATION?
giggle
Ah ha ha!
MY FAMILY'S GOING TO A BED AND BREAKFAST.
THAT SOUNDS COOL!
TO BE HONEST, ...
TAP
TAP
...I THINK EVERYONE'S MOOD RIGHT BEFORE A VACATION IS REALLY ANNOYING.
I DON'T HAVE ANY PLANS.
Lifeless
I WANNA STAY HERE AND FIND OUT MORE ABOUT DEMONS. THIS SUCKS...
HOO HOO... HOO HOO HOO!
THE DAY HAS FINALLY COME!
Whoa, intense...
Don't look at him!

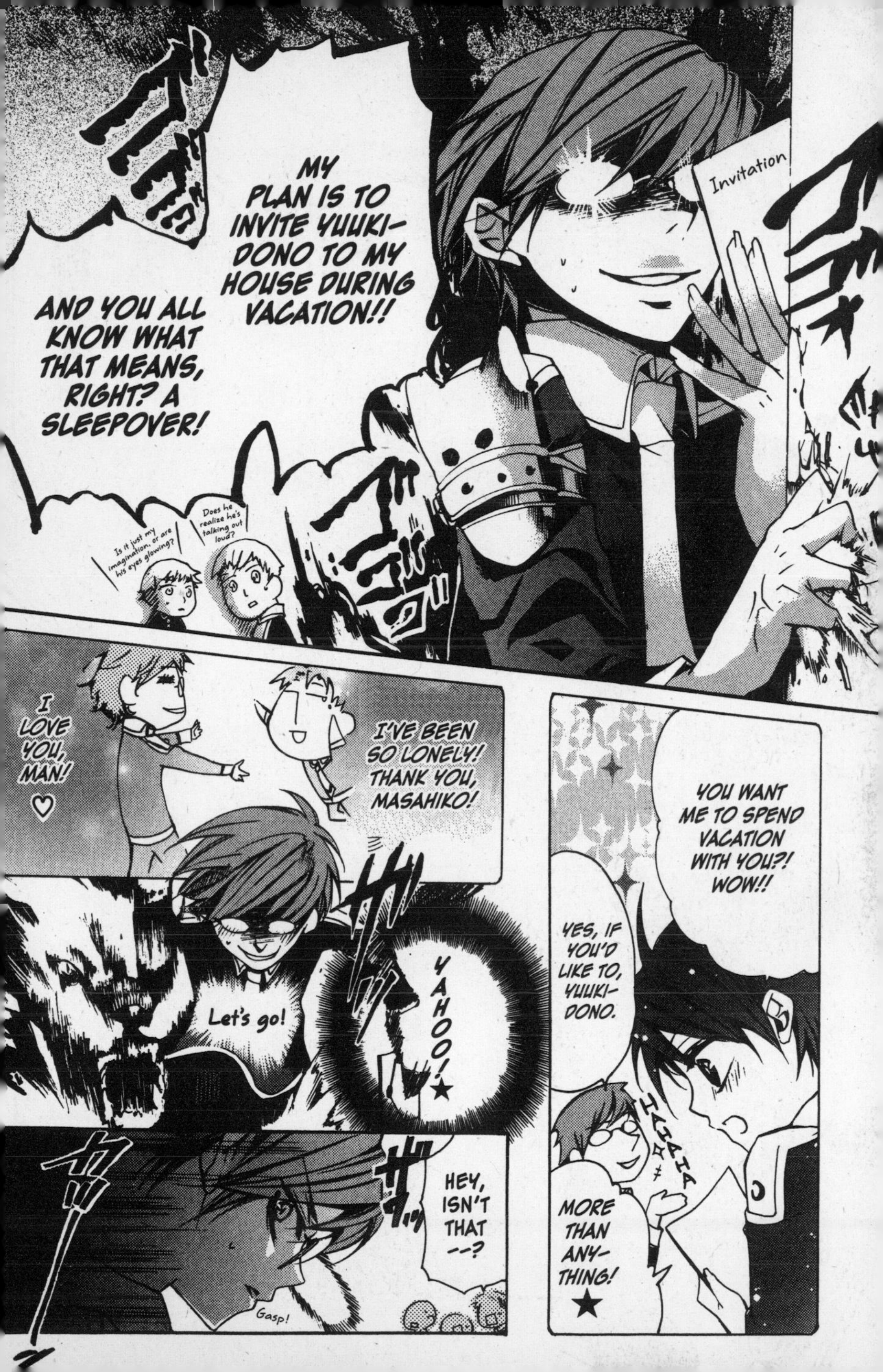
Invitation
MY PLAN IS TO INVITE YUUKI-DONO TO MY HOUSE DURING VACATION!!
AND YOU ALL KNOW WHAT THAT MEANS, RIGHT? A SLEEPOVER!
Does he realize he's talking out loud?
Is it just my imagination, or are his eyes glowing?
YOU WANT ME TO SPEND VACATION WITH YOU?! WOW!!
YES, IF YOU'D LIKE TO, YUUKI-DONO.
HAHAHA
MORE THAN ANY-THING! ★
I'VE BEEN SO LONELY! THANK YOU, MASAHIKO!
I LOVE YOU, MAN! ♡
YAHOO!★
Let's go!
HEY, ISN'T THAT --?
Gasp!

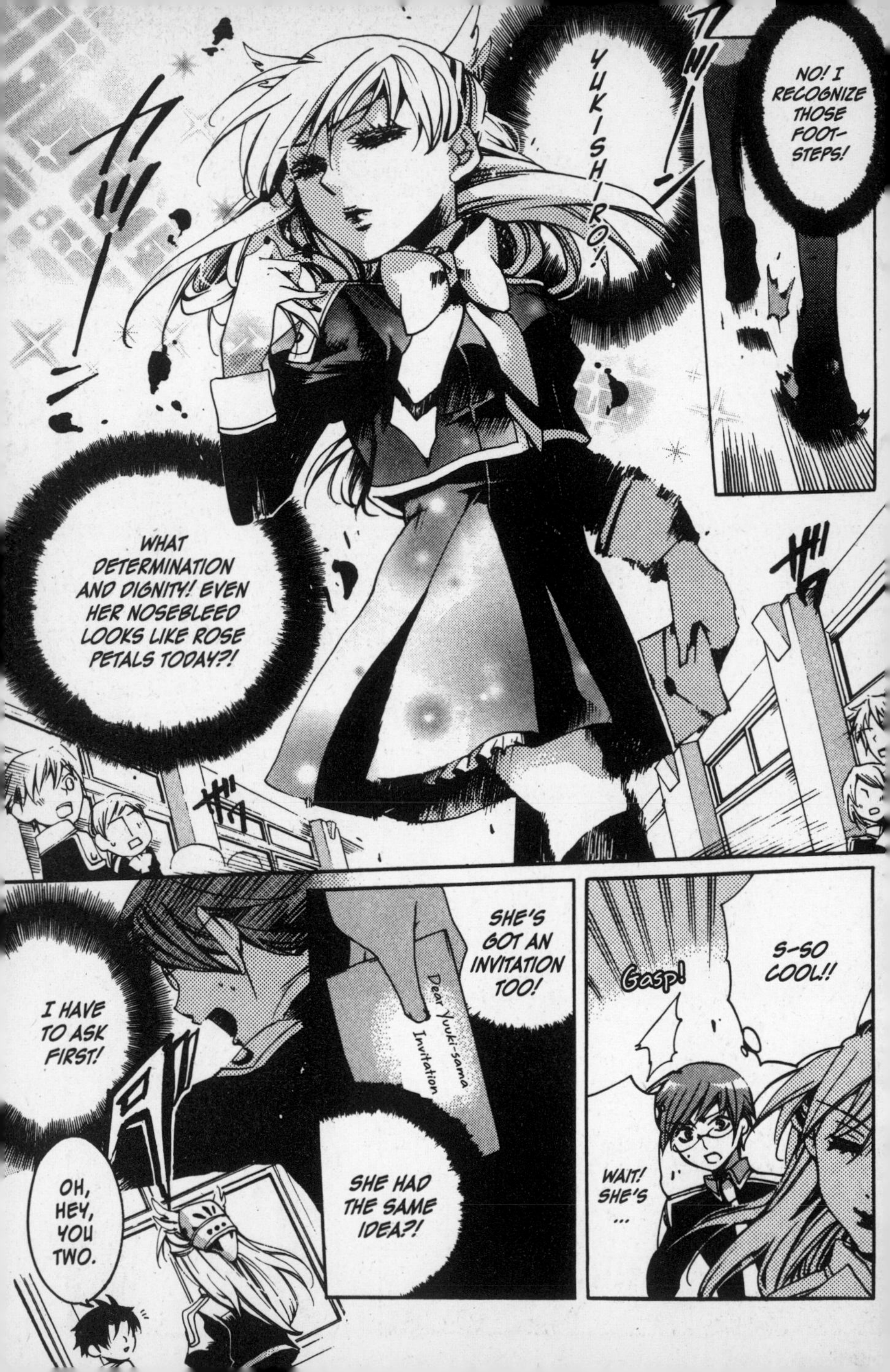
NO! I RECOGNIZE THOSE FOOT-STEPS!
YUKISHIRO...!
WHAT DETERMINATION AND DIGNITY! EVEN HER NOSEBLEED LOOKS LIKE ROSE PETALS TODAY?!
S-SO COOL!!
Gasp!
WAIT! SHE'S ...
SHE'S GOT AN INVITATION TOO!
Dear Yuuki-sama
Invitation
SHE HAD THE SAME IDEA?!
I HAVE TO ASK FIRST!
OH, HEY, YOU TWO.

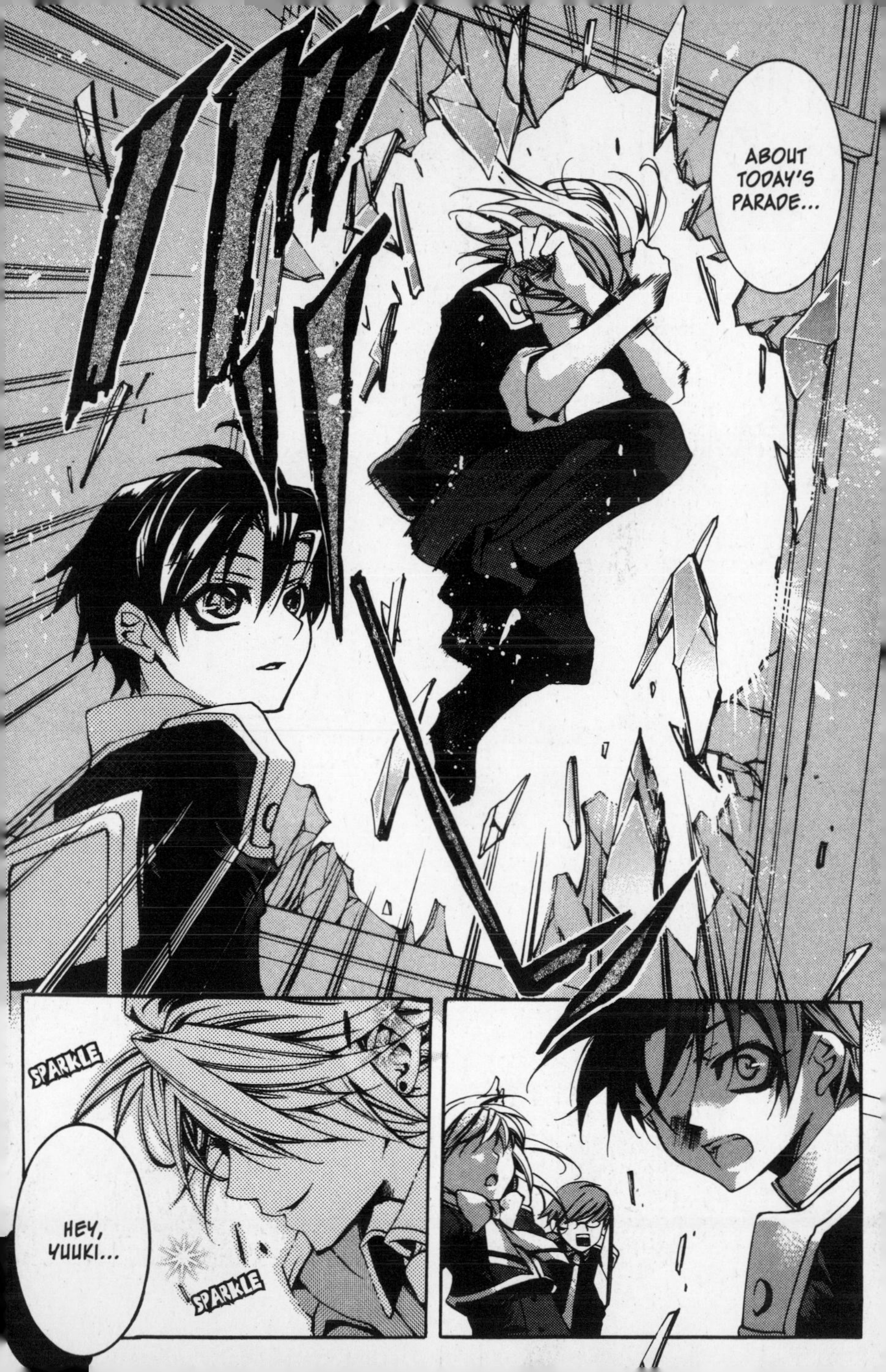
ABOUT TODAY'S PARADE...
SPARKLE
HEY, YUUKI...
SPARKLE

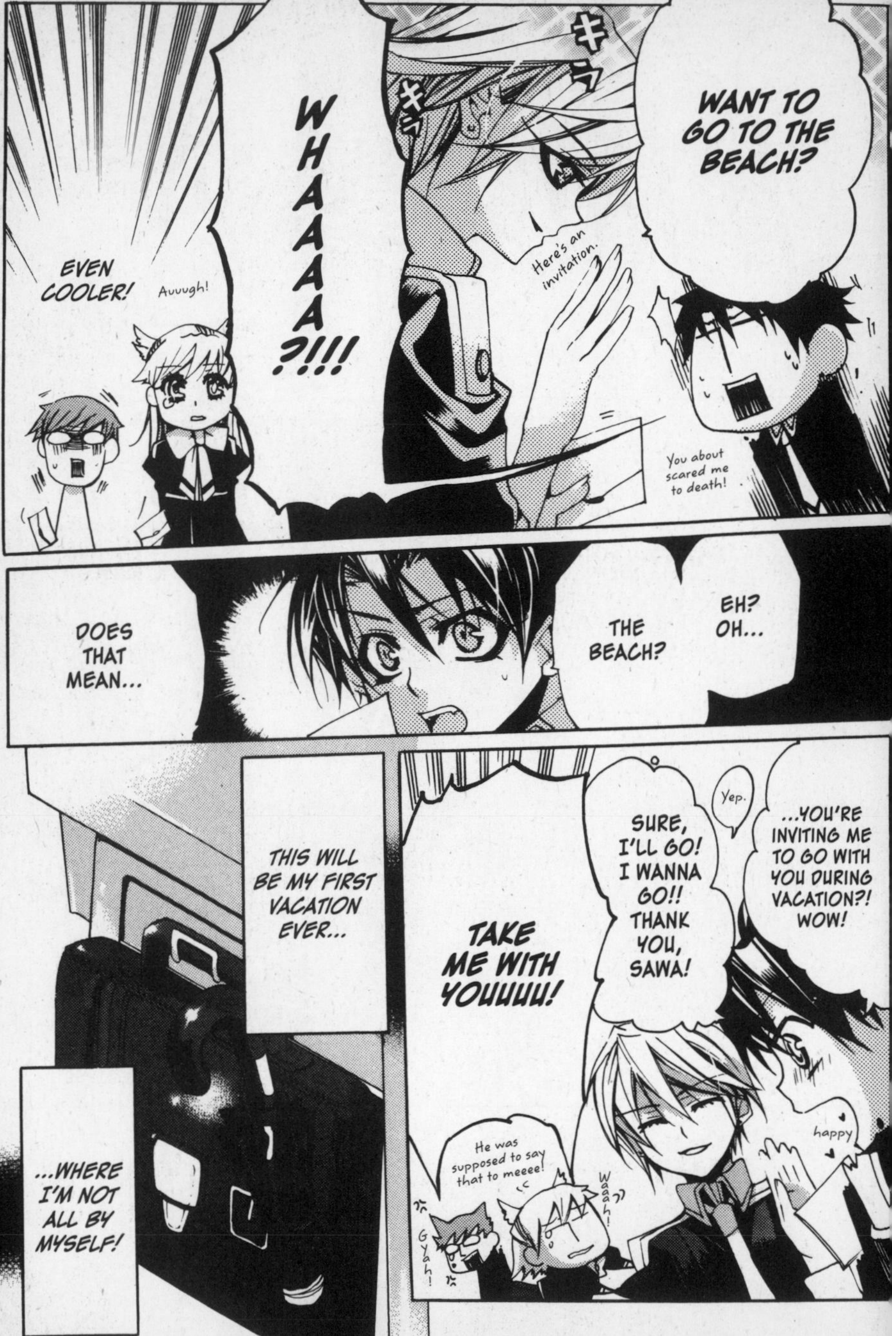
WANT TO GO TO THE BEACH?
Here's an invitation.
You about scared me to death!
WHAAAAA?!!!
Auuugh!
EVEN COOLER!
EH? OH...
THE BEACH?
DOES THAT MEAN...
...YOU'RE INVITING ME TO GO WITH YOU DURING VACATION?! WOW!
Yep.
SURE, I'LL GO! I WANNA GO!! THANK YOU, SAWA!
TAKE ME WITH YOUUUU!
happy
He was supposed to say that to meeee!
Waaah!
Gyah!
THIS WILL BE MY FIRST VACATION EVER...
...WHERE I'M NOT ALL BY MYSELF!

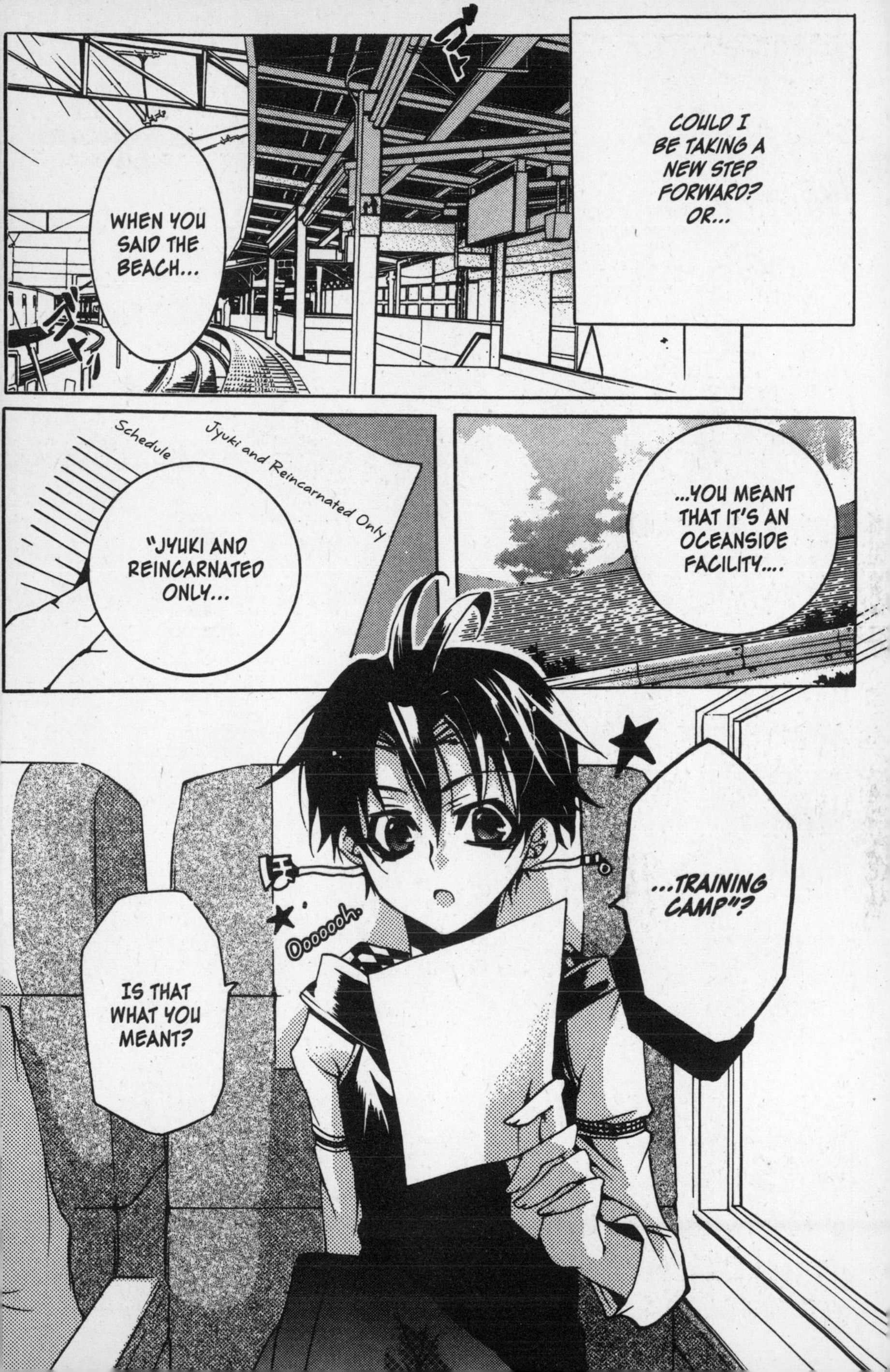
COULD I BE TAKING A NEW STEP FORWARD? OR...
WHEN YOU SAID THE BEACH...
...YOU MEANT THAT IT'S AN OCEANSIDE FACILITY....
Schedule
Jyuki and Reincarnated Only
"JYUKI AND REINCARNATED ONLY...
...TRAINING CAMP"?
Oooooh.
IS THAT WHAT YOU MEANT?

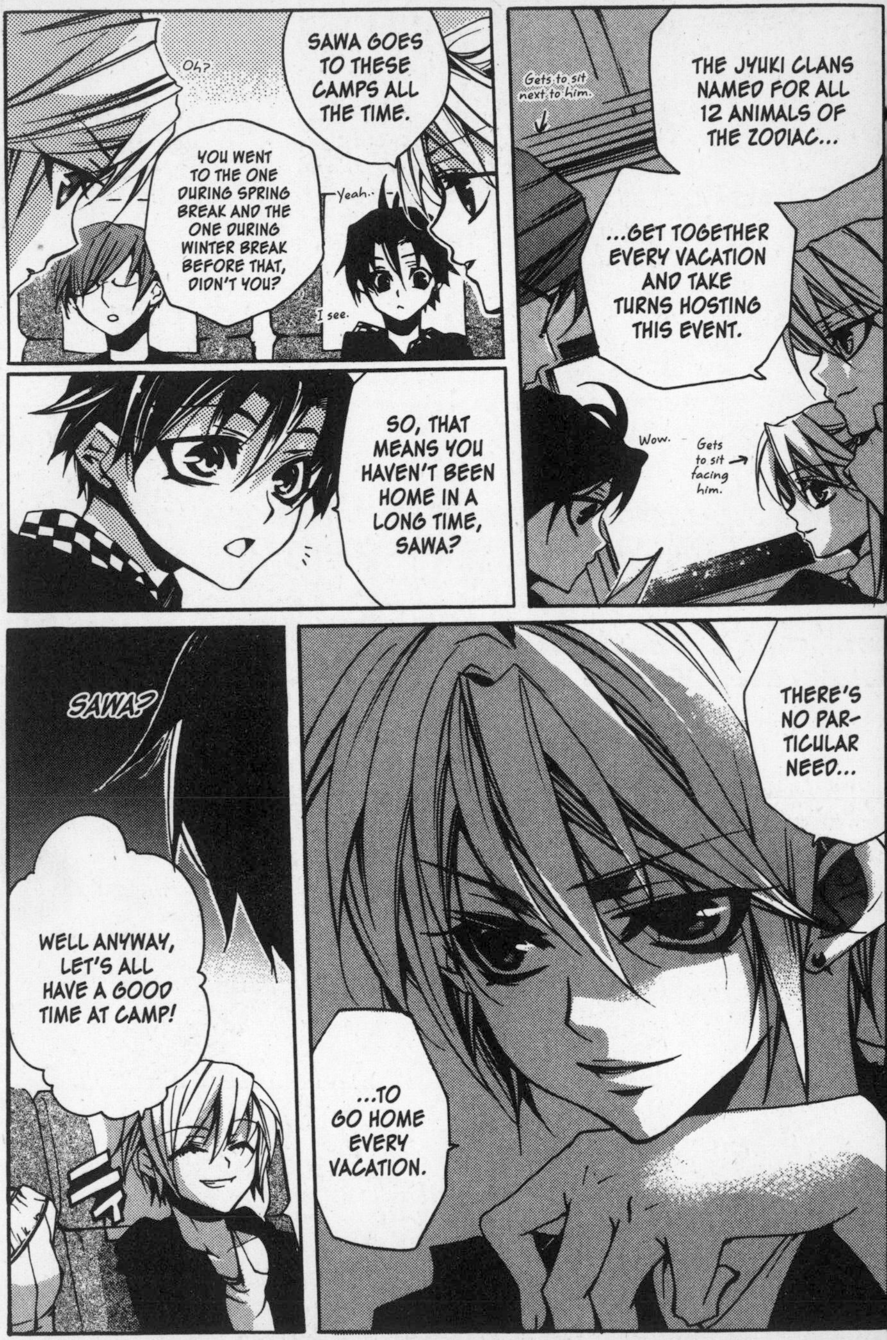
THE JYUKI CLANS NAMED FOR ALL 12 ANIMALS OF THE ZODIAC...
Gets to sit next to him.
...GET TOGETHER EVERY VACATION AND TAKE TURNS HOSTING THIS EVENT.
Gets to sit facing him.
Wow.
SAWA GOES TO THESE CAMPS ALL THE TIME.
Oh?
Yeah..
YOU WENT TO THE ONE DURING SPRING BREAK AND THE ONE DURING WINTER BREAK BEFORE THAT, DIDN'T YOU?
I see.
SO, THAT MEANS YOU HAVEN'T BEEN HOME IN A LONG TIME, SAWA?
THERE'S NO PAR-TICULAR NEED...
...TO GO HOME EVERY VACATION.
SAWA?
WELL ANYWAY, LET'S ALL HAVE A GOOD TIME AT CAMP!

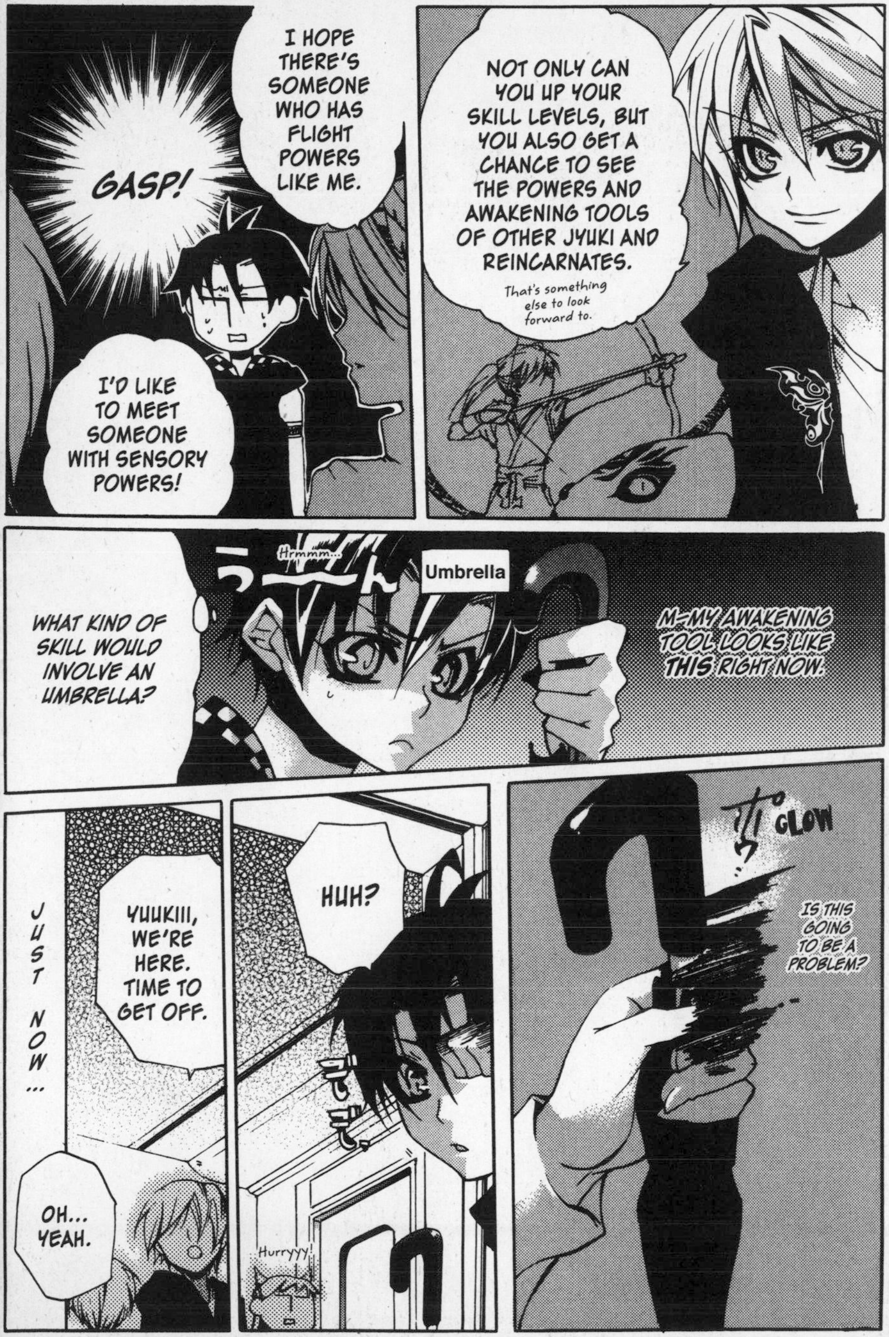
NOT ONLY CAN YOU UP YOUR SKILL LEVELS, BUT YOU ALSO GET A CHANCE TO SEE THE POWERS AND AWAKENING TOOLS OF OTHER JYUKI AND REINCARNATES.
That's something else to look forward to.
I HOPE THERE'S SOMEONE WHO HAS FLIGHT POWERS LIKE ME.
GASP!
I'D LIKE TO MEET SOMEONE WITH SENSORY POWERS!
M-MY AWAKENING TOOL LOOKS LIKE THIS RIGHT NOW.
Umbrella
Hrmmm...
WHAT KIND OF SKILL WOULD INVOLVE AN UMBRELLA?
GLOW
IS THIS GOING TO BE A PROBLEM?
HUH?
Hurryyy!
JUST NOW...
YUUKIII, WE'RE HERE. TIME TO GET OFF.
OH... YEAH.

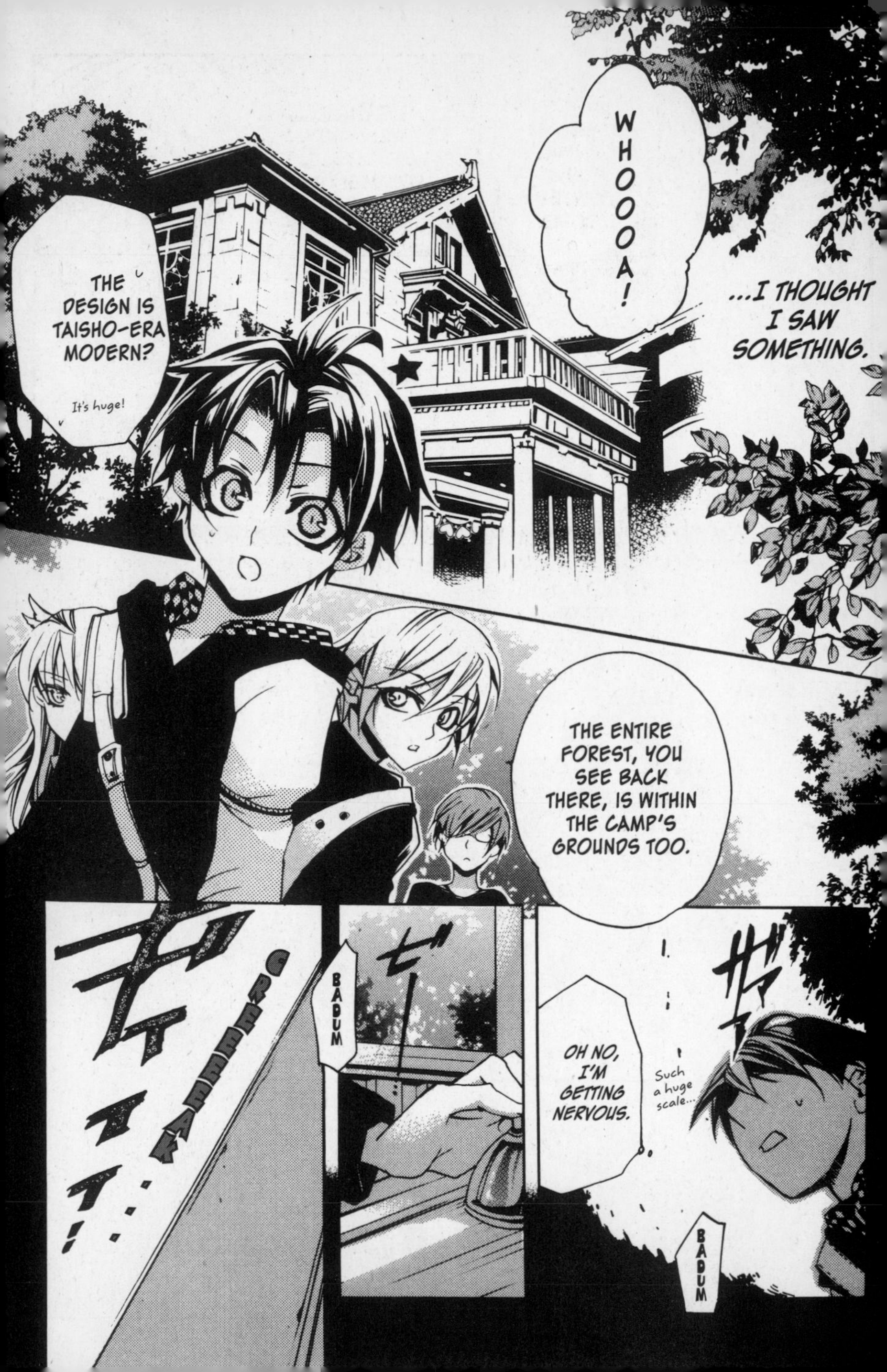
...I THOUGHT I SAW SOMETHING.
WHOOOOA!
THE DESIGN IS TAISHO-ERA MODERN?
It's huge!
THE ENTIRE FOREST, YOU SEE BACK THERE, IS WITHIN THE CAMP'S GROUNDS TOO.
BADUM
OH NO, I'M GETTING NERVOUS.
Such a huge scale...
BADUM
CREEEEAK

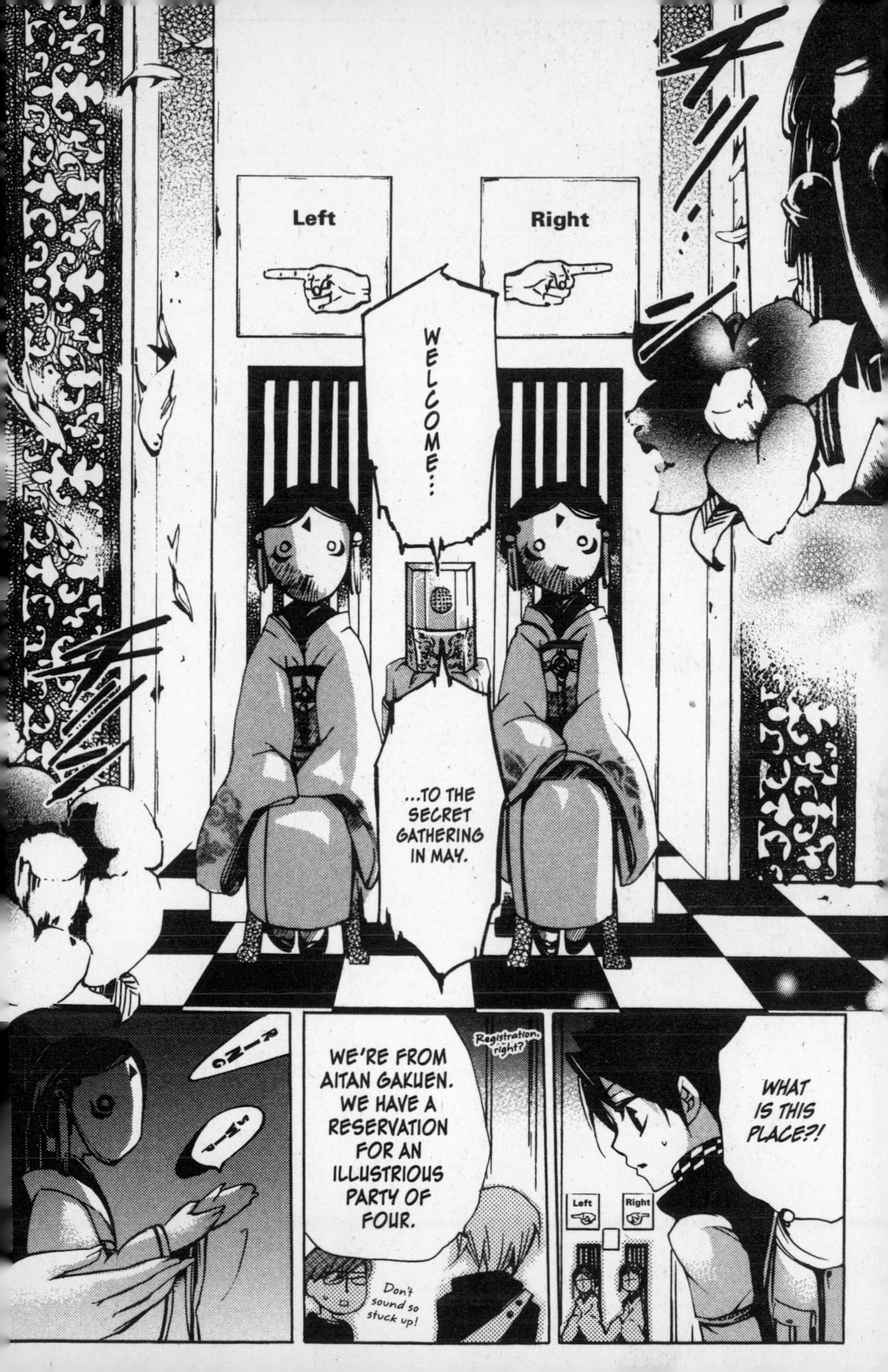
Right
Left
WELCOME...
...TO THE SECRET GATHERING IN MAY.
WHAT IS THIS PLACE?!
Right
Left
Registration, right?
WE'RE FROM AITAN GAKUEN. WE HAVE A RESERVATION FOR AN ILLUSTRIOUS PARTY OF FOUR.
Don't sound so stuck up!
RING

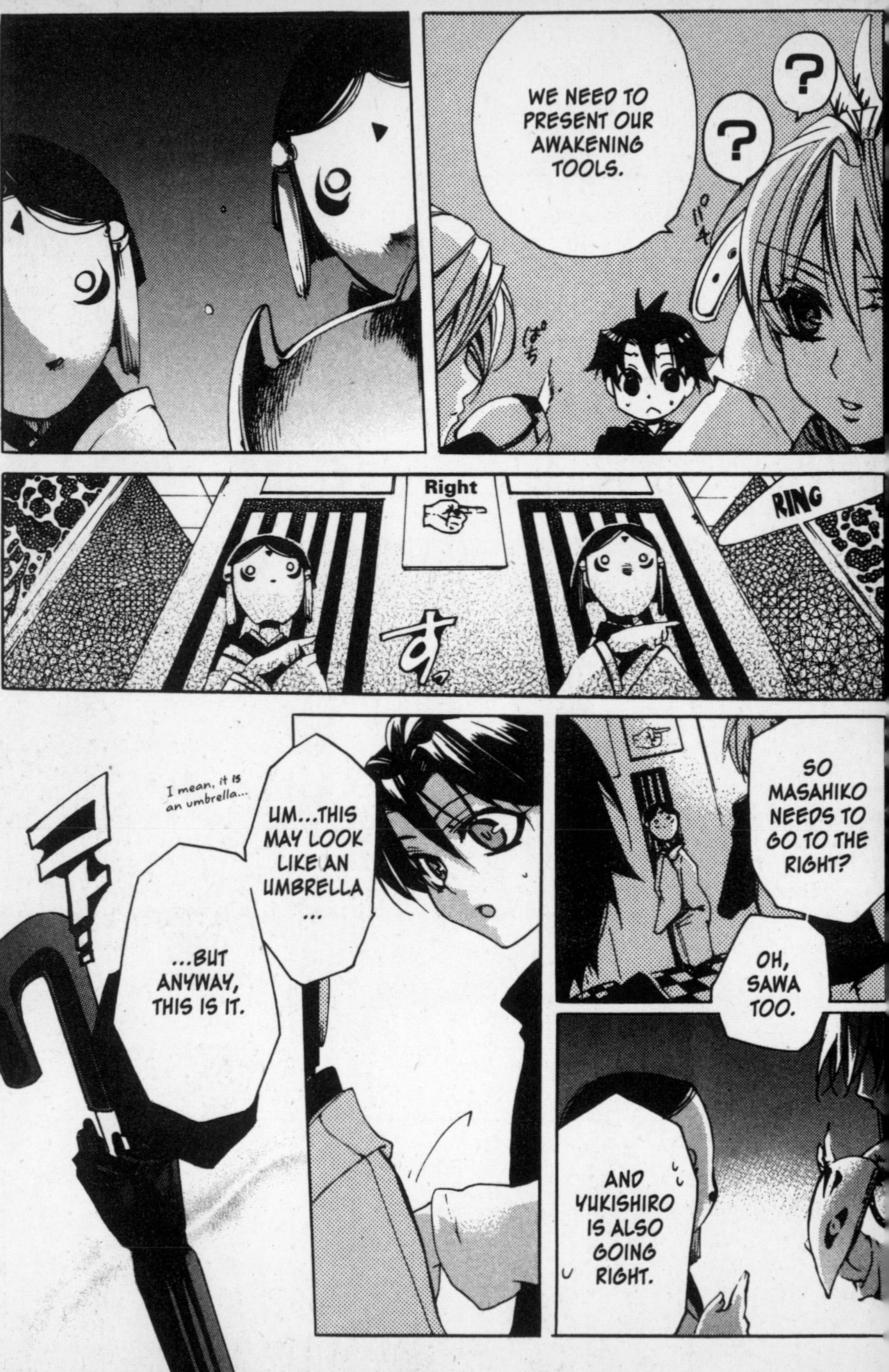
?
?
WE NEED TO PRESENT OUR AWAKENING TOOLS.
RING
Right
す
SO MASAHIKO NEEDS TO GO TO THE RIGHT?
OH, SAWA TOO.
AND YUKISHIRO IS ALSO GOING RIGHT.
UM...THIS MAY LOOK LIKE AN UMBRELLA ...
I mean, it is an umbrella...
...BUT ANYWAY, THIS IS IT.

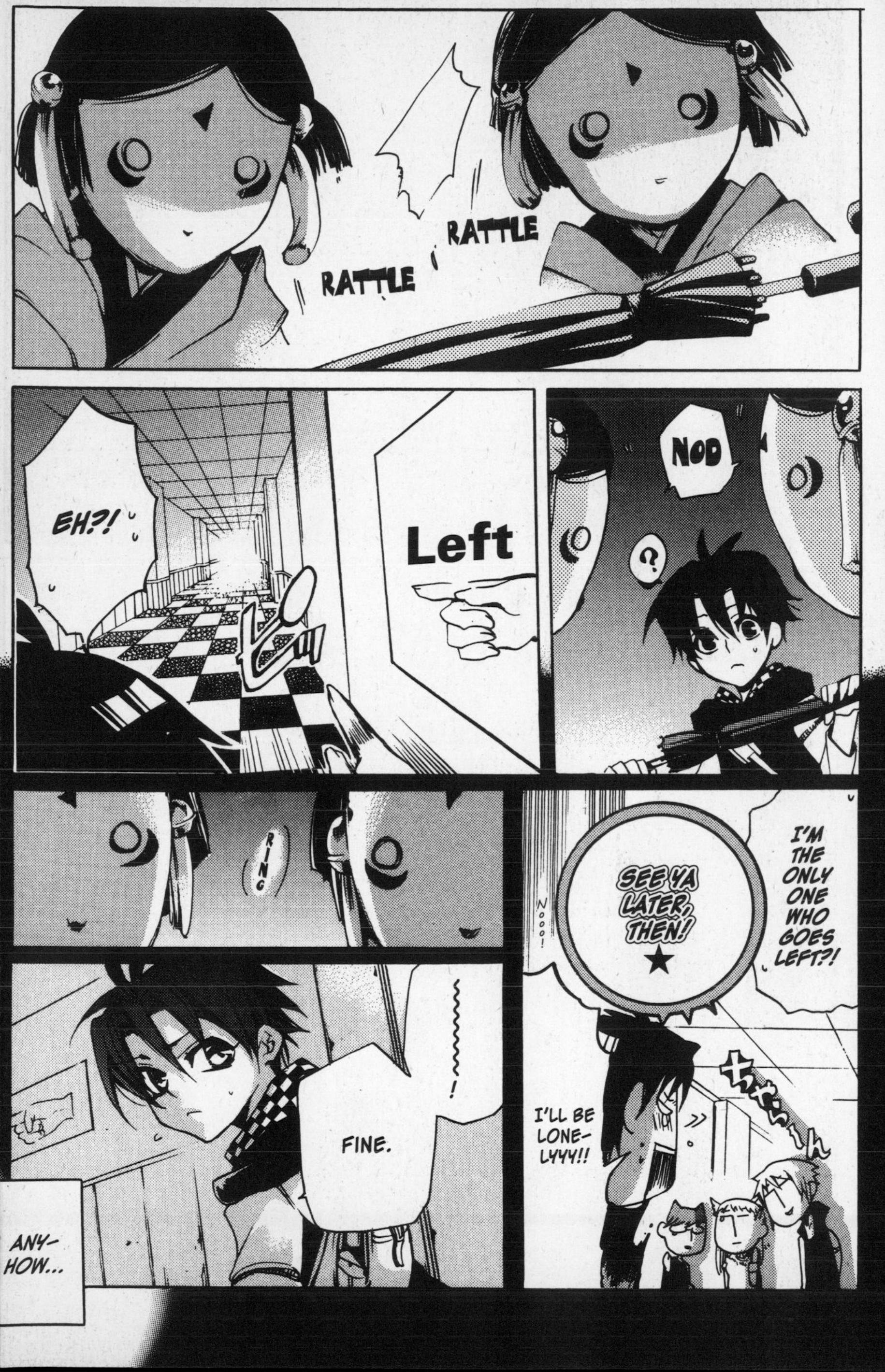
RATTLE
RATTLE
NOD
?
Left
EH?!
SEE YA LATER, THEN! ★
I'M THE ONLY ONE WHO GOES LEFT?!
NOOO!
I'LL BE LONE-LYYY!!
RING
~~~~~!
FINE.
ANY-HOW...
~~~~~

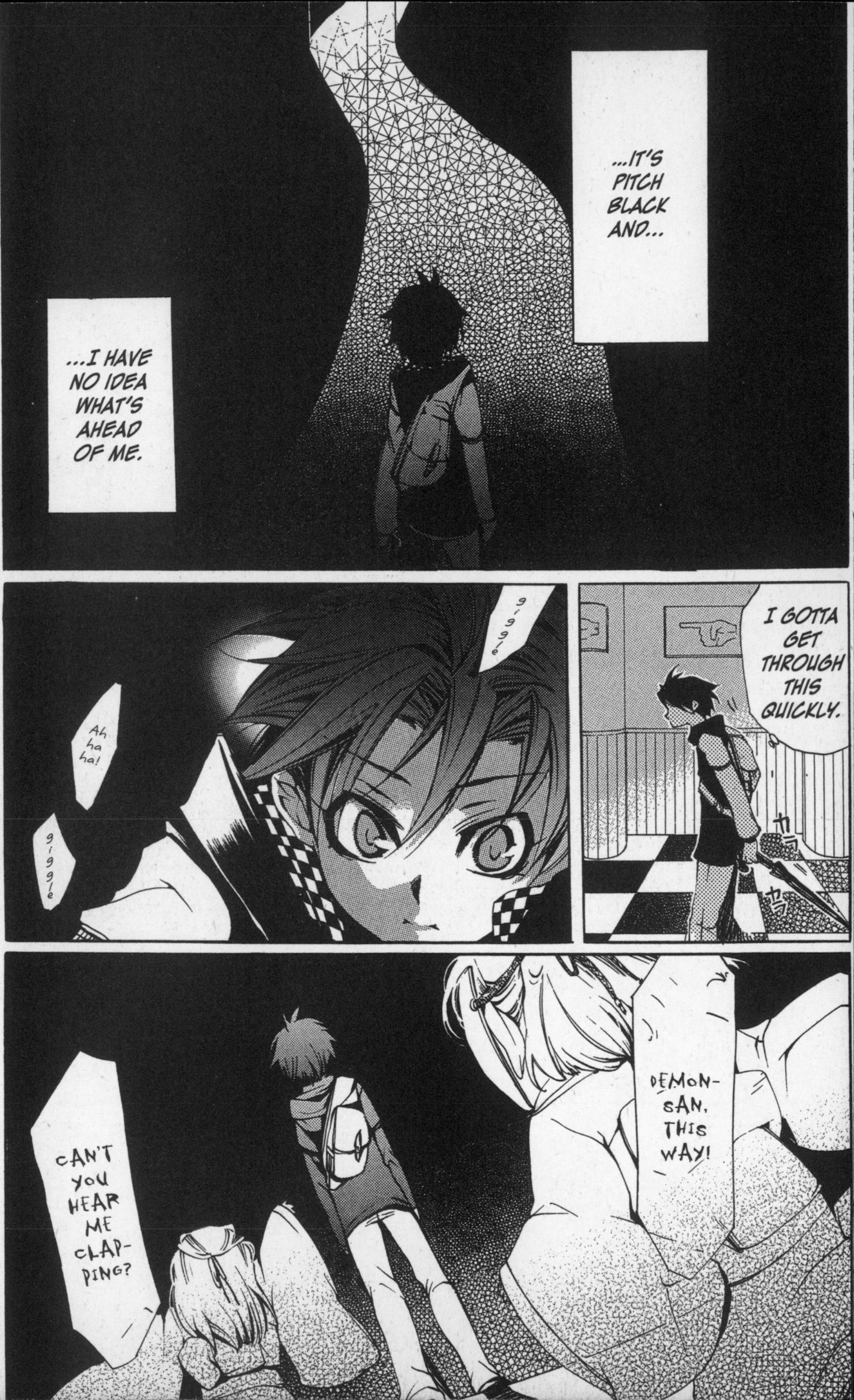
...IT'S PITCH BLACK AND...
...I HAVE NO IDEA WHAT'S AHEAD OF ME.
I GOTTA GET THROUGH THIS QUICKLY.
giggle
Ah ha ha!
giggle
DEMON-SAN, THIS WAY!
CAN'T YOU HEAR ME CLAPPING?

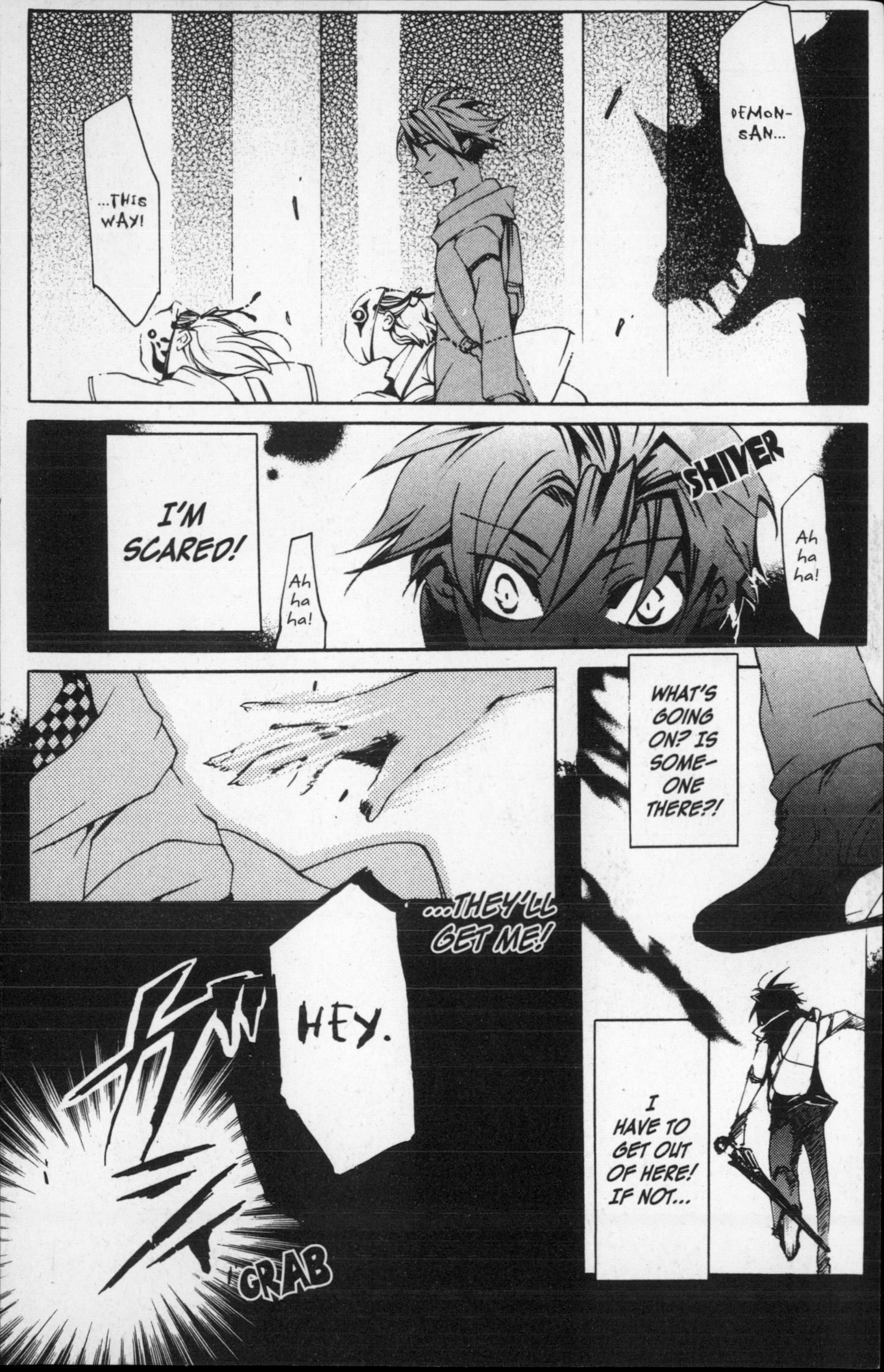
DEMON-SAN...
...THIS WAY!
SHIVER
Ah ha ha!
Ah ha ha!
I'M SCARED!
WHAT'S GOING ON? IS SOME-ONE THERE?!
I HAVE TO GET OUT OF HERE! IF NOT...
...THEY'LL GET ME!
HEY.
GRAB

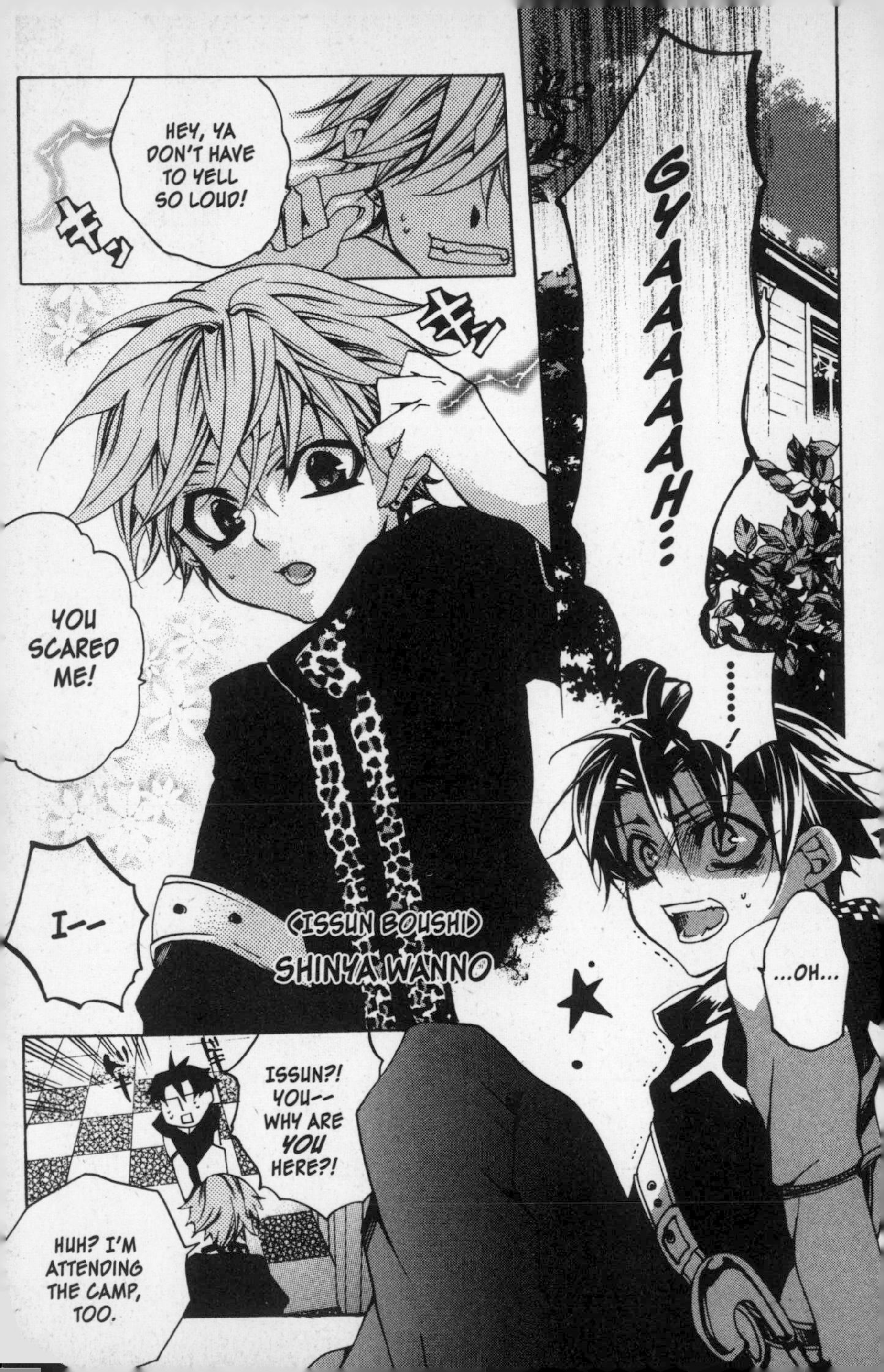
GYAAAAAH...
.....!
...OH...
HEY, YA DON'T HAVE TO YELL SO LOUD!
YOU SCARED ME!
I--
<ISSUN BOUSHI>
SHINYA WANNO
ISSUN?! YOU-- WHY ARE YOU HERE?!
HUH? I'M ATTENDING THE CAMP, TOO.

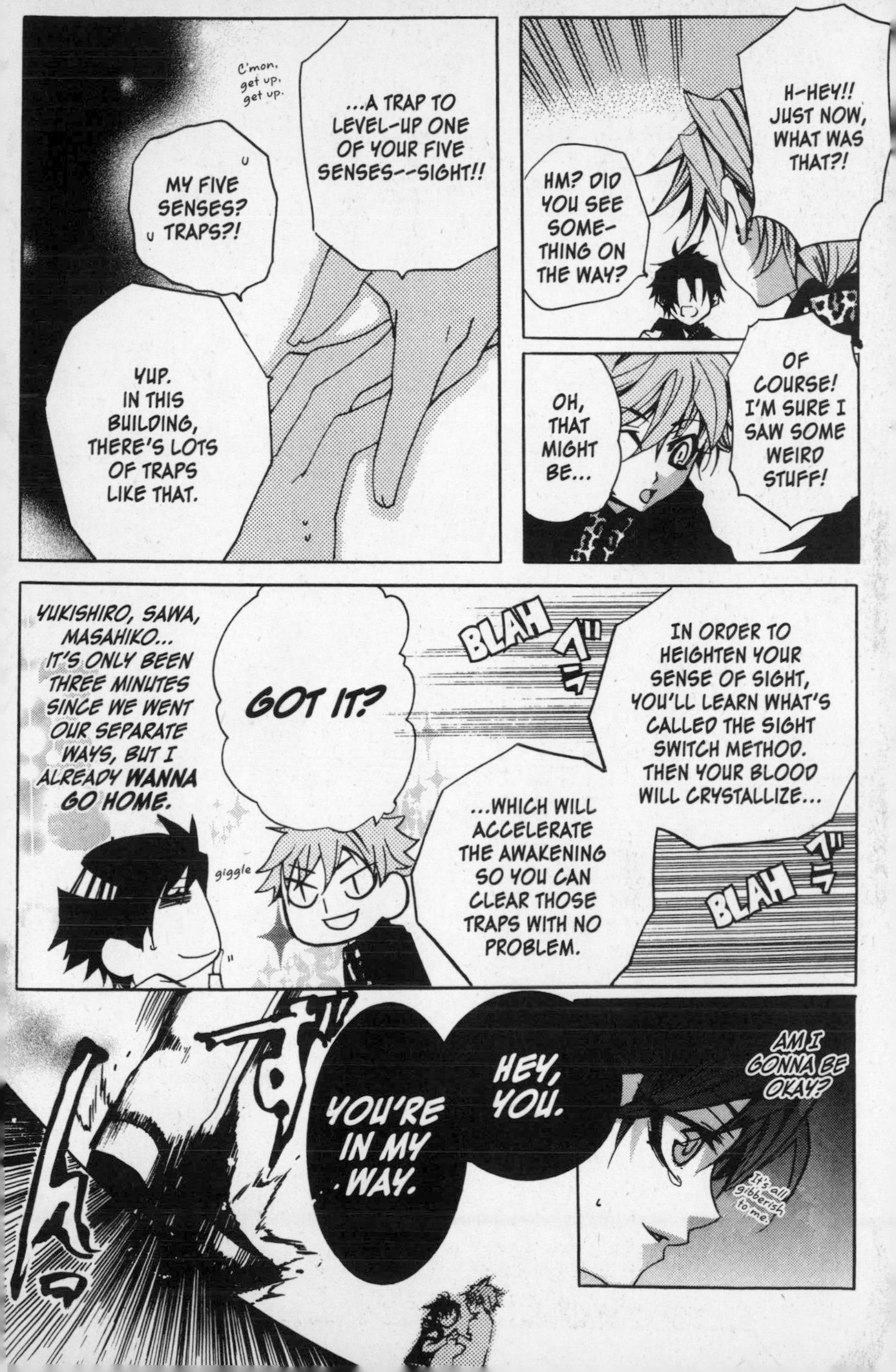
H-HEY!! JUST NOW, WHAT WAS THAT?!
HM? DID YOU SEE SOME-THING ON THE WAY?
OF COURSE! I'M SURE I SAW SOME WEIRD STUFF!
OH, THAT MIGHT BE...
...A TRAP TO LEVEL-UP ONE OF YOUR FIVE SENSES--SIGHT!!
C'mon, get up, get up.
MY FIVE SENSES? TRAPS?!
YUP. IN THIS BUILDING, THERE'S LOTS OF TRAPS LIKE THAT.
IN ORDER TO HEIGHTEN YOUR SENSE OF SIGHT, YOU'LL LEARN WHAT'S CALLED THE SIGHT SWITCH METHOD. THEN YOUR BLOOD WILL CRYSTALLIZE...
BLAH
BLAH
...WHICH WILL ACCELERATE THE AWAKENING SO YOU CAN CLEAR THOSE TRAPS WITH NO PROBLEM.
GOT IT?
YUKISHIRO, SAWA, MASAHIKO... IT'S ONLY BEEN THREE MINUTES SINCE WE WENT OUR SEPARATE WAYS, BUT I ALREADY WANNA GO HOME.
giggle
AM I GONNA BE OKAY?
It's all gibberish to me.
HEY, YOU.
YOU'RE IN MY WAY.

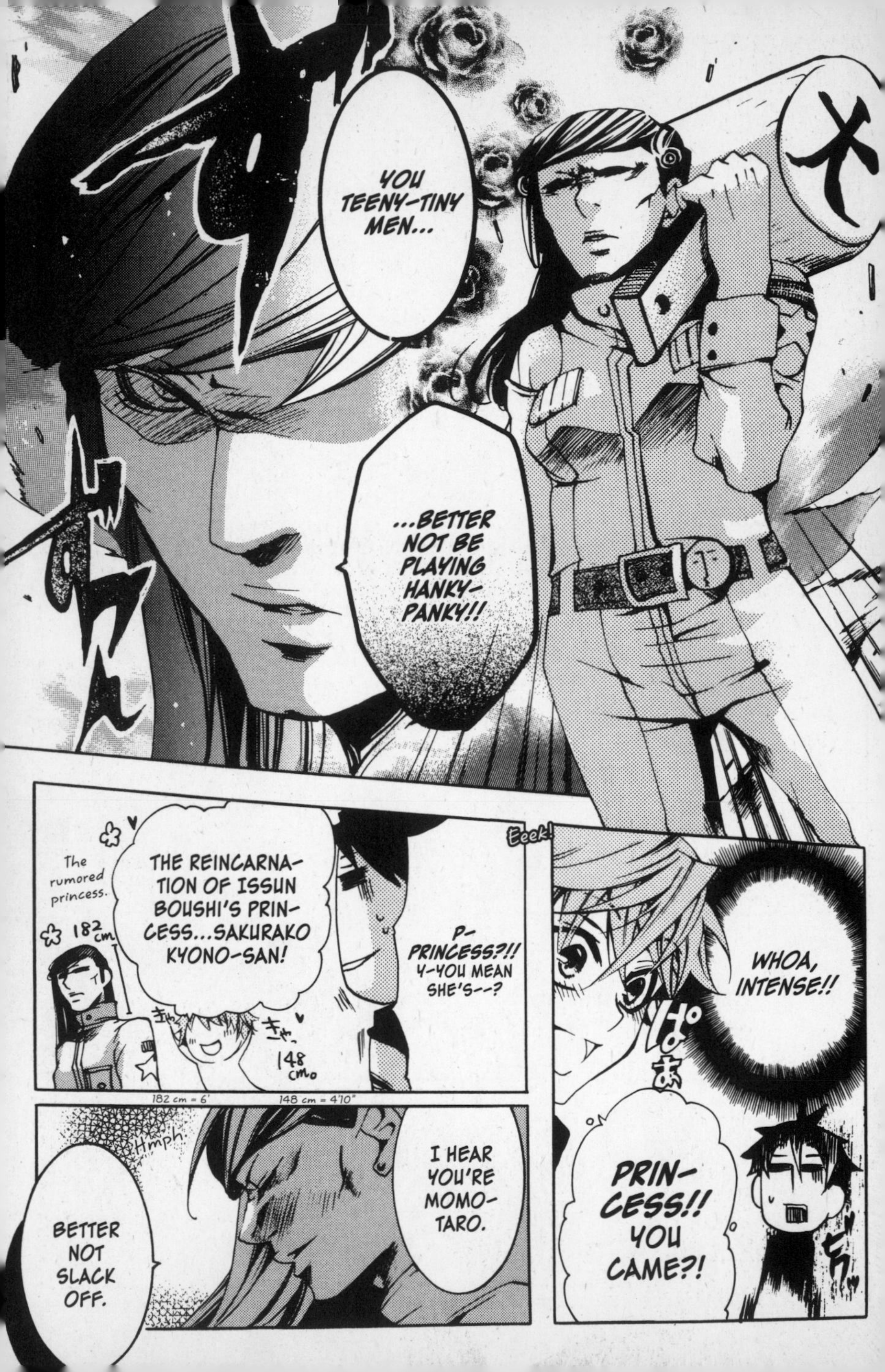
YOU TEENY-TINY MEN...
...BETTER NOT BE PLAYING HANKY-PANKY!!
Eeek!
WHOA, INTENSE!!
PRIN-CESS!! YOU CAME?!
P-PRINCESS?!! Y-YOU MEAN SHE'S--?
THE REINCARNA-TION OF ISSUN BOUSHI'S PRIN-CESS...SAKURAKO KYONO-SAN!
The rumored princess.
182 cm
148 cm.
182 cm = 6'
148 cm = 4'10"
I HEAR YOU'RE MOMO-TARO.
Hmph
BETTER NOT SLACK OFF.

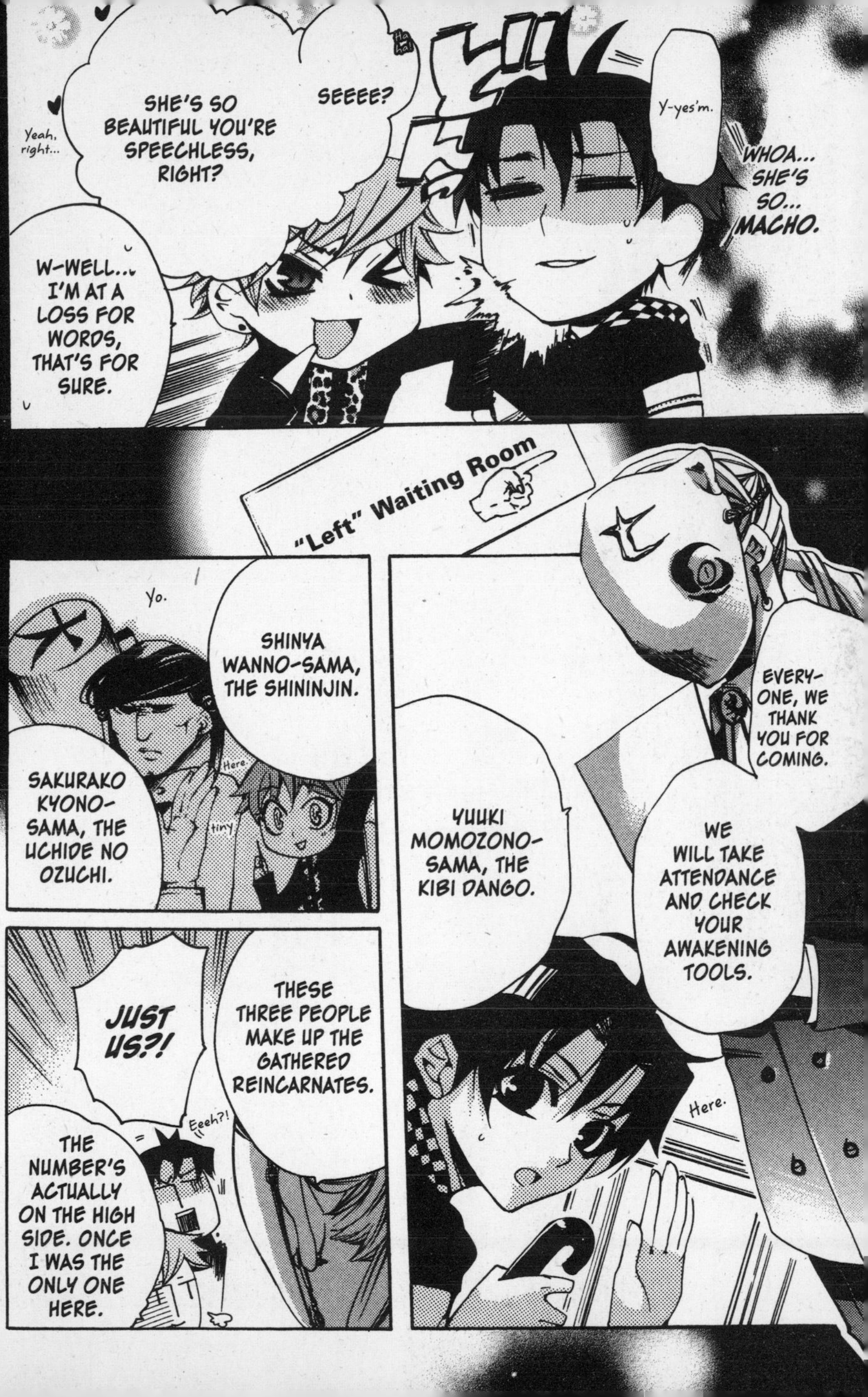
Y-yes'm.
WHOA... SHE'S SO... MACHO.
Ha ha!
SEEEE?
SHE'S SO BEAUTIFUL YOU'RE SPEECHLESS, RIGHT?
Yeah, right...
W-WELL... I'M AT A LOSS FOR WORDS, THAT'S FOR SURE.
"Left" Waiting Room
EVERYONE, WE THANK YOU FOR COMING.
WE WILL TAKE ATTENDANCE AND CHECK YOUR AWAKENING TOOLS.
YUUKI MOMOZONO-SAMA, THE KIBI DANGO.
Here.
SHINYA WANNO-SAMA, THE SHININJIN.
Yo.
SAKURAKO KYONO-SAMA, THE UCHIDE NO OZUCHI.
Here.
tiny
THESE THREE PEOPLE MAKE UP THE GATHERED REINCARNATES.
JUST US?!
Eeeh?!
THE NUMBER'S ACTUALLY ON THE HIGH SIDE. ONCE I WAS THE ONLY ONE HERE.

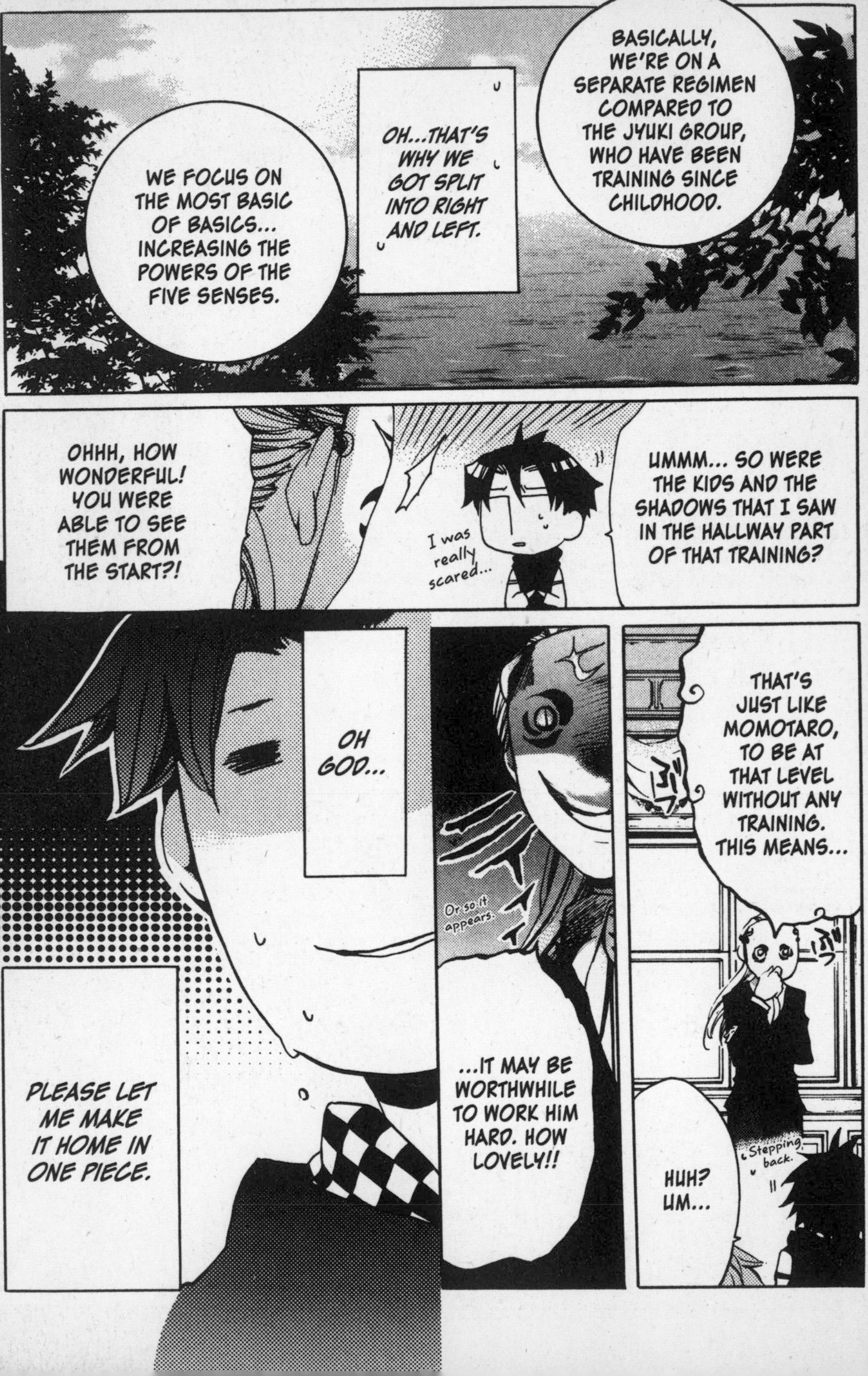
BASICALLY, WE'RE ON A SEPARATE REGIMEN COMPARED TO THE JYUKI GROUP, WHO HAVE BEEN TRAINING SINCE CHILDHOOD.
OH...THAT'S WHY WE GOT SPLIT INTO RIGHT AND LEFT.
WE FOCUS ON THE MOST BASIC OF BASICS... INCREASING THE POWERS OF THE FIVE SENSES.
UMMM... SO WERE THE KIDS AND THE SHADOWS THAT I SAW IN THE HALLWAY PART OF THAT TRAINING?
I was really scared...
OHHH, HOW WONDERFUL! YOU WERE ABLE TO SEE THEM FROM THE START?!
THAT'S JUST LIKE MOMOTARO, TO BE AT THAT LEVEL WITHOUT ANY TRAINING. THIS MEANS...
Stepping back.
HUH? UM...
Or so it appears.
...IT MAY BE WORTHWHILE TO WORK HIM HARD. HOW LOVELY!!
OH GOD...
PLEASE LET ME MAKE IT HOME IN ONE PIECE.

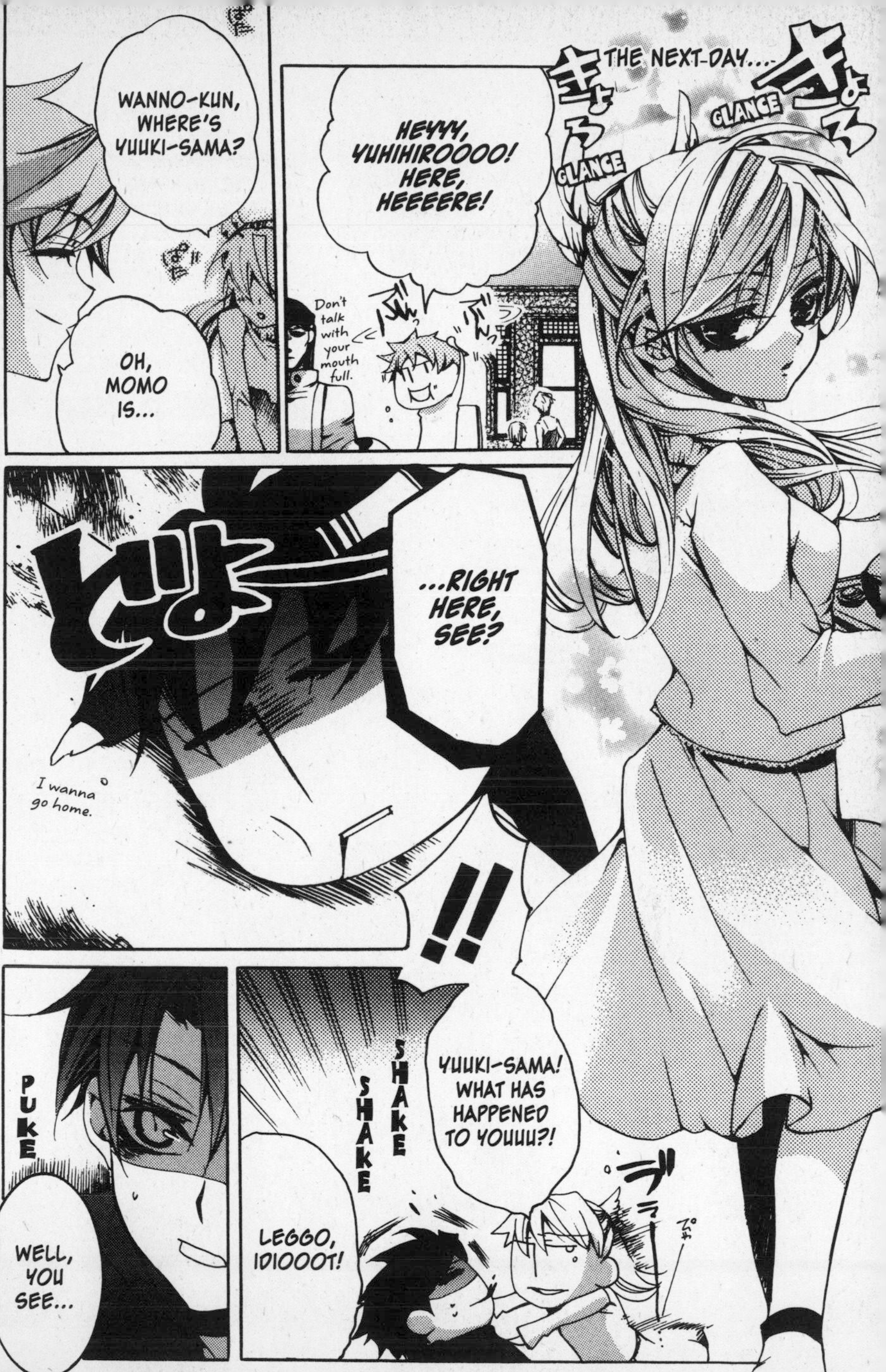

THE NEXT DAY....
GLANCE
GLANCE
HEYYY, YUHIHIROOOO! HERE, HEEEEERE!
Don't talk with your mouth full.
WANNO-KUN, WHERE'S YUUKI-SAMA?
OH, MOMO IS...
...RIGHT HERE, SEE?
I wanna go home.
!!
YUUKI-SAMA! WHAT HAS HAPPENED TO YOUUU?!
SHAKE
SHAKE
LEGGO, IDIOOOT!
PUKE
WELL, YOU SEE...

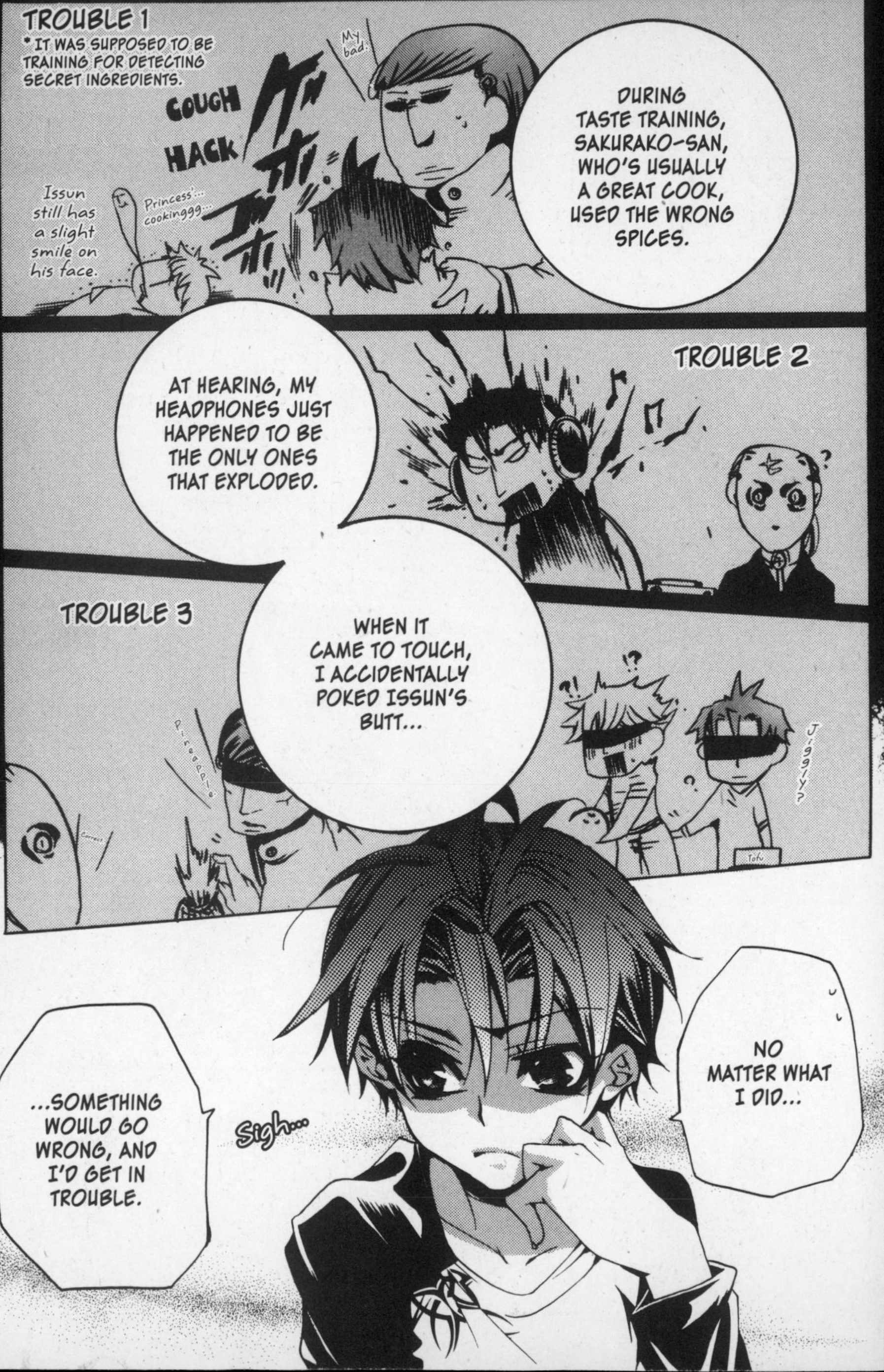
DURING TASTE TRAINING, SAKURAKO-SAN, WHO'S USUALLY A GREAT COOK, USED THE WRONG SPICES.
My bad.
TROUBLE 1
* IT WAS SUPPOSED TO BE TRAINING FOR DETECTING SECRET INGREDIENTS.
COUGH
HACK
Princess'... cookinggg...
Issun still has a slight smile on his face.
TROUBLE 2
AT HEARING, MY HEADPHONES JUST HAPPENED TO BE THE ONLY ONES THAT EXPLODED.
WHEN IT CAME TO TOUCH, I ACCIDENTALLY POKED ISSUN'S BUTT...
TROUBLE 3
Jiggly?
Tofu
Pineapple
Correct
NO MATTER WHAT I DID...
Sigh...
...SOMETHING WOULD GO WRONG, AND I'D GET IN TROUBLE.

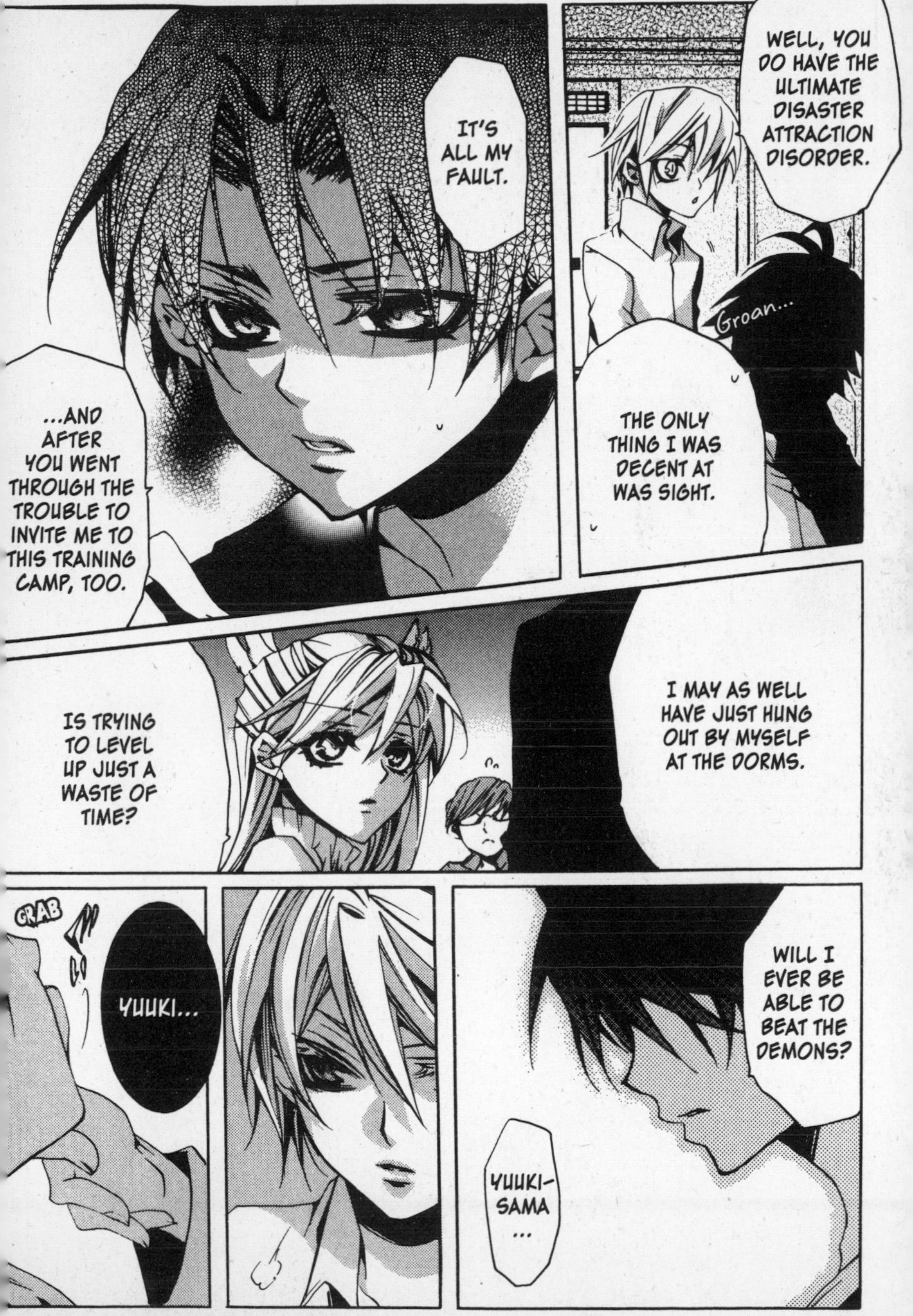
WELL, YOU DO HAVE THE ULTIMATE DISASTER ATTRACTION DISORDER.
Groan...
THE ONLY THING I WAS DECENT AT WAS SIGHT.
IT'S ALL MY FAULT.
...AND AFTER YOU WENT THROUGH THE TROUBLE TO INVITE ME TO THIS TRAINING CAMP, TOO.
I MAY AS WELL HAVE JUST HUNG OUT BY MYSELF AT THE DORMS.
IS TRYING TO LEVEL UP JUST A WASTE OF TIME?
WILL I EVER BE ABLE TO BEAT THE DEMONS?
YUUKI-SAMA ...
YUUKI...
GRAB

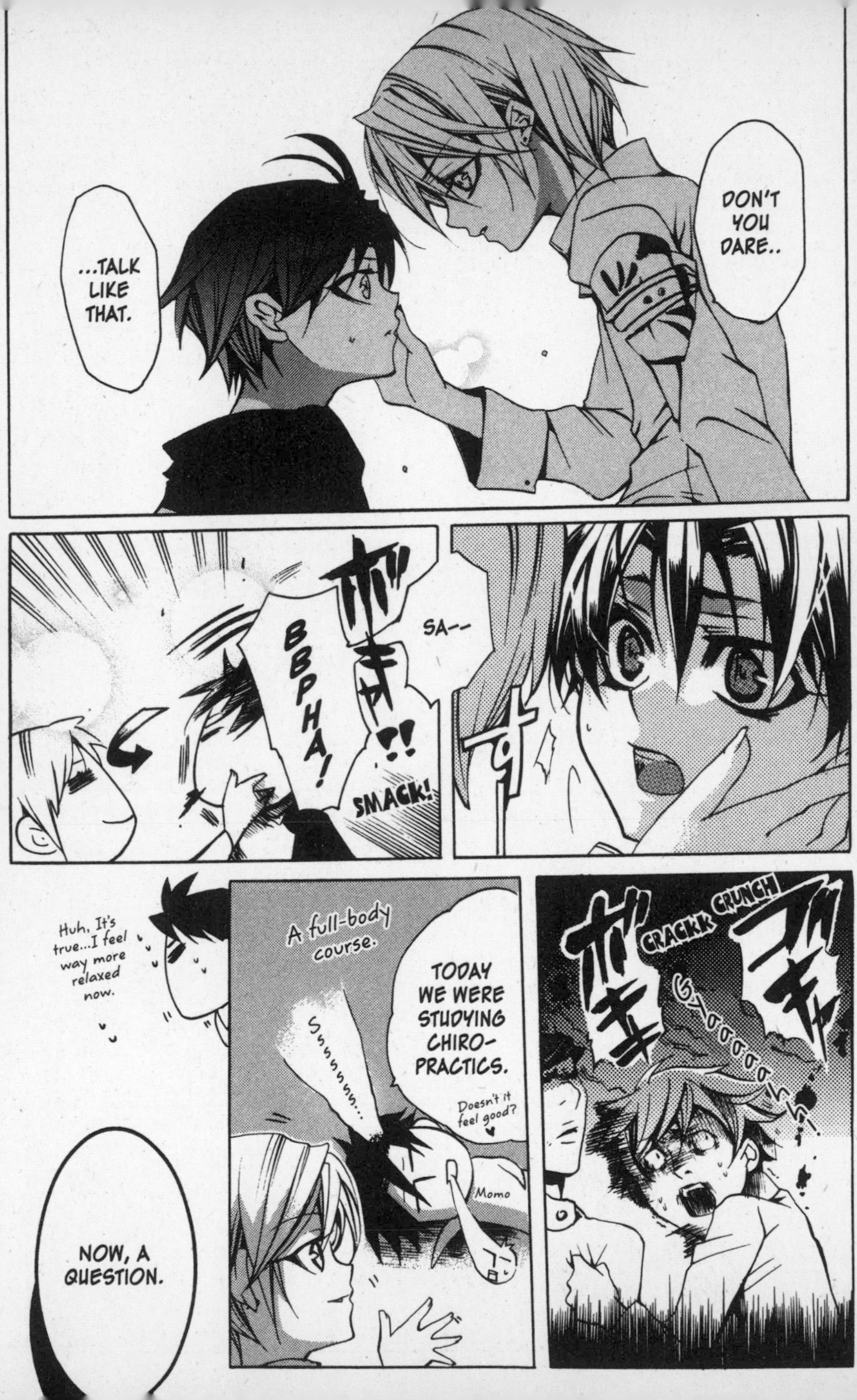
DON'T YOU DARE..
...TALK LIKE THAT.
SA--
BBPHA!
SMACK!
CRACKK
CRUNCH
Gyaaaaaaah...
A full-body course.
TODAY WE WERE STUDYING CHIRO-PRACTICS.
Ssssss...
Doesn't it feel good?
Momo
Huh, It's true...I feel way more relaxed now.
NOW, A QUESTION.

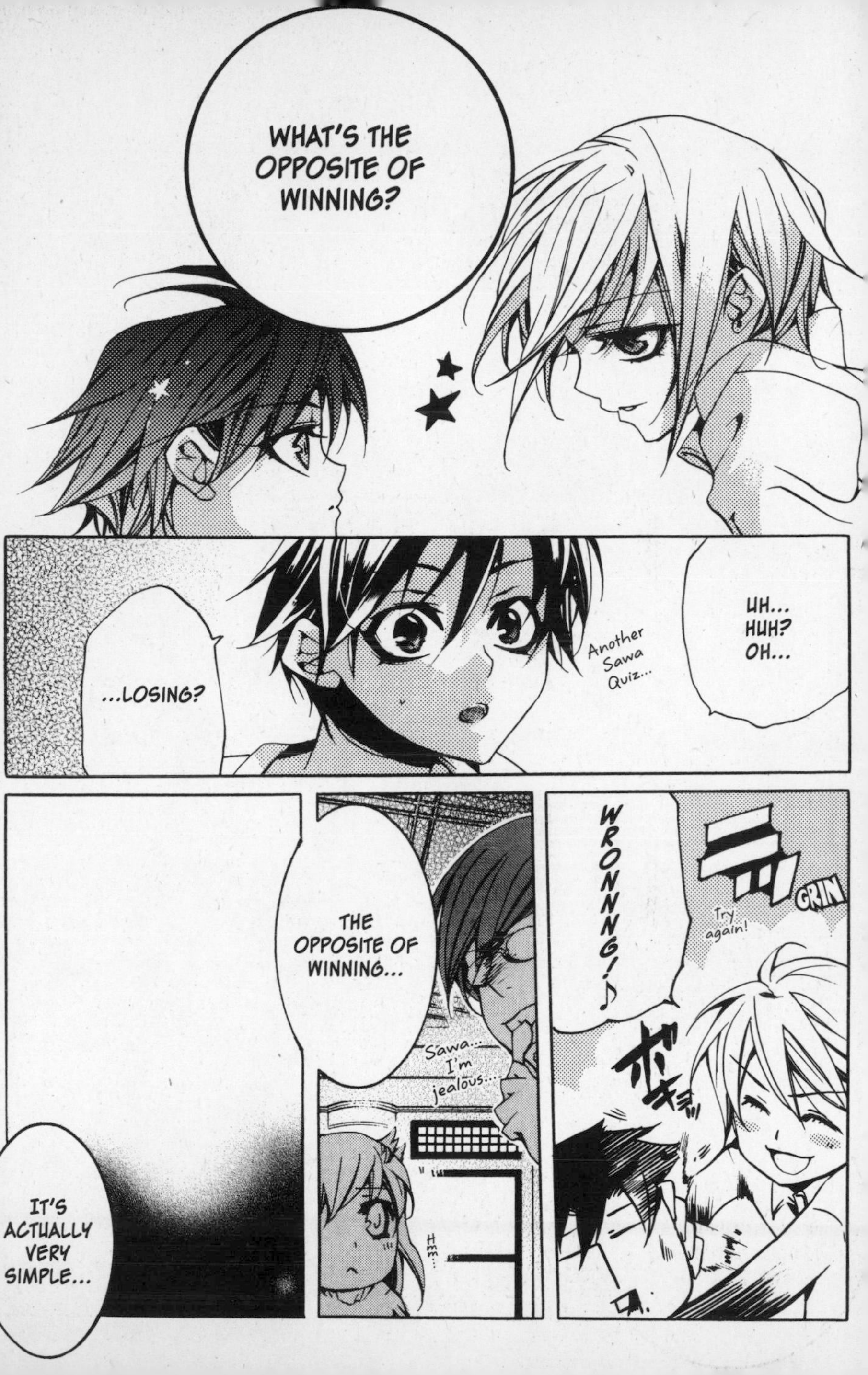
WHAT'S THE OPPOSITE OF WINNING?
UH... HUH? OH...
Another Sawa Quiz...
...LOSING?
WRONNNG! ♪
GRIN
Try again!
ボキッ
THE OPPOSITE OF WINNING...
Sawa... I'm jealous...
Hmm...
IT'S ACTUALLY VERY SIMPLE...

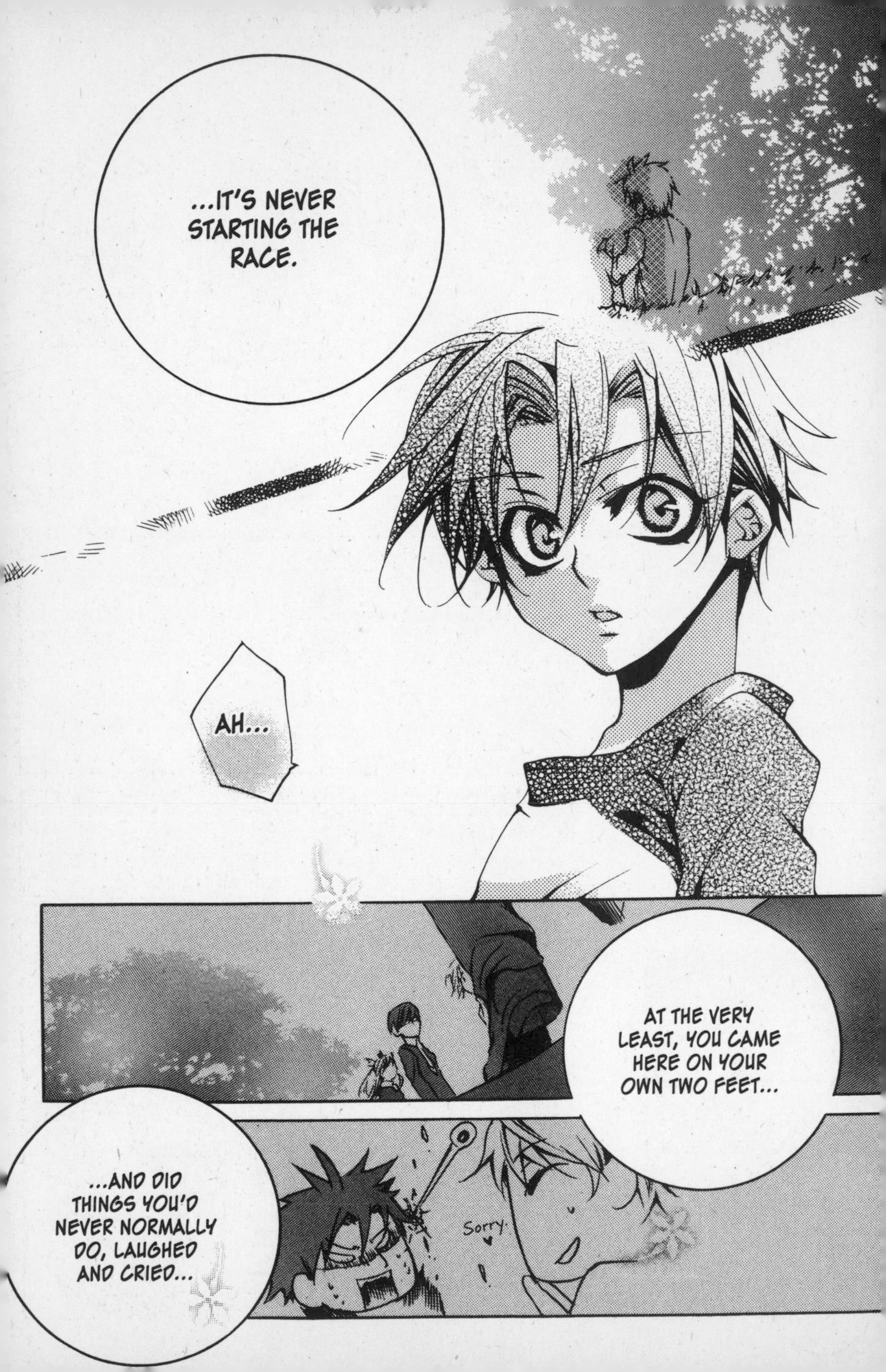
...IT'S NEVER STARTING THE RACE.
AH...
AT THE VERY LEAST, YOU CAME HERE ON YOUR OWN TWO FEET...
Sorry.
...AND DID THINGS YOU'D NEVER NORMALLY DO, LAUGHED AND CRIED...

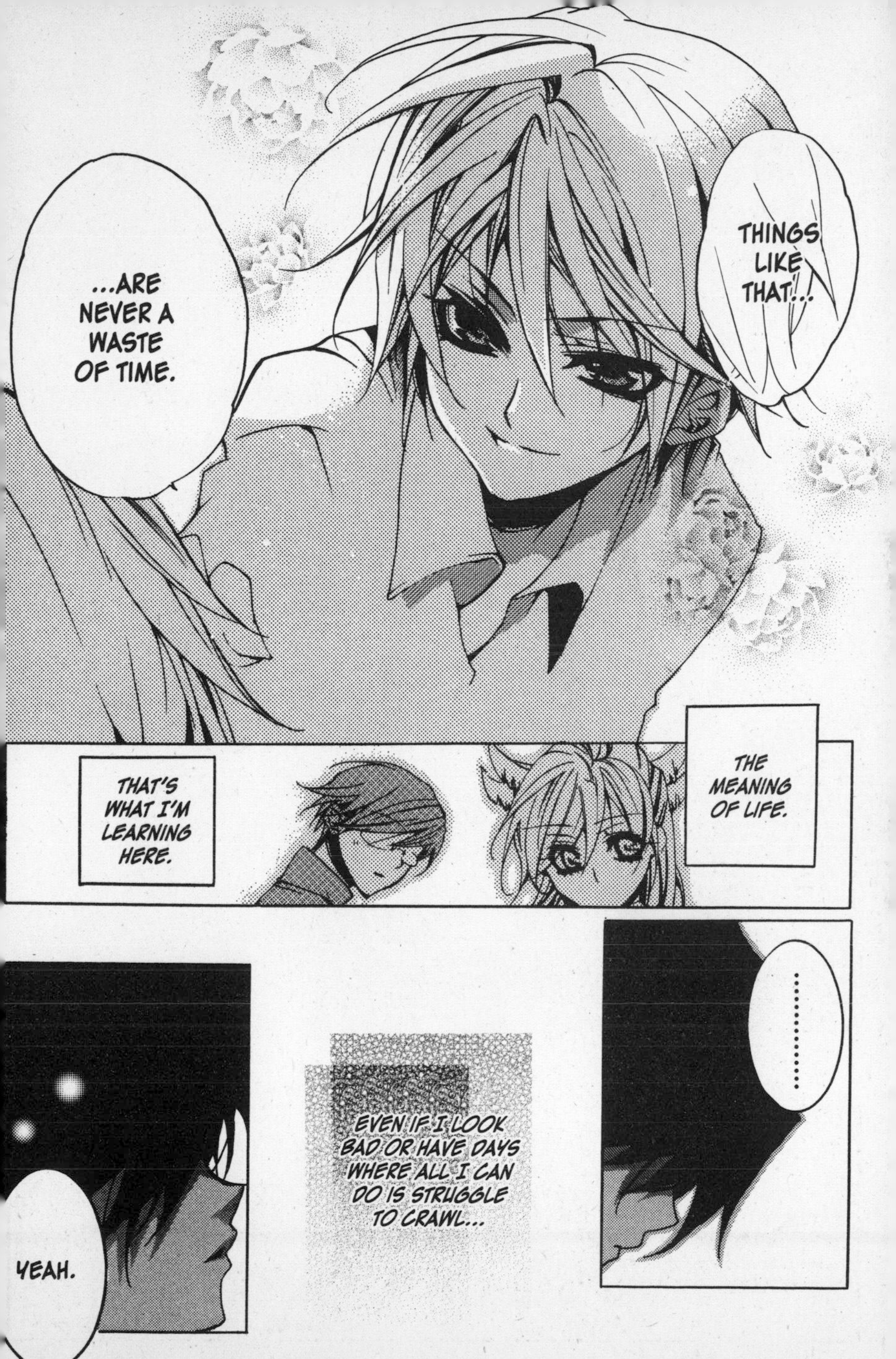
THINGS LIKE THAT...
...ARE NEVER A WASTE OF TIME.
THE MEANING OF LIFE.
THAT'S WHAT I'M LEARNING HERE.
......
EVEN IF I LOOK BAD OR HAVE DAYS WHERE ALL I CAN DO IS STRUGGLE TO CRAWL...
YEAH.

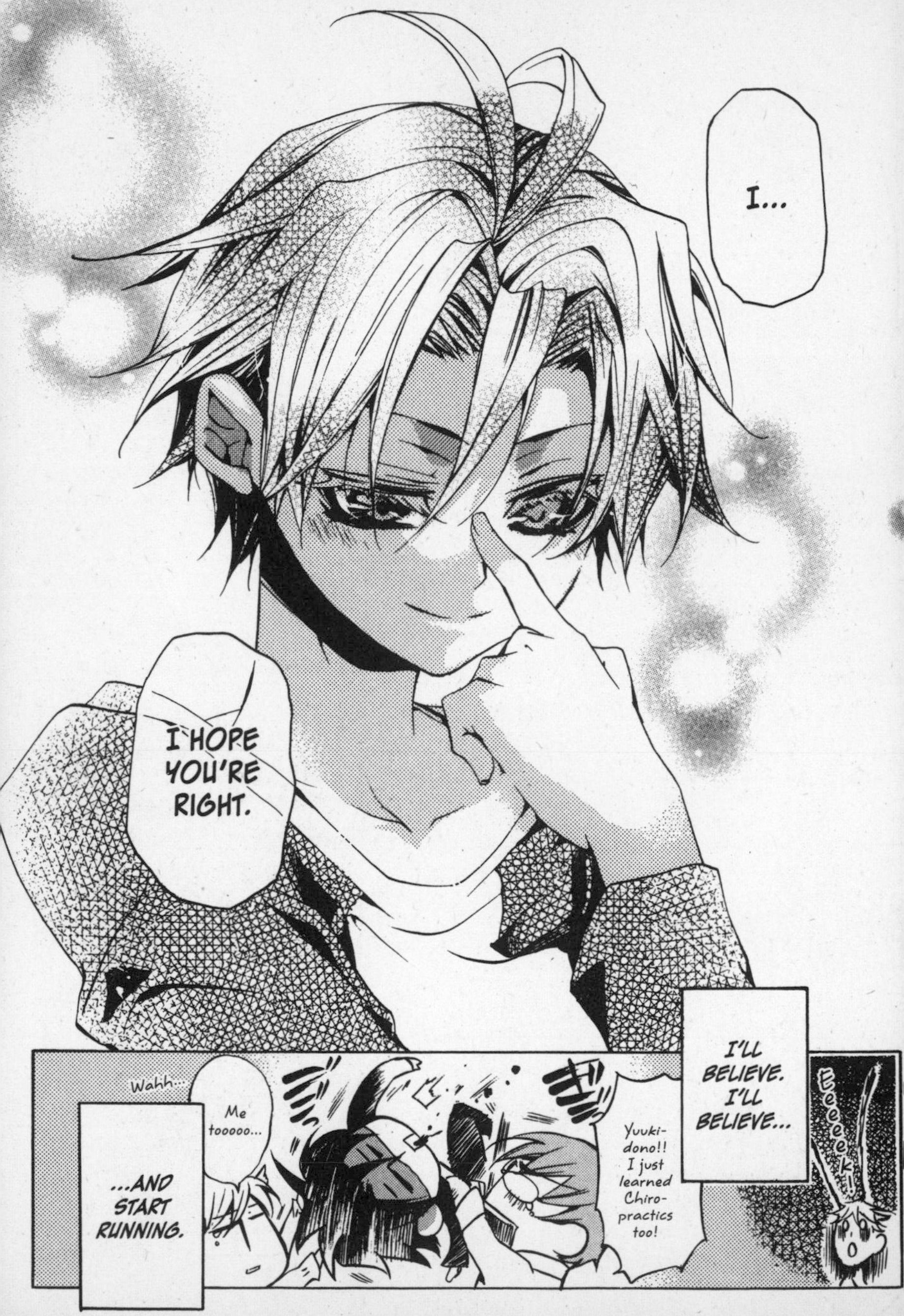
I...
I HOPE YOU'RE RIGHT.
Eeeeek!
I'LL BELIEVE. I'LL BELIEVE...
Yuuki-dono!! I just learned Chiro-practics too!
Me toooo...
Wahh...
...AND START RUNNING.

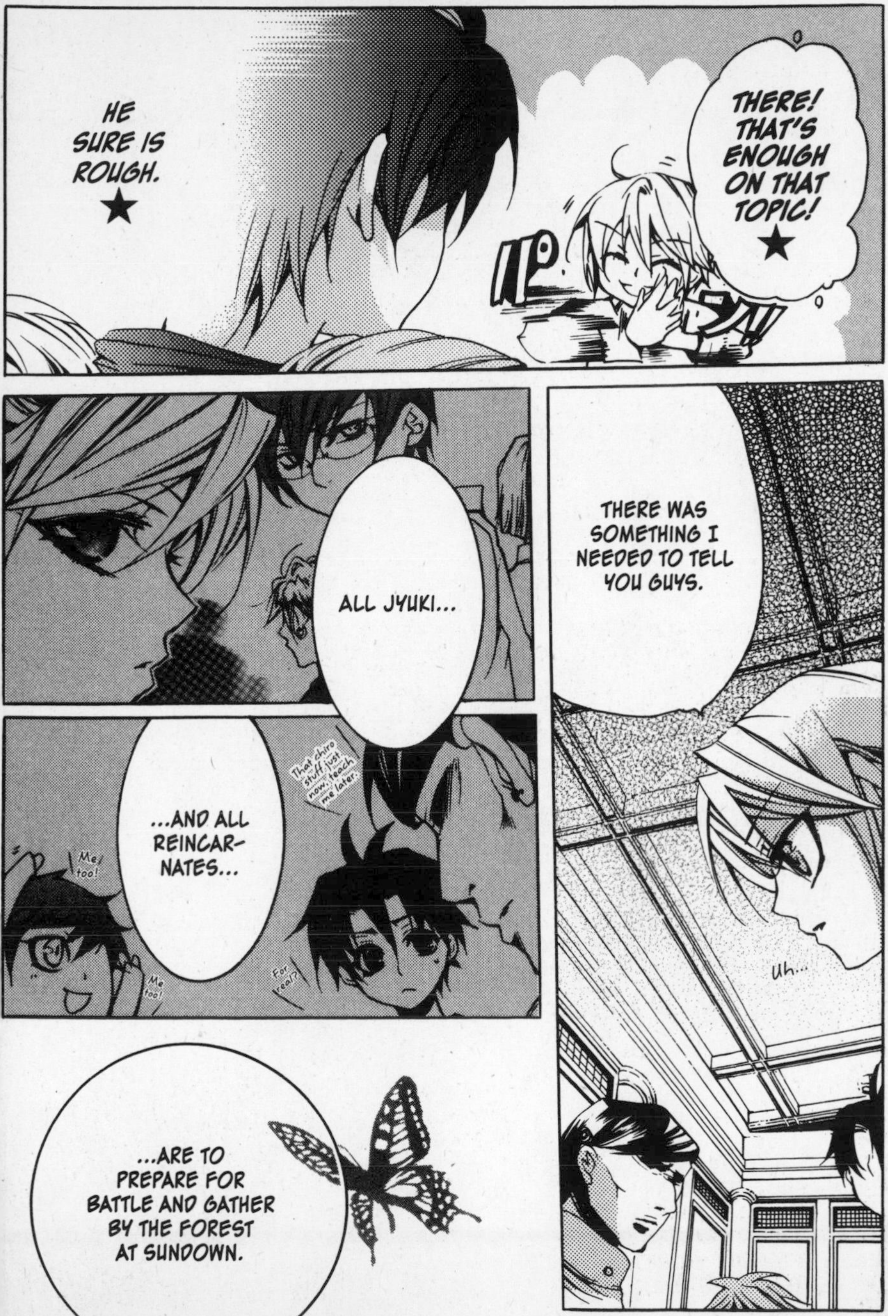
THERE! THAT'S ENOUGH ON THAT TOPIC! ★
HE SURE IS ROUGH. ★
THERE WAS SOMETHING I NEEDED TO TELL YOU GUYS.
Uh...
ALL JYUKI...
That chiro stuff just now, teach me later.
...AND ALL REINCARNATES...
For real?
Me too!
Me too!
...ARE TO PREPARE FOR BATTLE AND GATHER BY THE FOREST AT SUNDOWN.

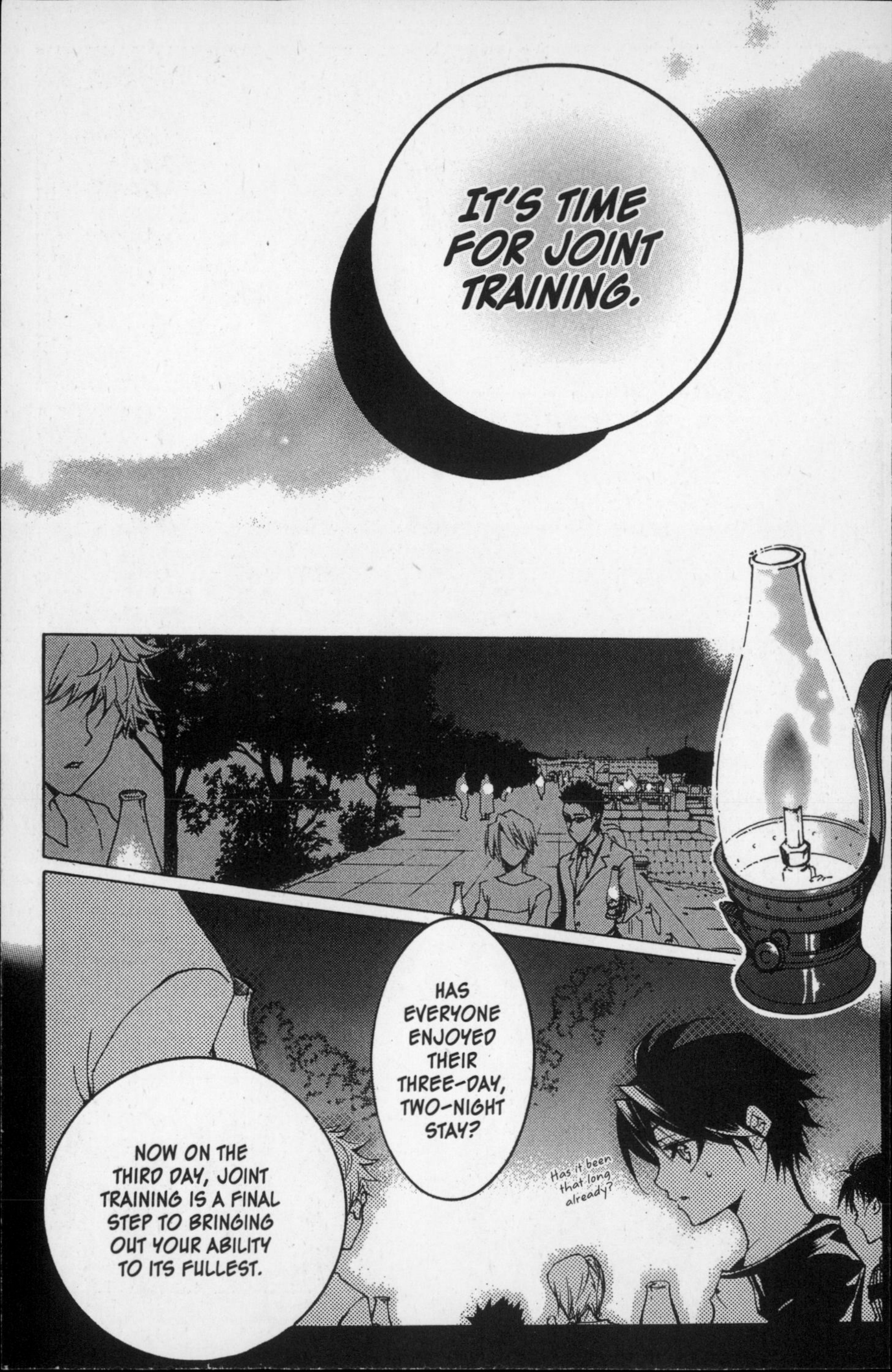
IT'S TIME FOR JOINT TRAINING.
HAS EVERYONE ENJOYED THEIR THREE-DAY, TWO-NIGHT STAY?
Has it been that long already?
NOW ON THE THIRD DAY, JOINT TRAINING IS A FINAL STEP TO BRINGING OUT YOUR ABILITY TO ITS FULLEST.

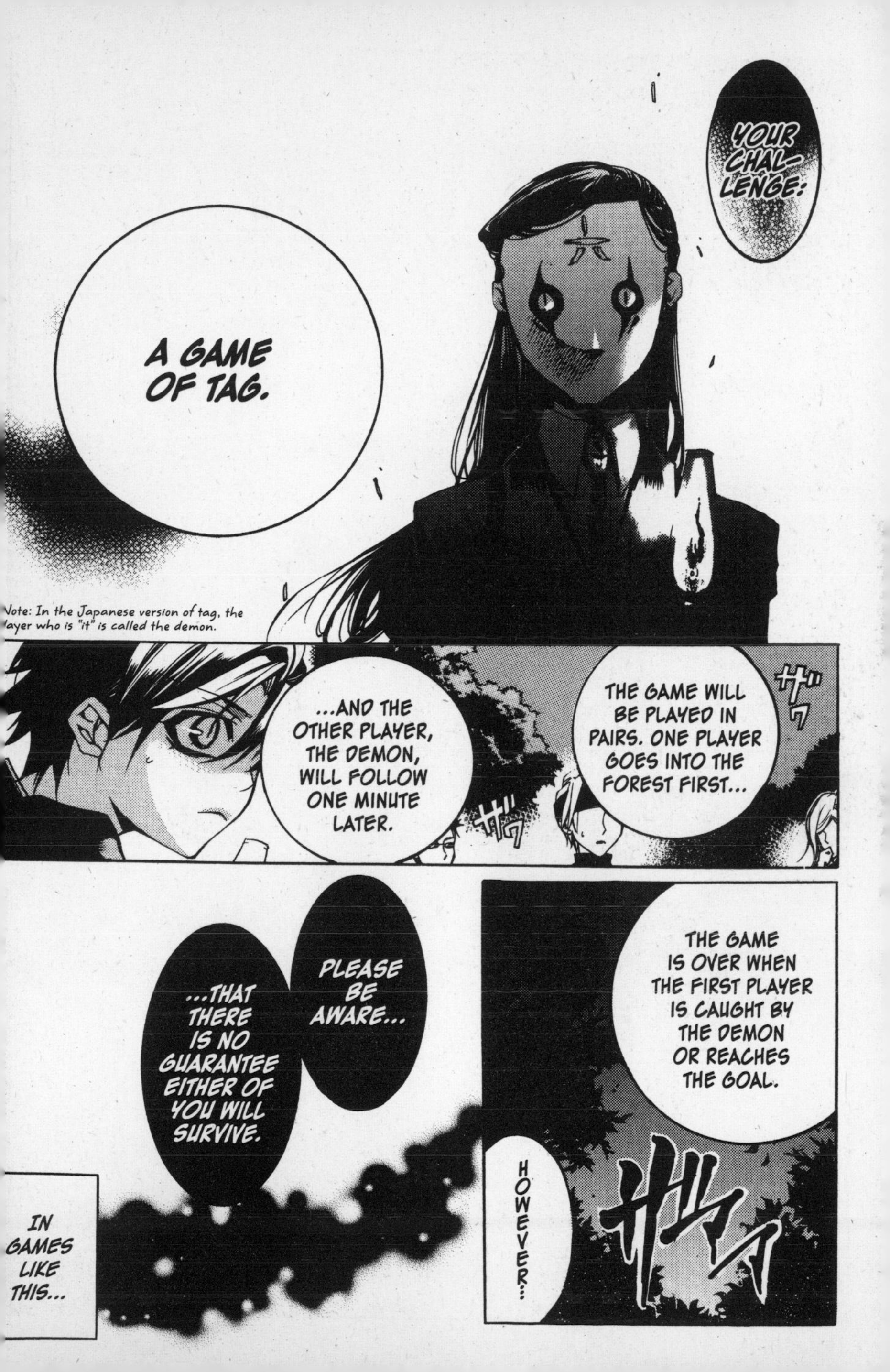
YOUR CHAL-LENGE:
A GAME OF TAG.
ザワ
THE GAME WILL BE PLAYED IN PAIRS. ONE PLAYER GOES INTO THE FOREST FIRST...
...AND THE OTHER PLAYER, THE DEMON, WILL FOLLOW ONE MINUTE LATER.
ザワ
THE GAME IS OVER WHEN THE FIRST PLAYER IS CAUGHT BY THE DEMON OR REACHES THE GOAL.
HOWEVER...
PLEASE BE AWARE...
...THAT THERE IS NO GUARANTEE EITHER OF YOU WILL SURVIVE.
IN GAMES LIKE THIS...

Note: In the Japanese version of tag, the player who is "it" is called the demon.

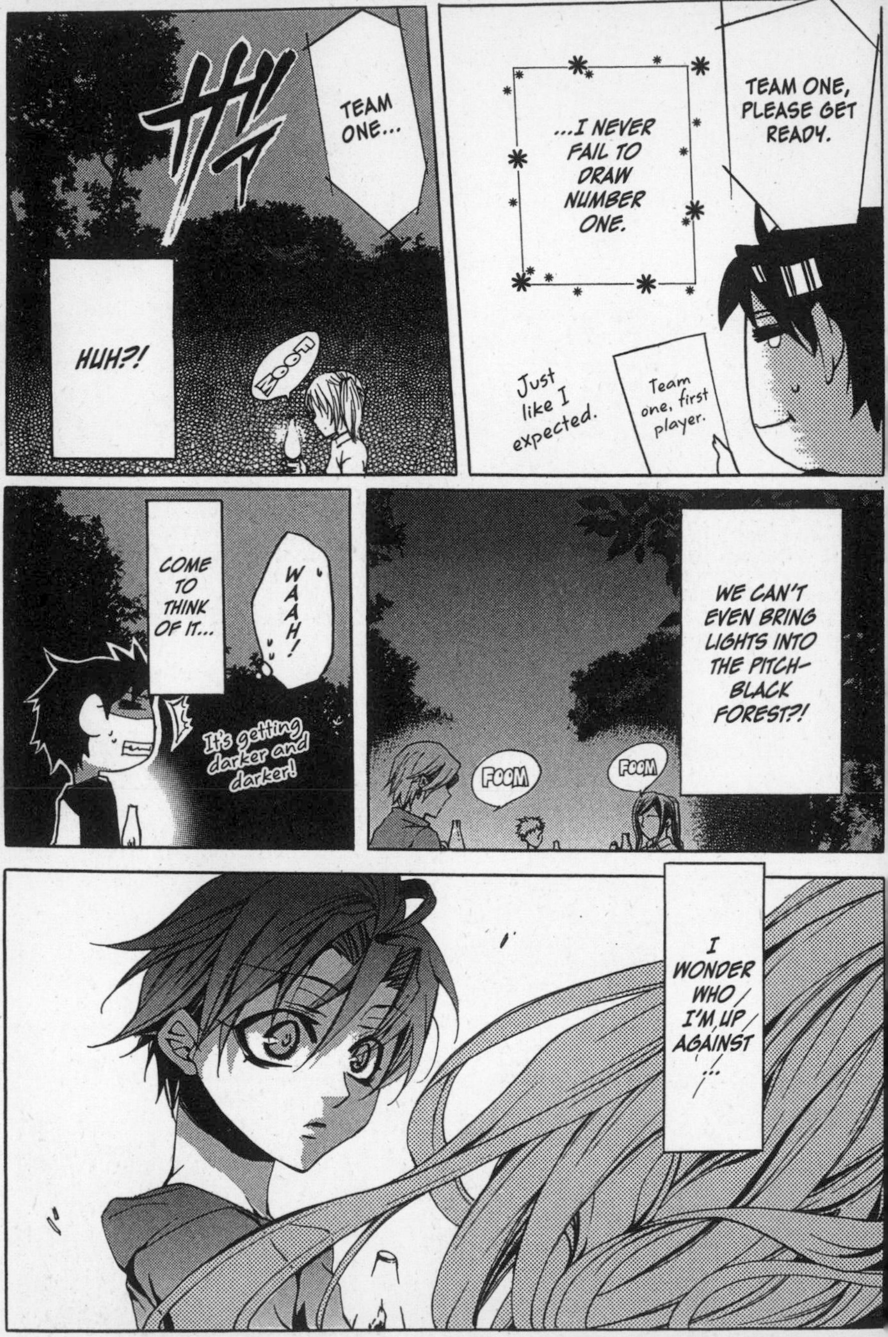
TEAM ONE, PLEASE GET READY.
...I NEVER FAIL TO DRAW NUMBER ONE.
Team one, first player.
Just like I expected.
TEAM ONE...
HUH?!
FOOM
WE CAN'T EVEN BRING LIGHTS INTO THE PITCH-BLACK FOREST?!
FOOM
FOOM
COME TO THINK OF IT...
WAAAH!
It's getting darker and darker!
I WONDER WHO I'M UP AGAINST...

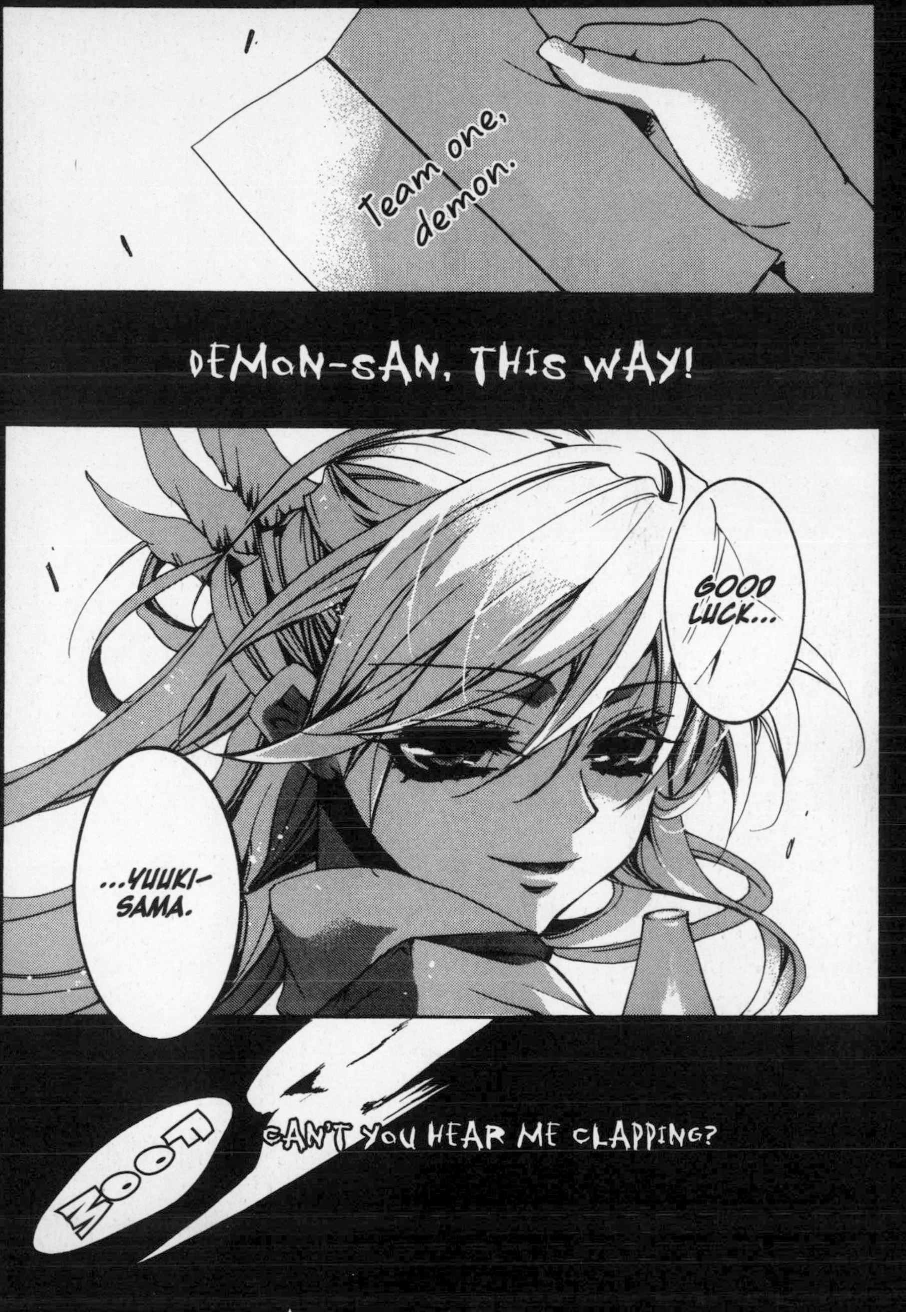
Team one, demon.
DEMON-SAN, THIS WAY!
GOOD LUCK...
...YUUKI-SAMA.
WOOF
CAN'T YOU HEAR ME CLAPPING?

★Chaper 6★END

Chapter 7

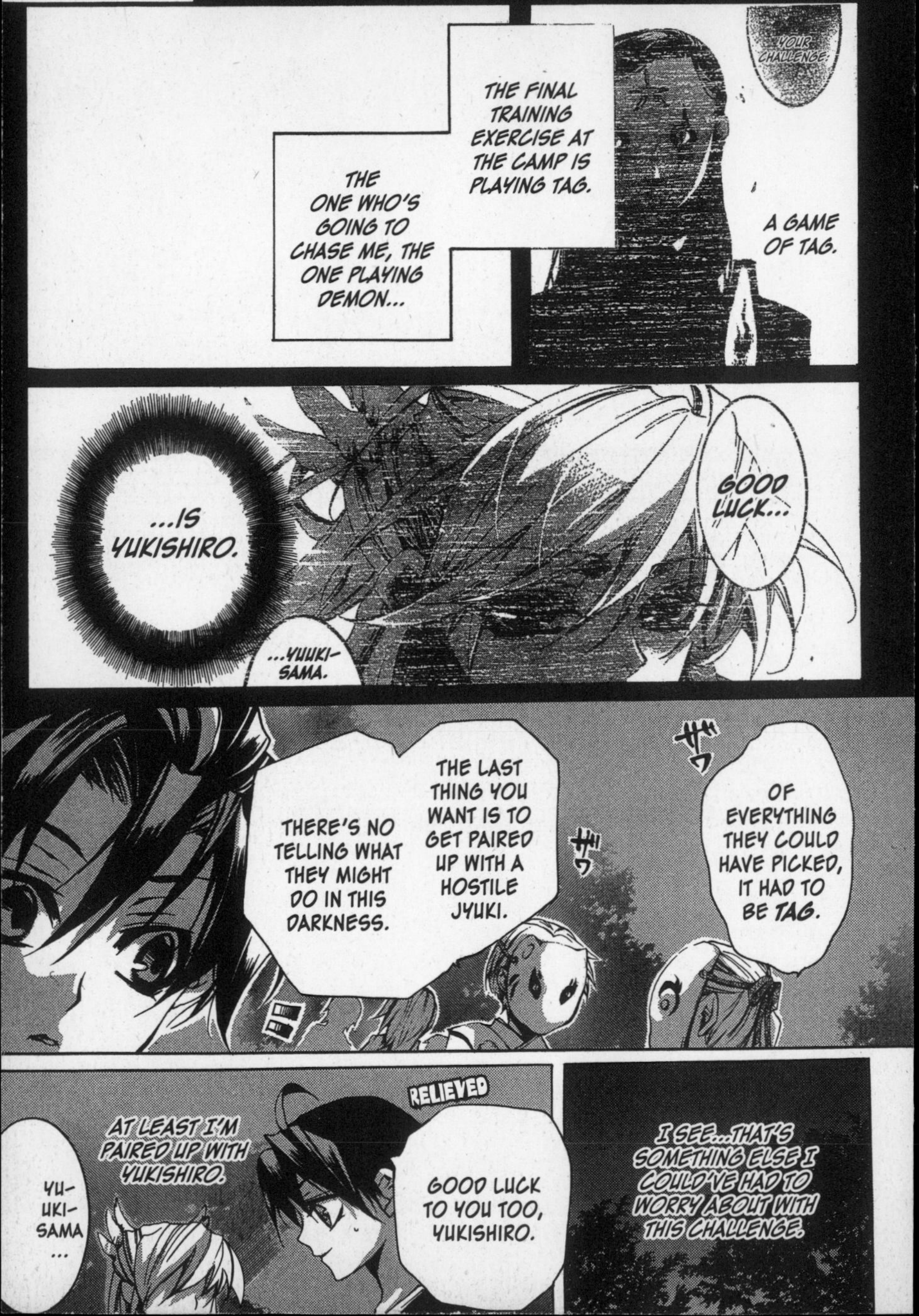
YOUR CHALLENGE.
A GAME OF TAG.
THE FINAL TRAINING EXERCISE AT THE CAMP IS PLAYING TAG.
THE ONE WHO'S GOING TO CHASE ME, THE ONE PLAYING DEMON...
GOOD LUCK...
...IS YUKISHIRO.
...YUUKI-SAMA.
OF EVERYTHING THEY COULD HAVE PICKED, IT HAD TO BE TAG.
THE LAST THING YOU WANT IS TO GET PAIRED UP WITH A HOSTILE JYUKI.
THERE'S NO TELLING WHAT THEY MIGHT DO IN THIS DARKNESS.
I SEE...THAT'S SOMETHING ELSE I COULD'VE HAD TO WORRY ABOUT WITH THIS CHALLENGE.
RELIEVED
GOOD LUCK TO YOU TOO, YUKISHIRO.
AT LEAST I'M PAIRED UP WITH YUKISHIRO.
YU-UKI-SAMA...

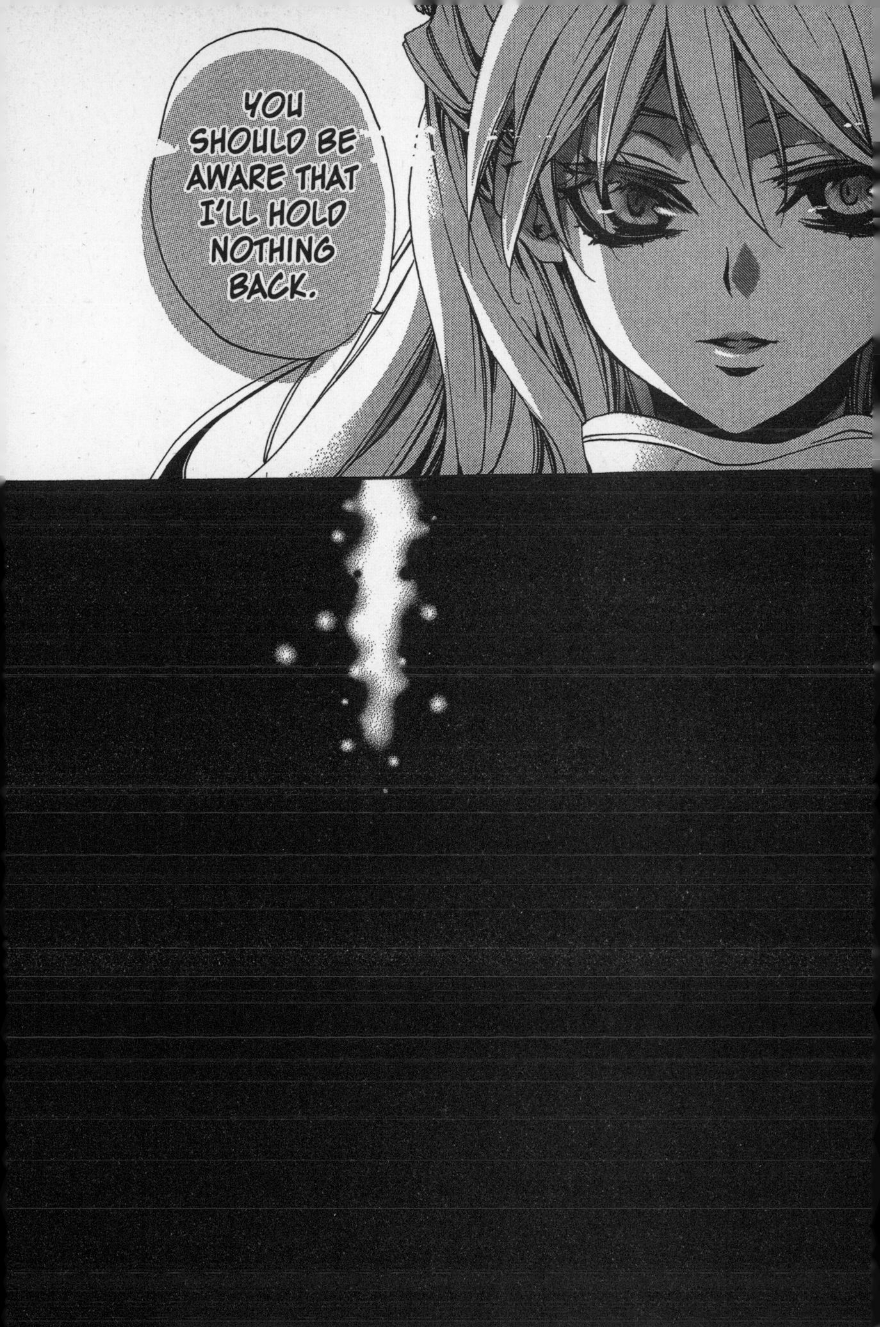
YOU SHOULD BE AWARE THAT I'LL HOLD NOTHING BACK.

Chapter 7: The Beasts' Secret Gathering in May, Part 2

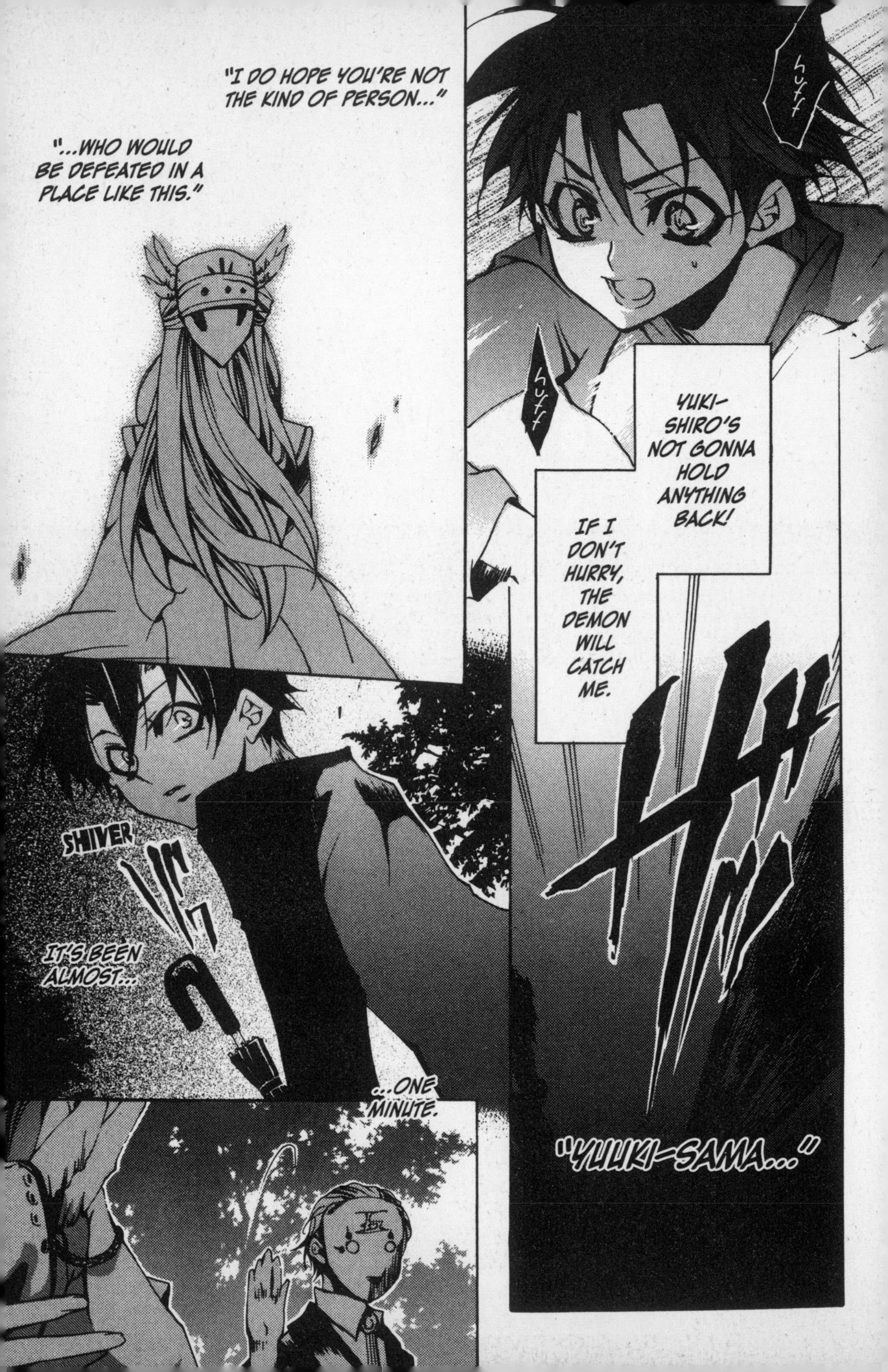
huff
huff
YUKI-SHIRO'S NOT GONNA HOLD ANYTHING BACK!
IF I DON'T HURRY, THE DEMON WILL CATCH ME.
"I DO HOPE YOU'RE NOT THE KIND OF PERSON..."
"...WHO WOULD BE DEFEATED IN A PLACE LIKE THIS."
"YUUKI-SAMA..."
SHIVER
IT'S BEEN ALMOST...
...ONE MINUTE.

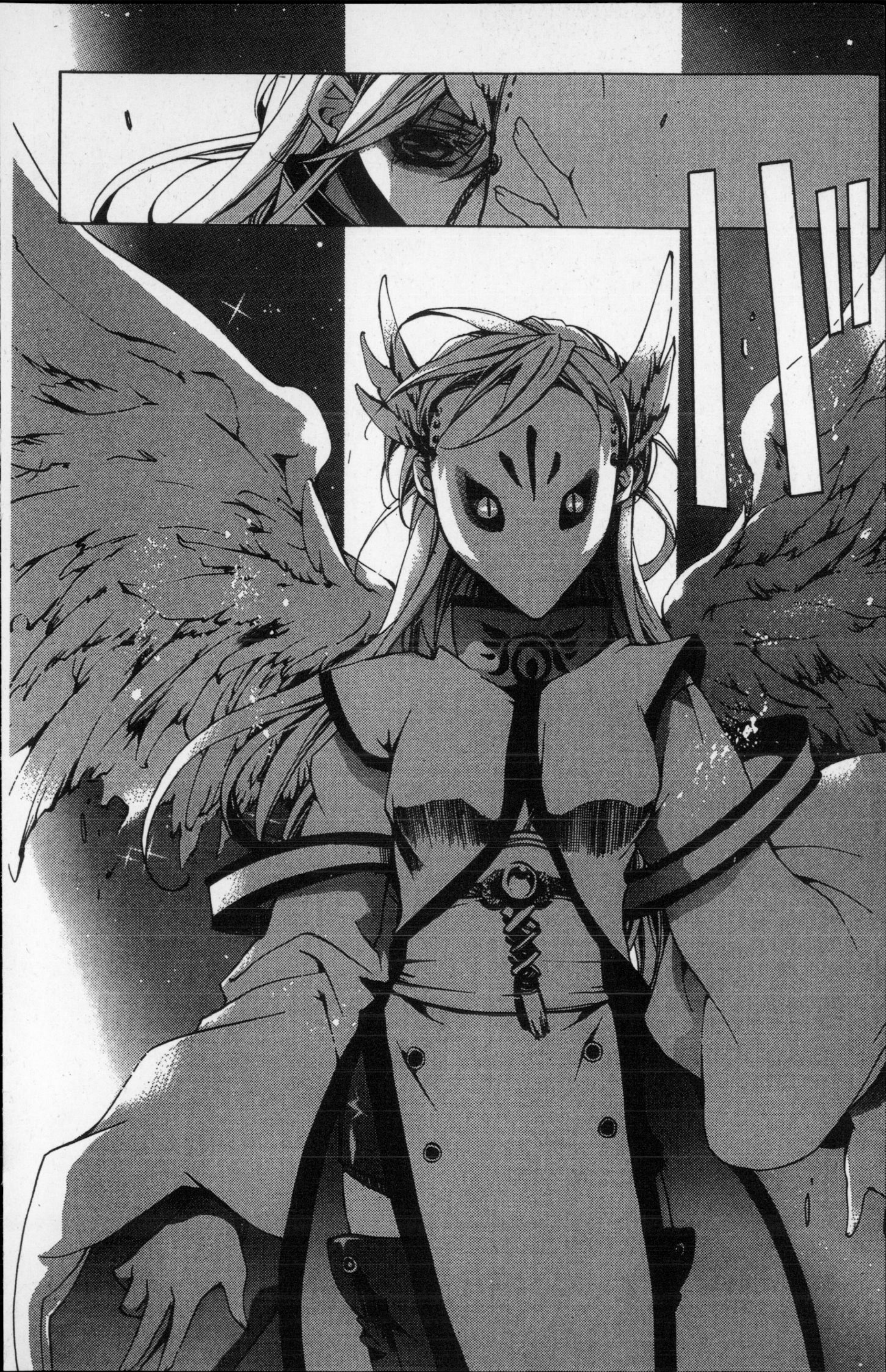

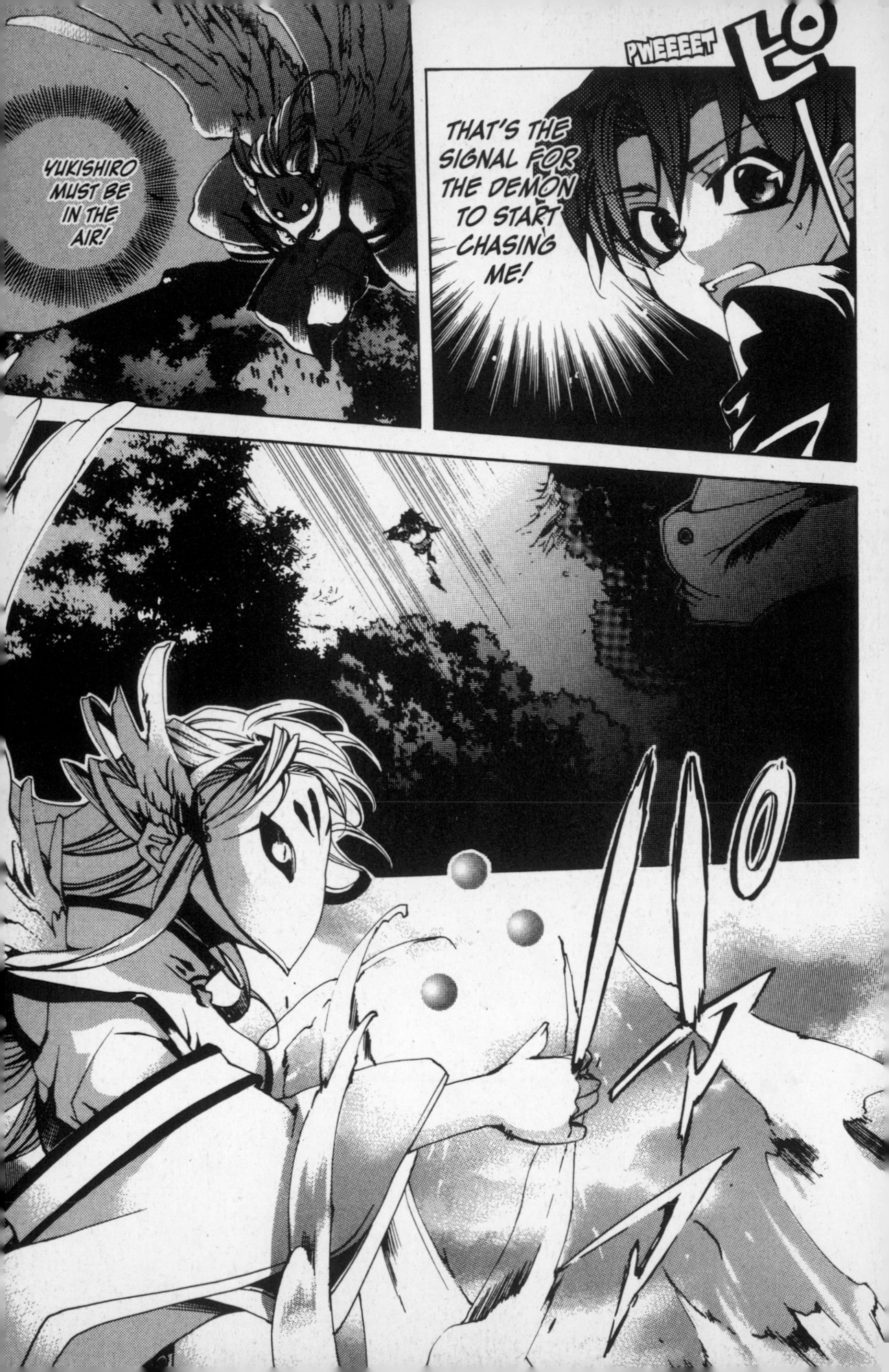
PWEEEET
THAT'S THE SIGNAL FOR THE DEMON TO START CHASING ME!
YUKISHIRO MUST BE IN THE AIR!

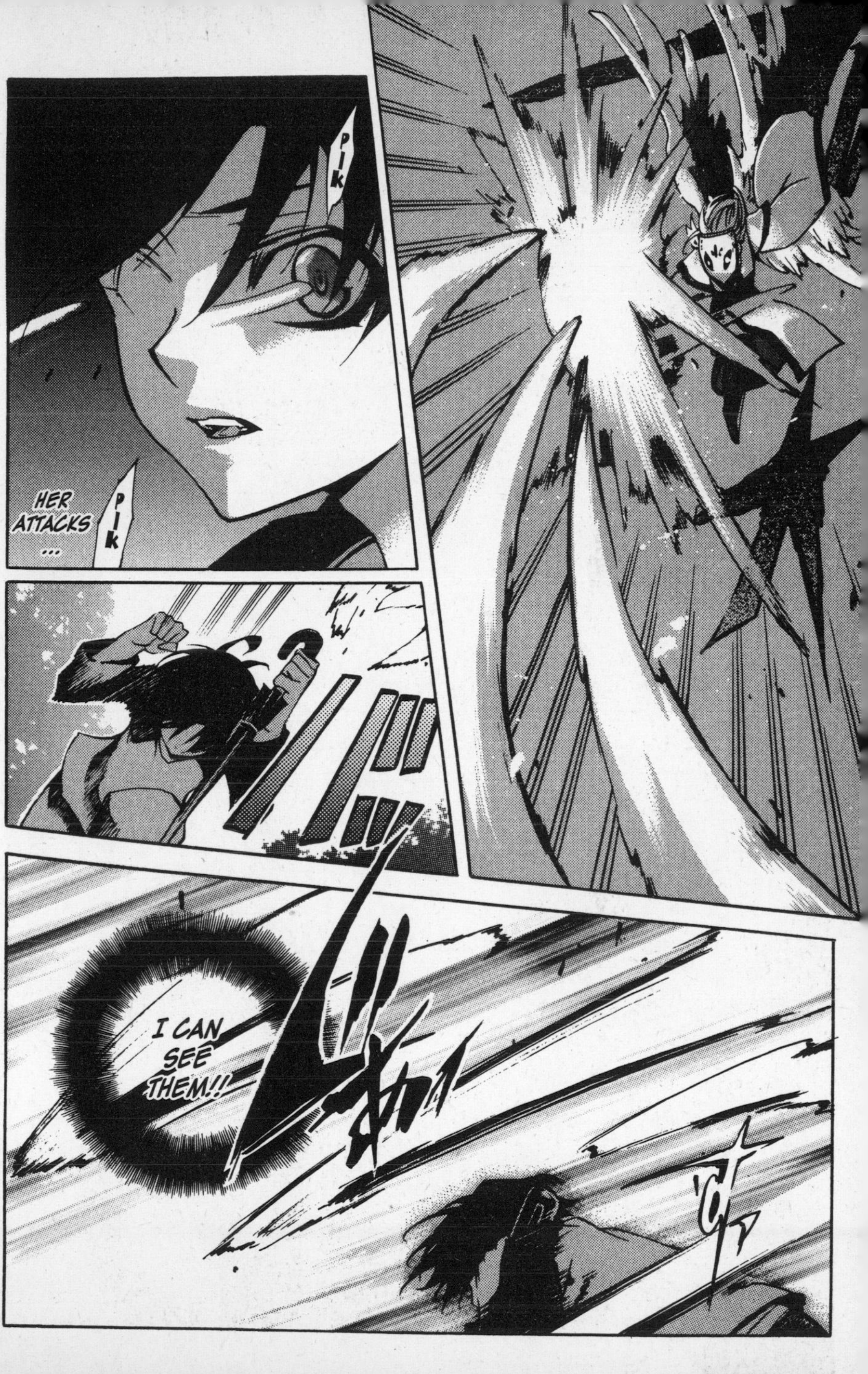
PIK
PIK
HER ATTACKS ...
I CAN SEE THEM!!

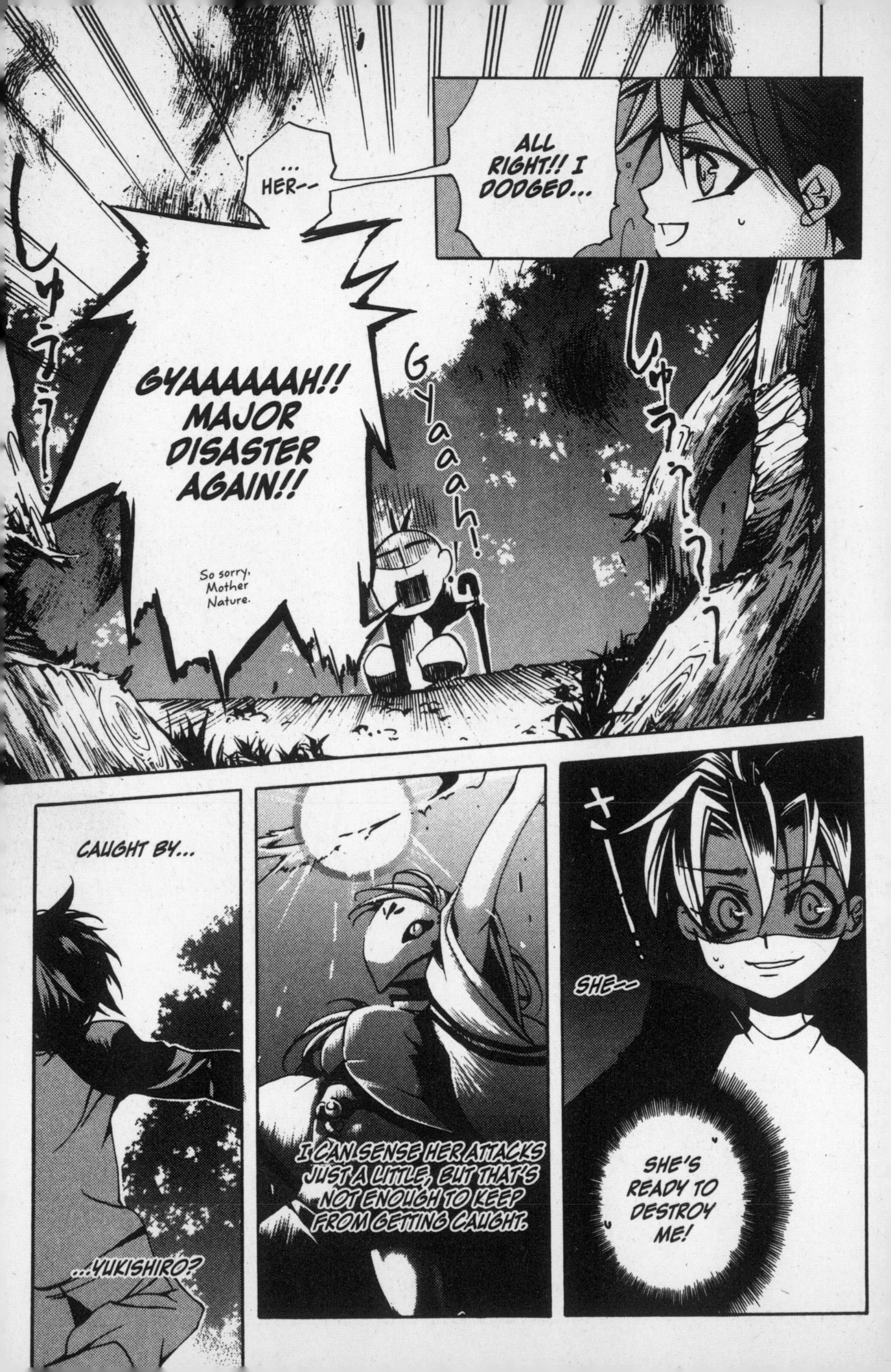
ALL RIGHT!! I DODGED...
... HER--
GYAAAAAAH!! MAJOR DISASTER AGAIN!!
Gyaaah!!
So sorry, Mother Nature.
SHE--
SHE'S READY TO DESTROY ME!
I CAN SENSE HER ATTACKS JUST A LITTLE, BUT THAT'S NOT ENOUGH TO KEEP FROM GETTING CAUGHT.
CAUGHT BY...
...YUKISHIRO?

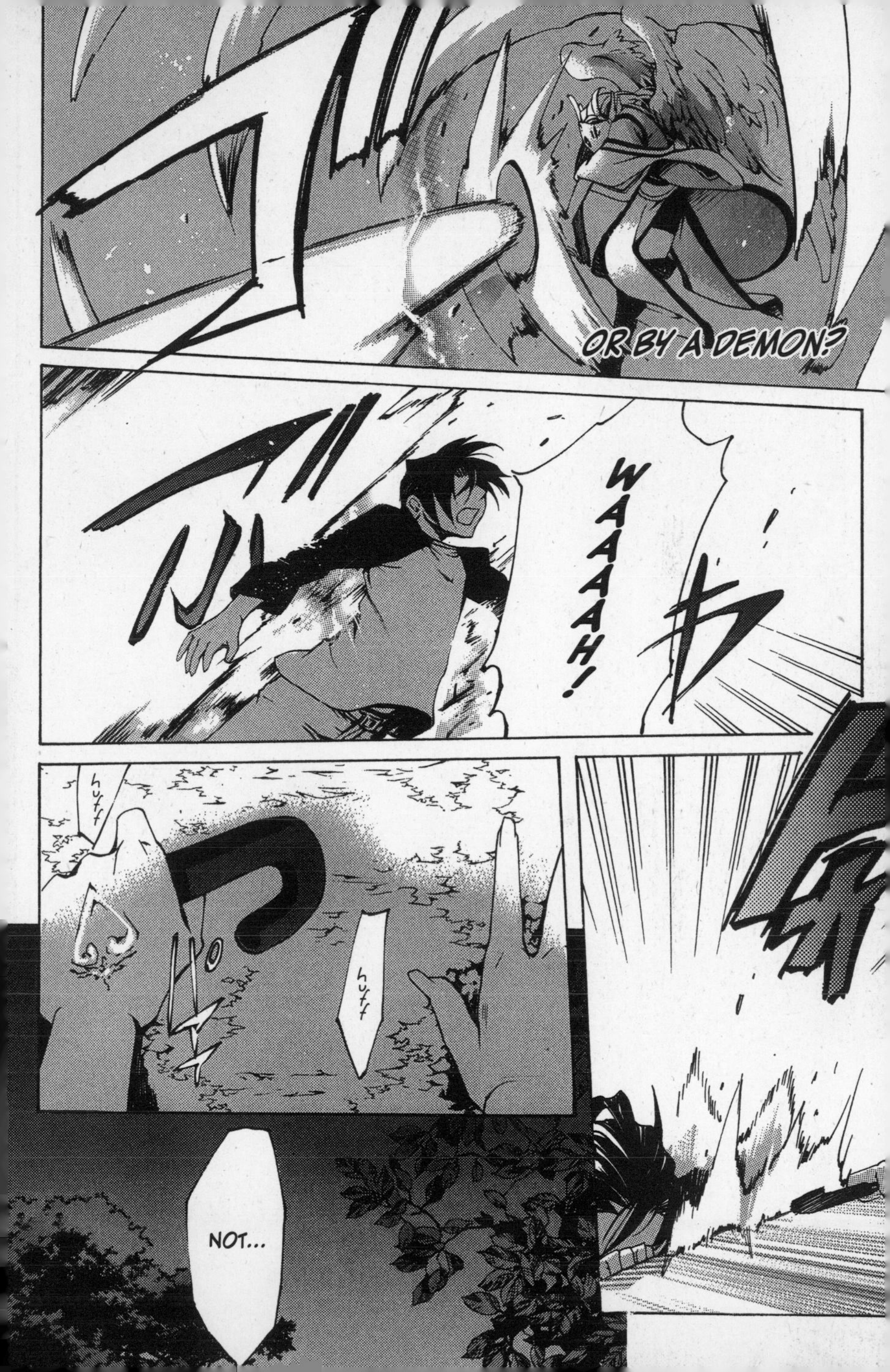

OR BY A DEMON?
WAAAAAH!
huff
huff
NOT...

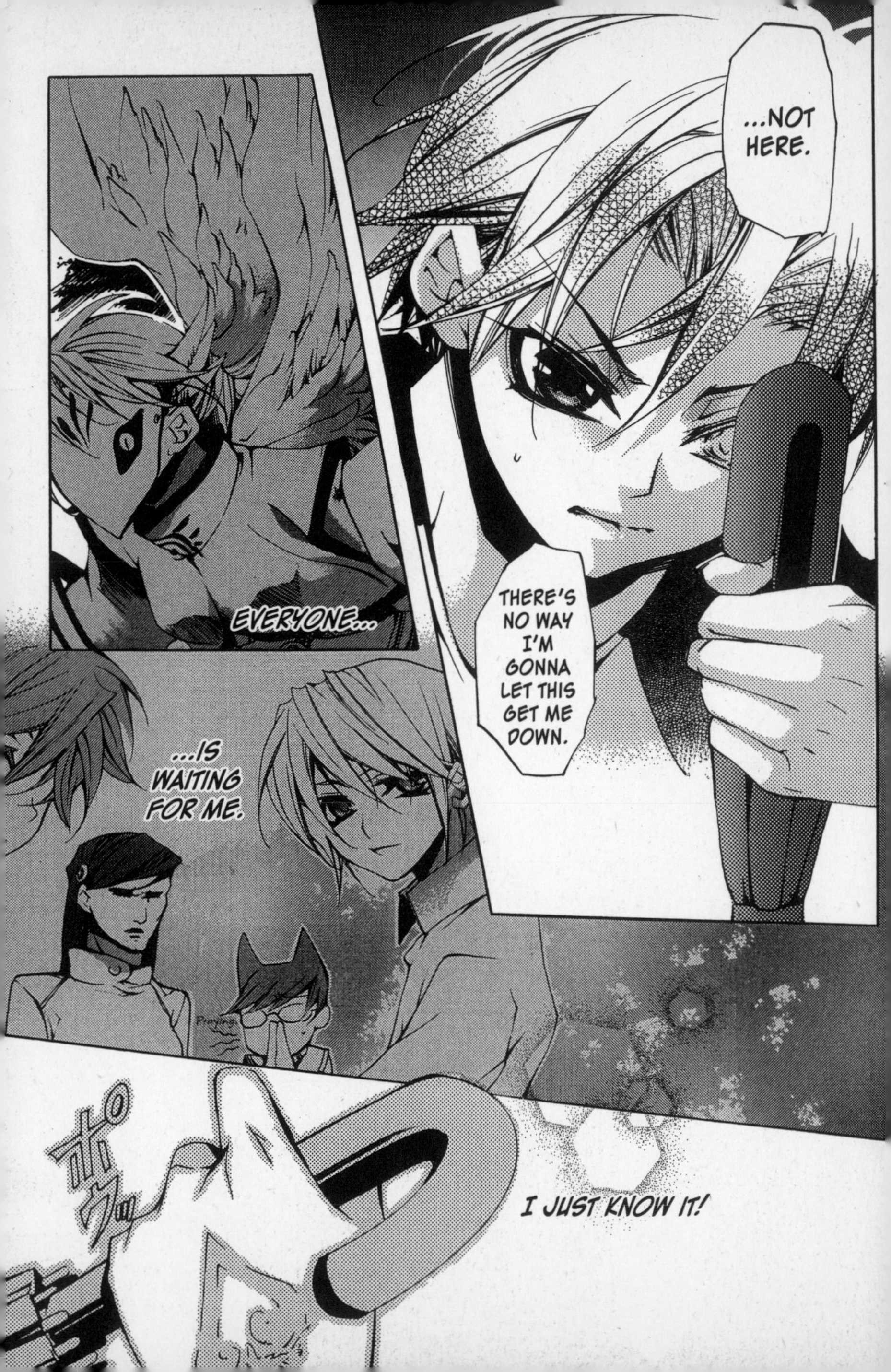
...NOT HERE.
THERE'S NO WAY I'M GONNA LET THIS GET ME DOWN.
EVERYONE...
...IS WAITING FOR ME.
Praying
I JUST KNOW IT!

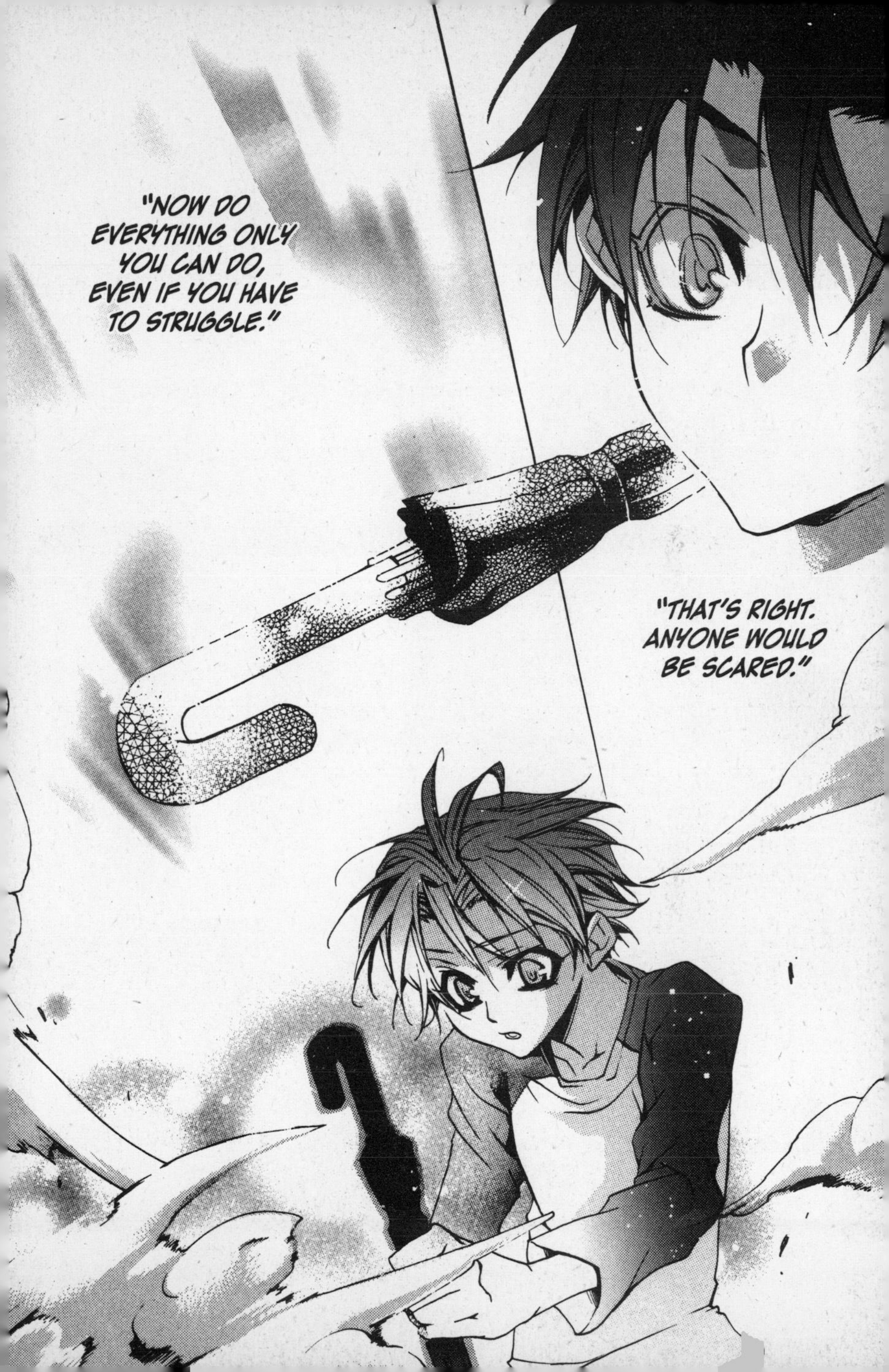
"THAT'S RIGHT. ANYONE WOULD BE SCARED."
"NOW DO EVERYTHING ONLY YOU CAN DO, EVEN IF YOU HAVE TO STRUGGLE."

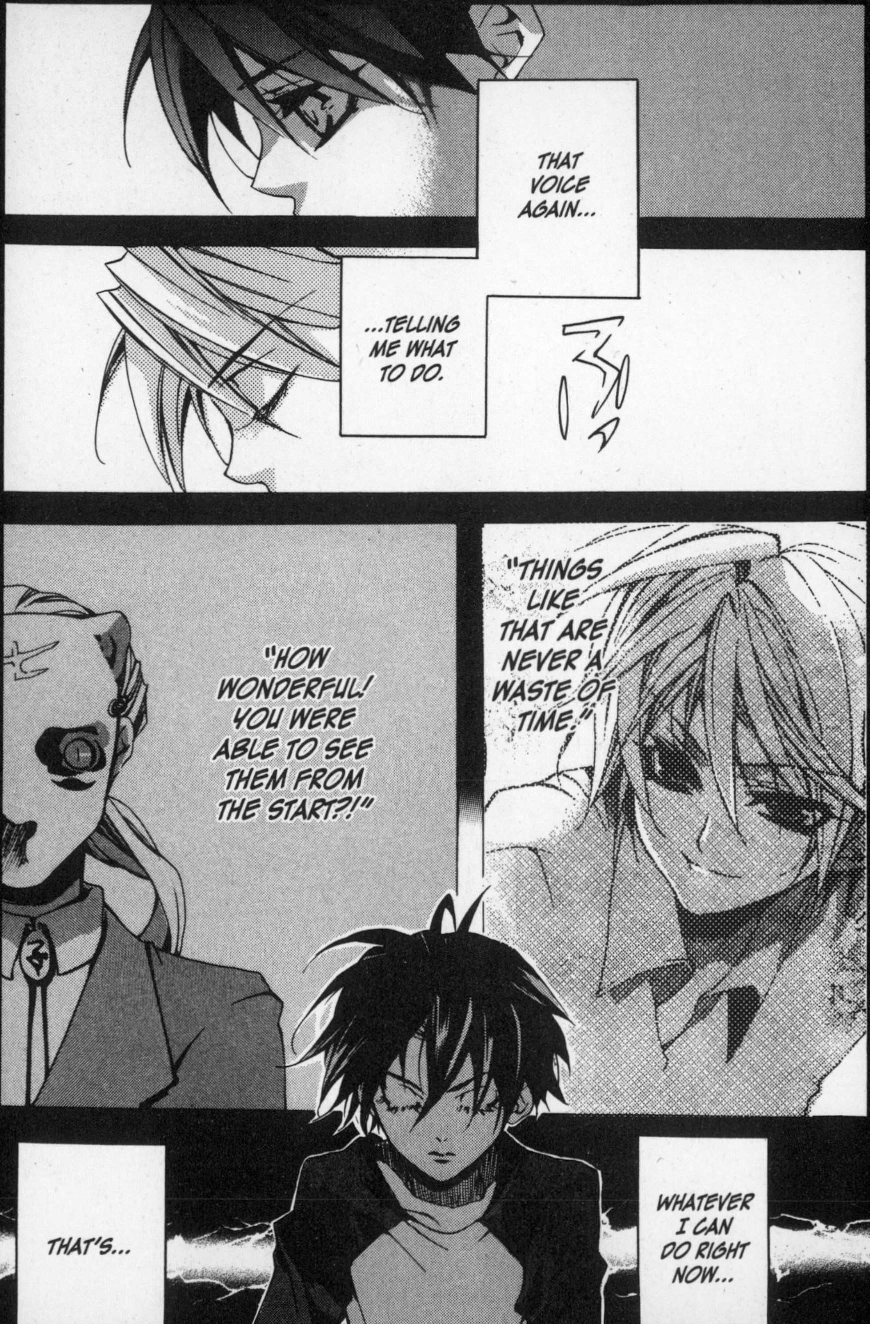
THAT VOICE AGAIN...
...TELLING ME WHAT TO DO.
"THINGS LIKE THAT ARE NEVER A WASTE OF TIME."
"HOW WONDERFUL! YOU WERE ABLE TO SEE THEM FROM THE START?!"
WHATEVER I CAN DO RIGHT NOW...
THAT'S...

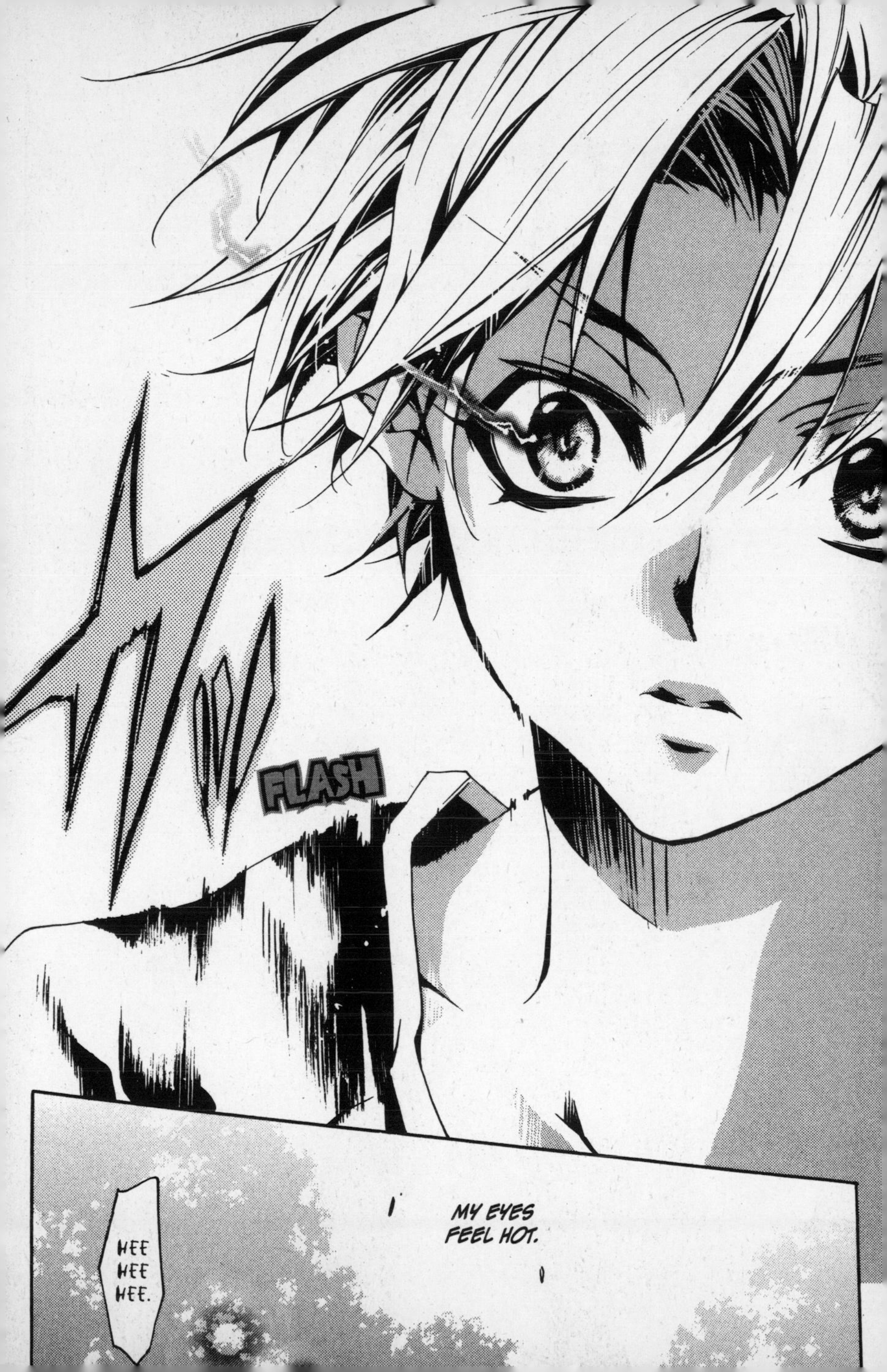
FLASH
MY EYES FEEL HOT.
HEE HEE HEE.

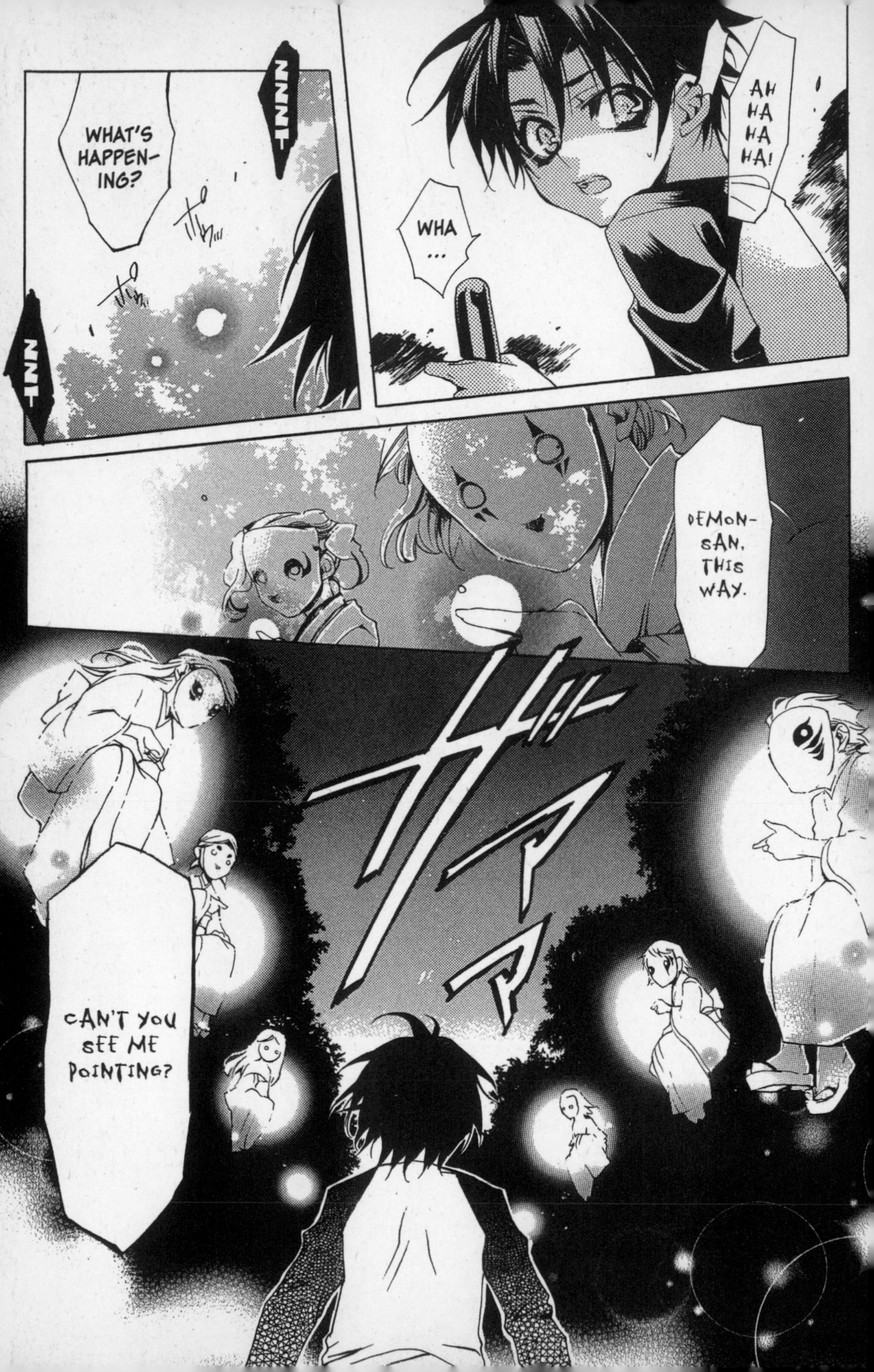
AH HA HA HA!
WHA ...
WHAT'S HAPPENING?
NNNT
NNNT
DEMON-SAN, THIS WAY.
CAN'T YOU SEE ME POINTING?

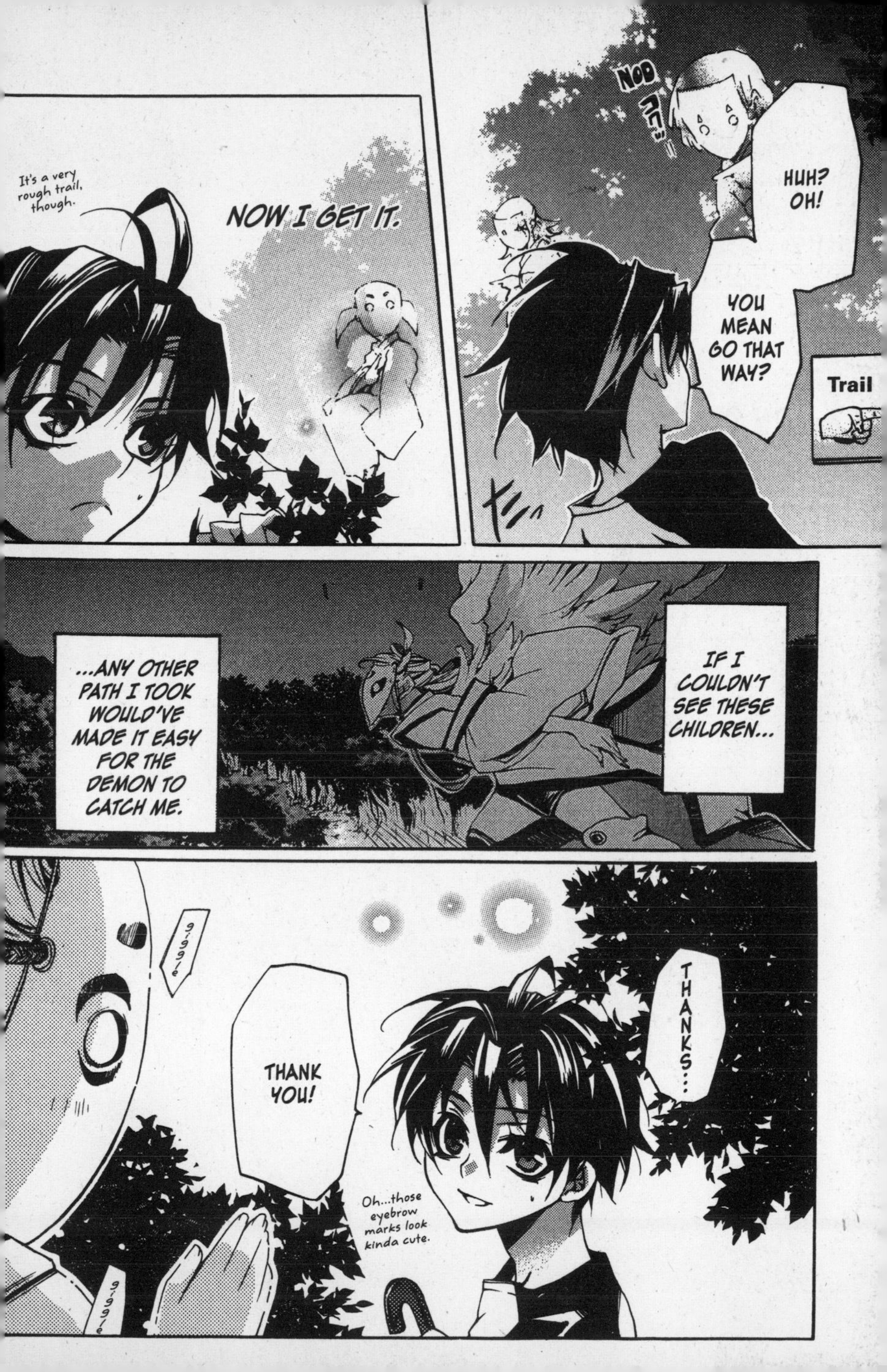
NOD
HUH? OH!
YOU MEAN GO THAT WAY?
Trail
NOW I GET IT.
It's a very rough trail, though.
IF I COULDN'T SEE THESE CHILDREN...
...ANY OTHER PATH I TOOK WOULD'VE MADE IT EASY FOR THE DEMON TO CATCH ME.
THANKS...
THANK YOU!
giggle
Oh...those eyebrow marks look kinda cute.
giggle

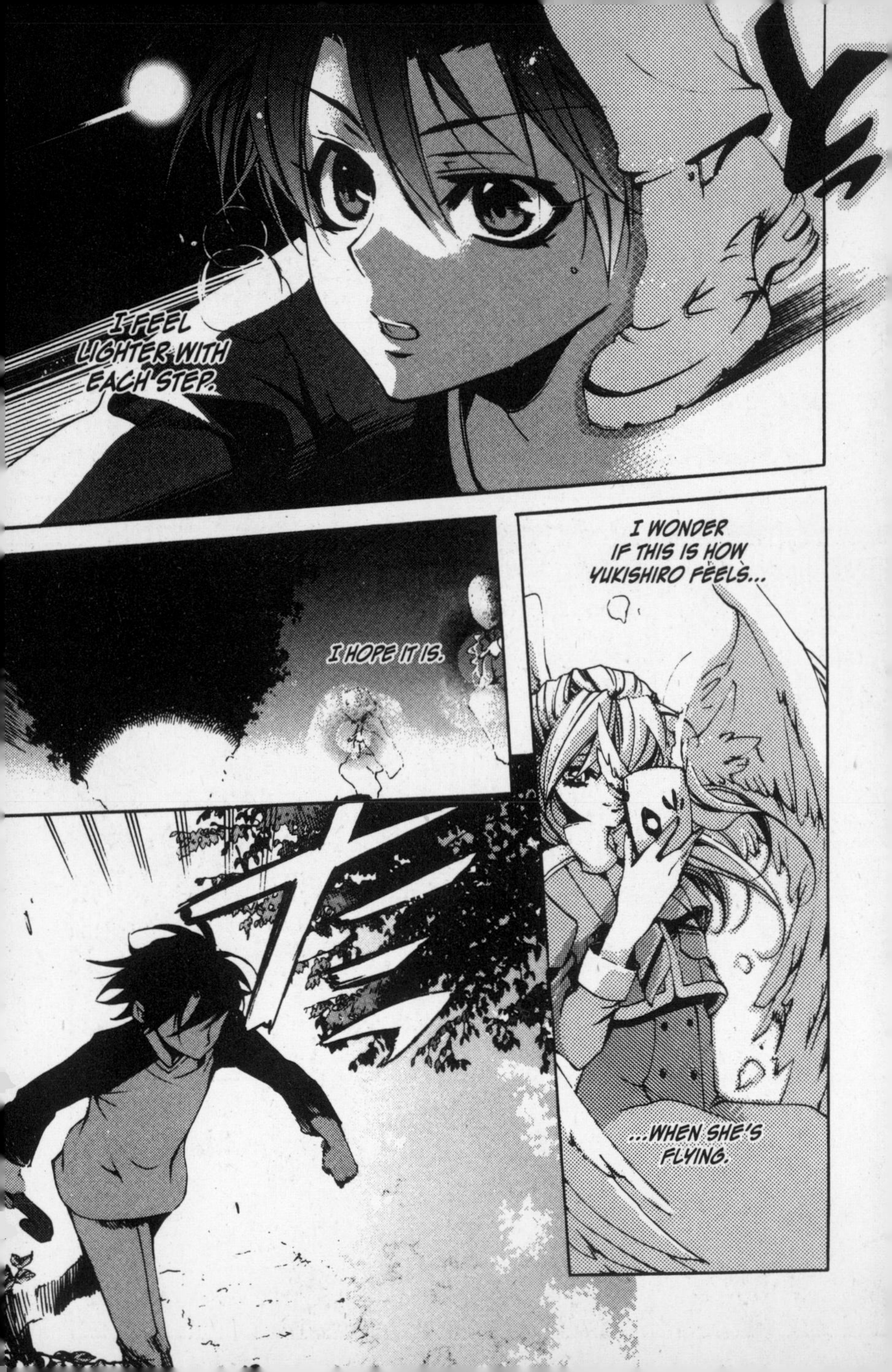
I FEEL LIGHTER WITH EACH STEP.
I WONDER IF THIS IS HOW YUKISHIRO FEELS...
...WHEN SHE'S FLYING.
I HOPE IT IS.

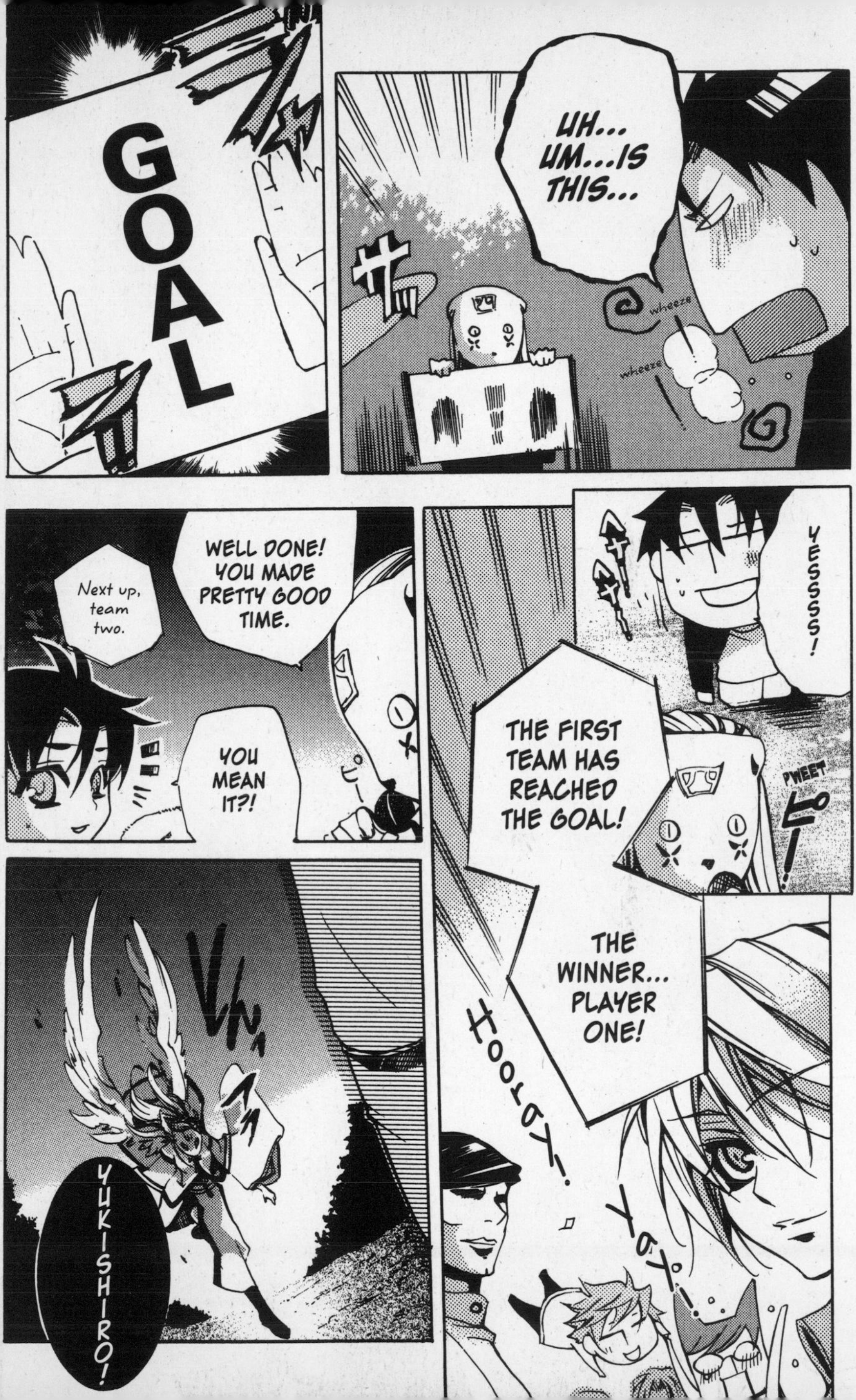
UH... UM...IS THIS...
wheeze
wheeze
GOAL
YESSSS!
THE FIRST TEAM HAS REACHED THE GOAL!
PWEET
THE WINNER... PLAYER ONE!
HOORAY!
YAAY!
WELL DONE! YOU MADE PRETTY GOOD TIME.
Next up, team two.
YOU MEAN IT?!
YUKISHIRO!

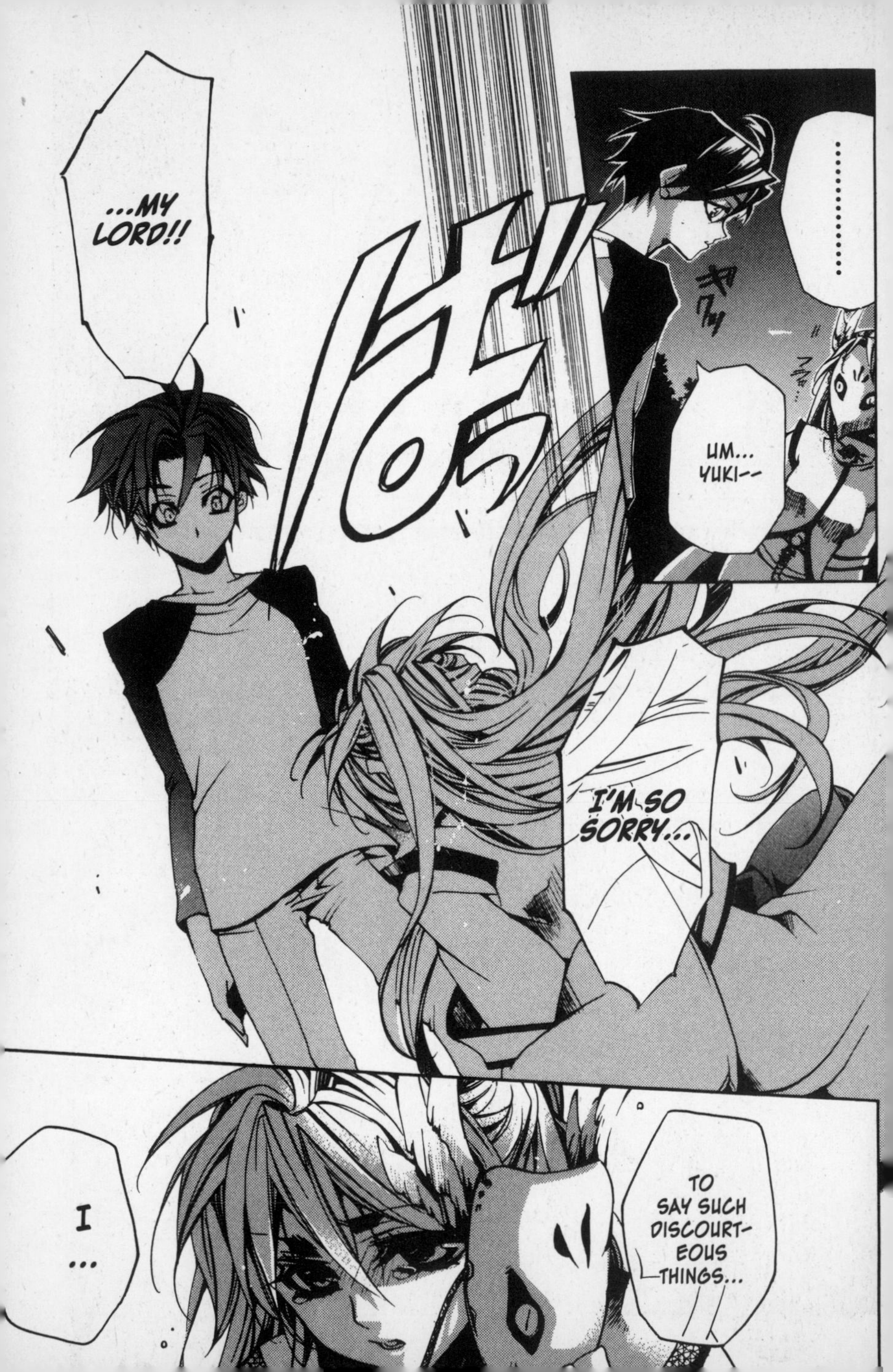
......
UM... YUKI--
...MY LORD!!
I'M SO SORRY...
TO SAY SUCH DISCOURT-EOUS THINGS...
I ...

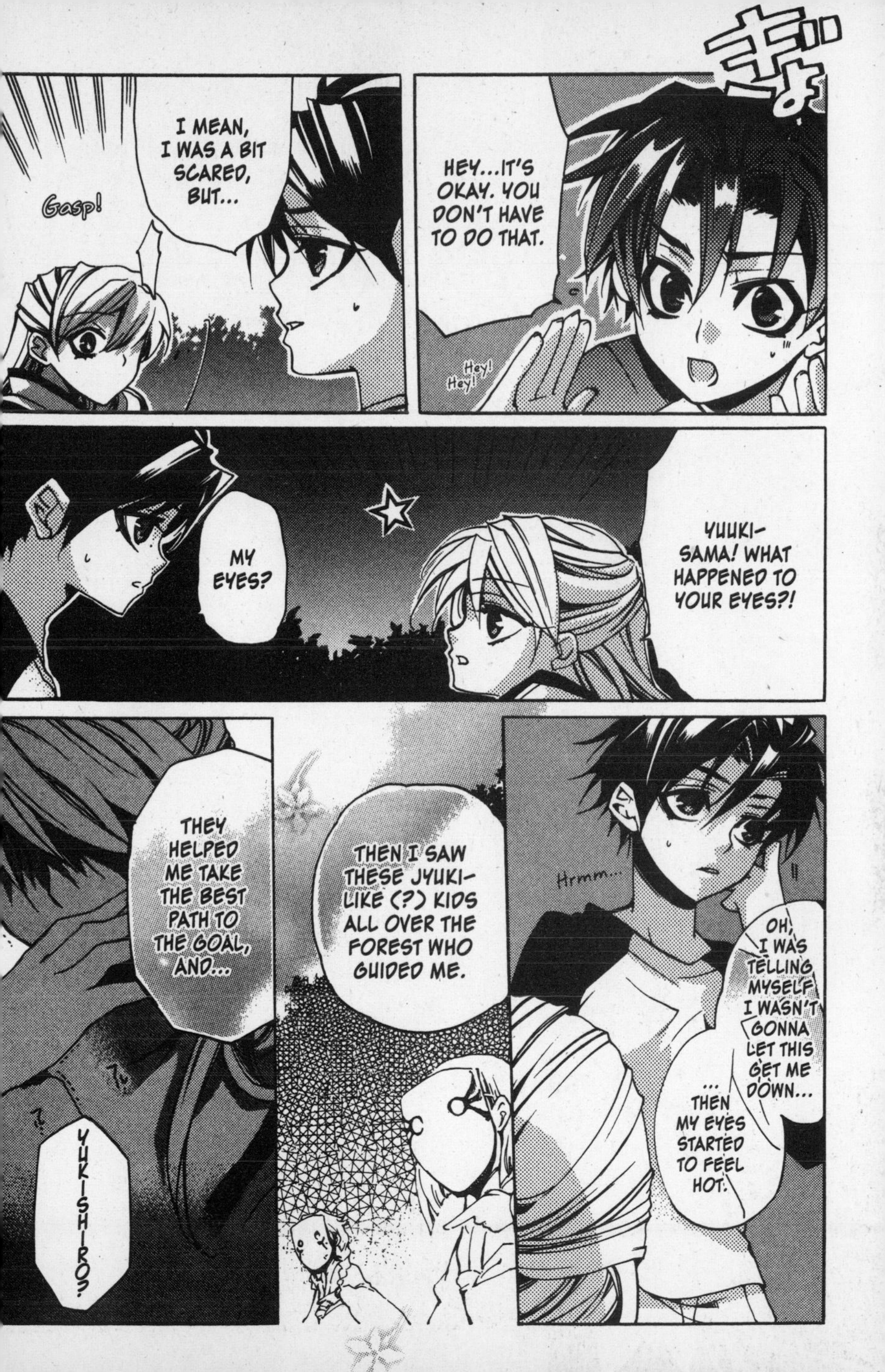
ぎょ
HEY...IT'S OKAY. YOU DON'T HAVE TO DO THAT.
Hey! Hey!
I MEAN, I WAS A BIT SCARED, BUT...
Gasp!
YUUKI-SAMA! WHAT HAPPENED TO YOUR EYES?!
MY EYES?
Hrmm...
OH, I WAS TELLING MYSELF I WASN'T GONNA LET THIS GET ME DOWN...
...THEN MY EYES STARTED TO FEEL HOT.
THEN I SAW THESE JYUKI-LIKE (?) KIDS ALL OVER THE FOREST WHO GUIDED ME.
THEY HELPED ME TAKE THE BEST PATH TO THE GOAL, AND...
YUKISHIRO?

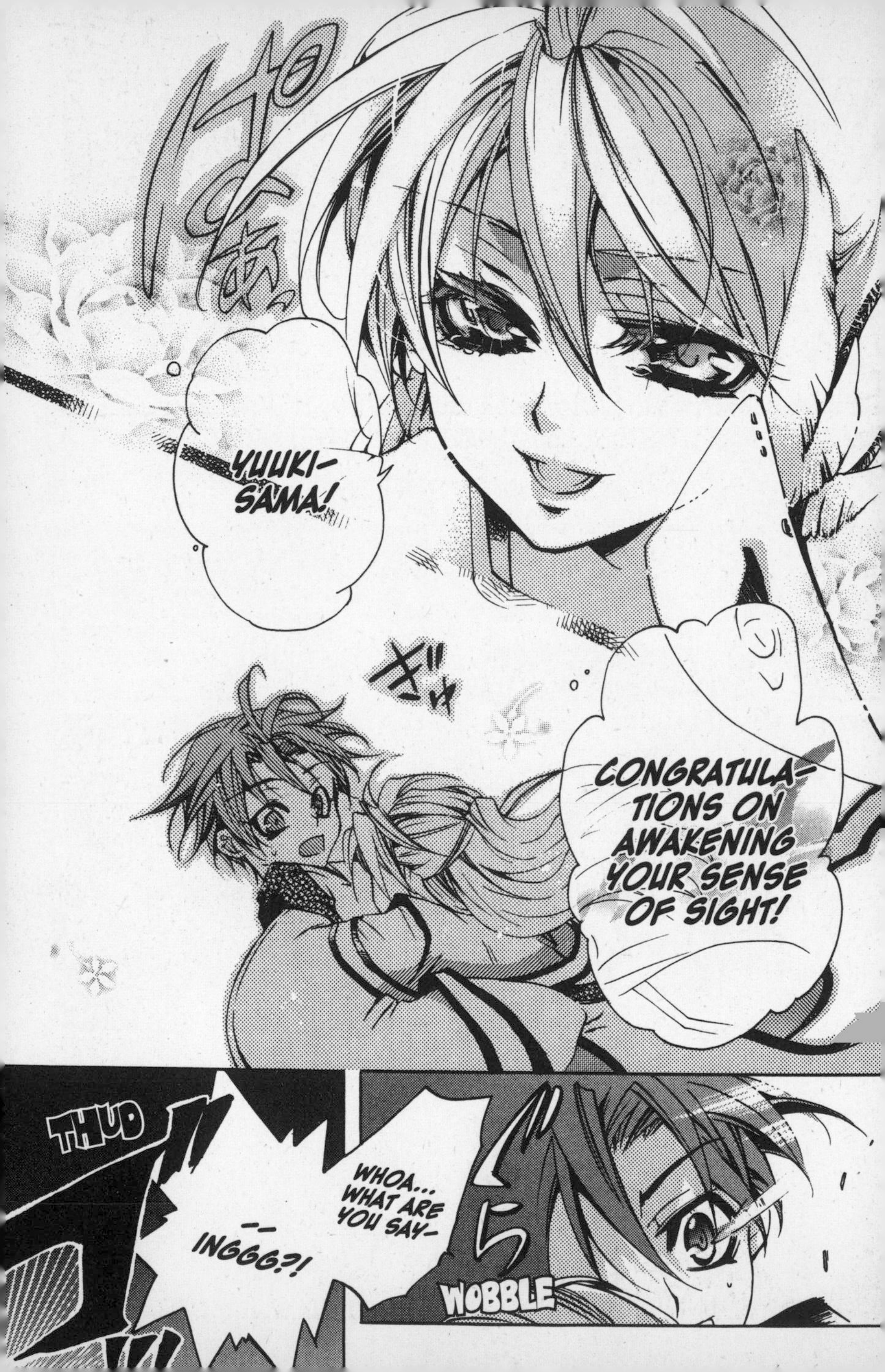
YUUKI-SAMA!
CONGRATULA-TIONS ON AWAKENING YOUR SENSE OF SIGHT!
WOBBLE
THUD
WHOA... WHAT ARE YOU SAY-
--INGGG?!

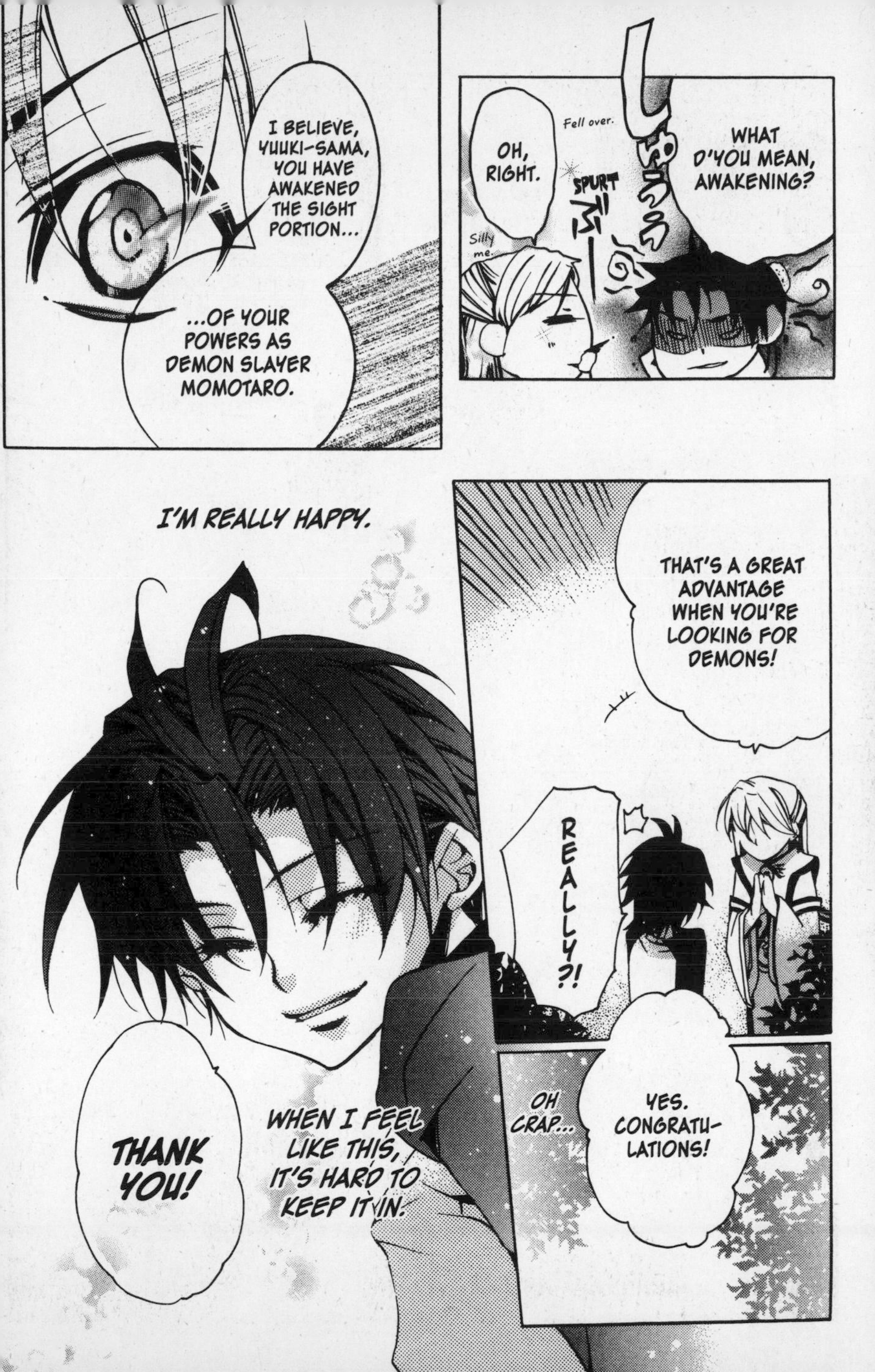
WHAT D'YOU MEAN, AWAKENING?
Fell over.
SPURT
OH, RIGHT.
Silly me.
I BELIEVE, YUUKI-SAMA, YOU HAVE AWAKENED THE SIGHT PORTION...
...OF YOUR POWERS AS DEMON SLAYER MOMOTARO.
THAT'S A GREAT ADVANTAGE WHEN YOU'RE LOOKING FOR DEMONS!
REALLY?!
YES. CONGRATULATIONS!
OH CRAP...
I'M REALLY HAPPY.
WHEN I FEEL LIKE THIS, IT'S HARD TO KEEP IT IN.
THANK YOU!

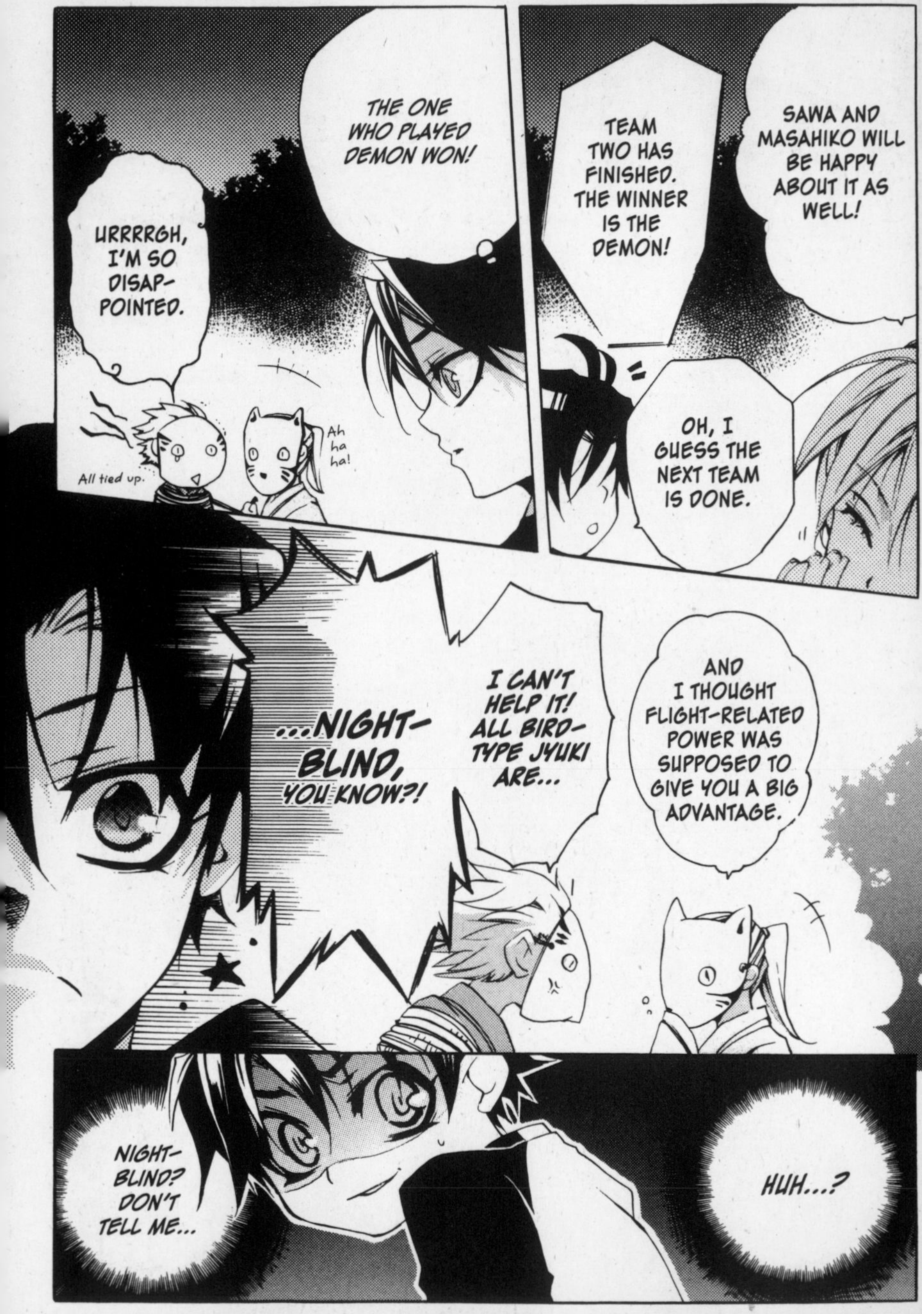
SAWA AND MASAHIKO WILL BE HAPPY ABOUT IT AS WELL!
TEAM TWO HAS FINISHED. THE WINNER IS THE DEMON!
OH, I GUESS THE NEXT TEAM IS DONE.
THE ONE WHO PLAYED DEMON WON!
URRRRGH, I'M SO DISAP-POINTED.
Ah ha ha!
All tied up.
AND I THOUGHT FLIGHT-RELATED POWER WAS SUPPOSED TO GIVE YOU A BIG ADVANTAGE.
I CAN'T HELP IT! ALL BIRD-TYPE JYUKI ARE...
...NIGHT-BLIND, YOU KNOW?!
HUH...?
NIGHT-BLIND? DON'T TELL ME...

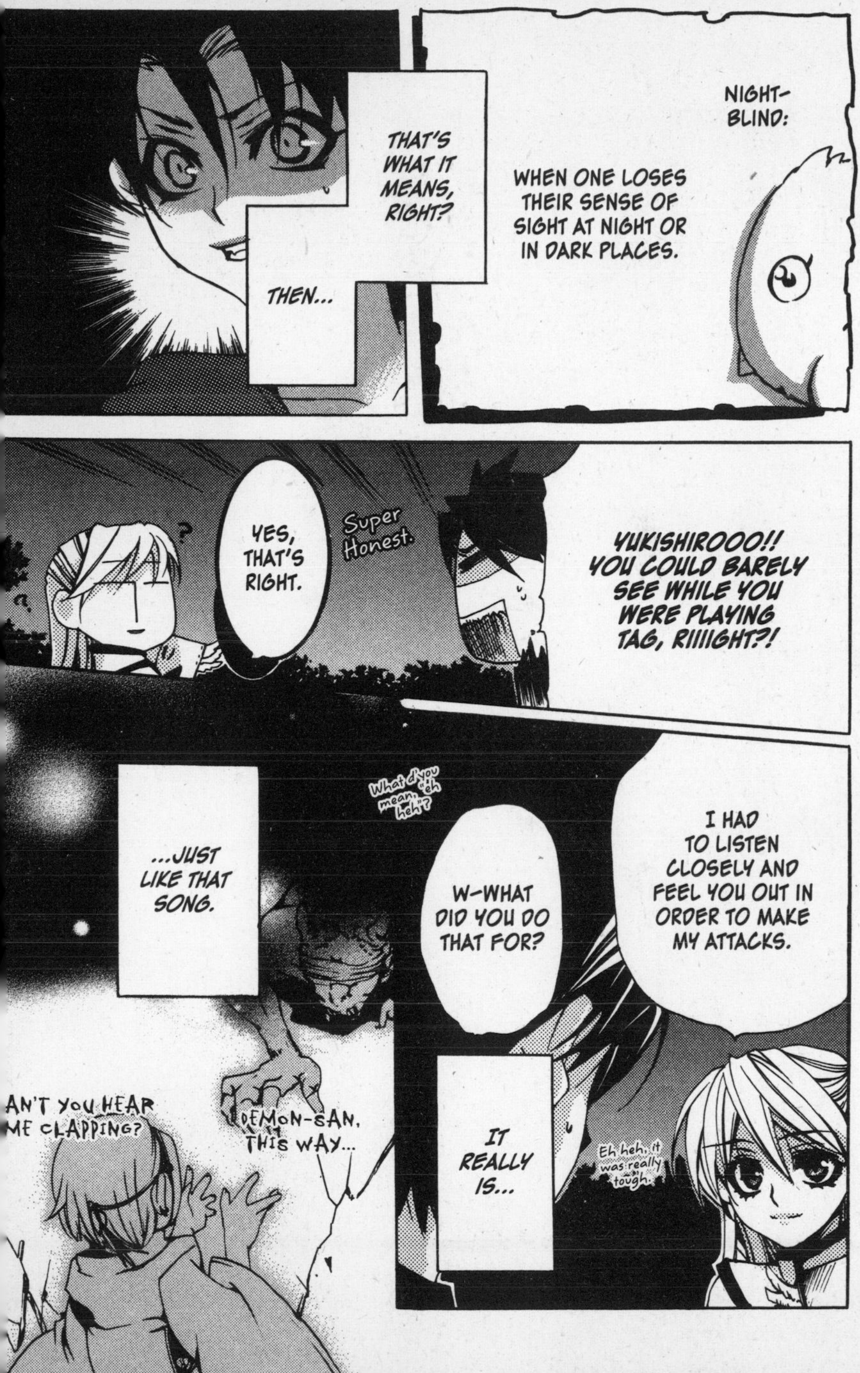
NIGHT-BLIND:
WHEN ONE LOSES THEIR SENSE OF SIGHT AT NIGHT OR IN DARK PLACES.
THAT'S WHAT IT MEANS, RIGHT?
THEN...
YUKISHIROOO!! YOU COULD BARELY SEE WHILE YOU WERE PLAYING TAG, RIIIIGHT?!
Super Honest.
YES, THAT'S RIGHT.
I HAD TO LISTEN CLOSELY AND FEEL YOU OUT IN ORDER TO MAKE MY ATTACKS.
Eh heh, it was really tough.
What d'you mean, "eh heh"?
W-WHAT DID YOU DO THAT FOR?
IT REALLY IS...
...JUST LIKE THAT SONG.
DEMON-SAN, THIS WAY...
AN'T YOU HEAR ME CLAPPING?

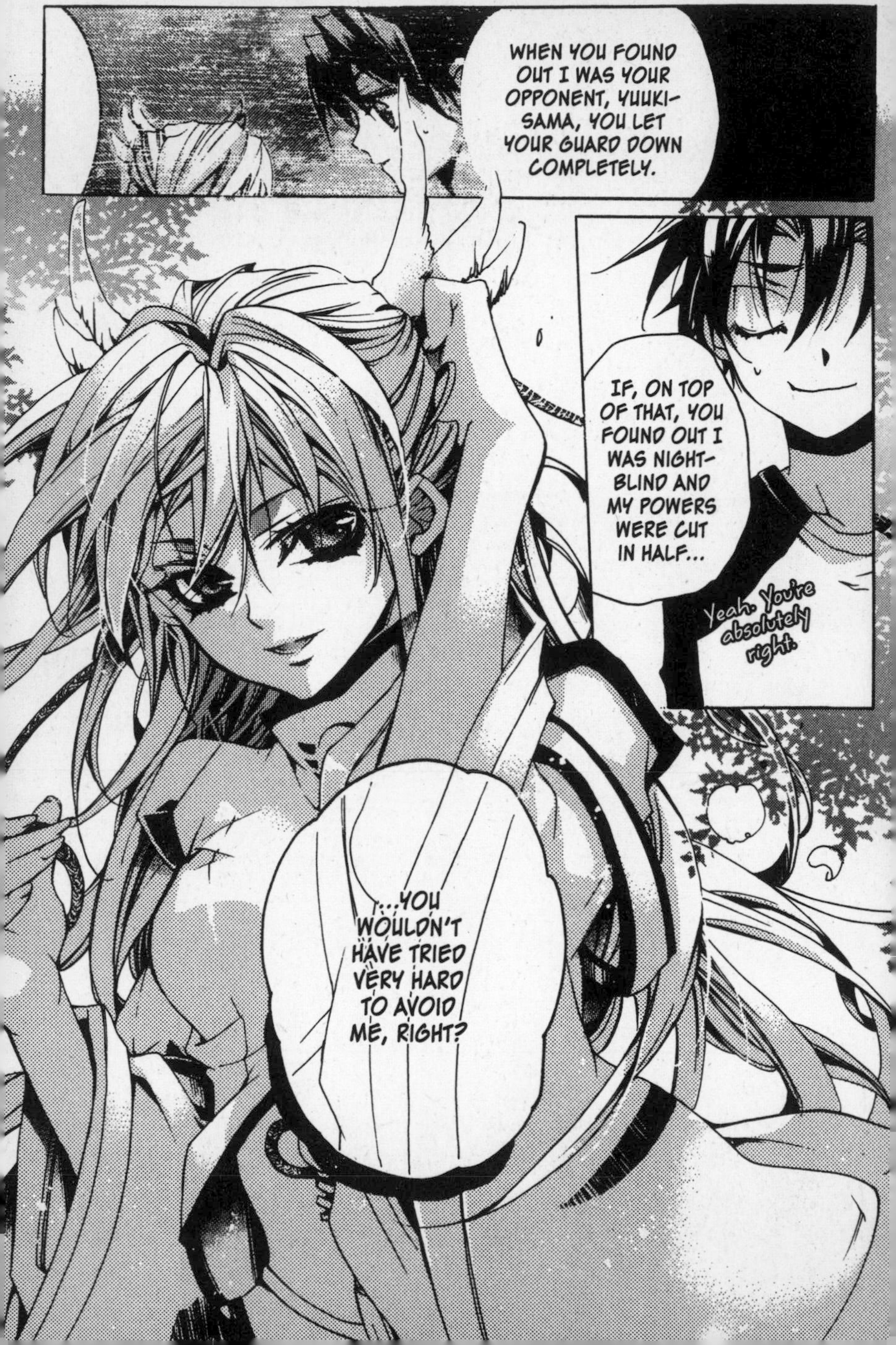
WHEN YOU FOUND OUT I WAS YOUR OPPONENT, YUUKI-SAMA, YOU LET YOUR GUARD DOWN COMPLETELY.
IF, ON TOP OF THAT, YOU FOUND OUT I WAS NIGHT-BLIND AND MY POWERS WERE CUT IN HALF...
Yeah. You're absolutely right.
...YOU WOULDN'T HAVE TRIED VERY HARD TO AVOID ME, RIGHT?

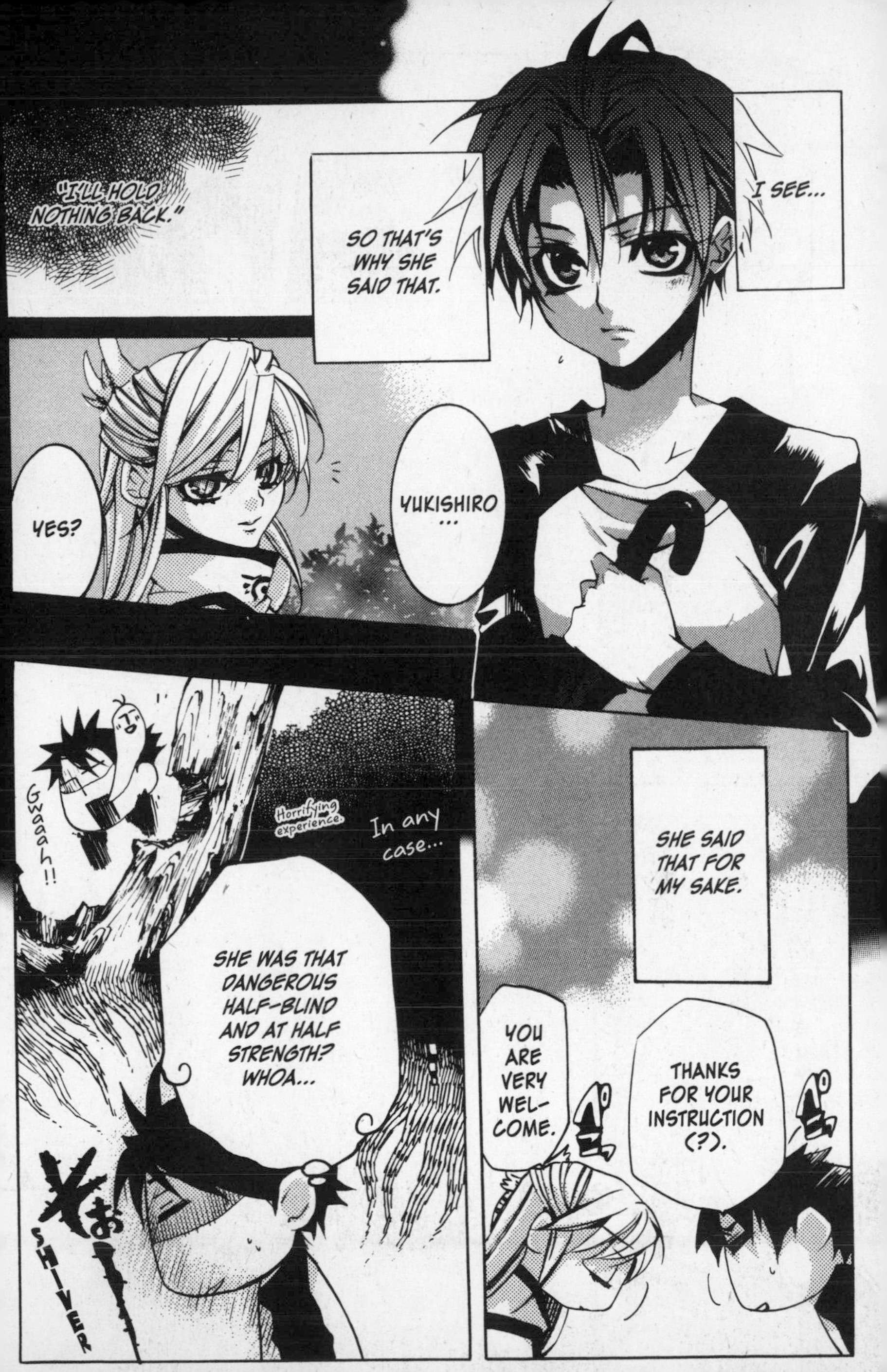
I SEE...
SO THAT'S WHY SHE SAID THAT.
"I'LL HOLD NOTHING BACK."
YUKISHIRO...
YES?
SHE SAID THAT FOR MY SAKE.
THANKS FOR YOUR INSTRUCTION (?).
YOU ARE VERY WEL-COME.
In any case...
SHE WAS THAT DANGEROUS HALF-BLIND AND AT HALF STRENGTH? WHOA...
Horrifying experience.
Gwaaah!!
SHIVER

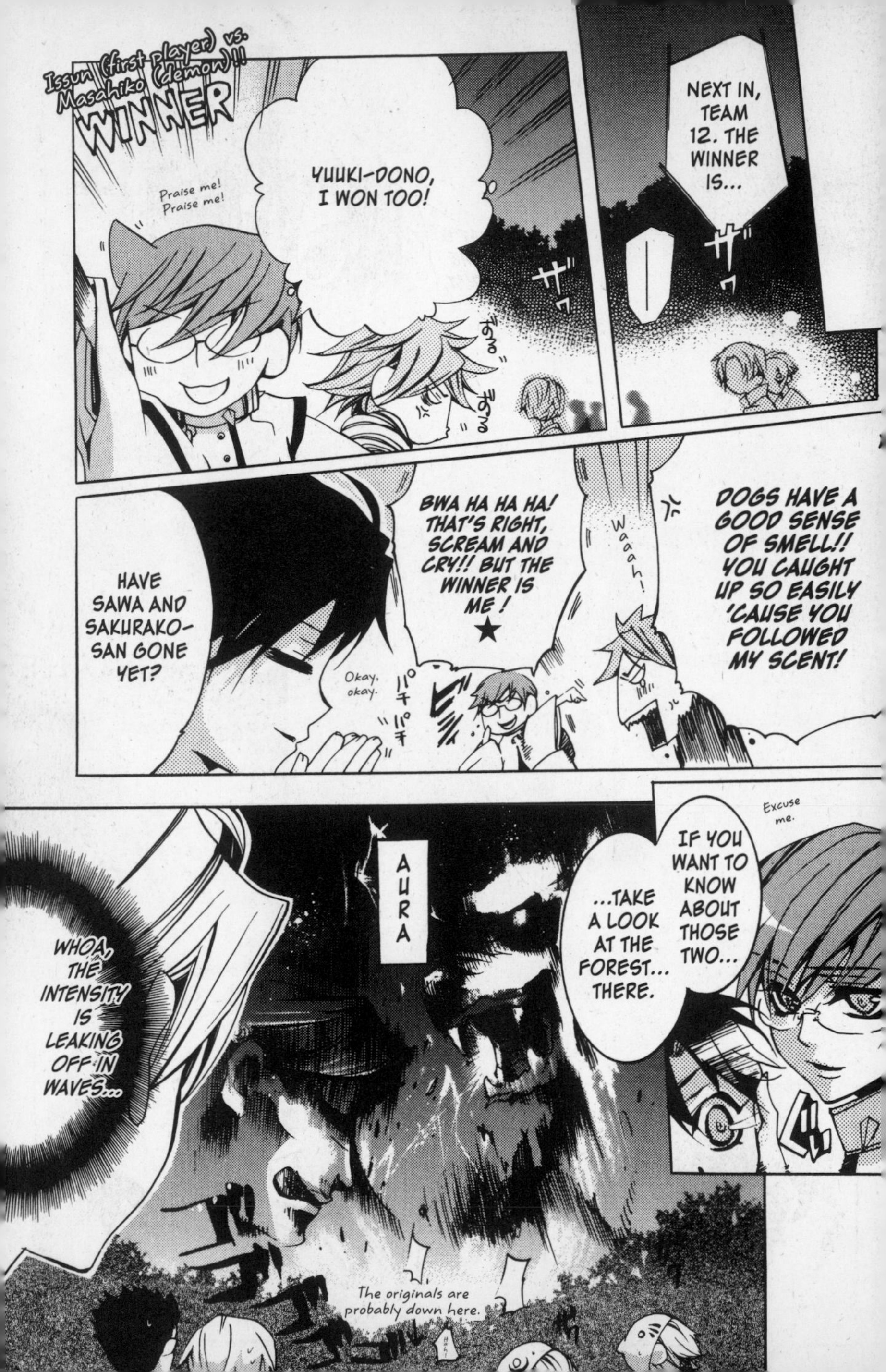
NEXT IN, TEAM 12. THE WINNER IS...
Issun (first player) vs. Masahiko (demon)!! WINNER
YUUKI-DONO, I WON TOO!
Praise me! Praise me!
DOGS HAVE A GOOD SENSE OF SMELL!! YOU CAUGHT UP SO EASILY 'CAUSE YOU FOLLOWED MY SCENT!
Waaah!
BWA HA HA HA! THAT'S RIGHT, SCREAM AND CRY!! BUT THE WINNER IS ME! ★
Okay, okay.
HAVE SAWA AND SAKURAKO-SAN GONE YET?
Excuse me.
IF YOU WANT TO KNOW ABOUT THOSE TWO...
...TAKE A LOOK AT THE FOREST... THERE.
AURA
WHOA, THE INTENSITY IS LEAKING OFF IN WAVES...
The originals are probably down here.

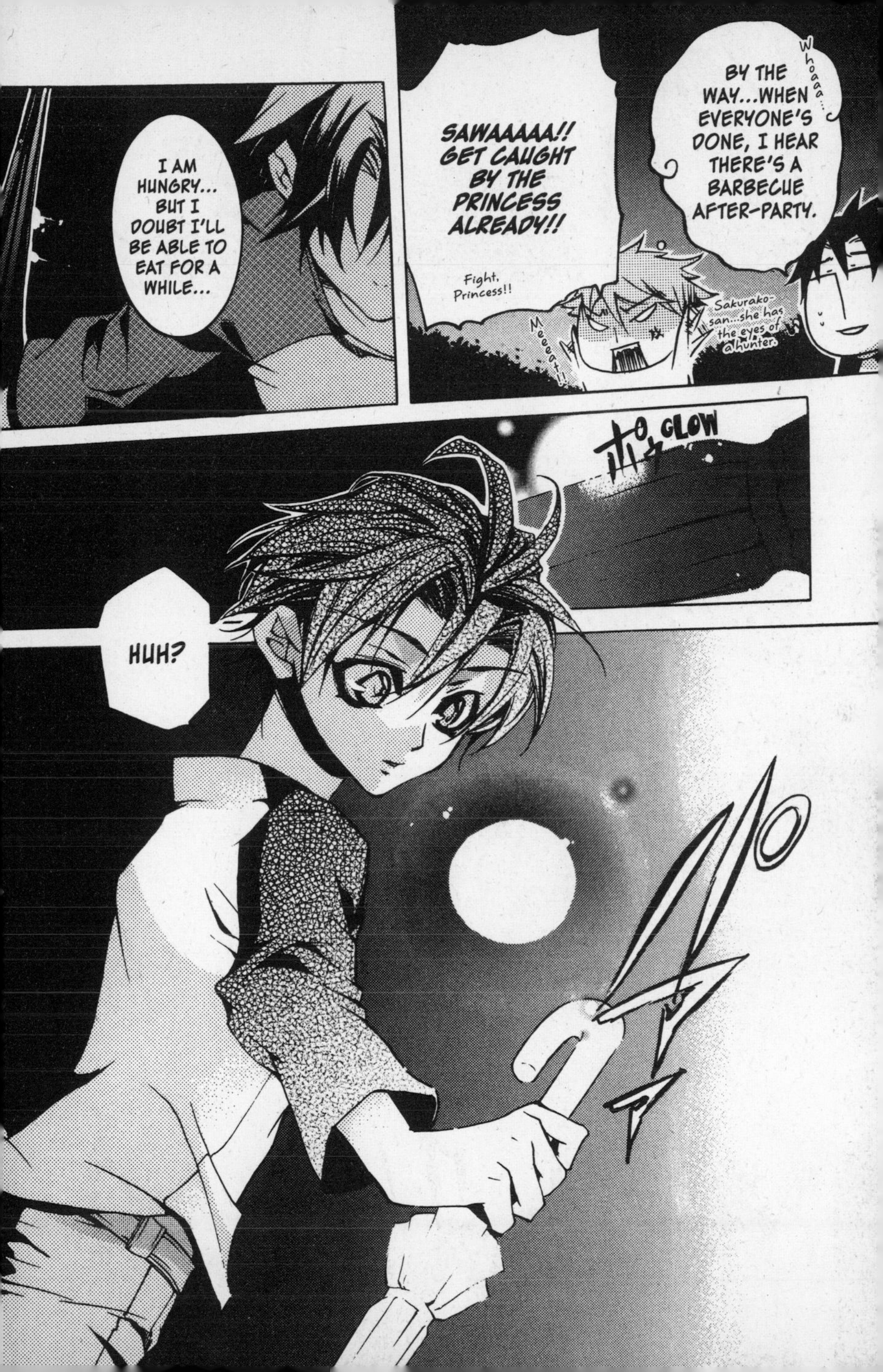
Whoaaa...
BY THE WAY...WHEN EVERYONE'S DONE, I HEAR THERE'S A BARBECUE AFTER-PARTY.
SAWAAAAAA!! GET CAUGHT BY THE PRINCESS ALREADY!!
Sakurako-san...she has the eyes of a hunter.
Fight, Princess!!
Meeeat!!
I AM HUNGRY... BUT I DOUBT I'LL BE ABLE TO EAT FOR A WHILE...
GLOW
HUH?

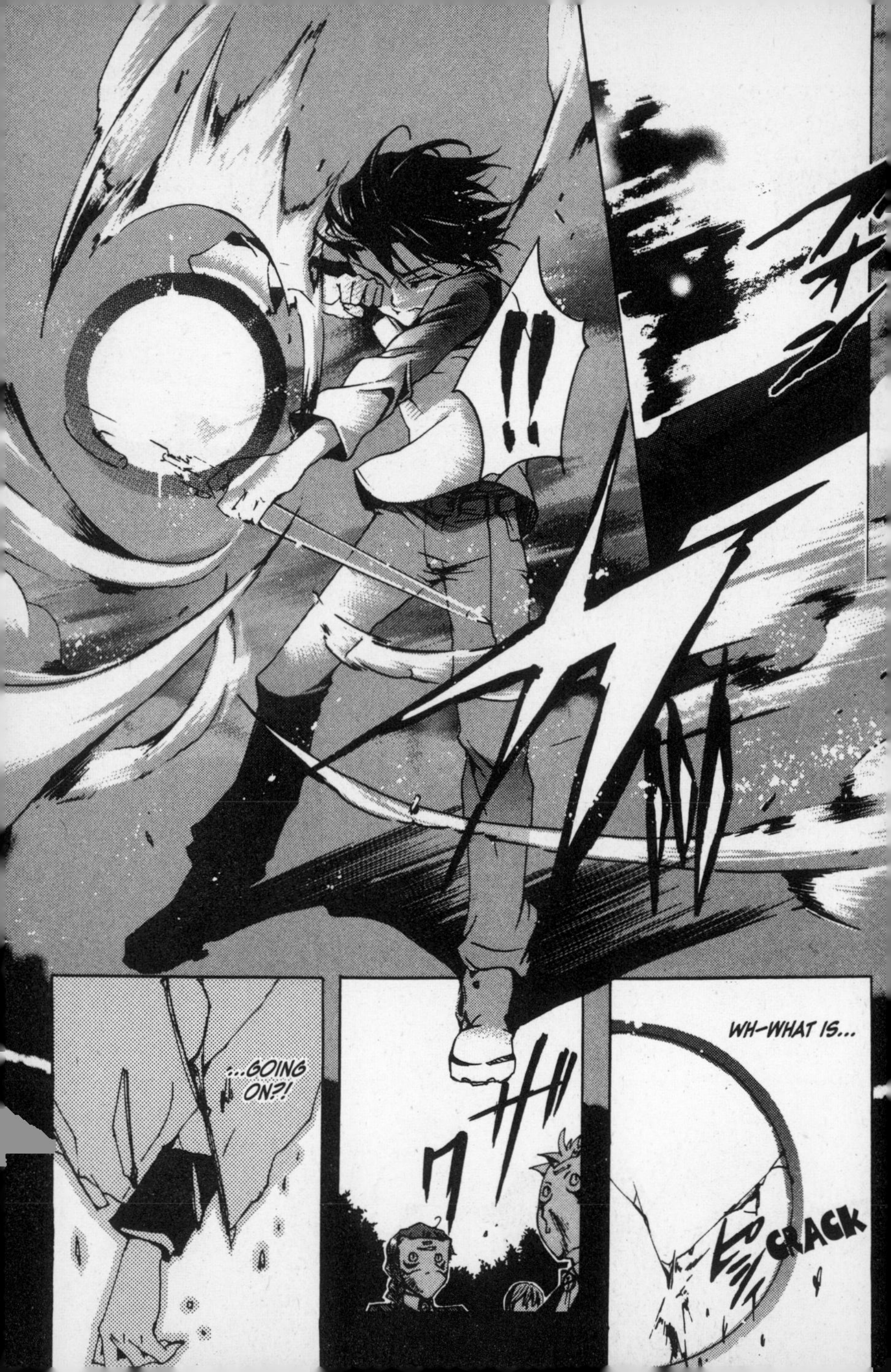
!!
WH-WHAT IS...
CRACK
...GOING ON?!

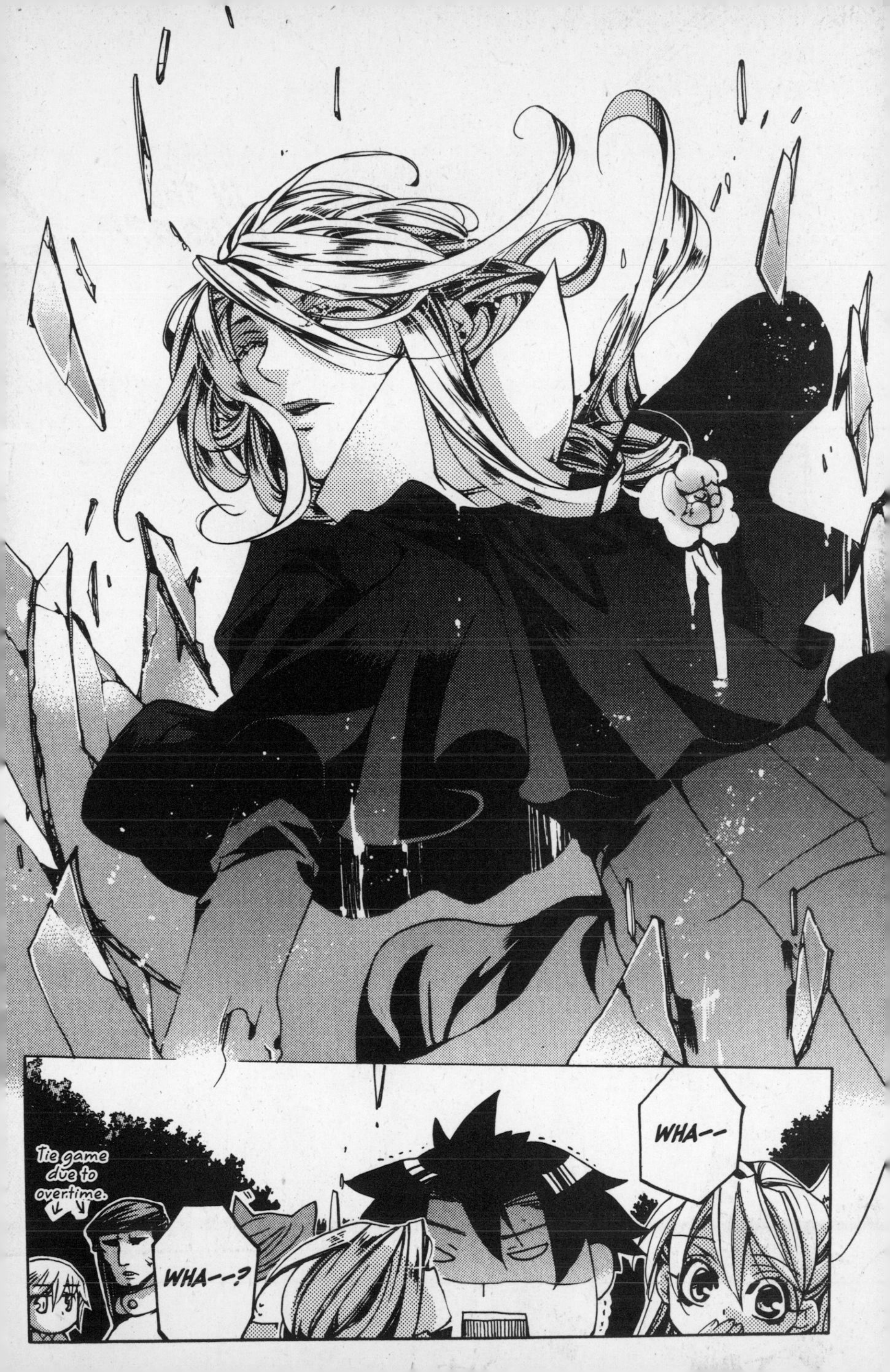
WHA--
WHA--?
Tie game due to overtime.

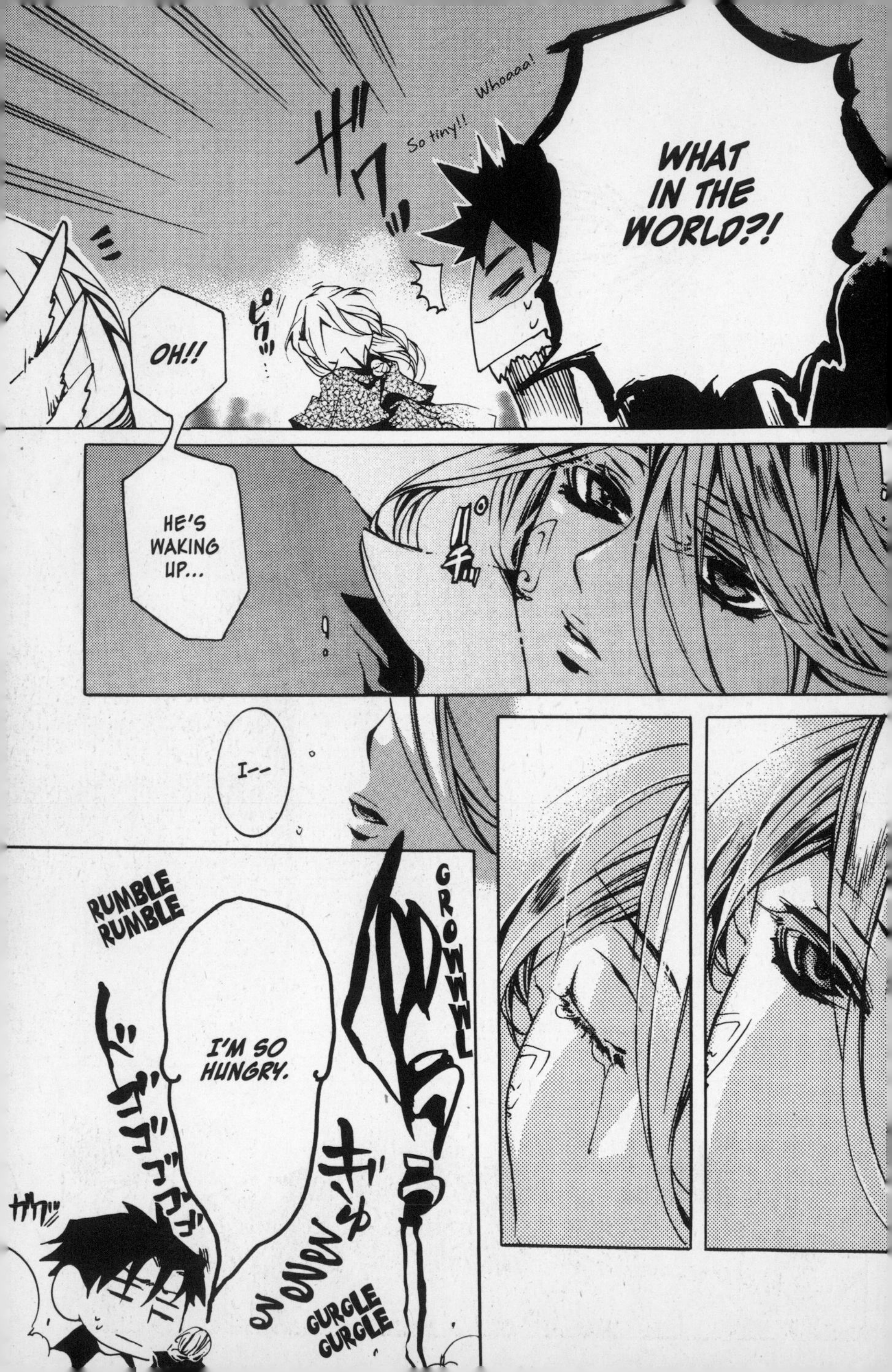
WHAT IN THE WORLD?!
Whoaaa!
So tiny!!
OH!!
HE'S WAKING UP...
I--
GROWWWL
I'M SO HUNGRY.
RUMBLE RUMBLE
GURGLE GURGLE

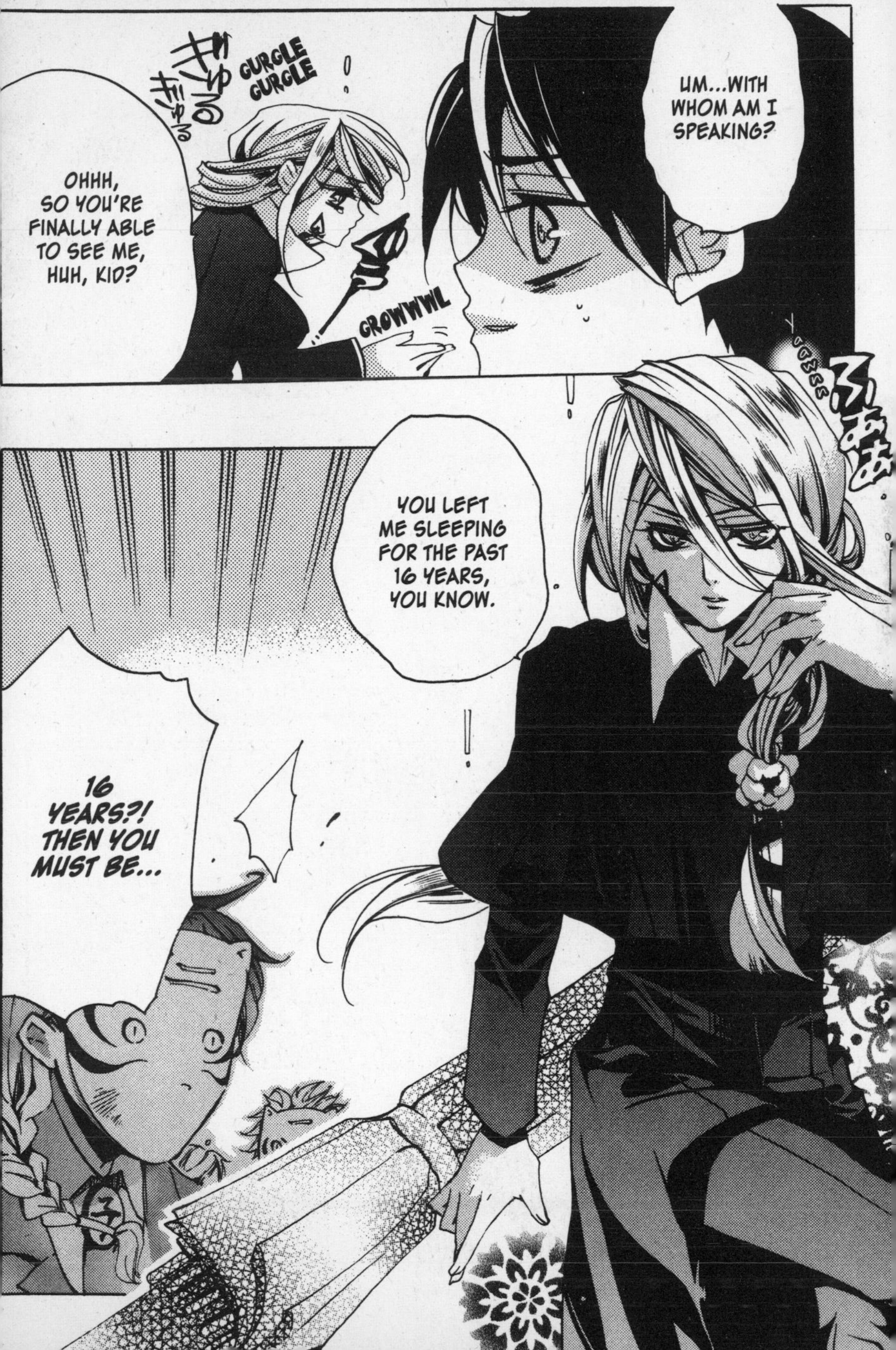
UM...WITH WHOM AM I SPEAKING?
GURGLE GURGLE
OHHH, SO YOU'RE FINALLY ABLE TO SEE ME, HUH, KID?
GROWWWL
Yaawnn
YOU LEFT ME SLEEPING FOR THE PAST 16 YEARS, YOU KNOW.
16 YEARS?! THEN YOU MUST BE...

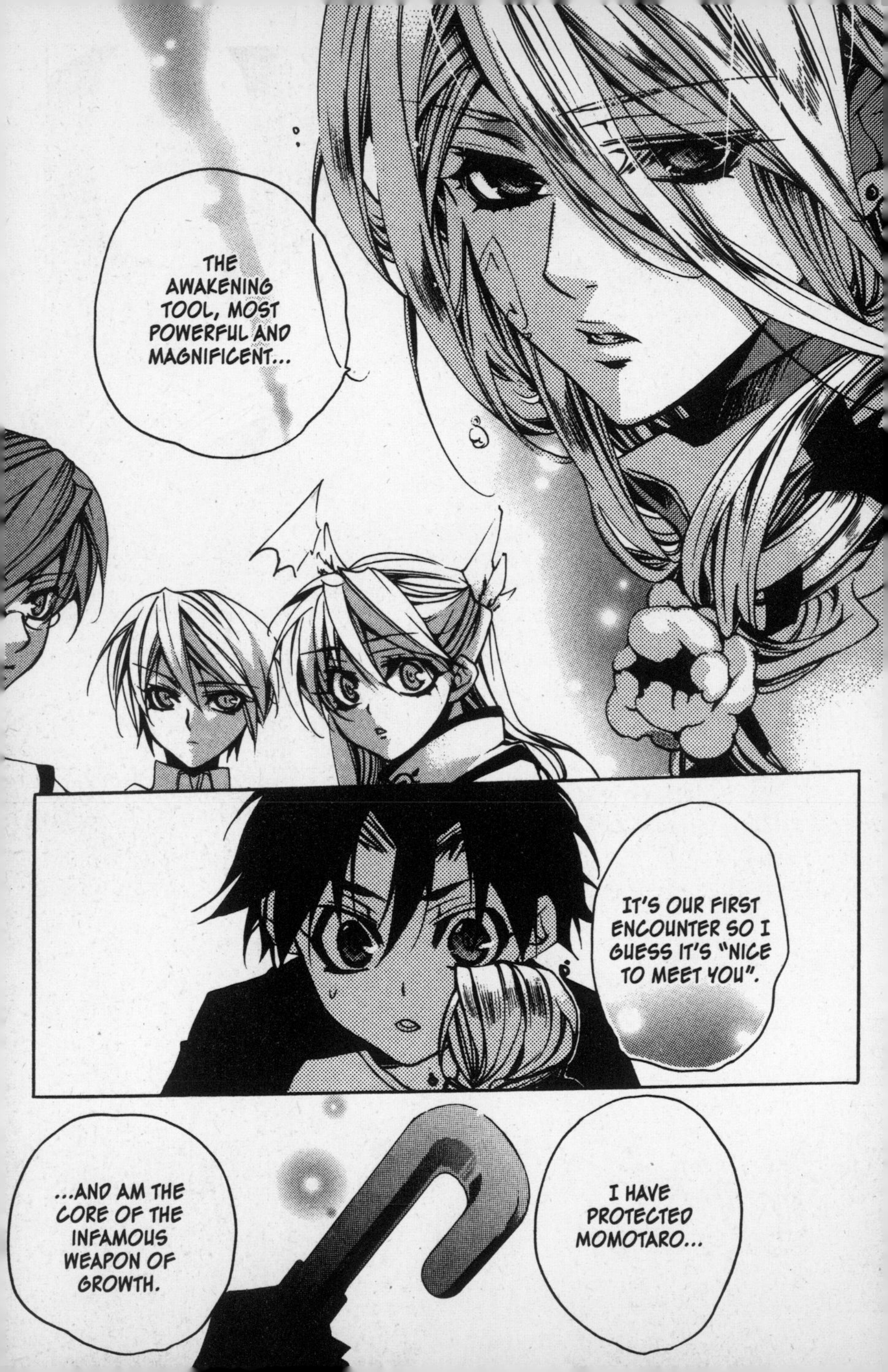
THE AWAKENING TOOL, MOST POWERFUL AND MAGNIFICENT...
IT'S OUR FIRST ENCOUNTER SO I GUESS IT'S "NICE TO MEET YOU".
I HAVE PROTECTED MOMOTARO...
...AND AM THE CORE OF THE INFAMOUS WEAPON OF GROWTH.

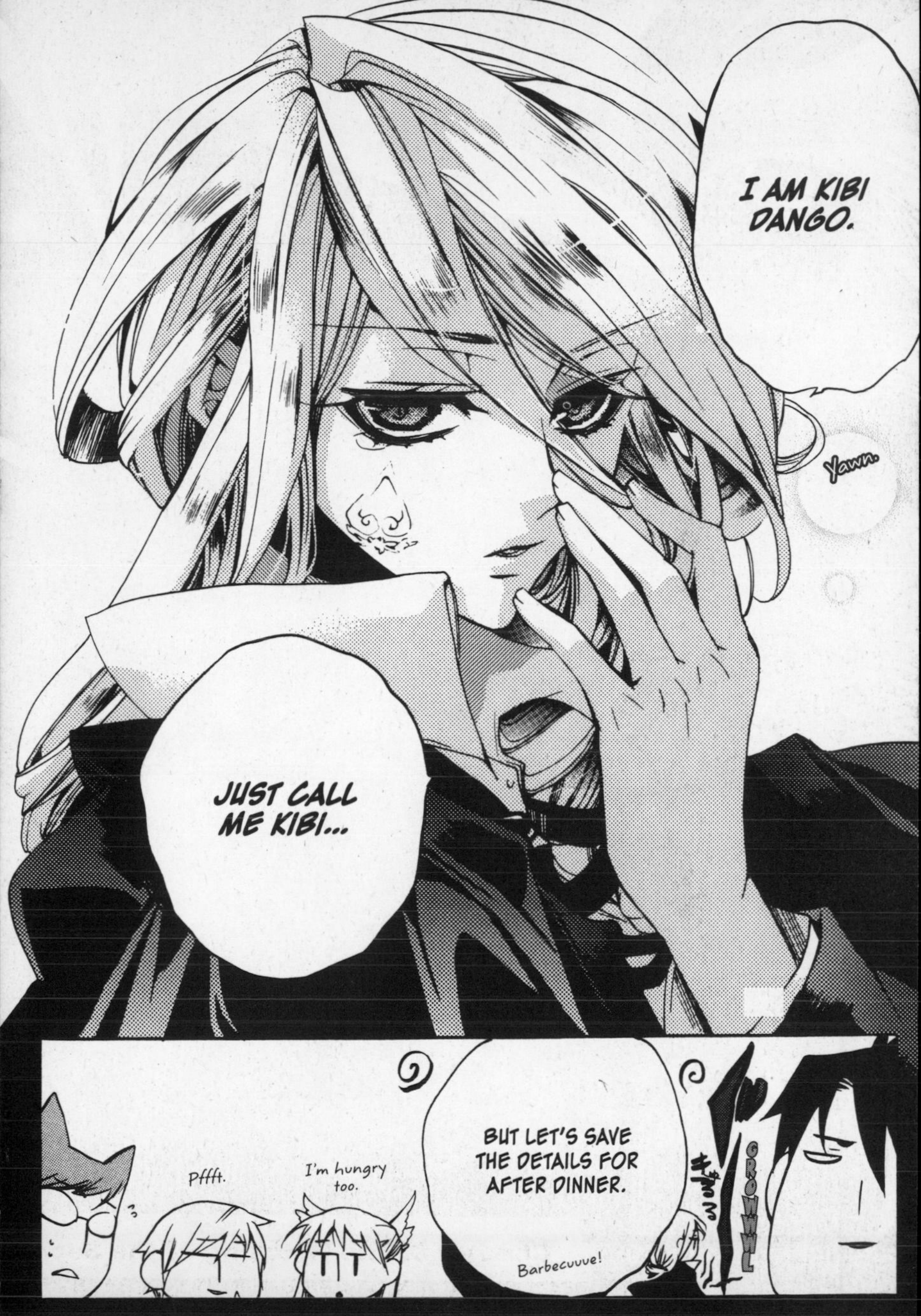
I AM KIBI DANGO.
Yawn.
JUST CALL ME KIBI...
GROWWL
BUT LET'S SAVE THE DETAILS FOR AFTER DINNER.
Barbecuuue!
I'm hungry too.
Pffft.

★ Chapter 7 ★ END

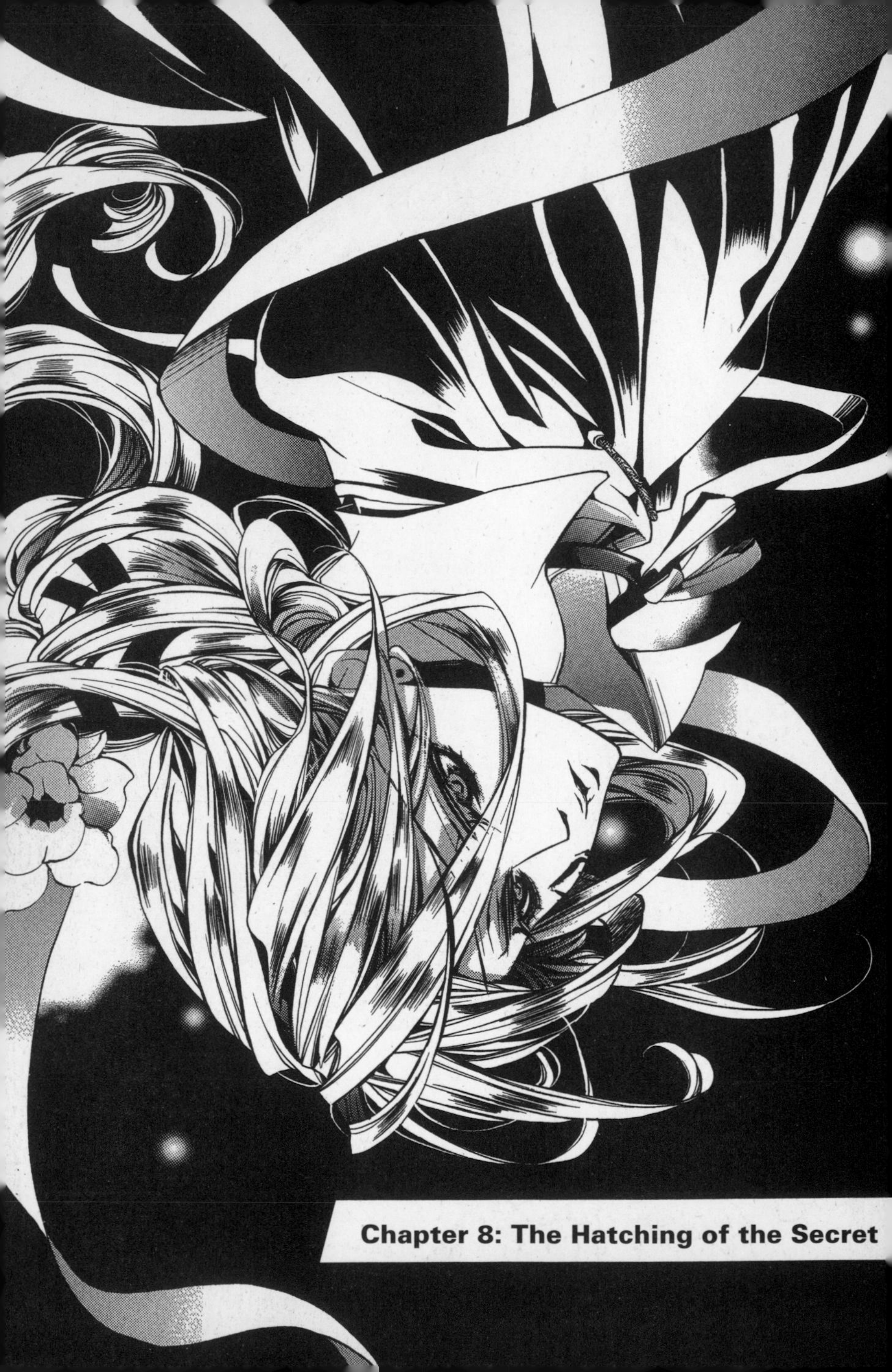
Chapter 8: The Hatching of the Secret

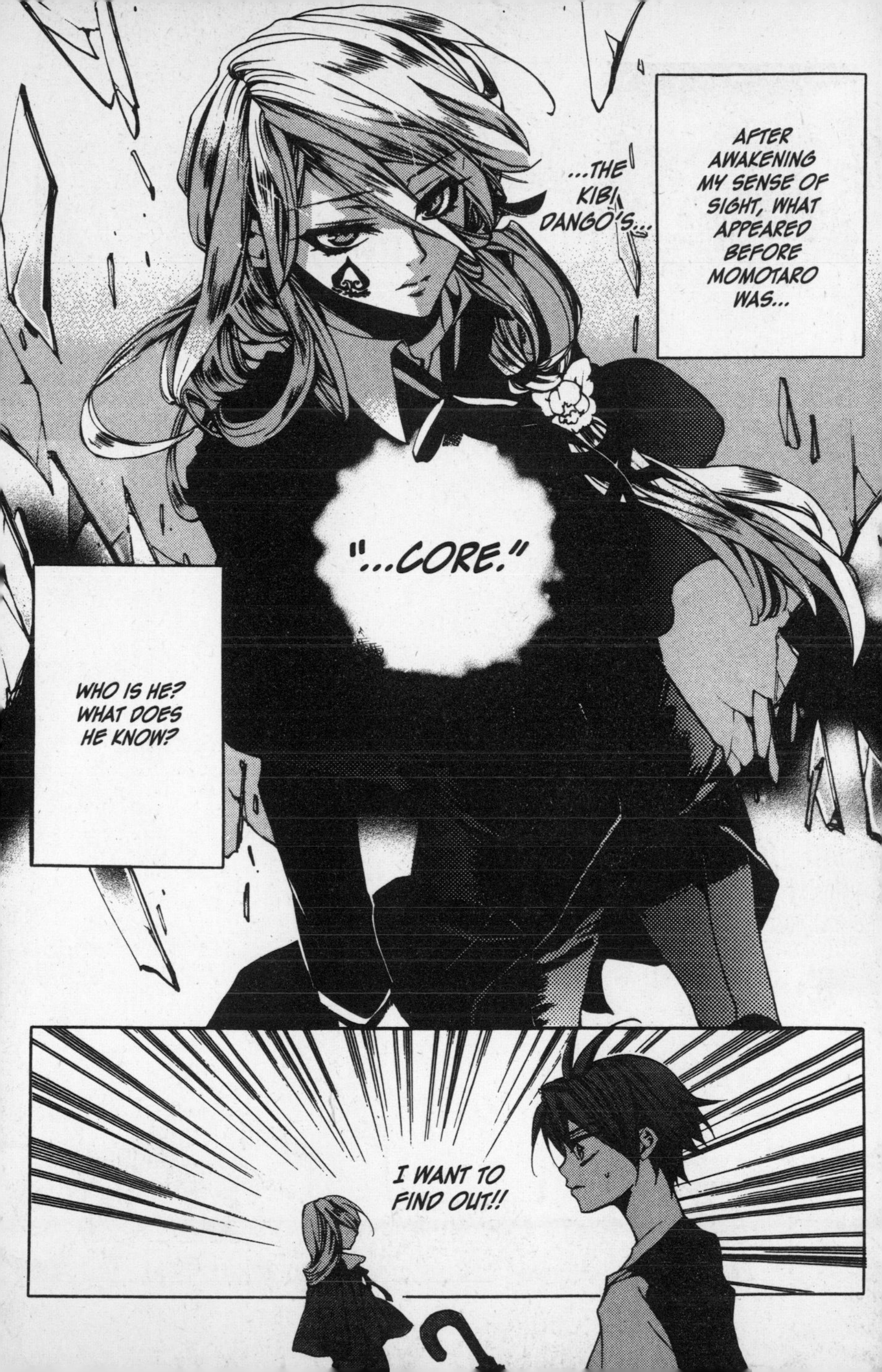
AFTER AWAKENING MY SENSE OF SIGHT, WHAT APPEARED BEFORE MOMOTARO WAS...
...THE KIBI DANGO'S...
"...CORE."
WHO IS HE? WHAT DOES HE KNOW?
I WANT TO FIND OUT!!

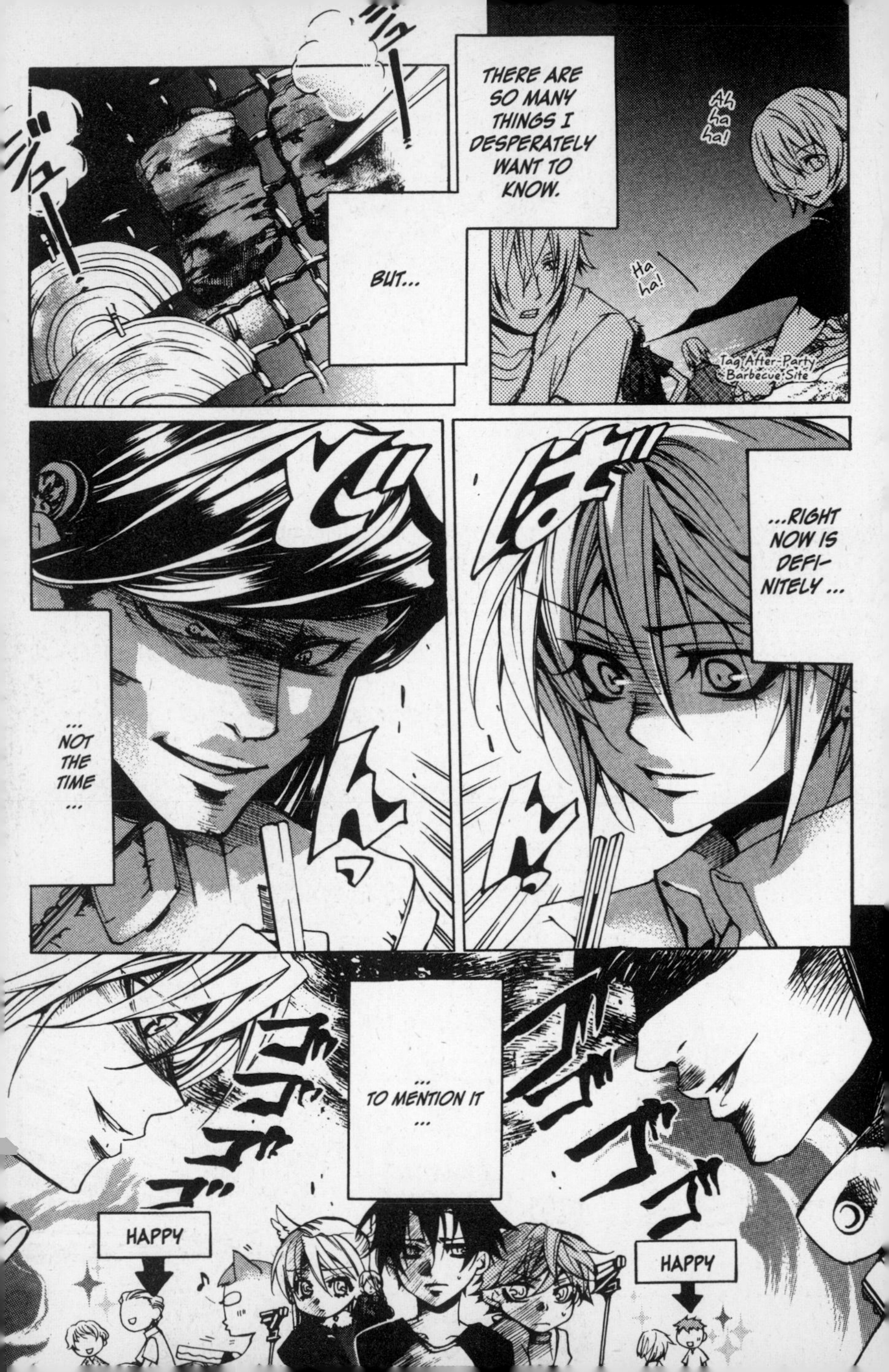
THERE ARE SO MANY THINGS I DESPERATELY WANT TO KNOW.
Ah ha ha!
Ha ha!
Tag After-Party Barbecue Site
BUT...
...RIGHT NOW IS DEFI-NITELY ...
... NOT THE TIME ...
... TO MENTION IT ...
HAPPY
HAPPY

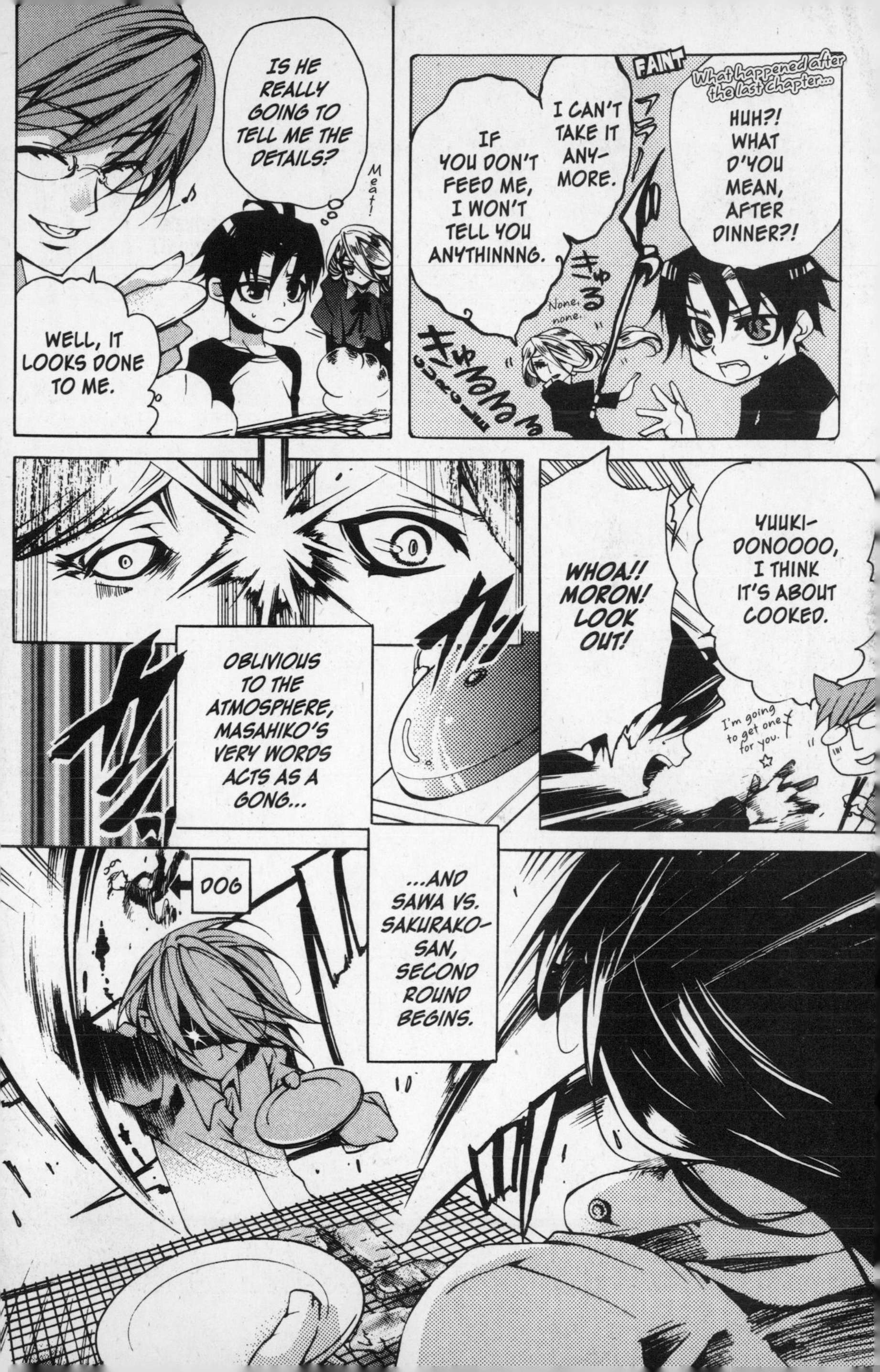
What happened after the last chapter...
FAINT
HUH?! WHAT D'YOU MEAN, AFTER DINNER?!
I CAN'T TAKE IT ANY-MORE.
IF YOU DON'T FEED ME, I WON'T TELL YOU ANYTHINNNG.
None, none.
IS HE REALLY GOING TO TELL ME THE DETAILS?
Meat!
WELL, IT LOOKS DONE TO ME.
YUUKI-DONOOOO, I THINK IT'S ABOUT COOKED.
I'm going to get one for you.
WHOA!! MORON! LOOK OUT!
OBLIVIOUS TO THE ATMOSPHERE, MASAHIKO'S VERY WORDS ACTS AS A GONG...
...AND SAWA VS. SAKURAKO-SAN, SECOND ROUND BEGINS.
DOG

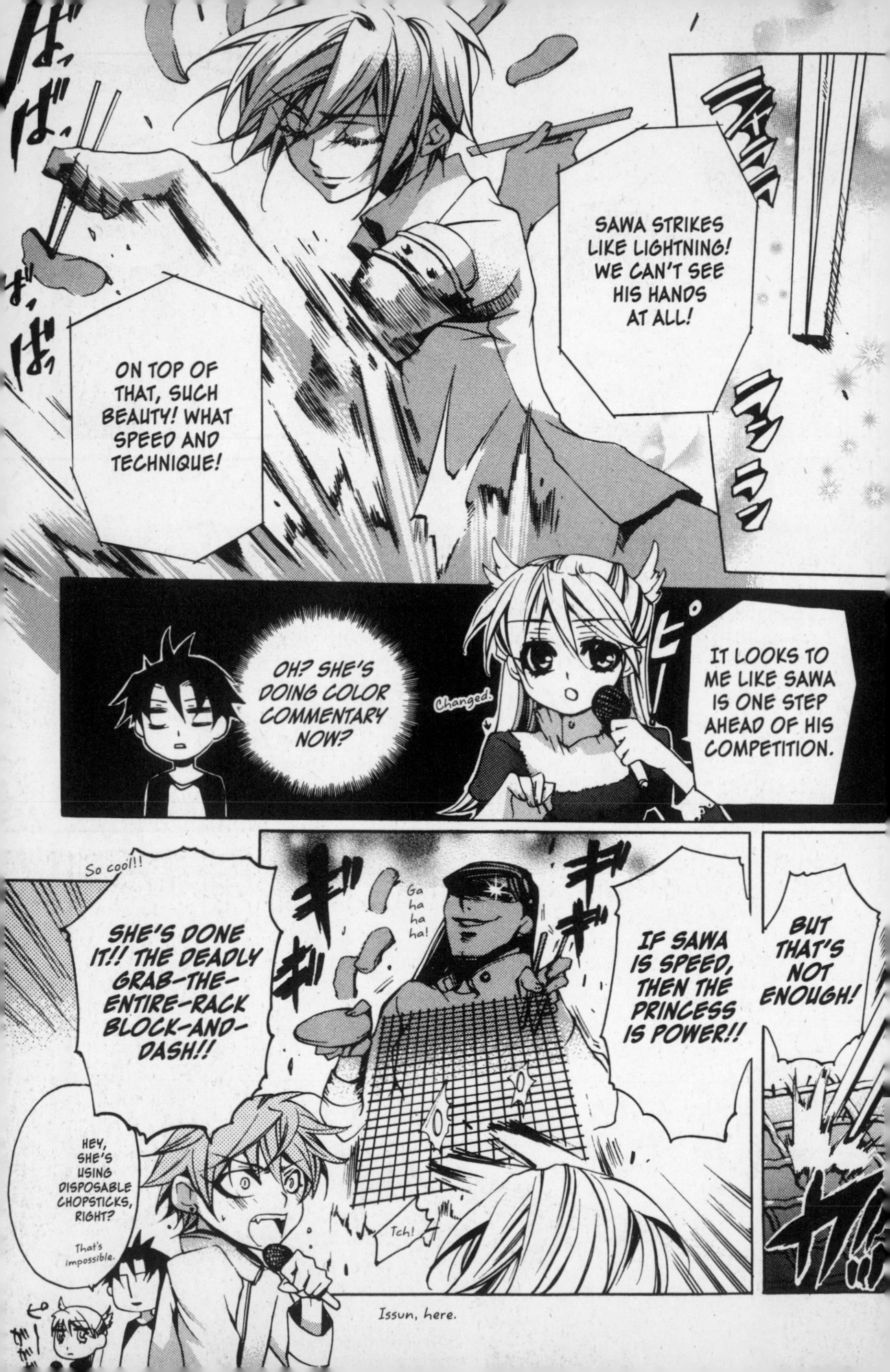
SAWA STRIKES LIKE LIGHTNING! WE CAN'T SEE HIS HANDS AT ALL!
ON TOP OF THAT, SUCH BEAUTY! WHAT SPEED AND TECHNIQUE!
IT LOOKS TO ME LIKE SAWA IS ONE STEP AHEAD OF HIS COMPETITION.
Changed.
OH? SHE'S DOING COLOR COMMENTARY NOW?
BUT THAT'S NOT ENOUGH!
IF SAWA IS SPEED, THEN THE PRINCESS IS POWER!!
Ga ha ha ha!
SHE'S DONE IT!! THE DEADLY GRAB-THE-ENTIRE-RACK BLOCK-AND-DASH!!
So cool!!
Tch!
HEY, SHE'S USING DISPOSABLE CHOPSTICKS, RIGHT?
That's impossible.
Issun, here.

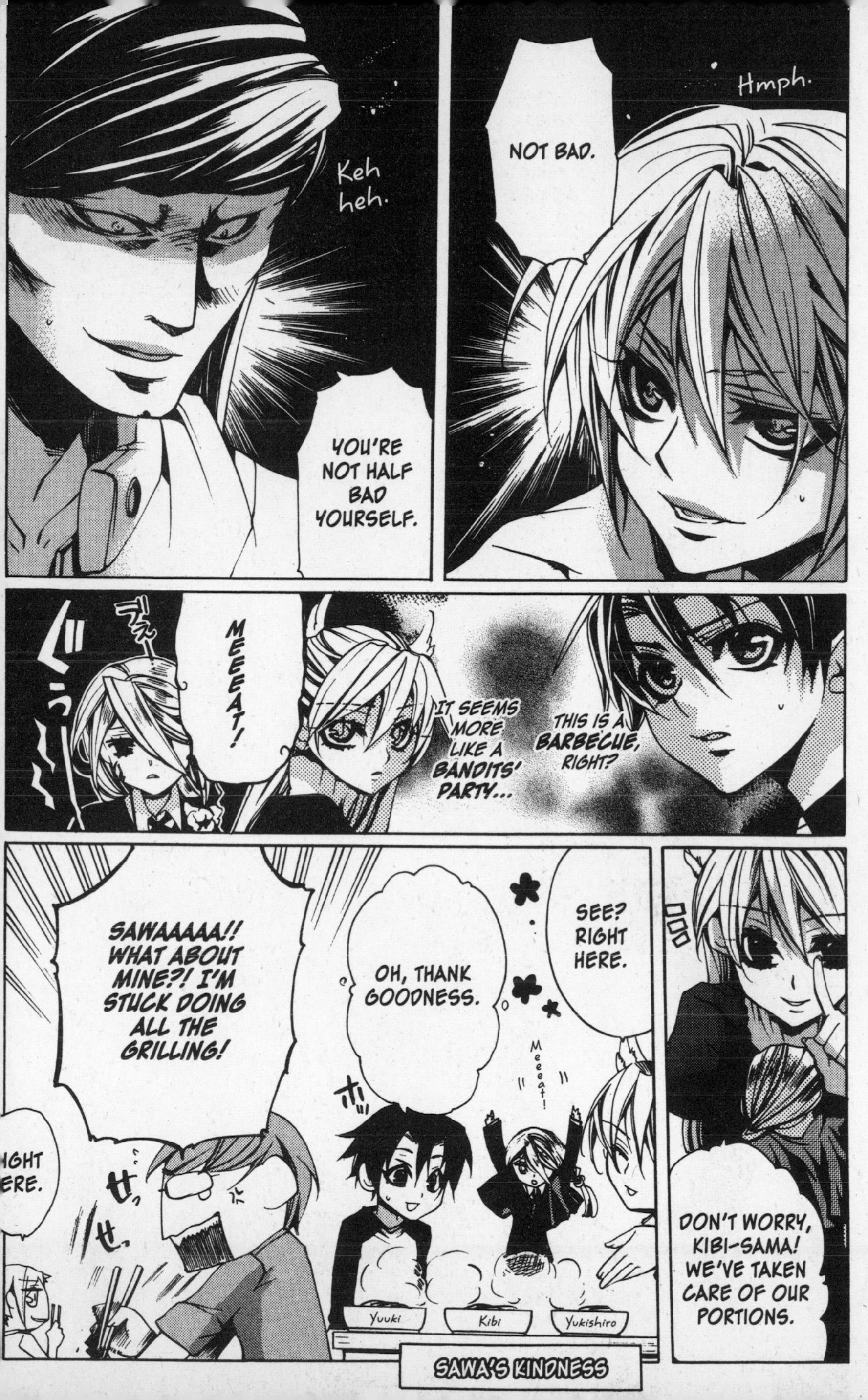
Hmph.
NOT BAD.
Keh heh.
YOU'RE NOT HALF BAD YOURSELF.
THIS IS A BARBECUE, RIGHT?
IT SEEMS MORE LIKE A BANDITS' PARTY...
MEEEEAT!
DON'T WORRY, KIBI-SAMA! WE'VE TAKEN CARE OF OUR PORTIONS.
SEE? RIGHT HERE.
OH, THANK GOODNESS.
ホッ
Meeeat!
SAWAAAAA!! WHAT ABOUT MINE?! I'M STUCK DOING ALL THE GRILLING!
せっ
せっ
Yuuki
Kibi
Yukishiro
SAWA'S KINDNESS

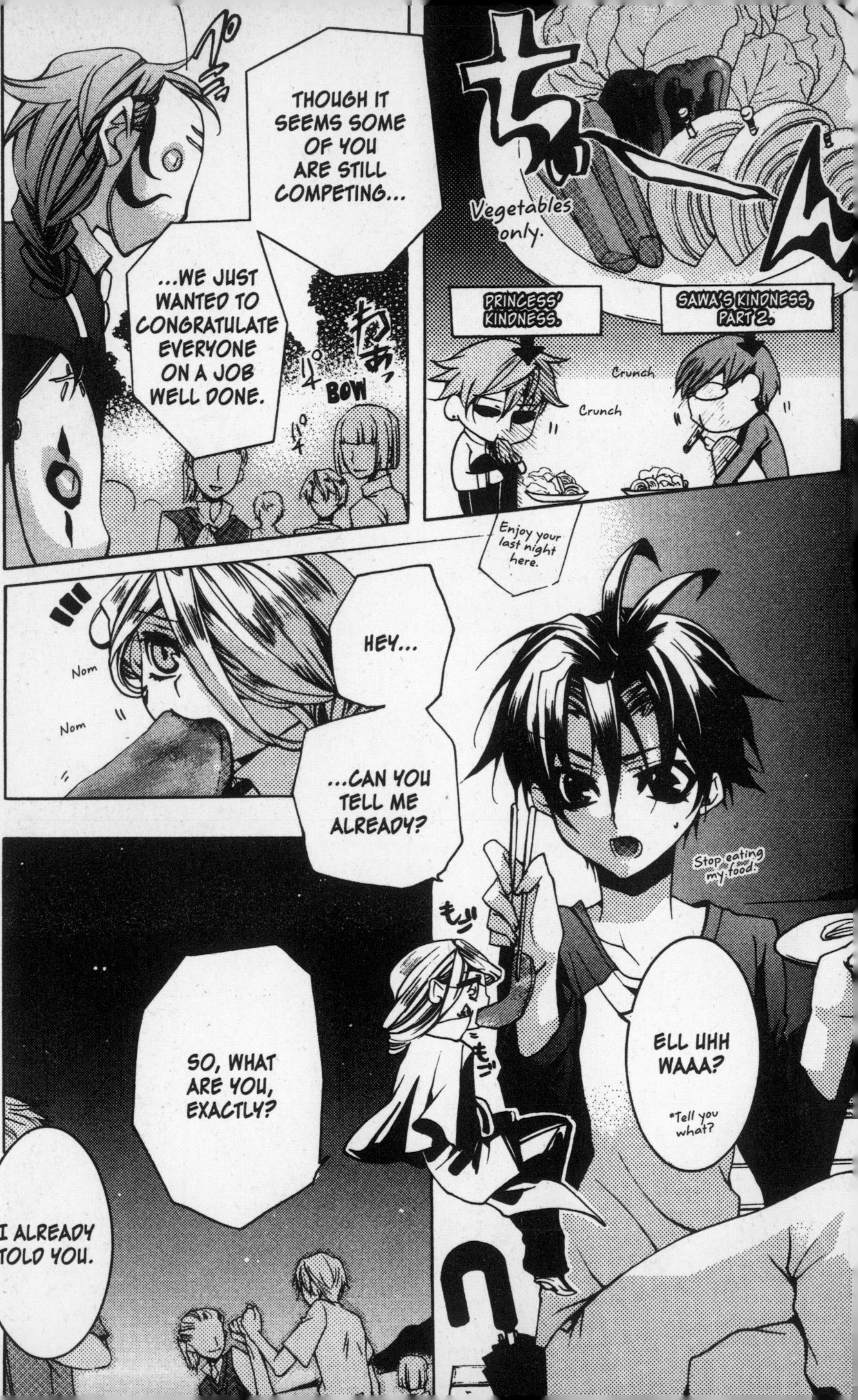

Vegetables only.
PRINCESS' KINDNESS.
SAWA'S KINDNESS, PART 2.
Crunch
Crunch
Enjoy your last night here.
THOUGH IT SEEMS SOME OF YOU ARE STILL COMPETING...
...WE JUST WANTED TO CONGRATULATE EVERYONE ON A JOB WELL DONE.
BOW
Nom
Nom
HEY...
...CAN YOU TELL ME ALREADY?
Stop eating my food.
ELL UHH WAAA?
*Tell you what?
SO, WHAT ARE YOU, EXACTLY?
I ALREADY TOLD YOU.

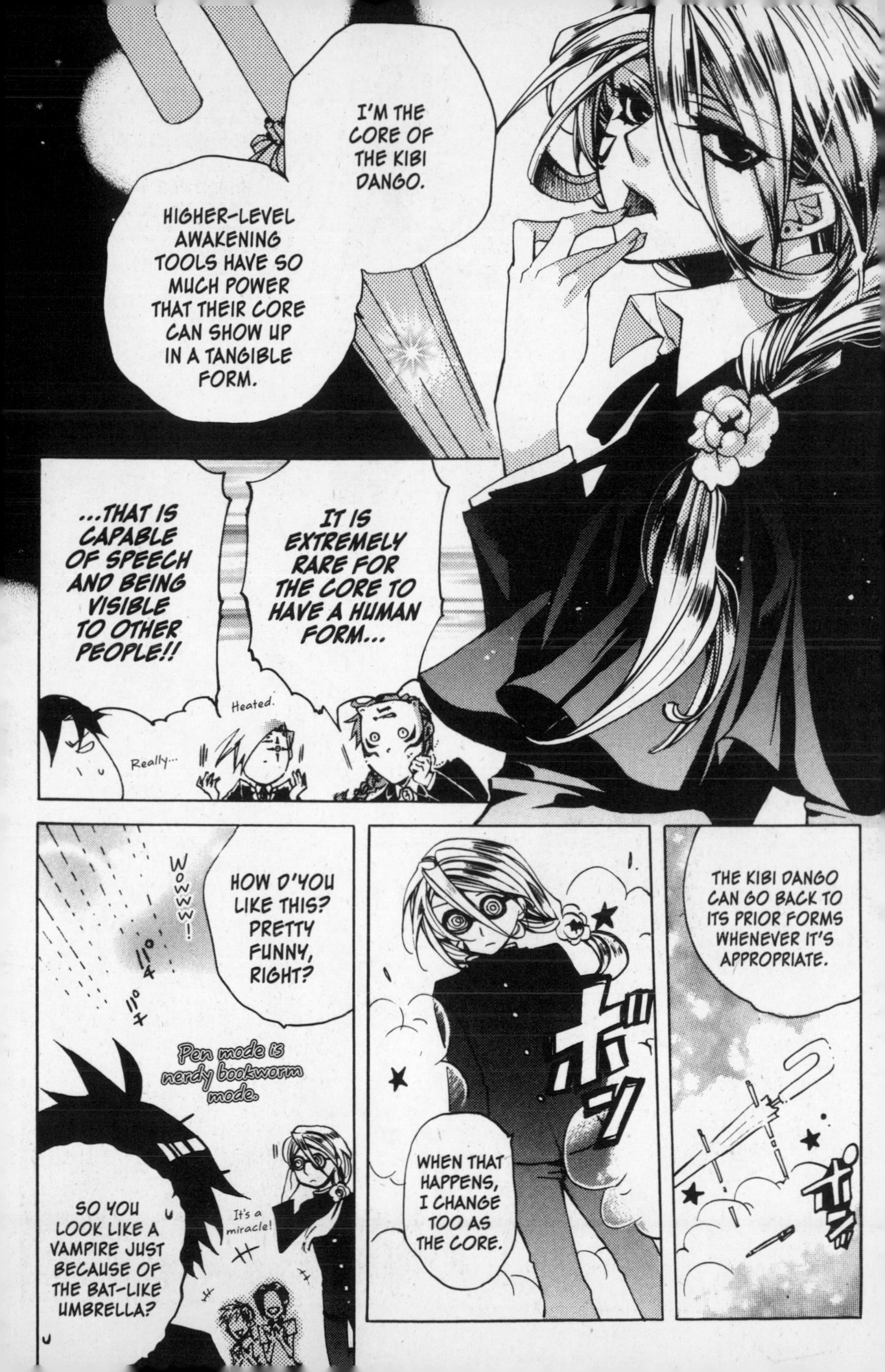
I'M THE CORE OF THE KIBI DANGO.
HIGHER-LEVEL AWAKENING TOOLS HAVE SO MUCH POWER THAT THEIR CORE CAN SHOW UP IN A TANGIBLE FORM.
IT IS EXTREMELY RARE FOR THE CORE TO HAVE A HUMAN FORM...
...THAT IS CAPABLE OF SPEECH AND BEING VISIBLE TO OTHER PEOPLE!!
Heated.
Really...
THE KIBI DANGO CAN GO BACK TO ITS PRIOR FORMS WHENEVER IT'S APPROPRIATE.
WHEN THAT HAPPENS, I CHANGE TOO AS THE CORE.
HOW D'YOU LIKE THIS? PRETTY FUNNY, RIGHT?
Wowww!
Pen mode is nerdy bookworm mode.
It's a miracle!
SO YOU LOOK LIKE A VAMPIRE JUST BECAUSE OF THE BAT-LIKE UMBRELLA?

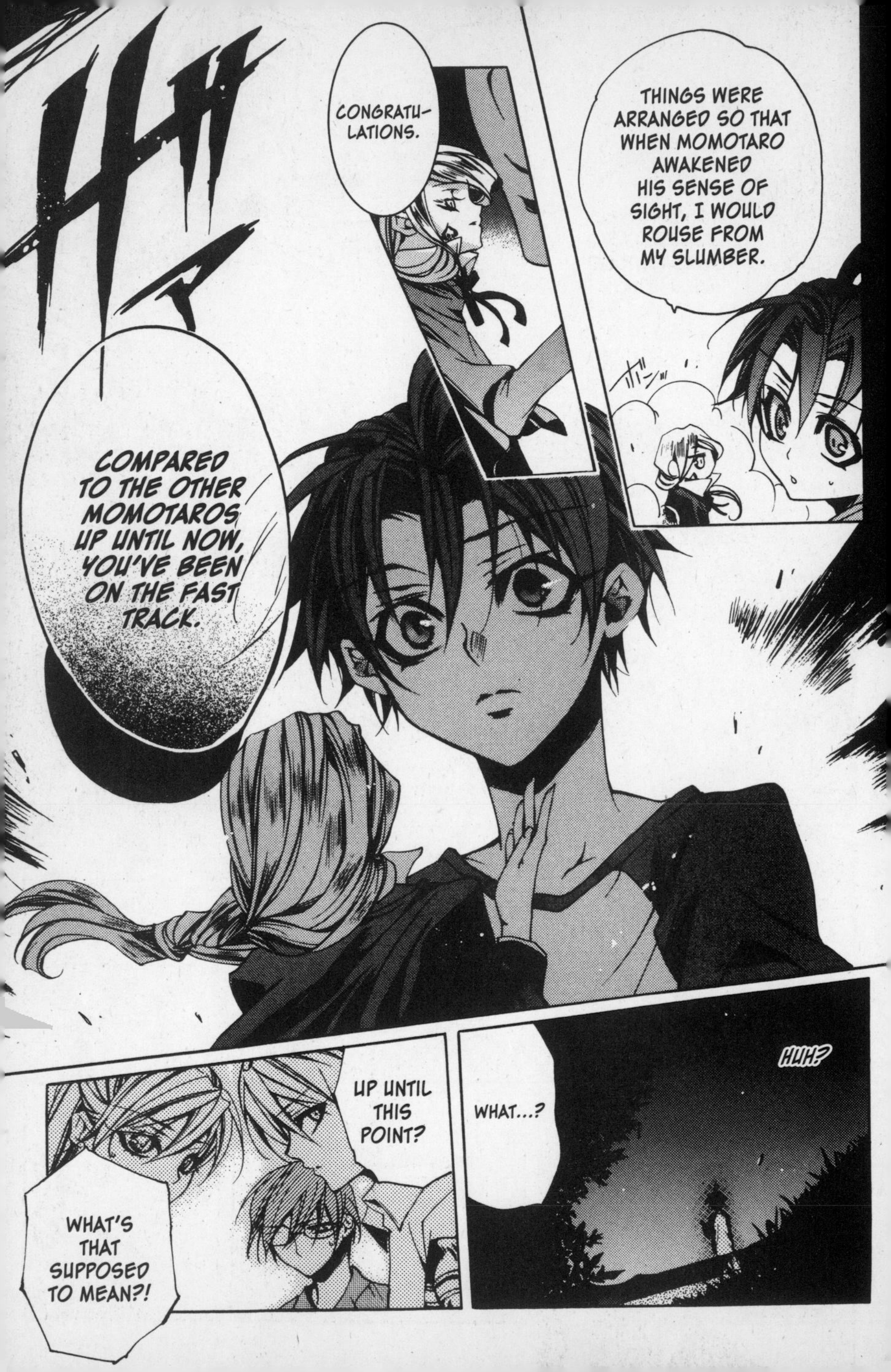
THINGS WERE ARRANGED SO THAT WHEN MOMOTARO AWAKENED HIS SENSE OF SIGHT, I WOULD ROUSE FROM MY SLUMBER.
CONGRATU-LATIONS.
COMPARED TO THE OTHER MOMOTAROS UP UNTIL NOW, YOU'VE BEEN ON THE FAST TRACK.
HUH?
WHAT...?
UP UNTIL THIS POINT?
WHAT'S THAT SUPPOSED TO MEAN?!

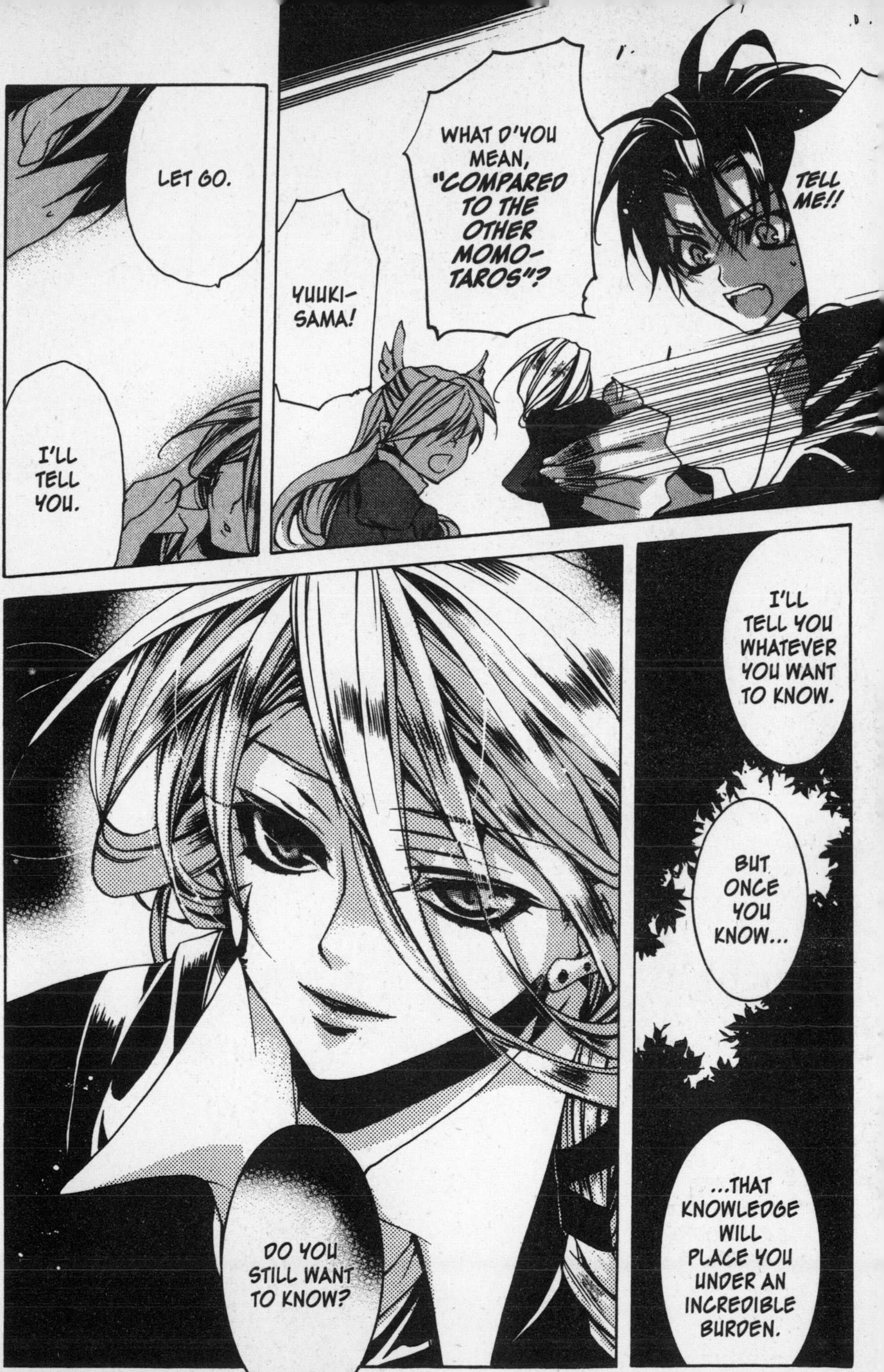
TELL ME!!
WHAT D'YOU MEAN, "COMPARED TO THE OTHER MOMO-TAROS"?
YUUKI-SAMA!
LET GO.
I'LL TELL YOU.
I'LL TELL YOU WHATEVER YOU WANT TO KNOW.
BUT ONCE YOU KNOW...
...THAT KNOWLEDGE WILL PLACE YOU UNDER AN INCREDIBLE BURDEN.
DO YOU STILL WANT TO KNOW?

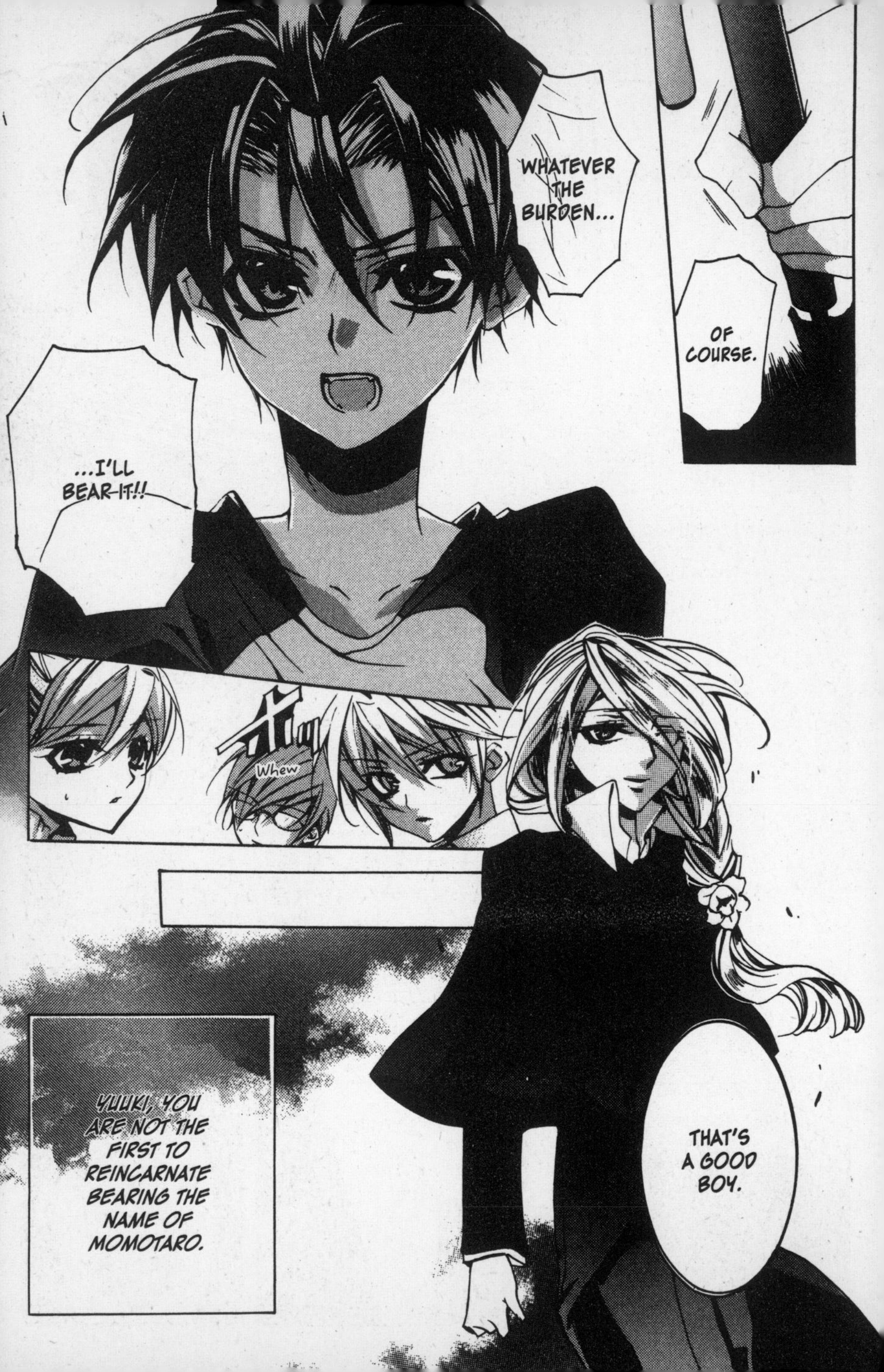
OF COURSE.
WHATEVER THE BURDEN...
...I'LL BEAR IT!!
Whew
THAT'S A GOOD BOY.
YUUKI, YOU ARE NOT THE FIRST TO REINCARNATE BEARING THE NAME OF MOMOTARO.

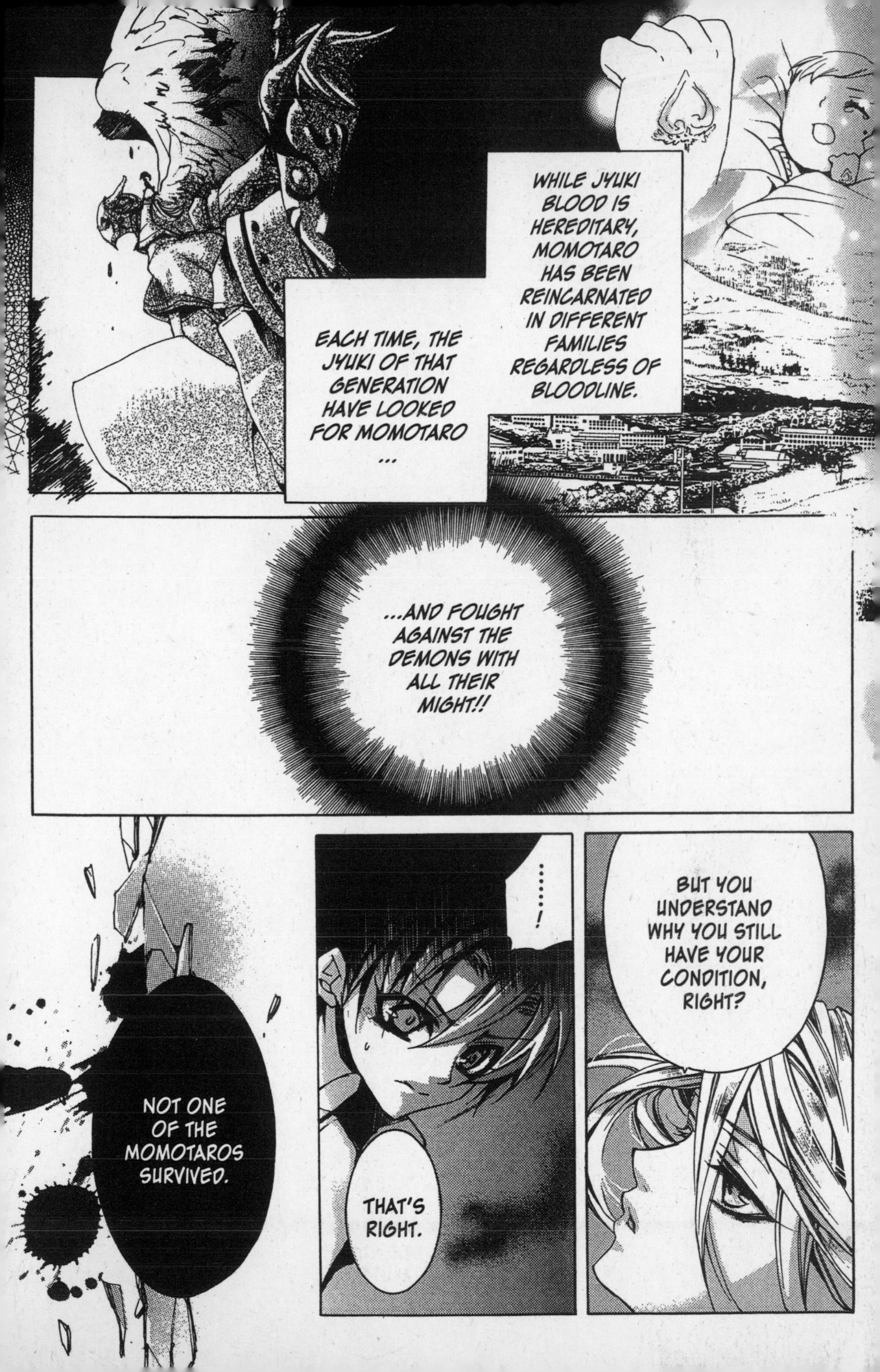
WHILE JYUKI BLOOD IS HEREDITARY, MOMOTARO HAS BEEN REINCARNATED IN DIFFERENT FAMILIES REGARDLESS OF BLOODLINE.
EACH TIME, THE JYUKI OF THAT GENERATION HAVE LOOKED FOR MOMOTARO ...
...AND FOUGHT AGAINST THE DEMONS WITH ALL THEIR MIGHT!!
BUT YOU UNDERSTAND WHY YOU STILL HAVE YOUR CONDITION, RIGHT?
......!
THAT'S RIGHT.
NOT ONE OF THE MOMOTAROS SURVIVED.

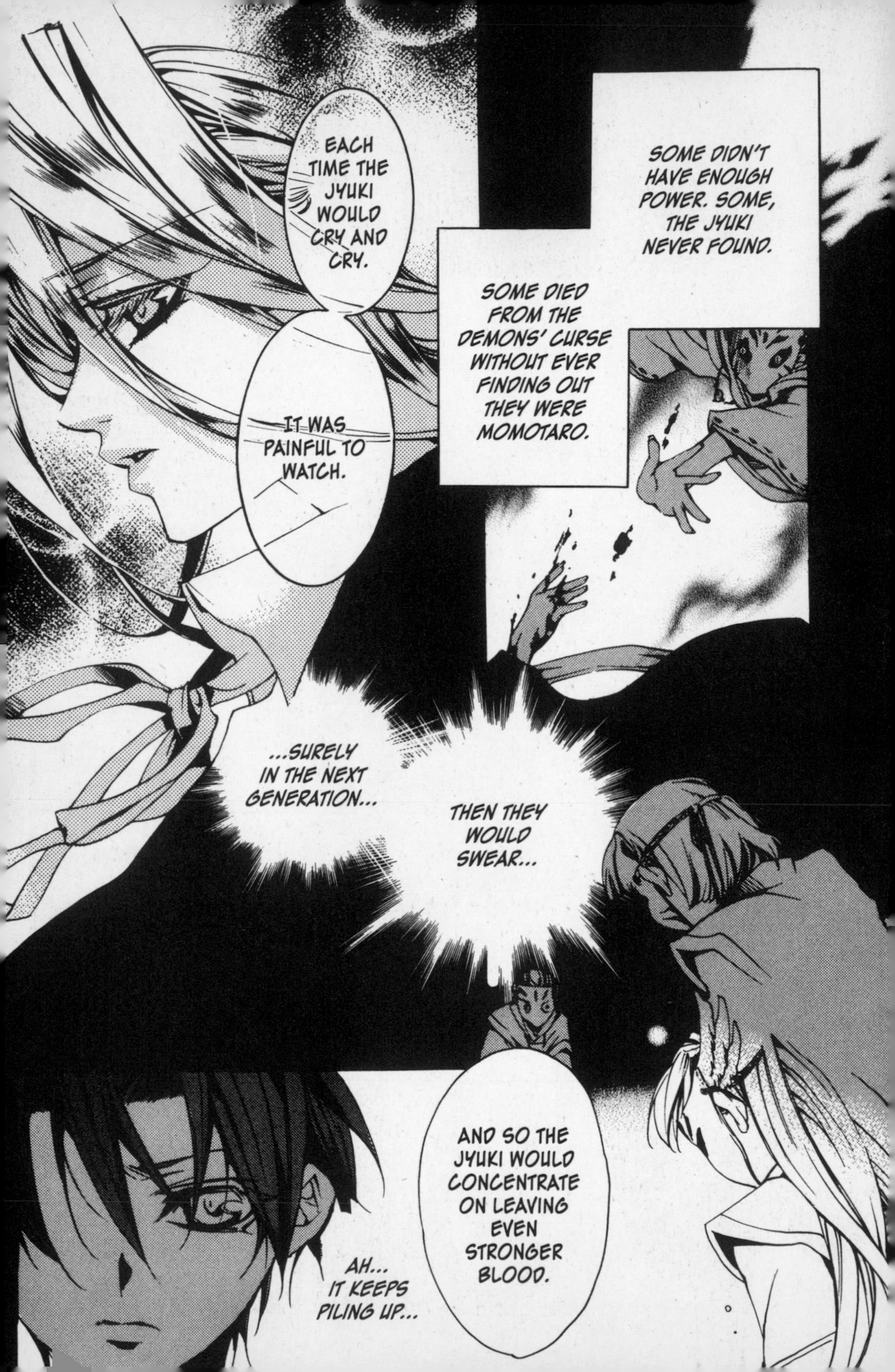
SOME DIDN'T HAVE ENOUGH POWER. SOME, THE JYUKI NEVER FOUND.
SOME DIED FROM THE DEMONS' CURSE WITHOUT EVER FINDING OUT THEY WERE MOMOTARO.
EACH TIME THE JYUKI WOULD CRY AND CRY.
IT WAS PAINFUL TO WATCH.
THEN THEY WOULD SWEAR...
...SURELY IN THE NEXT GENERATION...
AND SO THE JYUKI WOULD CONCENTRATE ON LEAVING EVEN STRONGER BLOOD.
AH... IT KEEPS PILING UP...

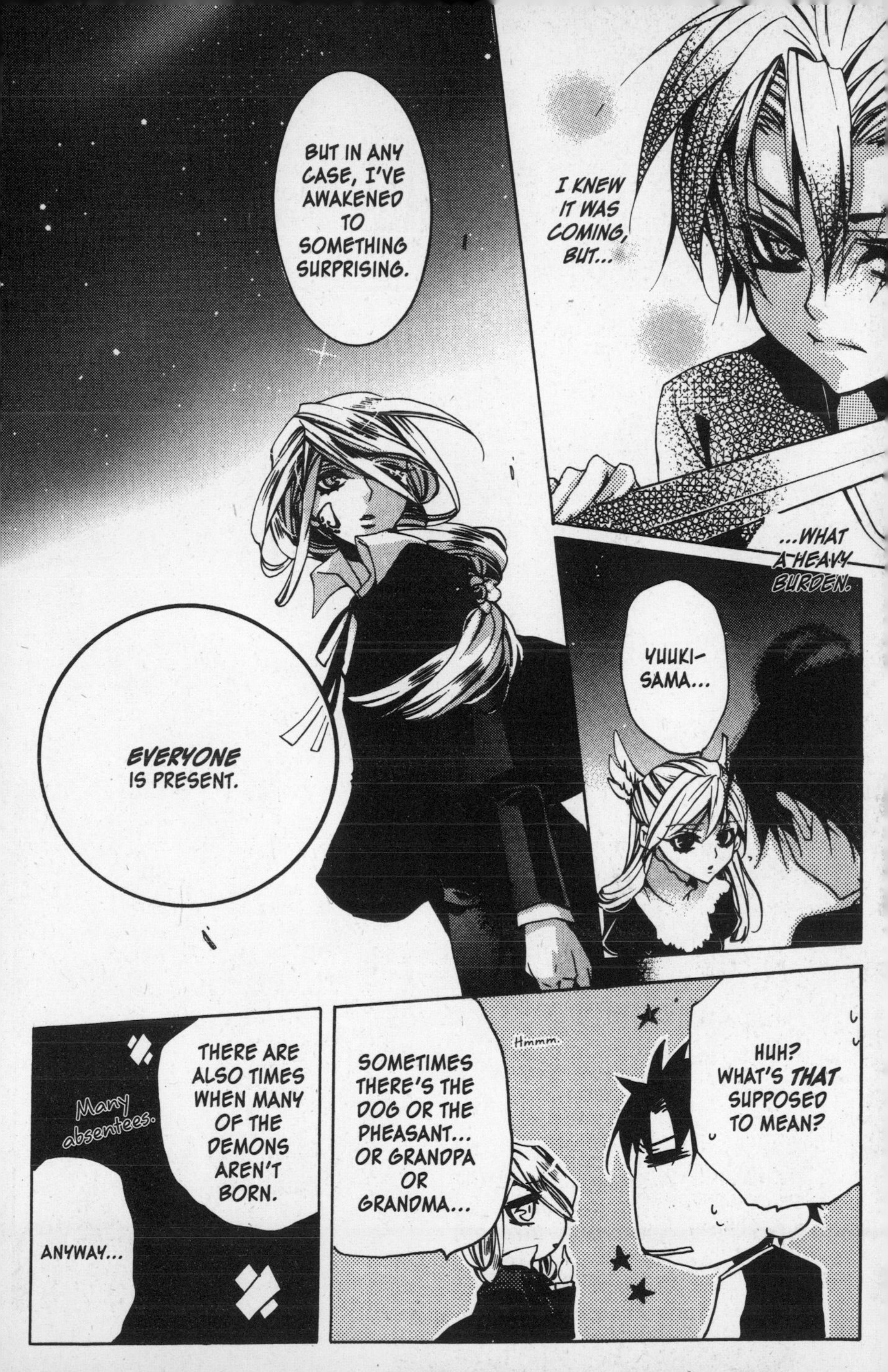
I KNEW IT WAS COMING, BUT...
...WHAT A HEAVY BURDEN.
YUUKI-SAMA...
BUT IN ANY CASE, I'VE AWAKENED TO SOMETHING SURPRISING.
EVERYONE IS PRESENT.
HUH? WHAT'S *THAT* SUPPOSED TO MEAN?
Hmmm.
SOMETIMES THERE'S THE DOG OR THE PHEASANT... OR GRANDPA OR GRANDMA...
THERE ARE ALSO TIMES WHEN MANY OF THE DEMONS AREN'T BORN.
Many absentees.
ANYWAY...

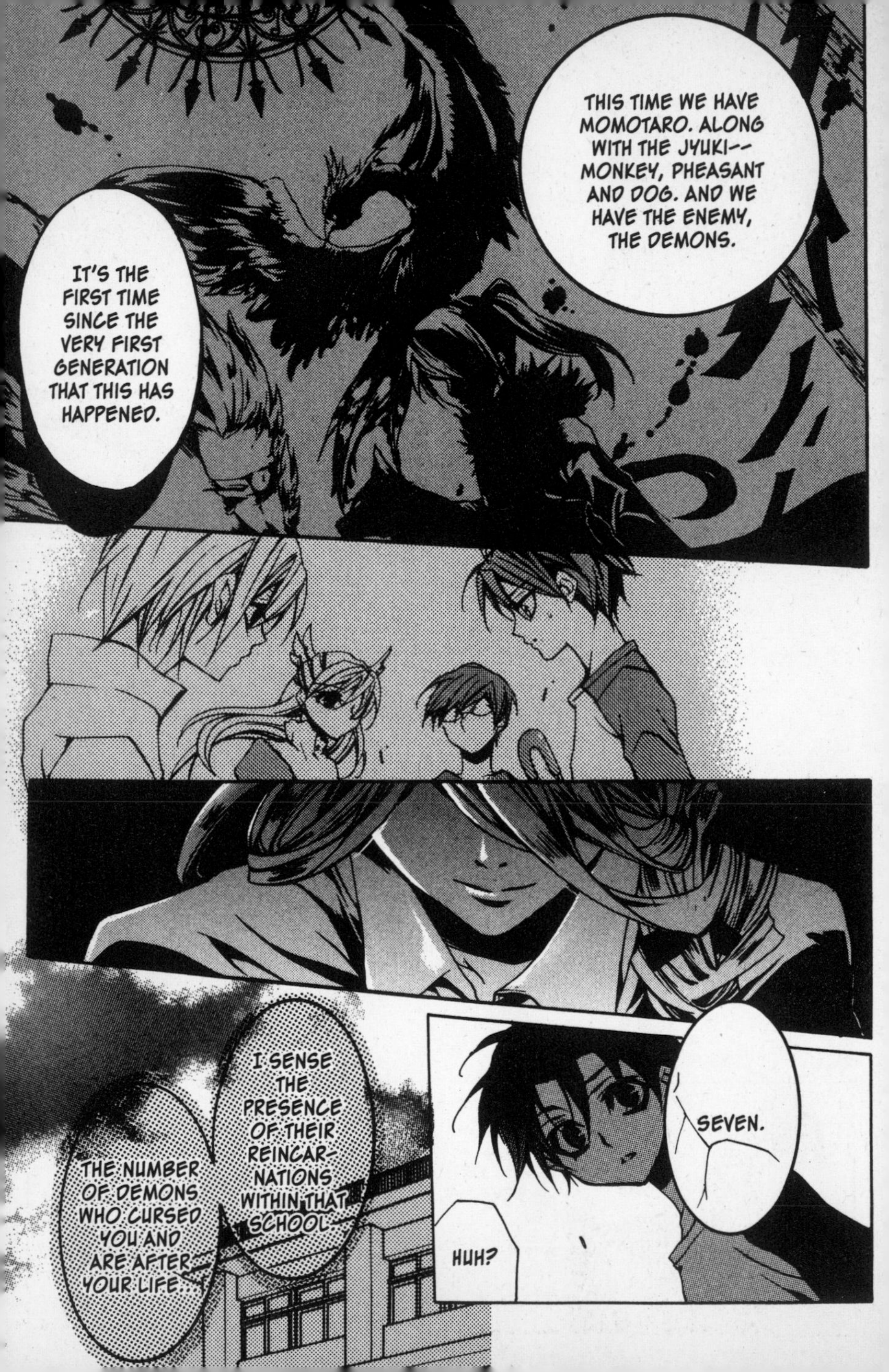
THIS TIME WE HAVE MOMOTARO. ALONG WITH THE JYUKI-- MONKEY, PHEASANT AND DOG. AND WE HAVE THE ENEMY, THE DEMONS.
IT'S THE FIRST TIME SINCE THE VERY FIRST GENERATION THAT THIS HAS HAPPENED.
SEVEN.
HUH?
I SENSE THE PRESENCE OF THEIR REINCAR-NATIONS WITHIN THAT SCHOOL.
THE NUMBER OF DEMONS WHO CURSED YOU AND ARE AFTER YOUR LIFE.

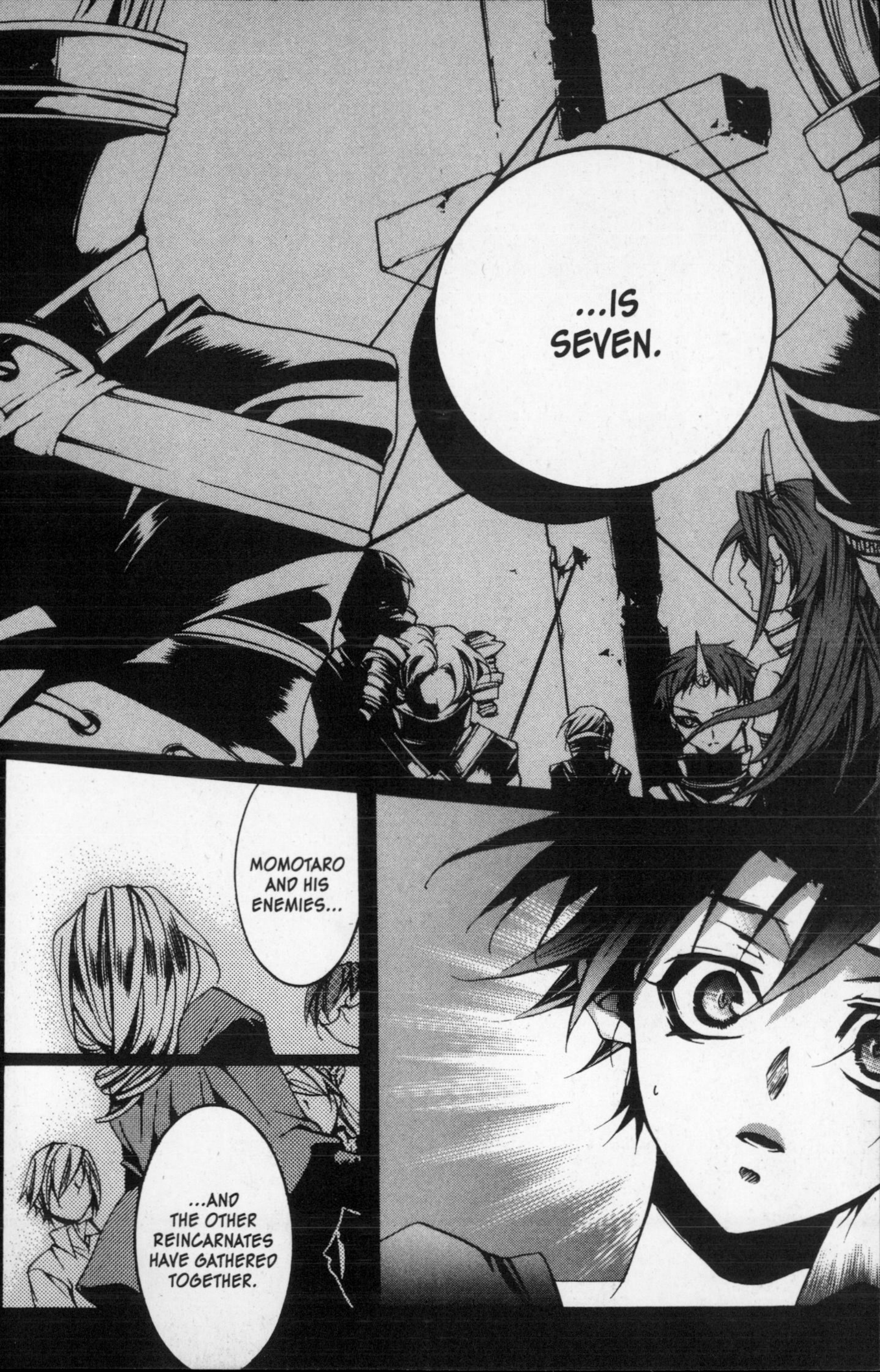
...IS SEVEN.
MOMOTARO AND HIS ENEMIES...
...AND THE OTHER REINCARNATES HAVE GATHERED TOGETHER.

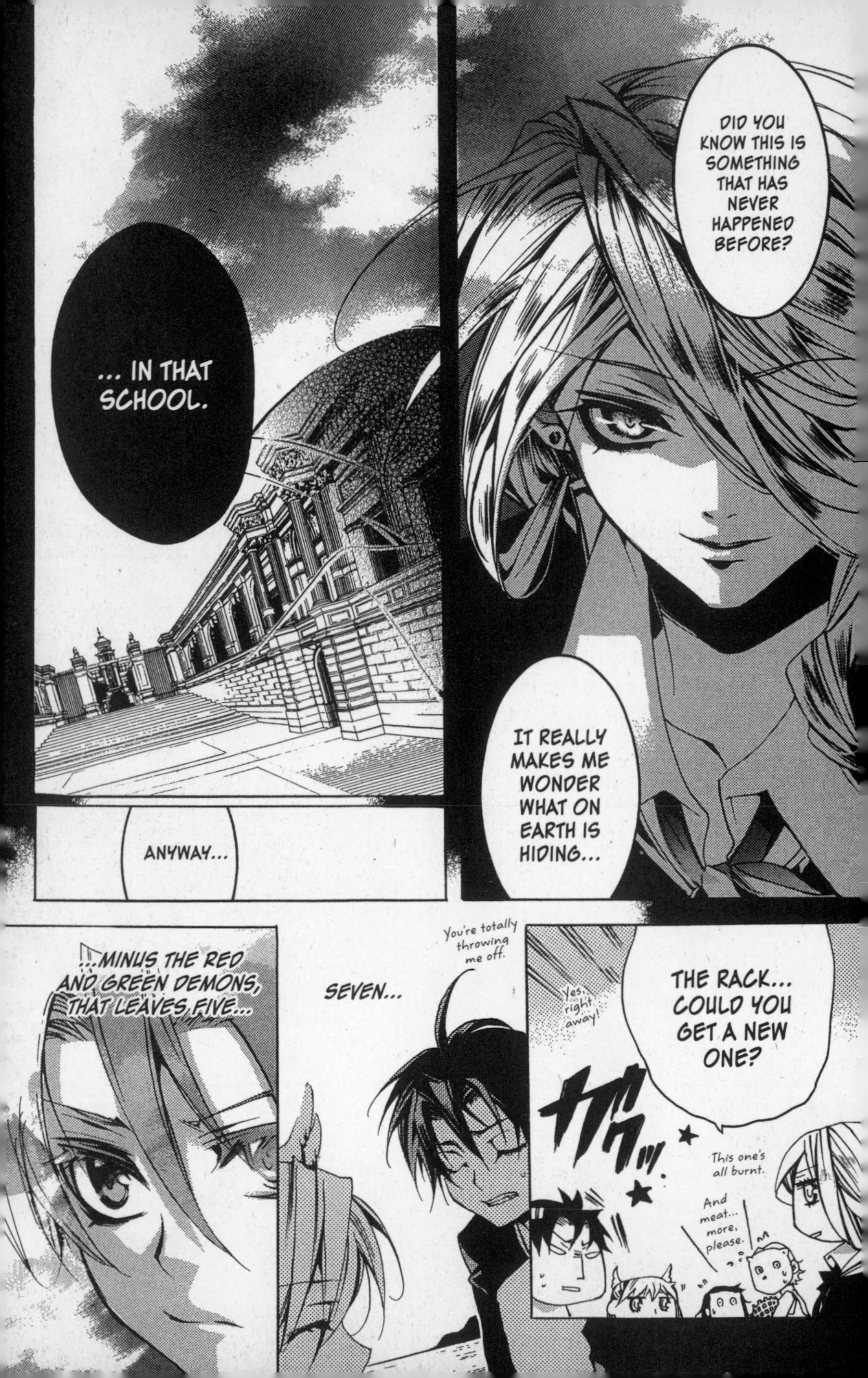
DID YOU KNOW THIS IS SOMETHING THAT HAS NEVER HAPPENED BEFORE?
IT REALLY MAKES ME WONDER WHAT ON EARTH IS HIDING...
... IN THAT SCHOOL.
ANYWAY...
THE RACK... COULD YOU GET A NEW ONE?
Yes, right away!
This one's all burnt.
And meat... more, please.
You're totally throwing me off.
SEVEN...
...MINUS THE RED AND GREEN DEMONS, THAT LEAVES FIVE...

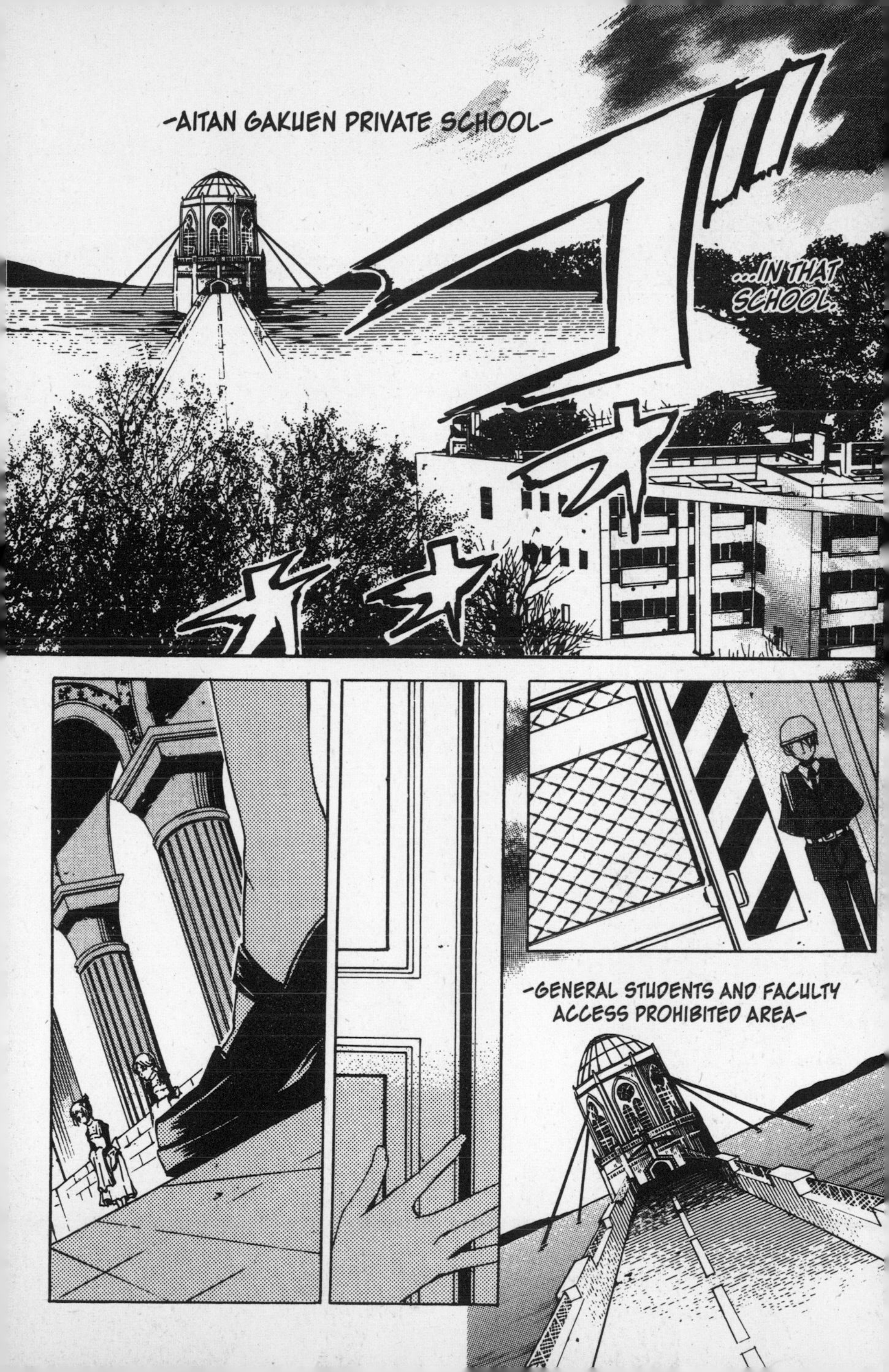
-AITAN GAKUEN PRIVATE SCHOOL-
...IN THAT SCHOOL.
-GENERAL STUDENTS AND FACULTY ACCESS PROHIBITED AREA-

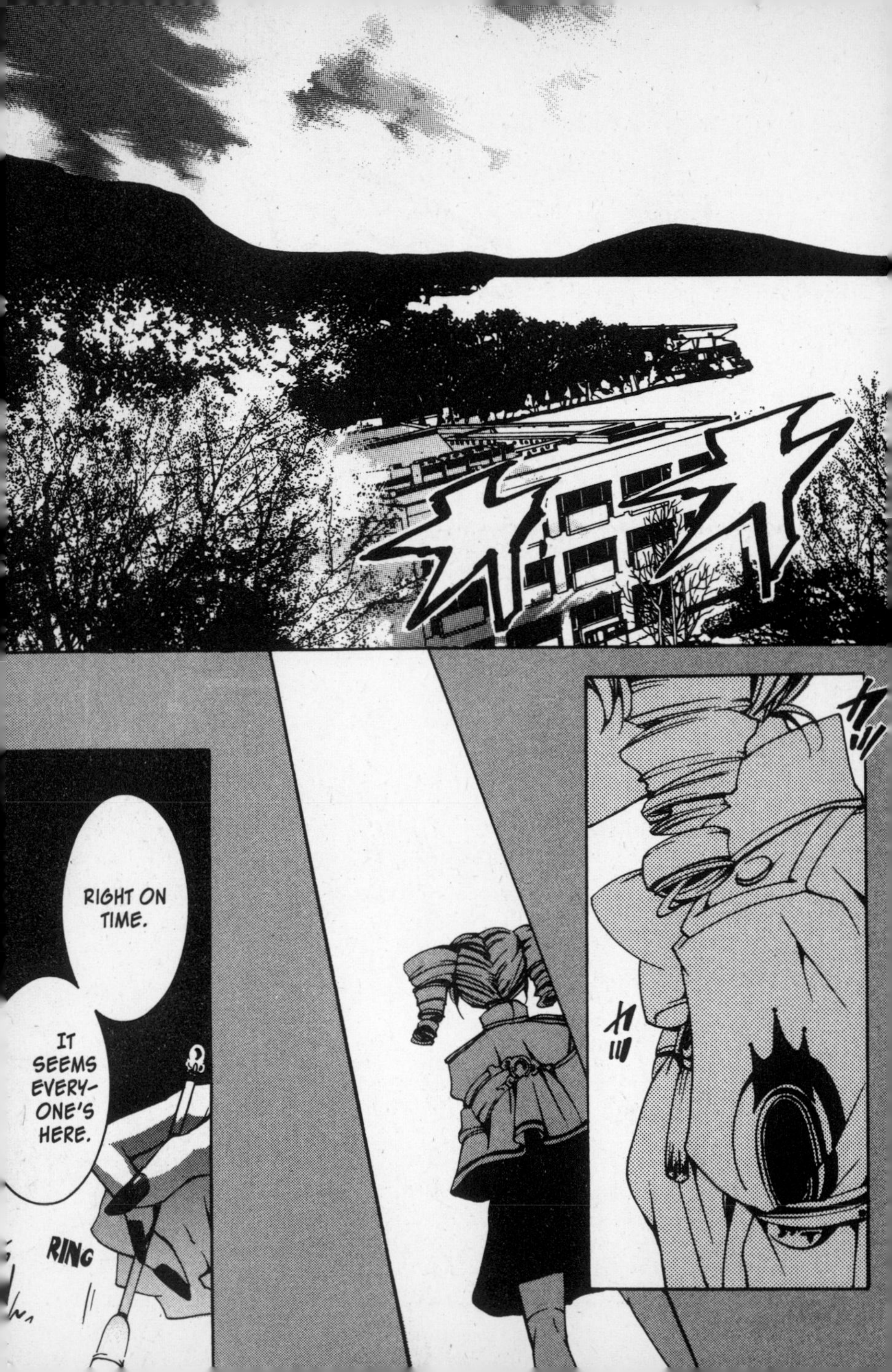
RIGHT ON TIME.
IT SEEMS EVERY-ONE'S HERE.
RING

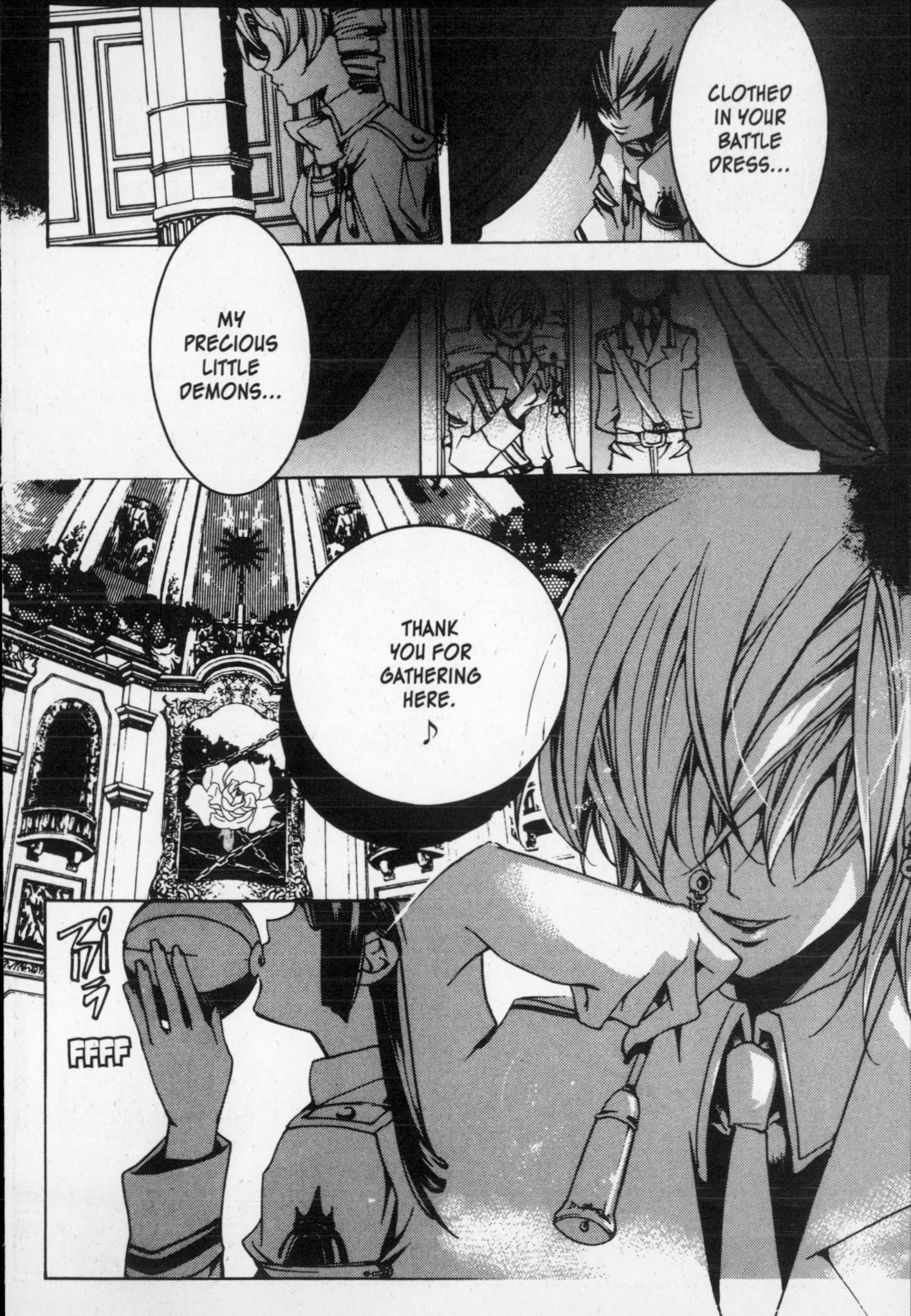
CLOTHED IN YOUR BATTLE DRESS...
MY PRECIOUS LITTLE DEMONS...
THANK YOU FOR GATHERING HERE. ♪
FFFF

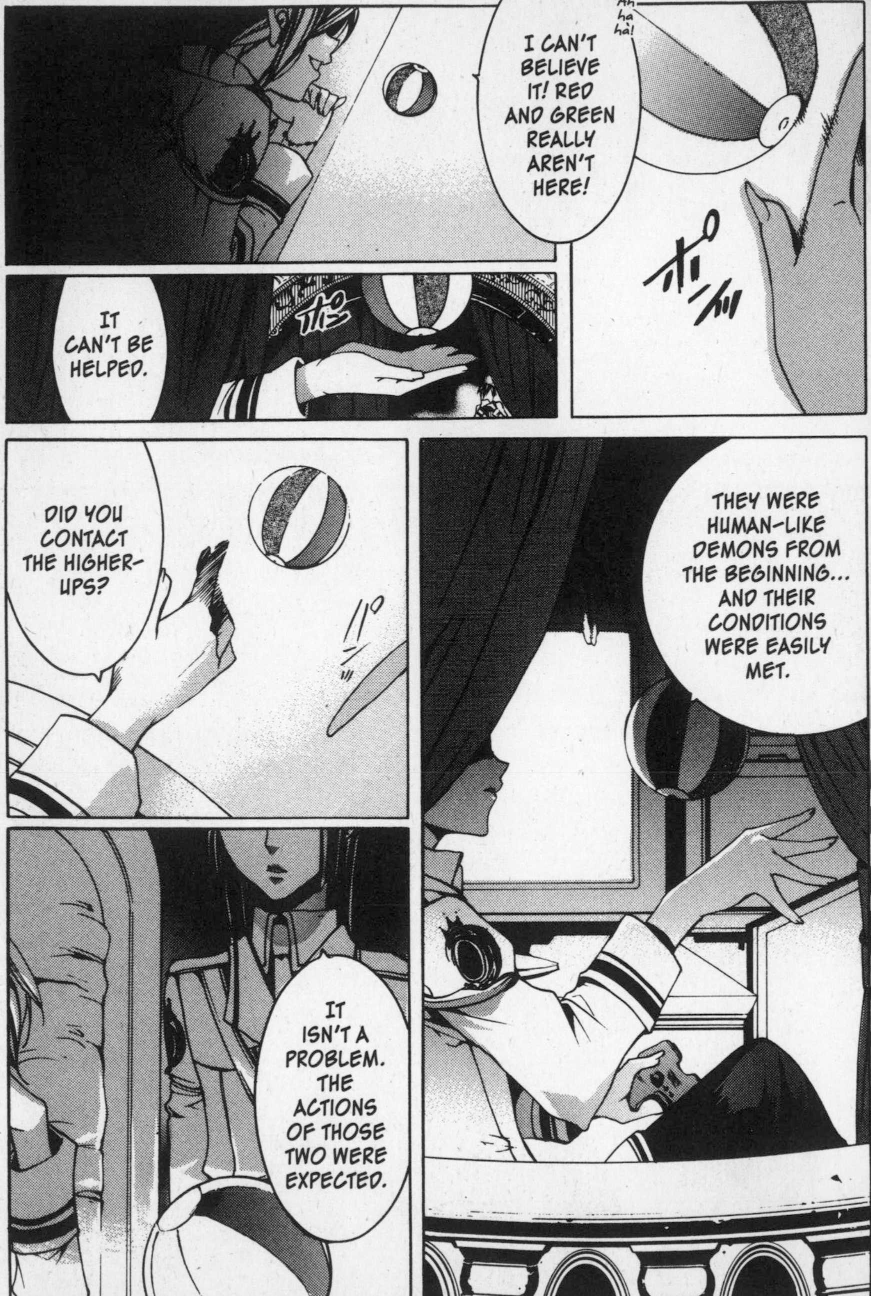
Ah ha ha!
I CAN'T BELIEVE IT! RED AND GREEN REALLY AREN'T HERE!
IT CAN'T BE HELPED.
THEY WERE HUMAN-LIKE DEMONS FROM THE BEGINNING... AND THEIR CONDITIONS WERE EASILY MET.
DID YOU CONTACT THE HIGHER-UPS?
IT ISN'T A PROBLEM. THE ACTIONS OF THOSE TWO WERE EXPECTED.

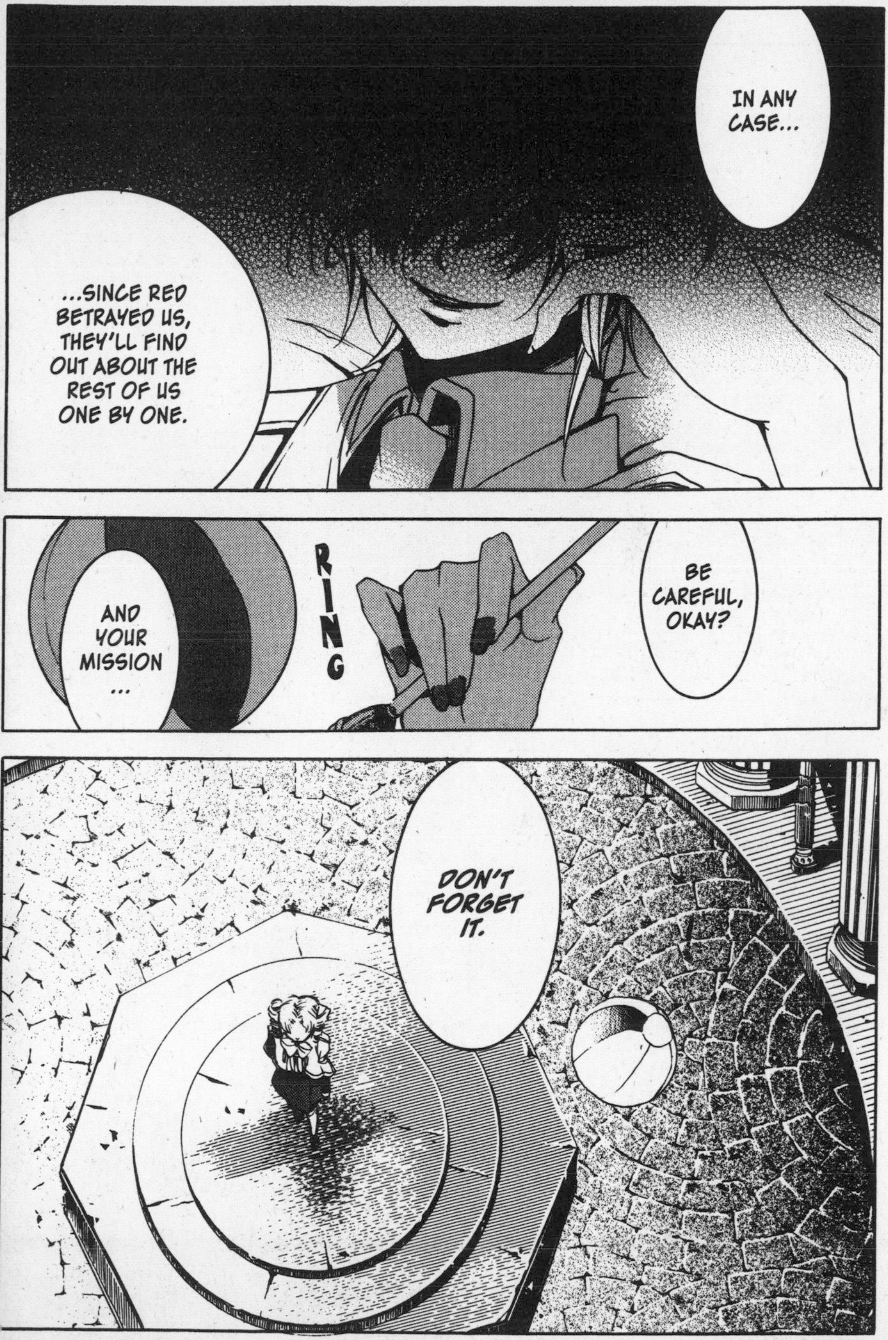
IN ANY CASE...
...SINCE RED BETRAYED US, THEY'LL FIND OUT ABOUT THE REST OF US ONE BY ONE.
BE CAREFUL, OKAY?
RING
AND YOUR MISSION ...
DON'T FORGET IT.

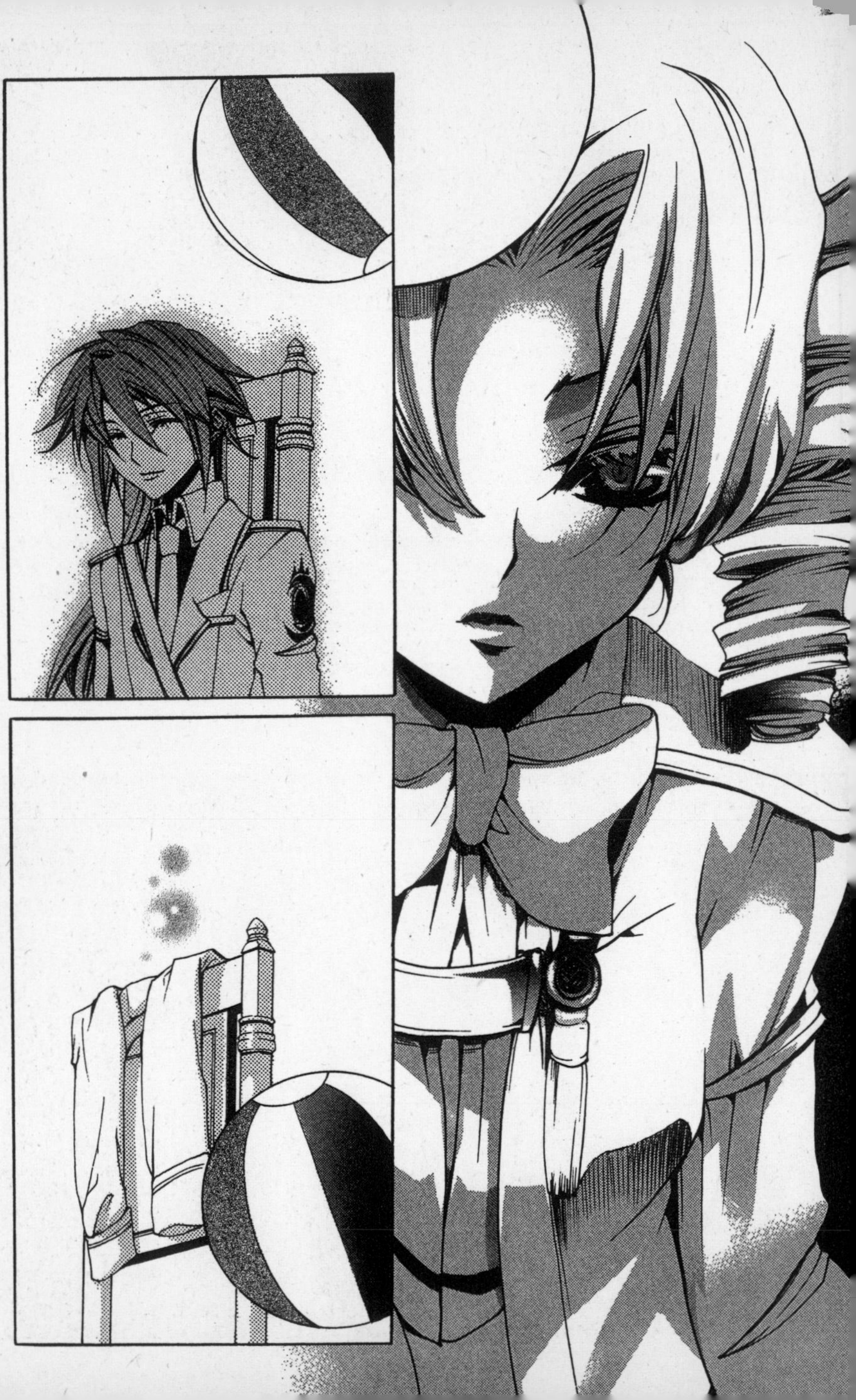

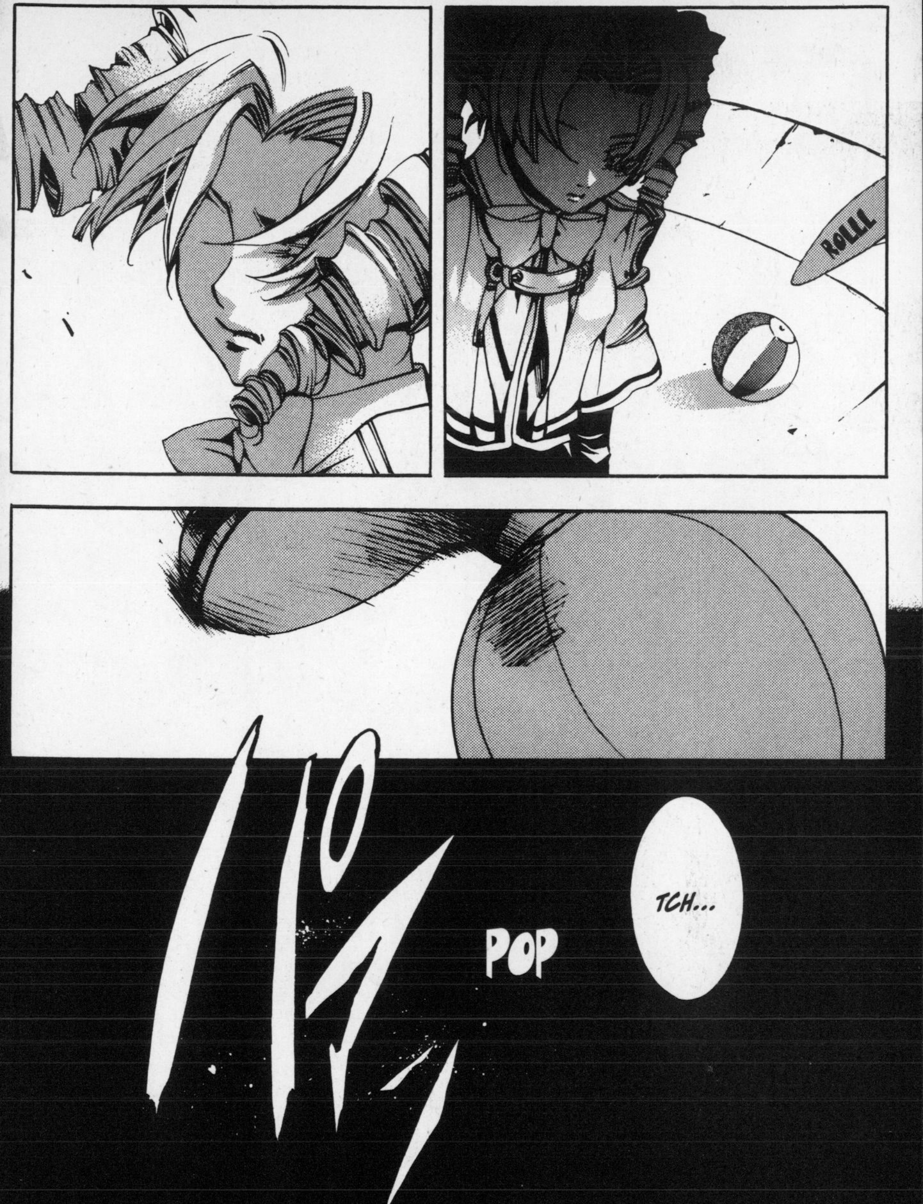
ROLLL
TCH...
POP

Chapter 9

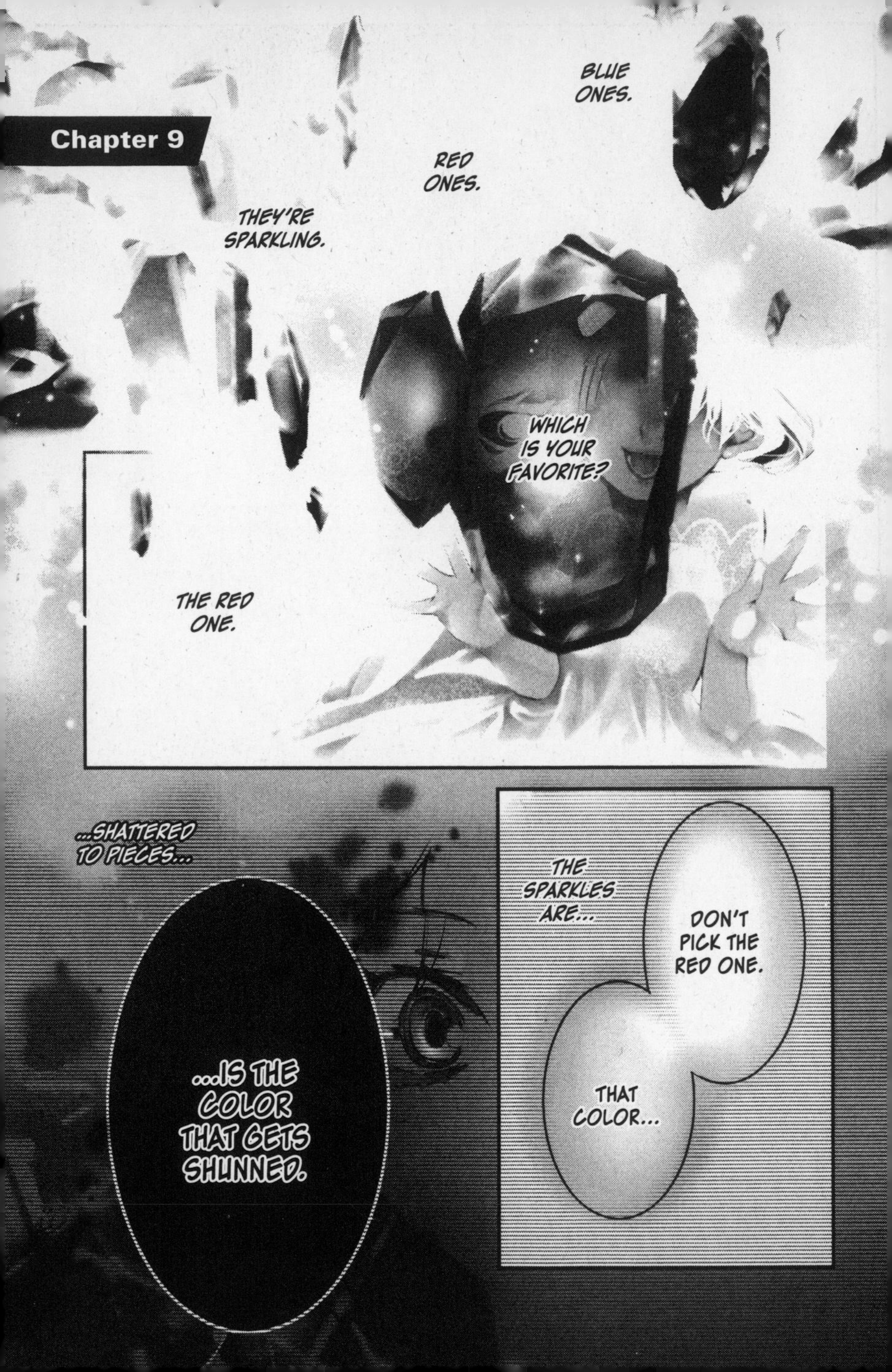

BLUE ONES.
RED ONES.
THEY'RE SPARKLING.
WHICH IS YOUR FAVORITE?
THE RED ONE.
THE SPARKLES ARE...
DON'T PICK THE RED ONE.
THAT COLOR...
...SHATTERED TO PIECES...
...IS THE COLOR THAT GETS SHUNNED.

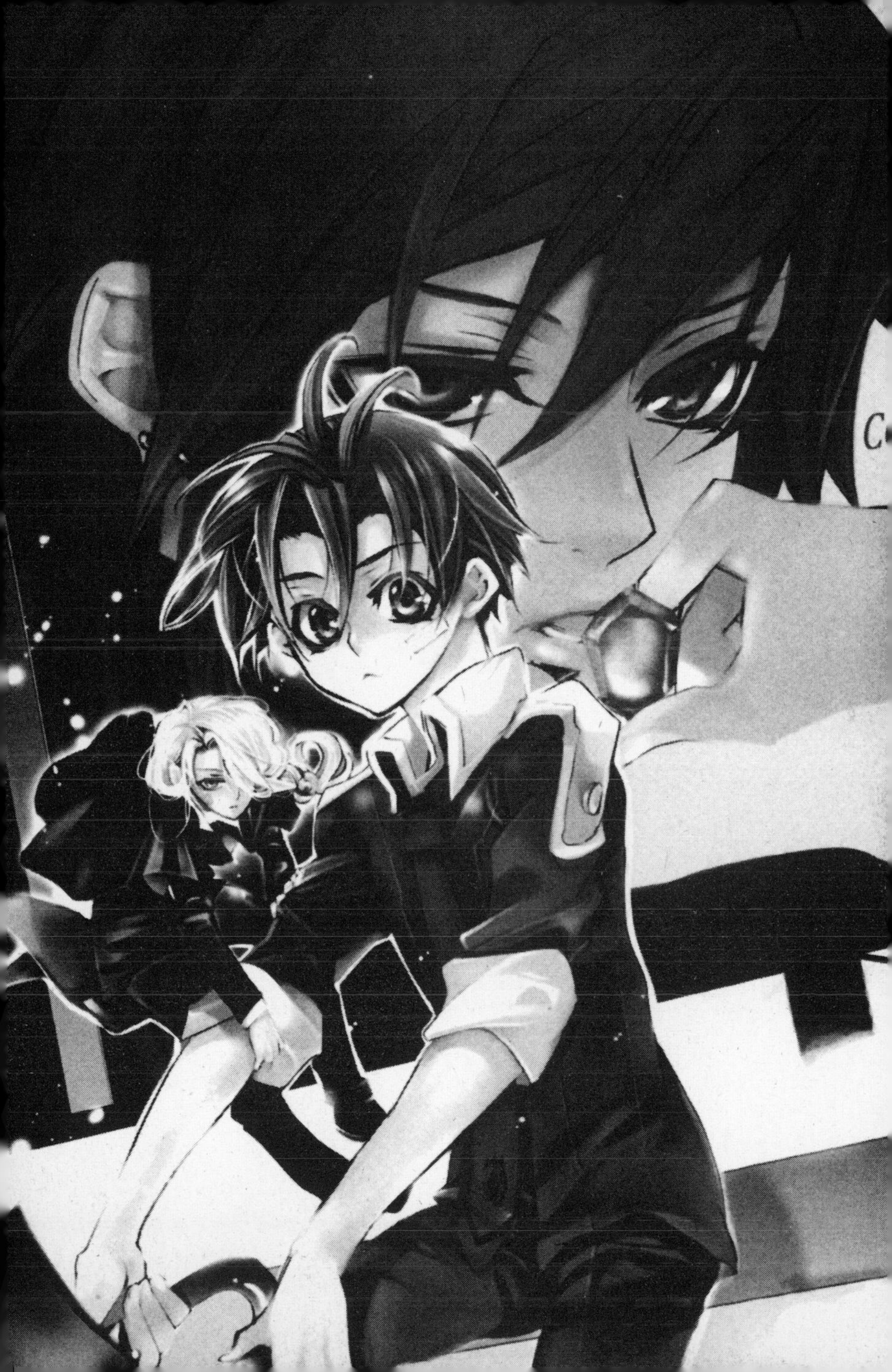

Chapter 9: The Contradiction in the Contract, Part 1

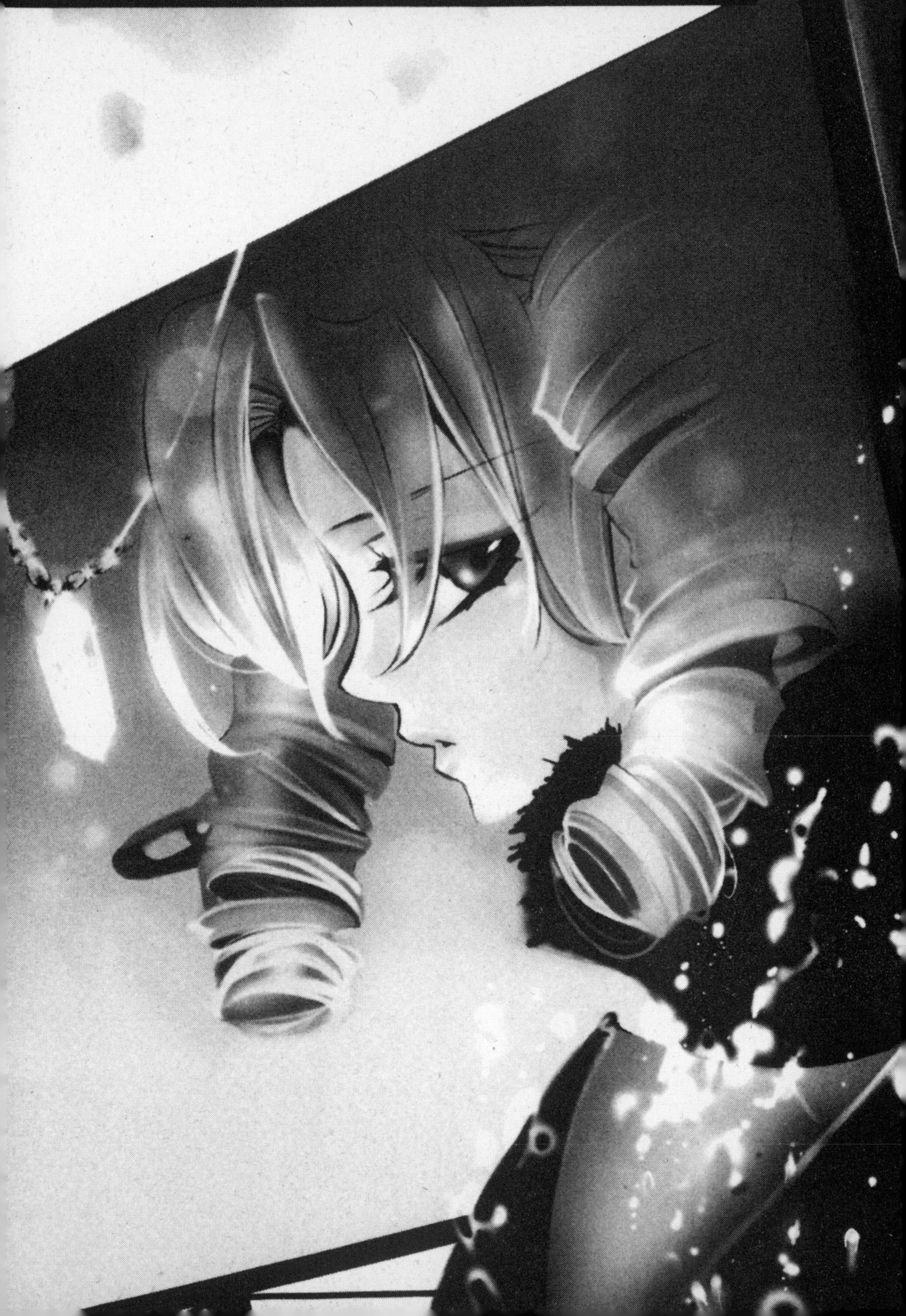

桃組プラス戦記

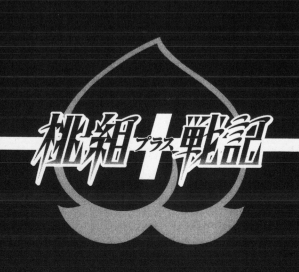

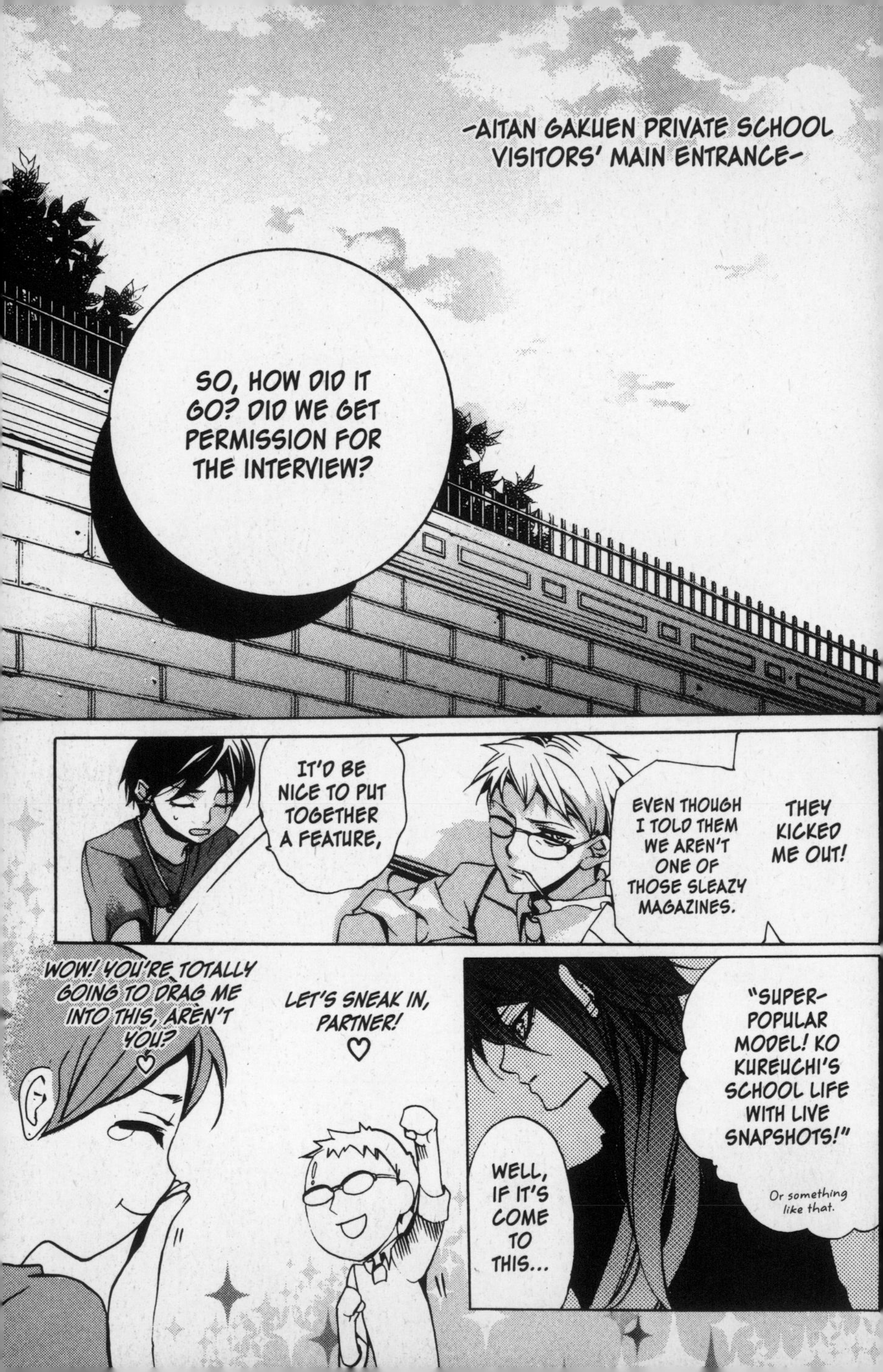
-AITAN GAKUEN PRIVATE SCHOOL VISITORS' MAIN ENTRANCE-
SO, HOW DID IT GO? DID WE GET PERMISSION FOR THE INTERVIEW?
THEY KICKED ME OUT!
EVEN THOUGH I TOLD THEM WE AREN'T ONE OF THOSE SLEAZY MAGAZINES.
IT'D BE NICE TO PUT TOGETHER A FEATURE,
"SUPER-POPULAR MODEL! KO KUREUCHI'S SCHOOL LIFE WITH LIVE SNAPSHOTS!"
Or something like that.
WELL, IF IT'S COME TO THIS...
LET'S SNEAK IN, PARTNER! ♡
WOW! YOU'RE TOTALLY GOING TO DRAG ME INTO THIS, AREN'T YOU? ♡

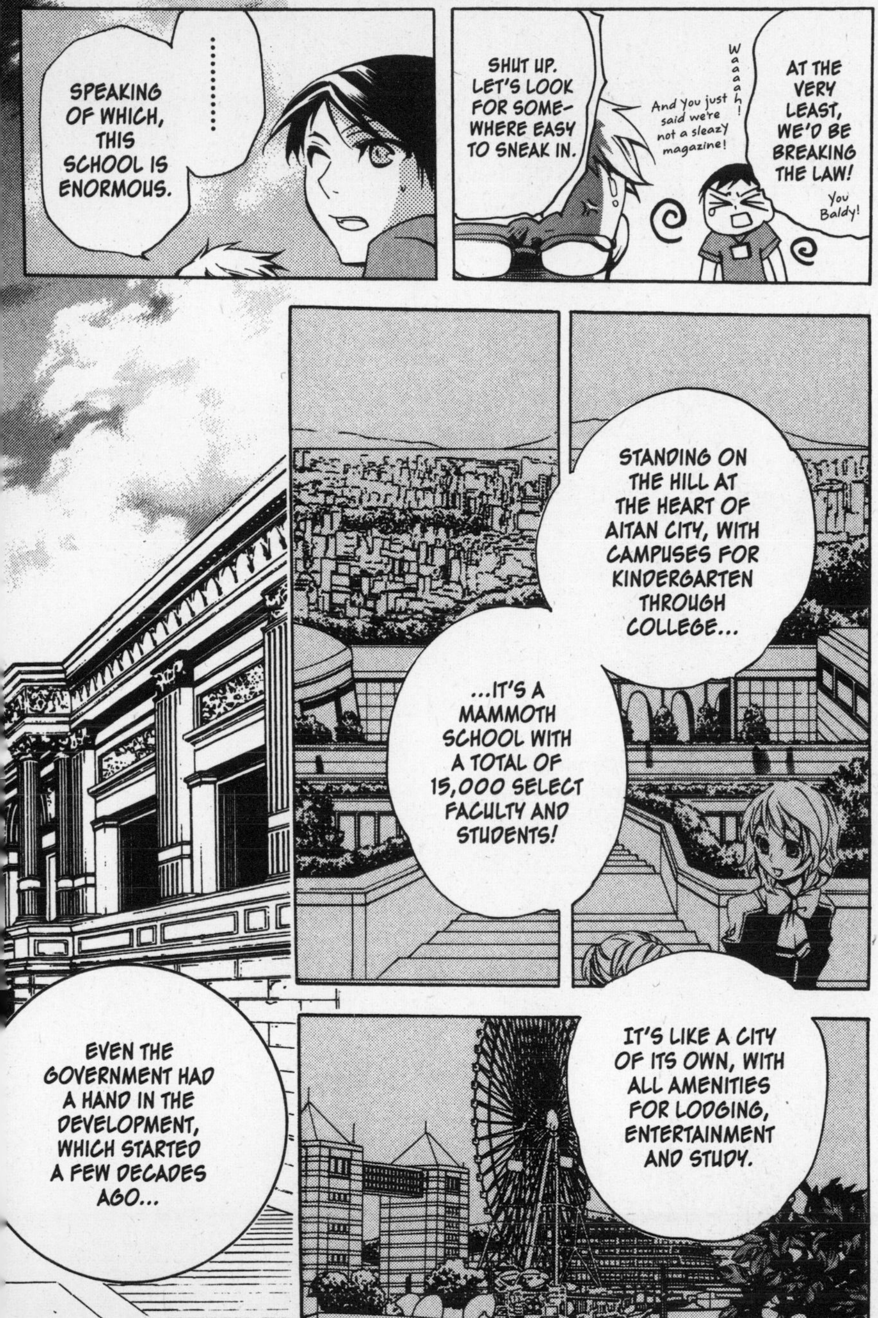
AT THE VERY LEAST, WE'D BE BREAKING THE LAW!
You Baldy!
Waaaah!
And You just said we're not a sleazy magazine!
SHUT UP. LET'S LOOK FOR SOME-WHERE EASY TO SNEAK IN.
......
SPEAKING OF WHICH, THIS SCHOOL IS ENORMOUS.
STANDING ON THE HILL AT THE HEART OF AITAN CITY, WITH CAMPUSES FOR KINDERGARTEN THROUGH COLLEGE...
...IT'S A MAMMOTH SCHOOL WITH A TOTAL OF 15,000 SELECT FACULTY AND STUDENTS!
IT'S LIKE A CITY OF ITS OWN, WITH ALL AMENITIES FOR LODGING, ENTERTAINMENT AND STUDY.
EVEN THE GOVERNMENT HAD A HAND IN THE DEVELOPMENT, WHICH STARTED A FEW DECADES AGO...

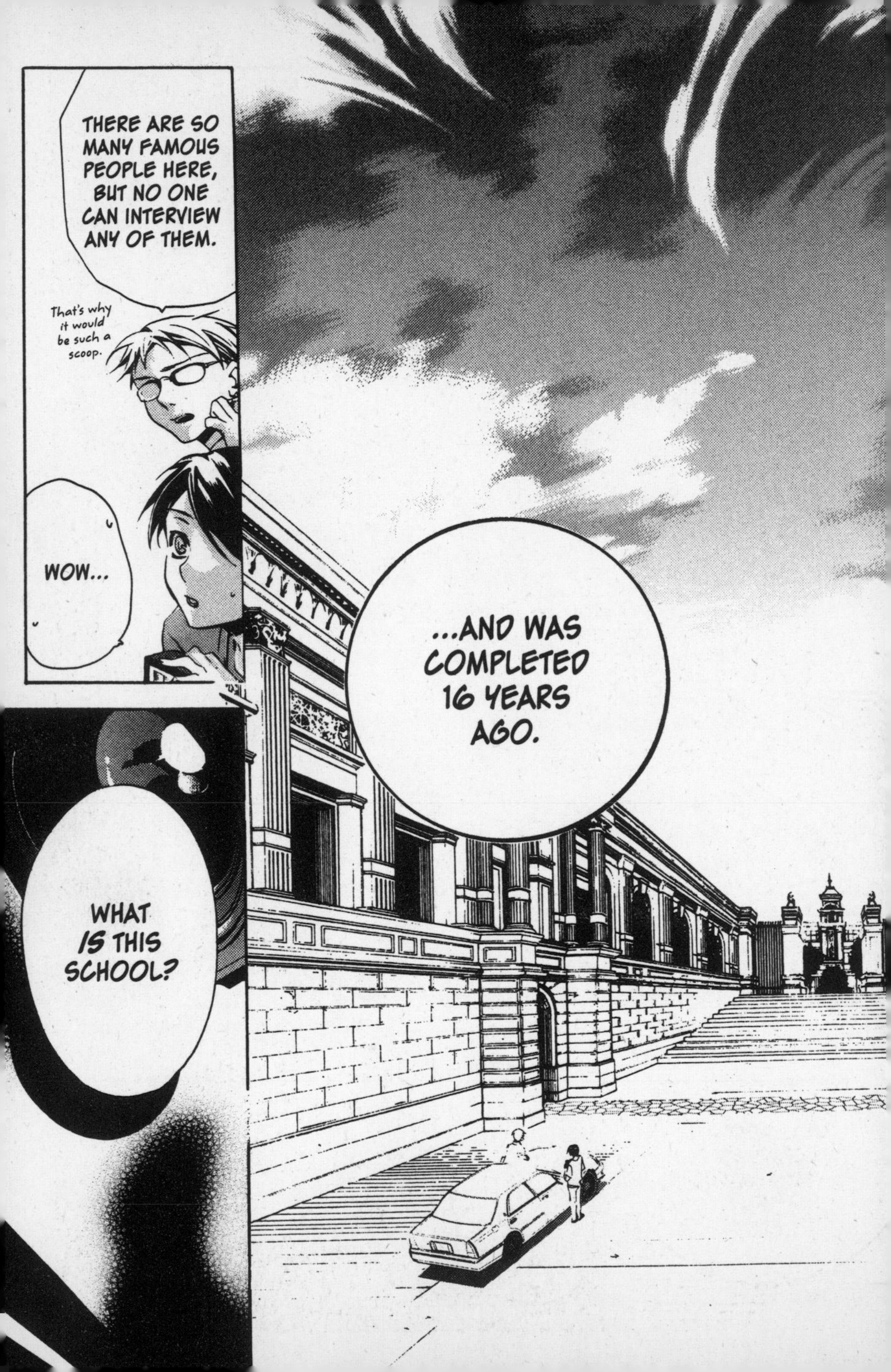
...AND WAS COMPLETED 16 YEARS AGO.
THERE ARE SO MANY FAMOUS PEOPLE HERE, BUT NO ONE CAN INTERVIEW ANY OF THEM.
That's why it would be such a scoop.
WOW...
WHAT *IS* THIS SCHOOL?

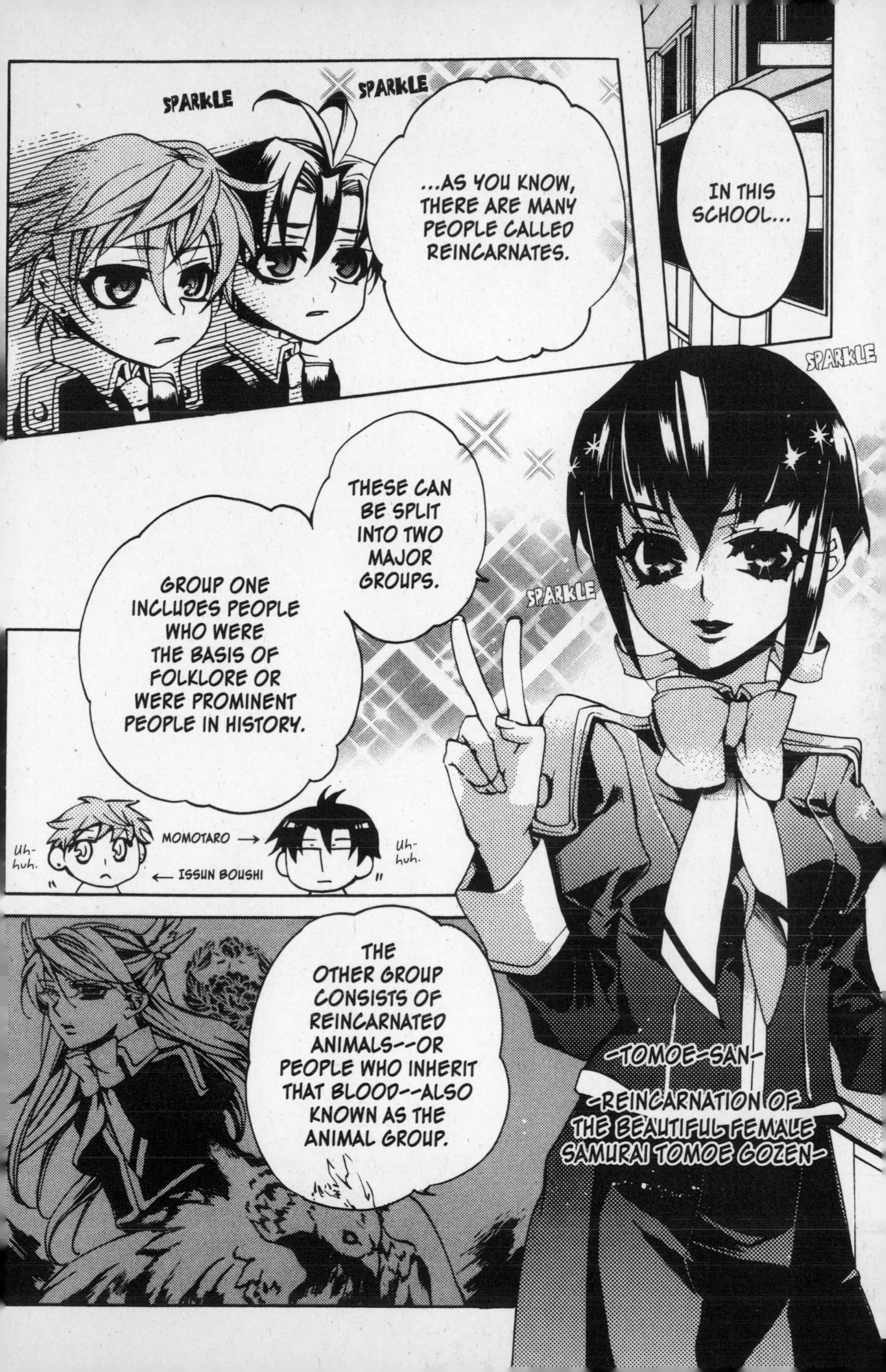
IN THIS SCHOOL...
SPARKLE
SPARKLE
...AS YOU KNOW, THERE ARE MANY PEOPLE CALLED REINCARNATES.
SPARKLE
THESE CAN BE SPLIT INTO TWO MAJOR GROUPS.
SPARKLE
GROUP ONE INCLUDES PEOPLE WHO WERE THE BASIS OF FOLKLORE OR WERE PROMINENT PEOPLE IN HISTORY.
-TOMOE-SAN-
-REINCARNATION OF THE BEAUTIFUL FEMALE SAMURAI TOMOE GOZEN-
Uh-huh.
MOMOTARO →
← ISSUN BOUSHI
Uh-huh.
THE OTHER GROUP CONSISTS OF REINCARNATED ANIMALS--OR PEOPLE WHO INHERIT THAT BLOOD--ALSO KNOWN AS THE ANIMAL GROUP.

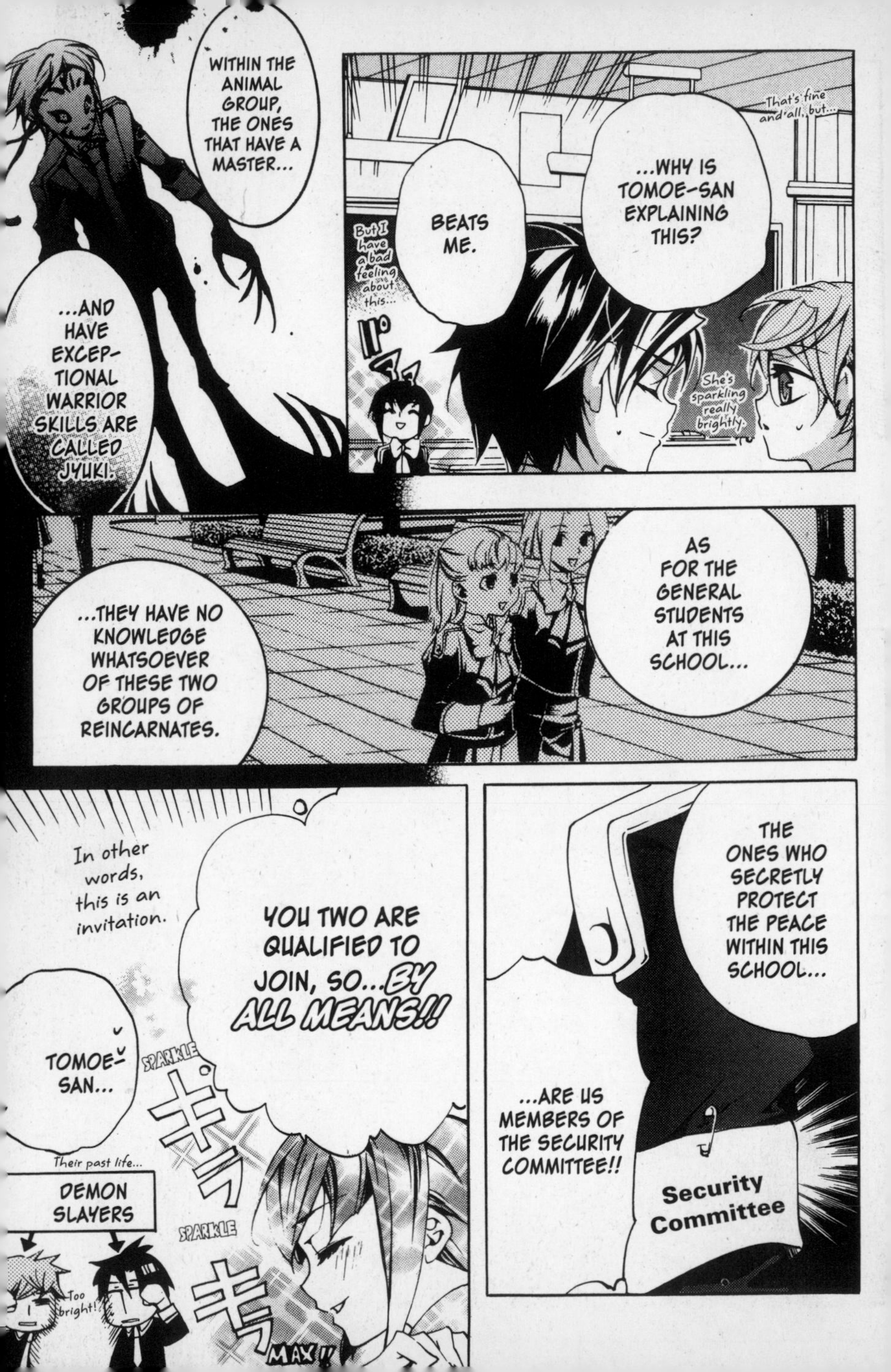
That's fine and all, but...
...WHY IS TOMOE-SAN EXPLAINING THIS?
BEATS ME.
But I have a bad feeling about this...
She's sparkling really brightly.
WITHIN THE ANIMAL GROUP, THE ONES THAT HAVE A MASTER...
...AND HAVE EXCEPTIONAL WARRIOR SKILLS ARE CALLED JYUKI.
AS FOR THE GENERAL STUDENTS AT THIS SCHOOL...
...THEY HAVE NO KNOWLEDGE WHATSOEVER OF THESE TWO GROUPS OF REINCARNATES.
THE ONES WHO SECRETLY PROTECT THE PEACE WITHIN THIS SCHOOL...
...ARE US MEMBERS OF THE SECURITY COMMITTEE!!
Security Committee
YOU TWO ARE QUALIFIED TO JOIN, SO...BY ALL MEANS!!
In other words, this is an invitation.
TOMOE-SAN...
SPARKLE
SPARKLE
MAX!!
Their past life...
DEMON SLAYERS
Too bright!!

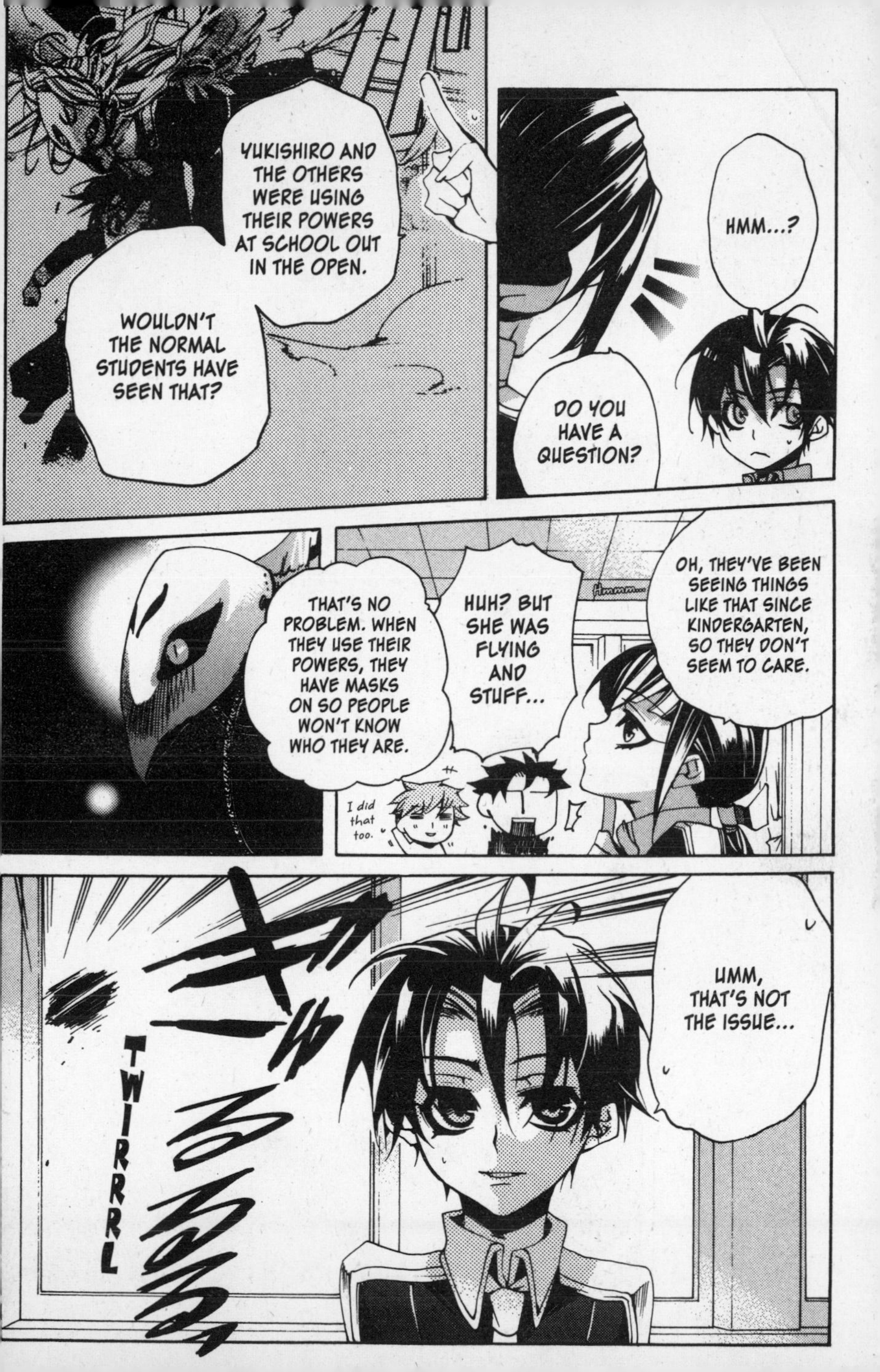
HMM...?
DO YOU HAVE A QUESTION?
YUKISHIRO AND THE OTHERS WERE USING THEIR POWERS AT SCHOOL OUT IN THE OPEN.
WOULDN'T THE NORMAL STUDENTS HAVE SEEN THAT?
OH, THEY'VE BEEN SEEING THINGS LIKE THAT SINCE KINDERGARTEN, SO THEY DON'T SEEM TO CARE.
Hmmm...
HUH? BUT SHE WAS FLYING AND STUFF...
I did that too.
THAT'S NO PROBLEM. WHEN THEY USE THEIR POWERS, THEY HAVE MASKS ON SO PEOPLE WON'T KNOW WHO THEY ARE.
UMM, THAT'S NOT THE ISSUE...
TWIRRRL

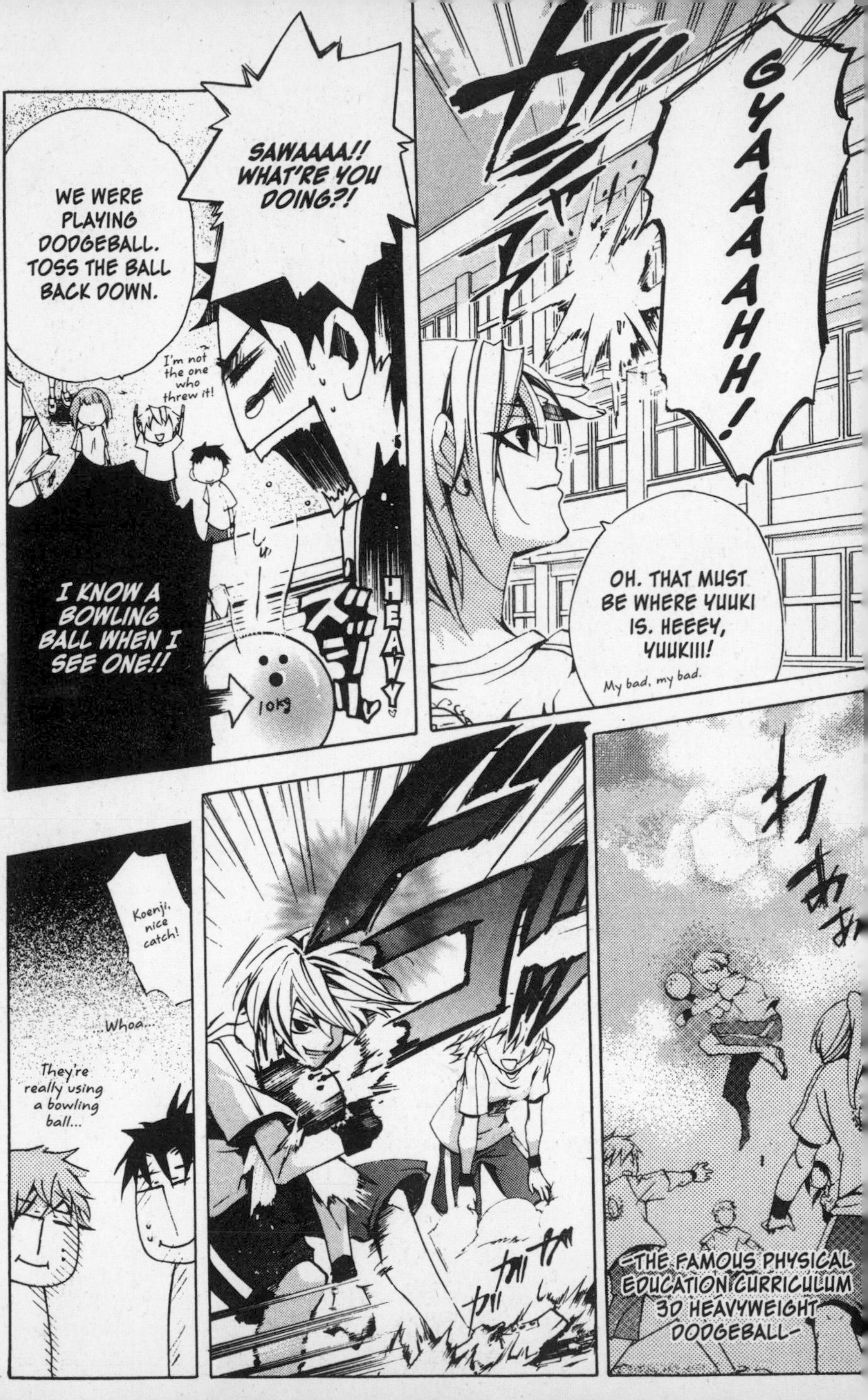
GYAAAAAHH!
OH. THAT MUST BE WHERE YUUKI IS. HEEEY, YUUKIII!
My bad, my bad.
SAWAAAA!! WHAT'RE YOU DOING?!
WE WERE PLAYING DODGEBALL. TOSS THE BALL BACK DOWN.
I'm not the one who threw it!
I KNOW A BOWLING BALL WHEN I SEE ONE!!
HEAVY
10kg
-THE FAMOUS PHYSICAL EDUCATION CURRICULUM 3D HEAVYWEIGHT DODGEBALL-
Koenji, nice catch!
...Whoa...
They're really using a bowling ball...

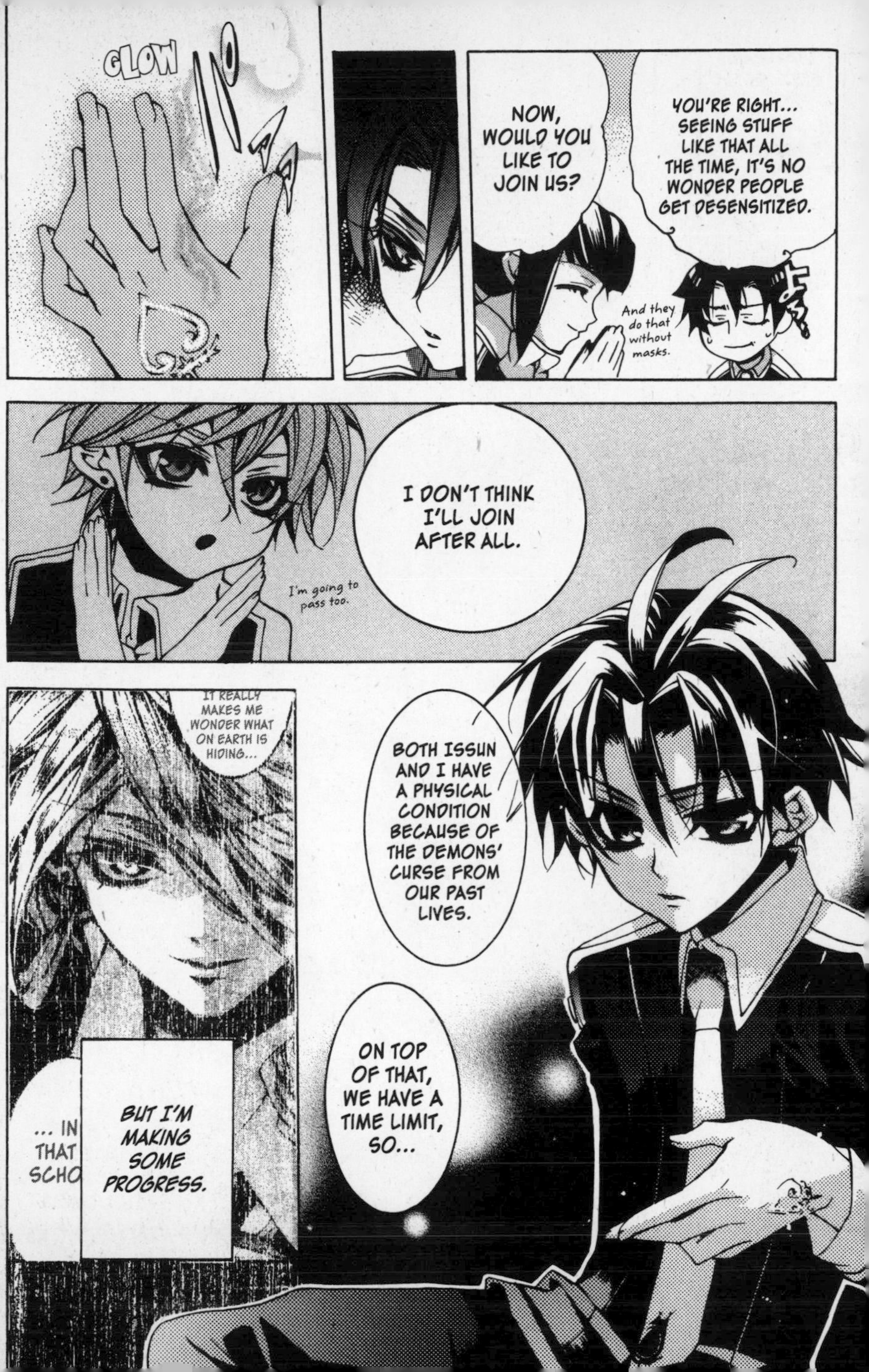
YOU'RE RIGHT... SEEING STUFF LIKE THAT ALL THE TIME, IT'S NO WONDER PEOPLE GET DESENSITIZED.
NOW, WOULD YOU LIKE TO JOIN US?
And they do that without masks.
GLOW
I DON'T THINK I'LL JOIN AFTER ALL.
I'm going to pass too.
BOTH ISSUN AND I HAVE A PHYSICAL CONDITION BECAUSE OF THE DEMONS' CURSE FROM OUR PAST LIVES.
ON TOP OF THAT, WE HAVE A TIME LIMIT, SO...
IT REALLY MAKES ME WONDER WHAT ON EARTH IS HIDING...
BUT I'M MAKING SOME PROGRESS.
... IN THAT SCHO

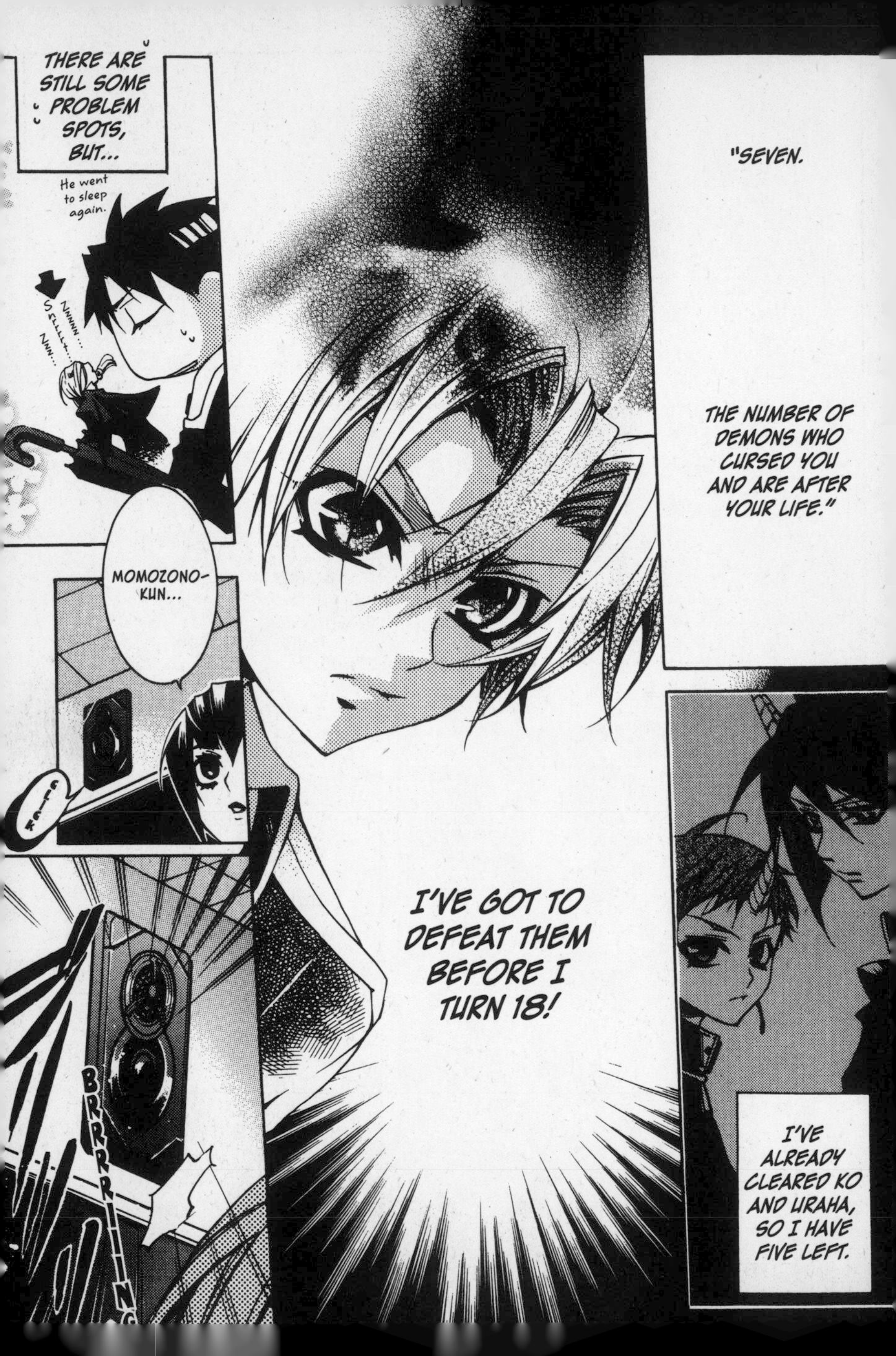
"SEVEN.
THE NUMBER OF DEMONS WHO CURSED YOU AND ARE AFTER YOUR LIFE."
I'VE ALREADY CLEARED KO AND URAHA, SO I HAVE FIVE LEFT.
I'VE GOT TO DEFEAT THEM BEFORE I TURN 18!
THERE ARE STILL SOME PROBLEM SPOTS, BUT...
He went to sleep again.
MOMOZONO-KUN...
CLICK
BRRRRIIING

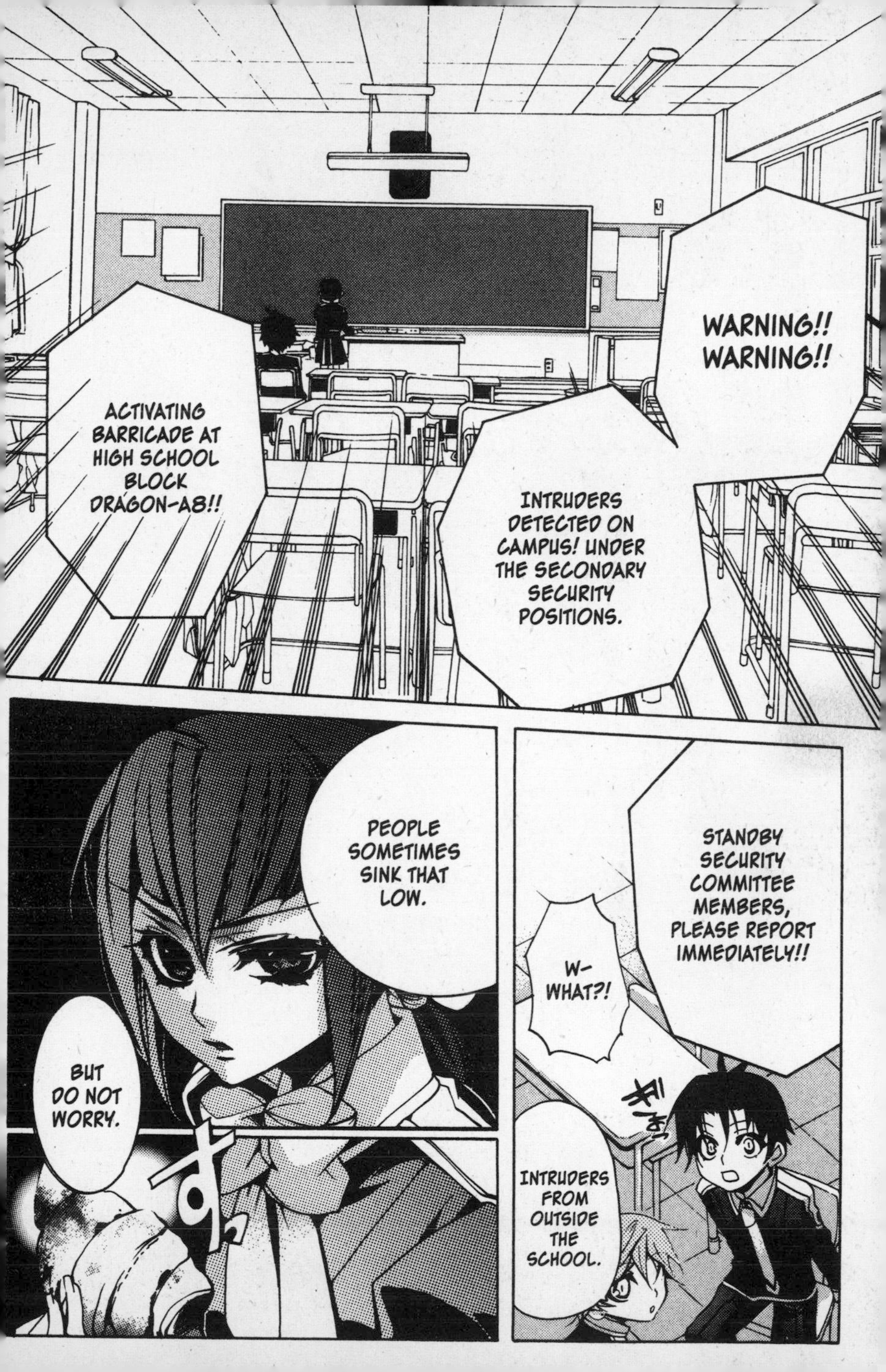
WARNING!! WARNING!!
INTRUDERS DETECTED ON CAMPUS! UNDER THE SECONDARY SECURITY POSITIONS.
ACTIVATING BARRICADE AT HIGH SCHOOL BLOCK DRAGON-A8!!
STANDBY SECURITY COMMITTEE MEMBERS, PLEASE REPORT IMMEDIATELY!!
W-WHAT?!
INTRUDERS FROM OUTSIDE THE SCHOOL.
PEOPLE SOMETIMES SINK THAT LOW.
BUT DO NOT WORRY.

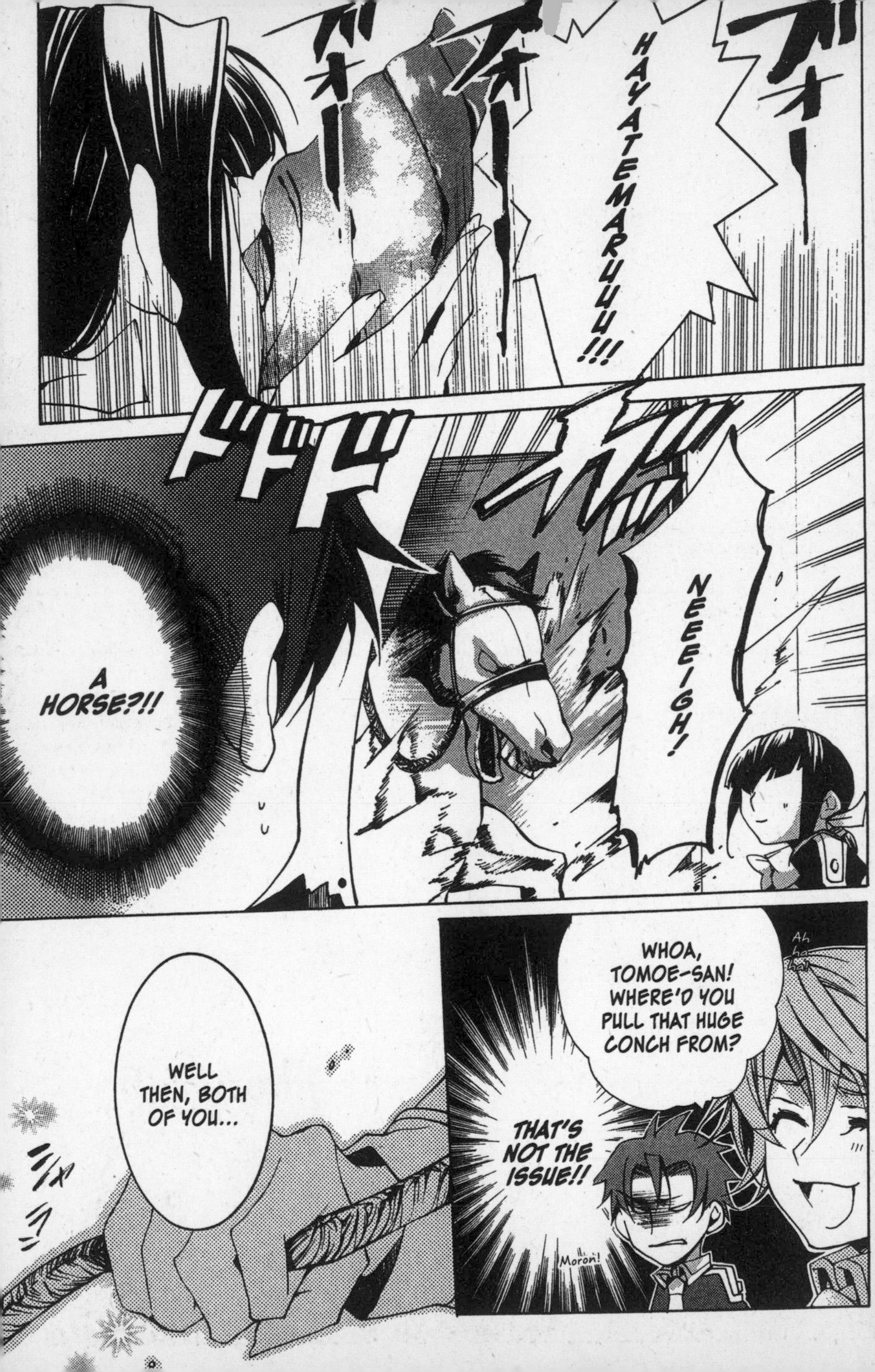
HAYATEMARUUUU!!!
NEEEIGH!
A HORSE?!!
WHOA, TOMOE-SAN! WHERE'D YOU PULL THAT HUGE CONCH FROM?
Ah ha ha!
THAT'S NOT THE ISSUE!!
Moron!
WELL THEN, BOTH OF YOU...

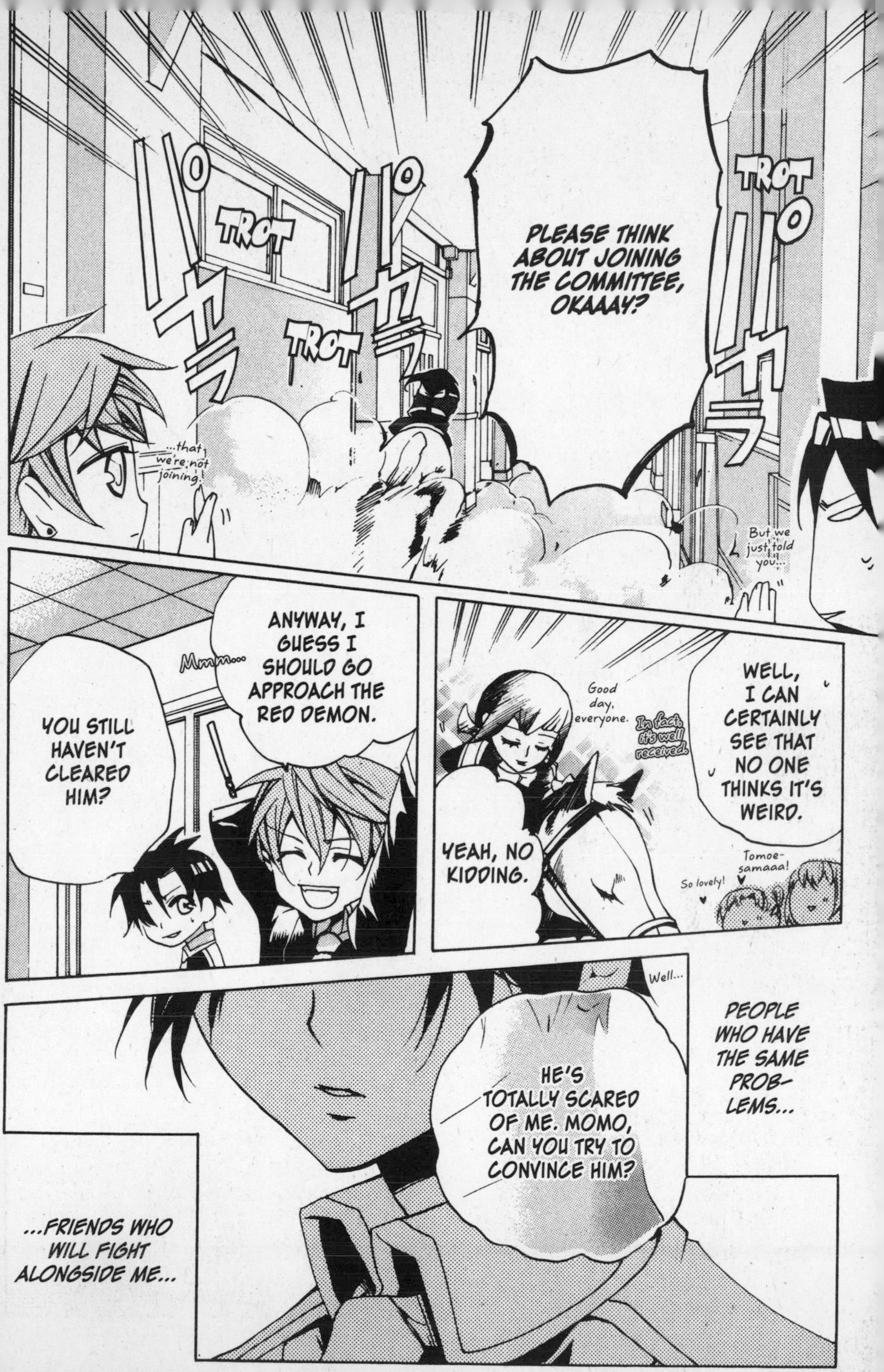
TROT
パカラ
PLEASE THINK ABOUT JOINING THE COMMITTEE, OKAAAY?
But we just told you...
パカラ
TROT
TROT
パカラ
...that we're not joining.
WELL, I CAN CERTAINLY SEE THAT NO ONE THINKS IT'S WEIRD.
Good day, everyone.
In fact, it's well received.
Tomoe-samaaa!
So lovely!
YEAH, NO KIDDING.
ANYWAY, I GUESS I SHOULD GO APPROACH THE RED DEMON.
Mmm...
YOU STILL HAVEN'T CLEARED HIM?
Well...
PEOPLE WHO HAVE THE SAME PROB-LEMS...
HE'S TOTALLY SCARED OF ME. MOMO, CAN YOU TRY TO CONVINCE HIM?
...FRIENDS WHO WILL FIGHT ALONGSIDE ME...

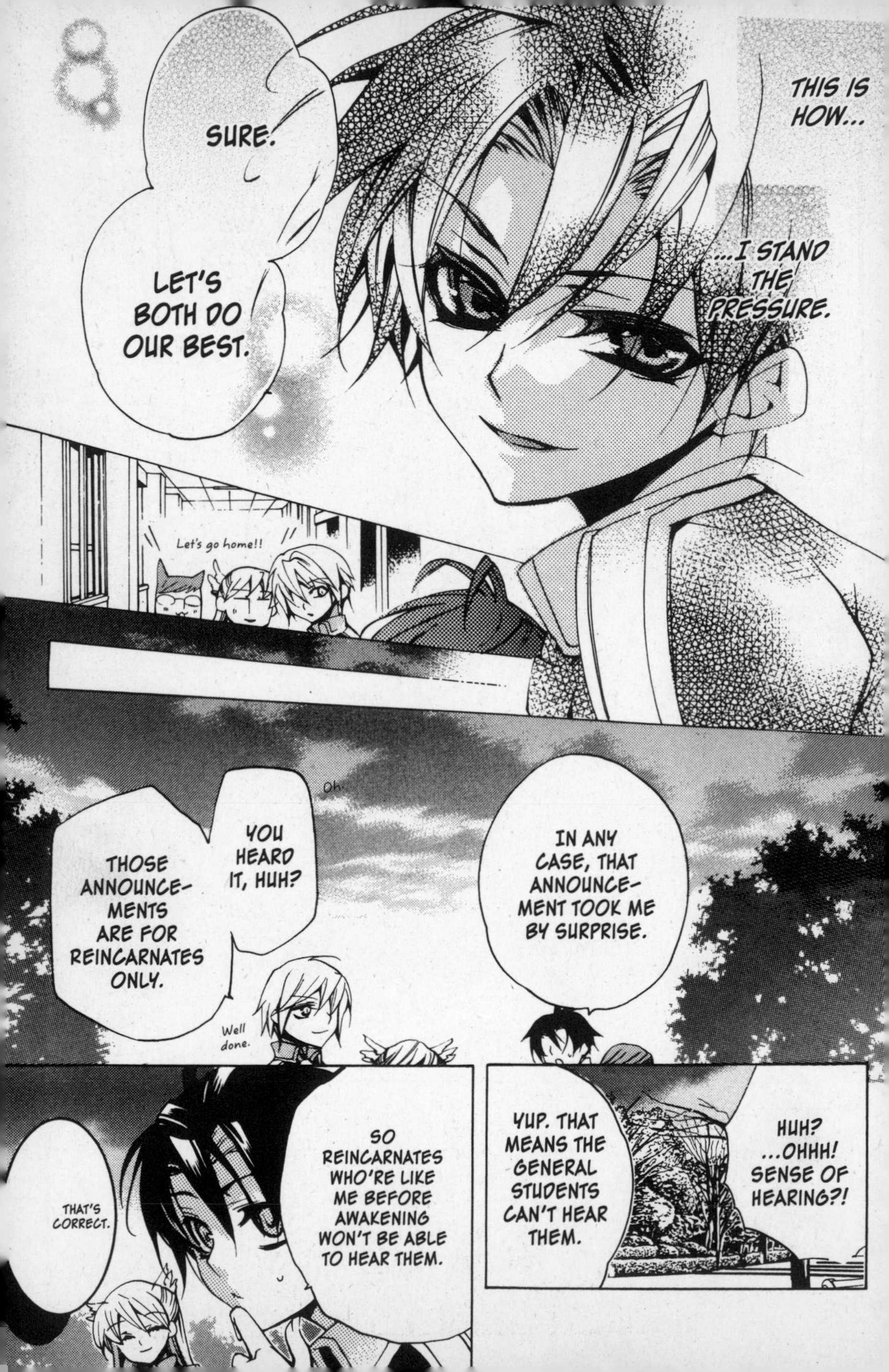
THIS IS HOW...
...I STAND THE PRESSURE.
SURE. LET'S BOTH DO OUR BEST.
Let's go home!!
IN ANY CASE, THAT ANNOUNCEMENT TOOK ME BY SURPRISE.
Oh.
YOU HEARD IT, HUH?
THOSE ANNOUNCEMENTS ARE FOR REINCARNATES ONLY.
Well done.
HUH? ...OHHH! SENSE OF HEARING?!
YUP. THAT MEANS THE GENERAL STUDENTS CAN'T HEAR THEM.
SO REINCARNATES WHO'RE LIKE ME BEFORE AWAKENING WON'T BE ABLE TO HEAR THEM.
THAT'S CORRECT.

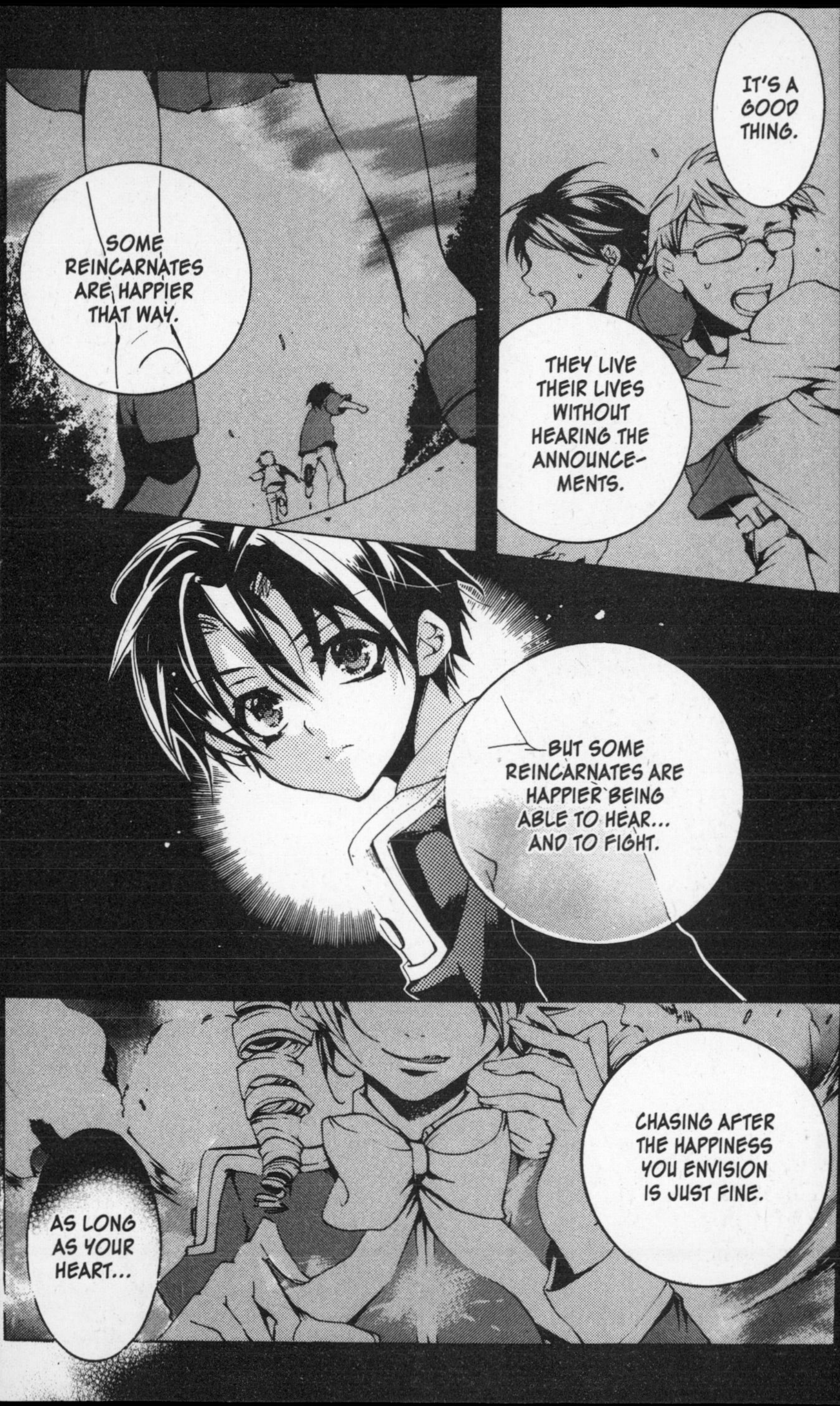
IT'S A GOOD THING.
THEY LIVE THEIR LIVES WITHOUT HEARING THE ANNOUNCE-MENTS.
SOME REINCARNATES ARE HAPPIER THAT WAY.
BUT SOME REINCARNATES ARE HAPPIER BEING ABLE TO HEAR... AND TO FIGHT.
CHASING AFTER THE HAPPINESS YOU ENVISION IS JUST FINE.
AS LONG AS YOUR HEART...

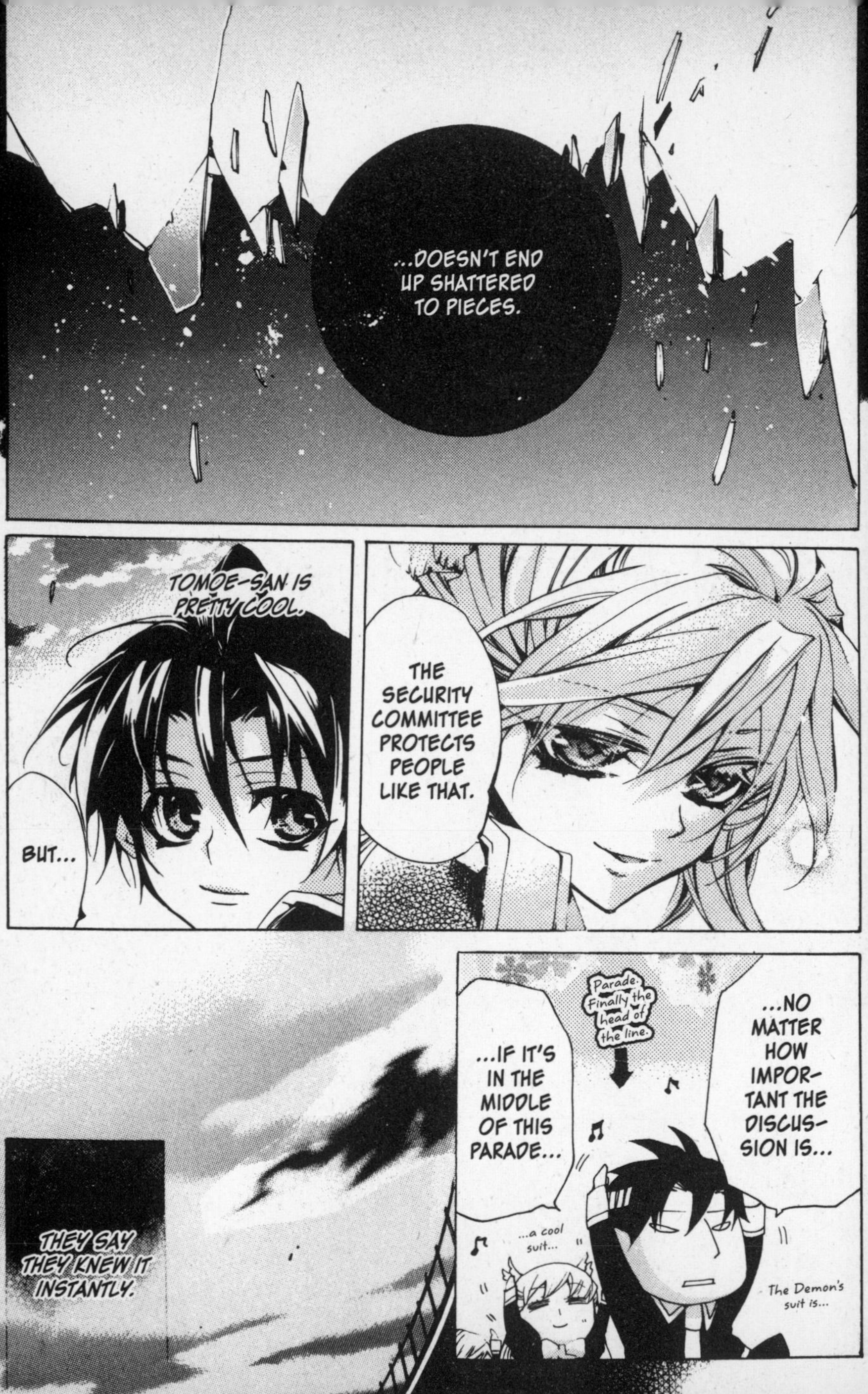
...DOESN'T END UP SHATTERED TO PIECES.
THE SECURITY COMMITTEE PROTECTS PEOPLE LIKE THAT.
TOMOE-SAN IS PRETTY COOL.
BUT...
...NO MATTER HOW IMPOR-TANT THE DISCUS-SION IS...
Parade. Finally the head of the line.
...IF IT'S IN THE MIDDLE OF THIS PARADE...
The Demon's suit is...
...a cool suit...
THEY SAY THEY KNEW IT INSTANTLY.

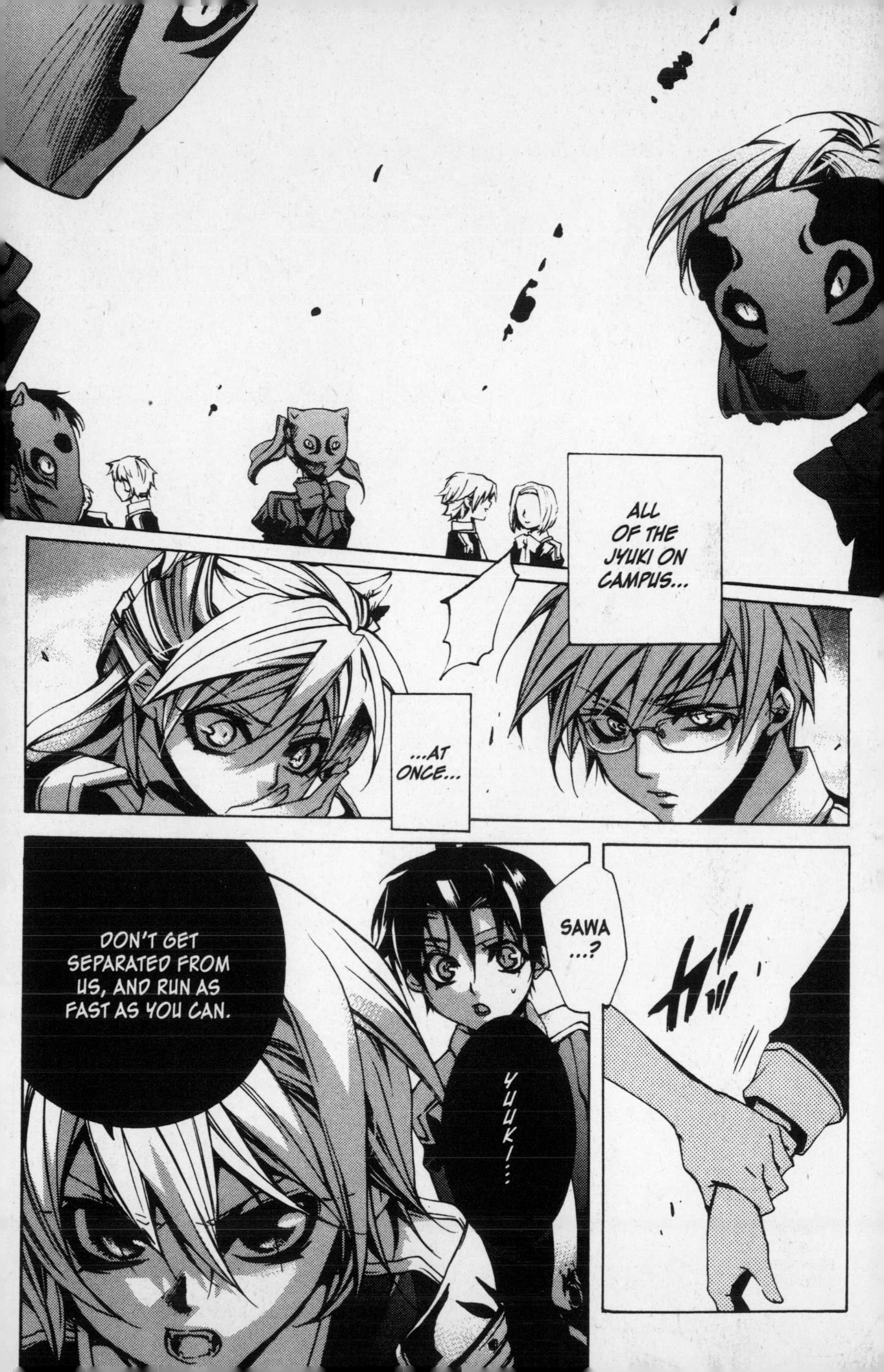
ALL OF THE JYUKI ON CAMPUS...
...AT ONCE...
SAWA ...?
YUUKI!...
DON'T GET SEPARATED FROM US, AND RUN AS FAST AS YOU CAN.

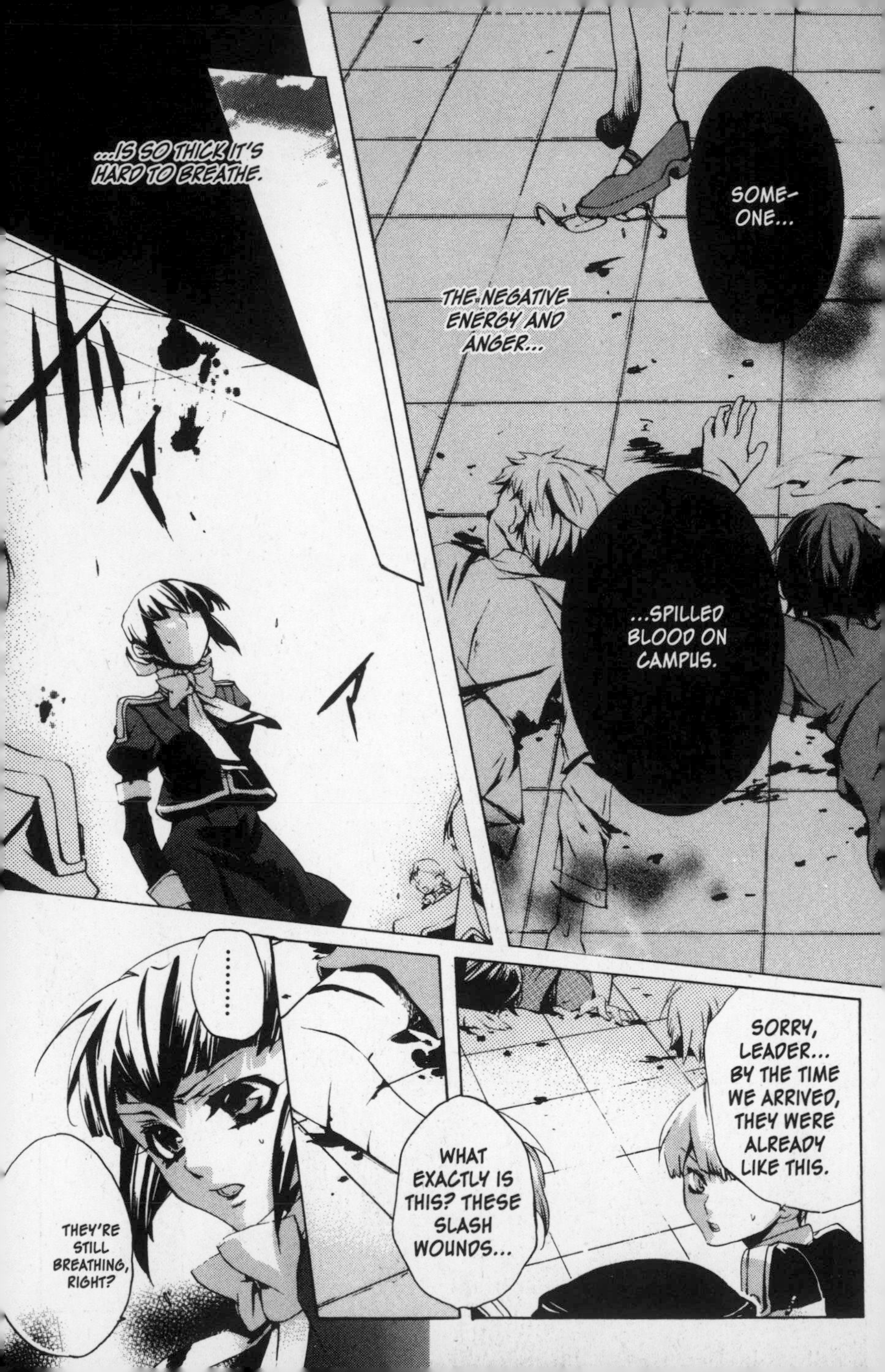
SOME-ONE...
...SPILLED BLOOD ON CAMPUS.
THE NEGATIVE ENERGY AND ANGER...
...IS SO THICK IT'S HARD TO BREATHE.
SORRY, LEADER... BY THE TIME WE ARRIVED, THEY WERE ALREADY LIKE THIS.
......
WHAT EXACTLY IS THIS? THESE SLASH WOUNDS...
THEY'RE STILL BREATHING, RIGHT?

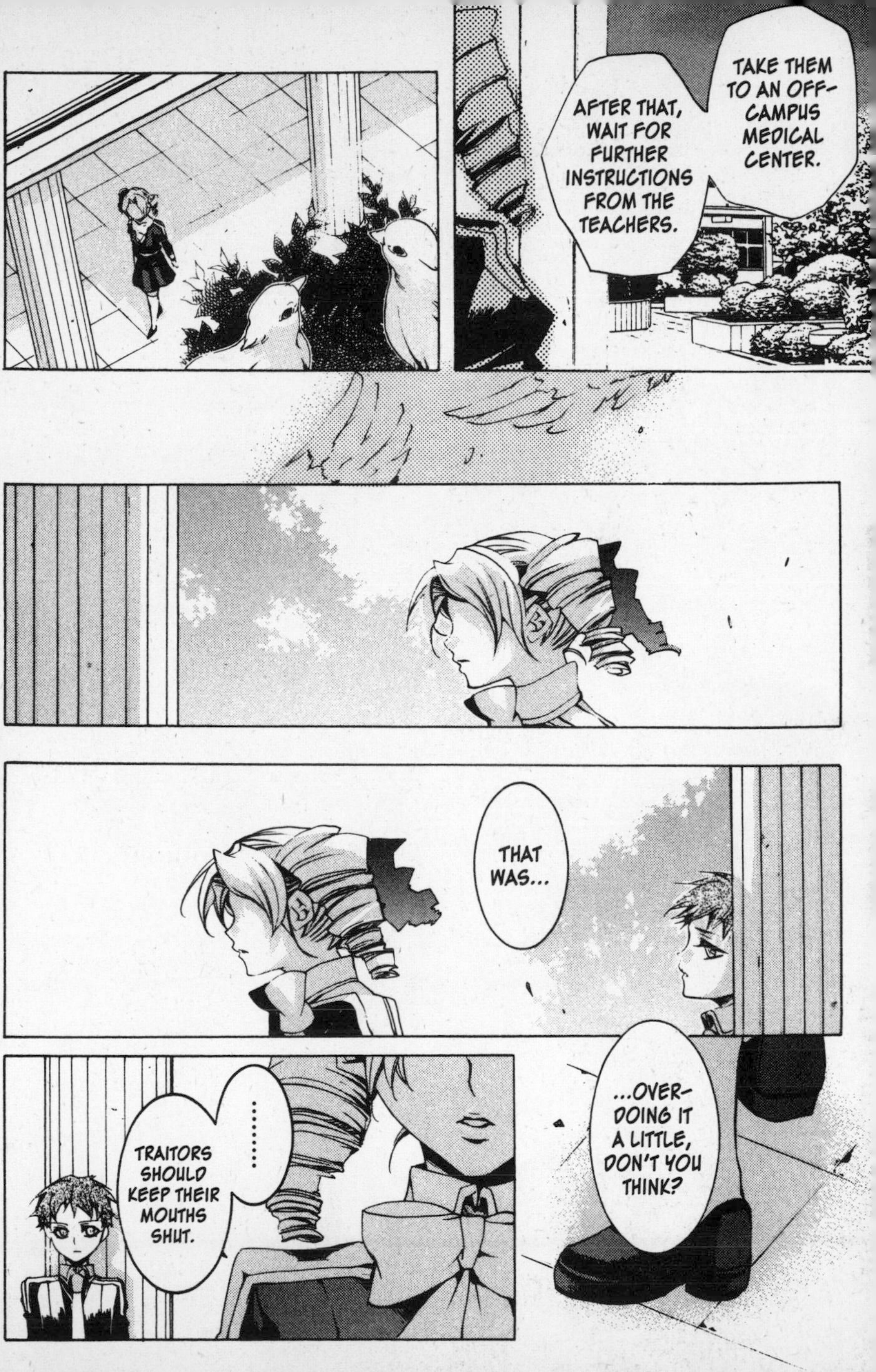
TAKE THEM TO AN OFF-CAMPUS MEDICAL CENTER.
AFTER THAT, WAIT FOR FURTHER INSTRUCTIONS FROM THE TEACHERS.
THAT WAS...
...OVER-DOING IT A LITTLE, DON'T YOU THINK?
....
TRAITORS SHOULD KEEP THEIR MOUTHS SHUT.

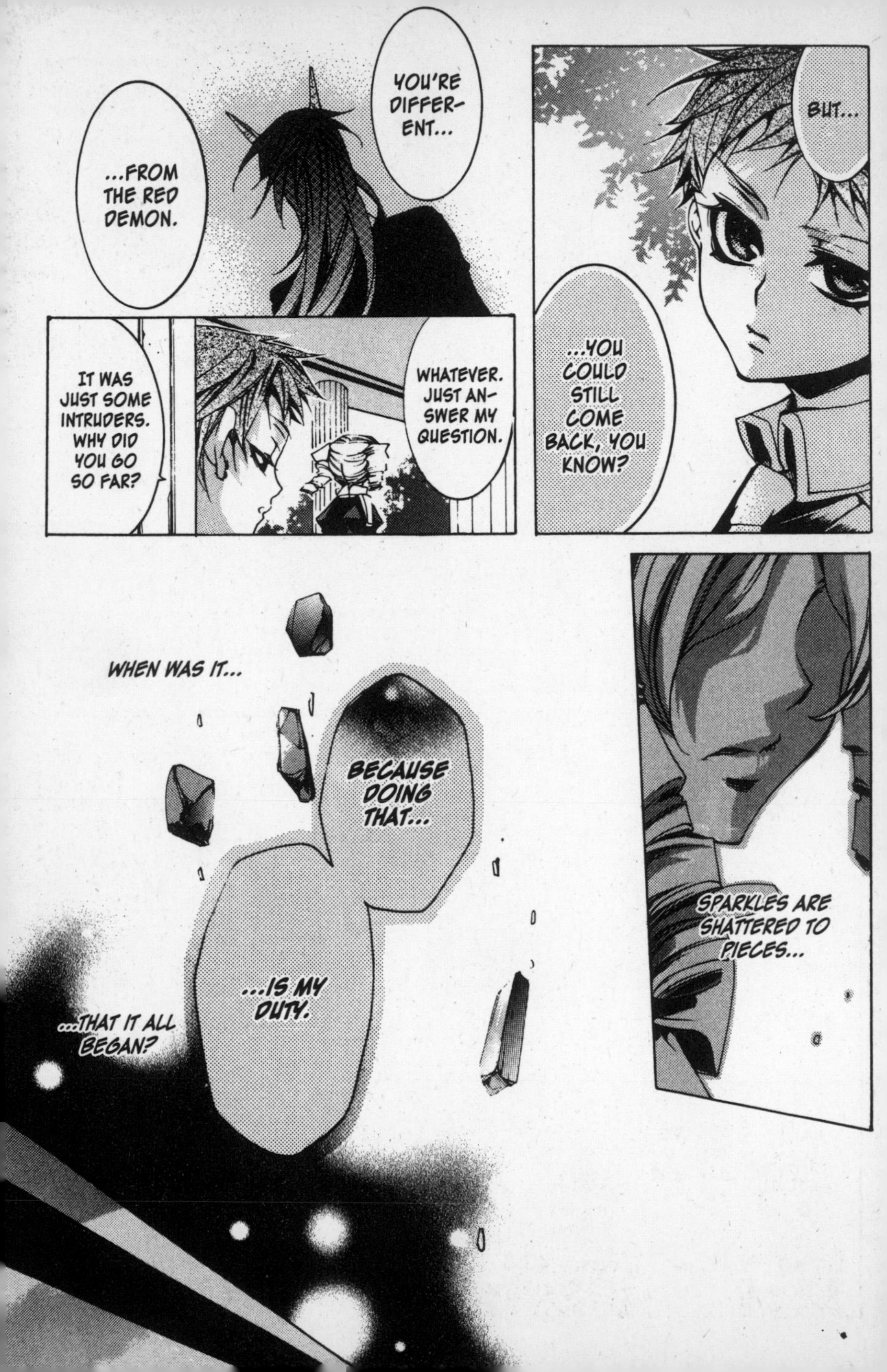
BUT...
...YOU COULD STILL COME BACK, YOU KNOW?
YOU'RE DIFFERENT...
...FROM THE RED DEMON.
WHATEVER. JUST ANSWER MY QUESTION.
IT WAS JUST SOME INTRUDERS. WHY DID YOU GO SO FAR?
SPARKLES ARE SHATTERED TO PIECES...
WHEN WAS IT...
BECAUSE DOING THAT...
...IS MY DUTY.
...THAT IT ALL BEGAN?

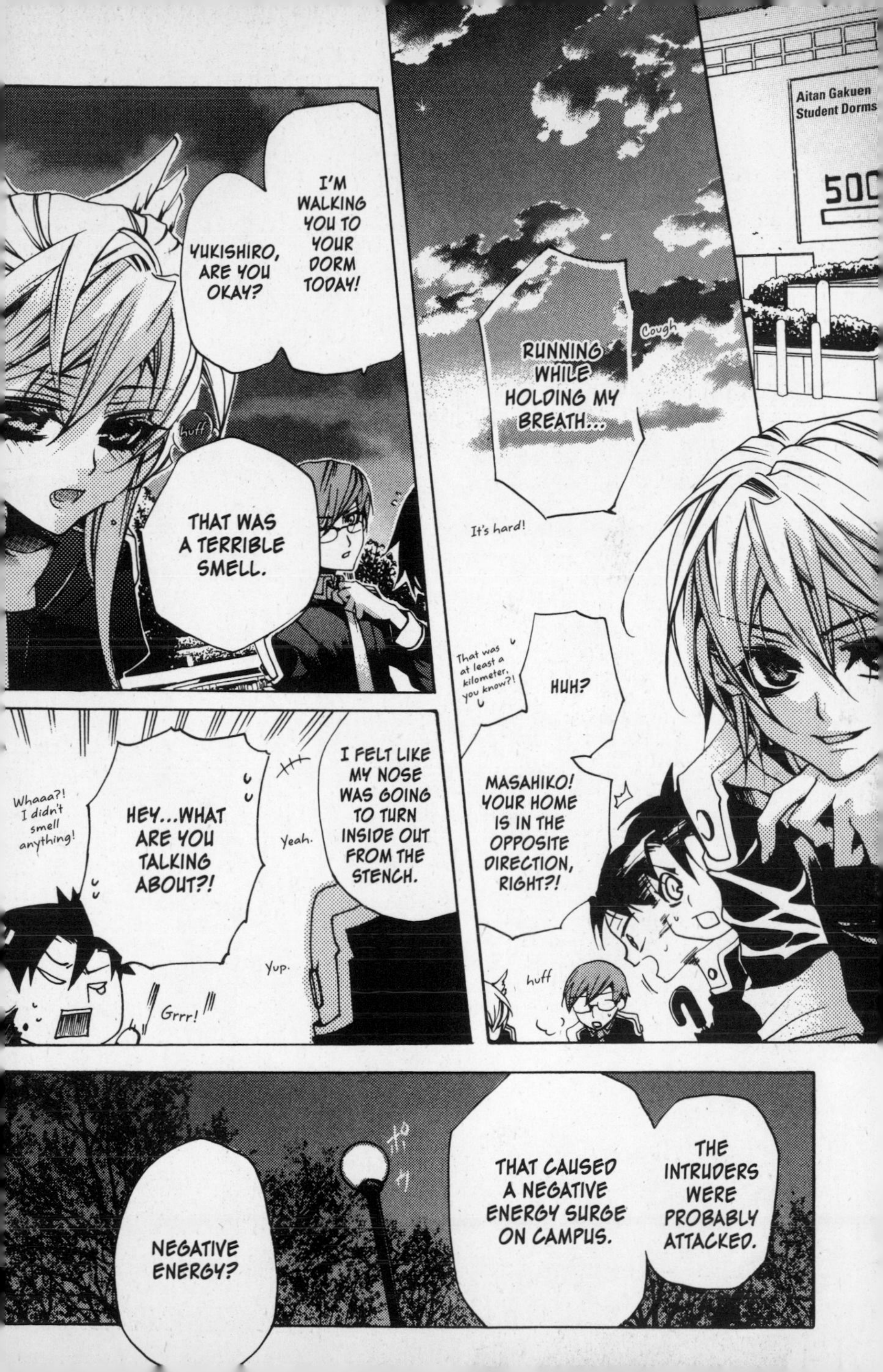
Aitan Gakuen Student Dorms
500
RUNNING WHILE HOLDING MY BREATH...
Cough
It's hard!
HUH?
That was at least a kilometer, you know?!
MASAHIKO! YOUR HOME IS IN THE OPPOSITE DIRECTION, RIGHT?!
huff
I'M WALKING YOU TO YOUR DORM TODAY!
YUKISHIRO, ARE YOU OKAY?
huff
THAT WAS A TERRIBLE SMELL.
I FELT LIKE MY NOSE WAS GOING TO TURN INSIDE OUT FROM THE STENCH.
Yeah.
Yup.
HEY...WHAT ARE YOU TALKING ABOUT?!
Whaaa?! I didn't smell anything!
Grrr!
THE INTRUDERS WERE PROBABLY ATTACKED.
THAT CAUSED A NEGATIVE ENERGY SURGE ON CAMPUS.
NEGATIVE ENERGY?

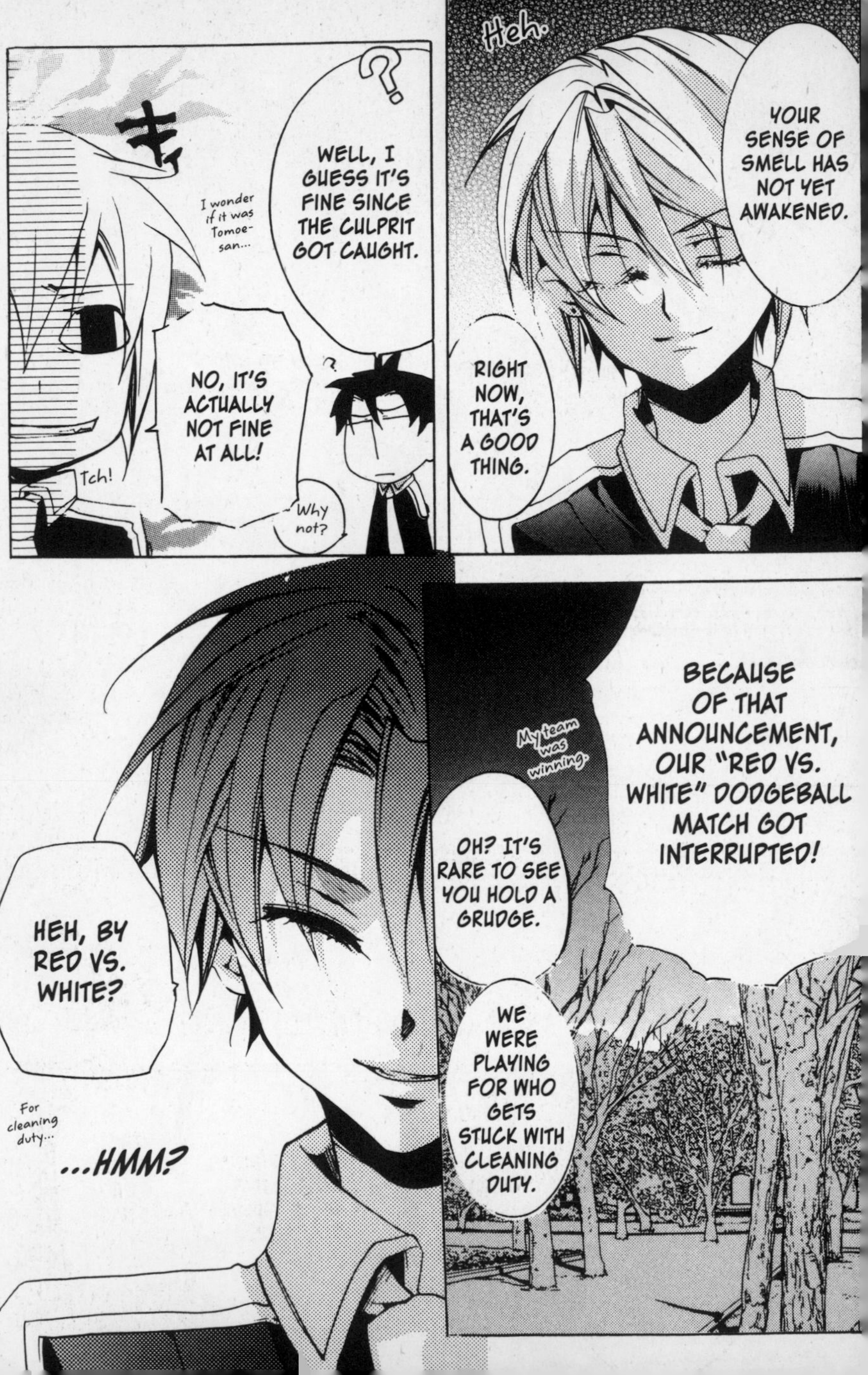
Heh.
YOUR SENSE OF SMELL HAS NOT YET AWAKENED.
RIGHT NOW, THAT'S A GOOD THING.
?
キ
WELL, I GUESS IT'S FINE SINCE THE CULPRIT GOT CAUGHT.
I wonder if it was Tomoe-san...
NO, IT'S ACTUALLY NOT FINE AT ALL!
?
Why not?
Tch!
BECAUSE OF THAT ANNOUNCEMENT, OUR "RED VS. WHITE" DODGEBALL MATCH GOT INTERRUPTED!
My team was winning.
OH? IT'S RARE TO SEE YOU HOLD A GRUDGE.
WE WERE PLAYING FOR WHO GETS STUCK WITH CLEANING DUTY.
HEH, BY RED VS. WHITE?
For cleaning duty...
...HMM?

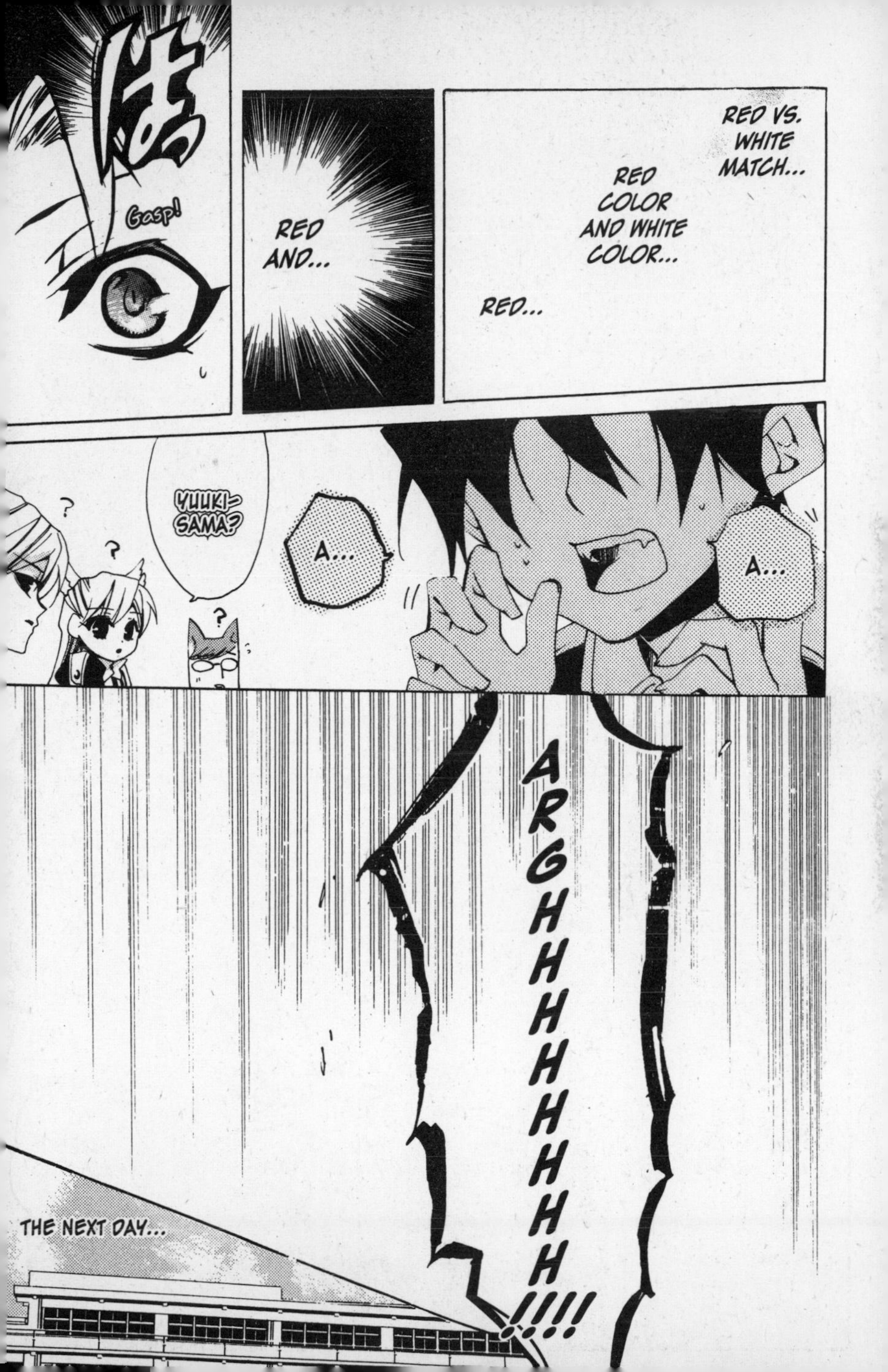
RED VS. WHITE MATCH...
RED COLOR AND WHITE COLOR...
RED...
RED AND...
Gasp!
A...
A...
YUUKI-SAMA?
ARGHHHHHHHH!!!!
THE NEXT DAY...

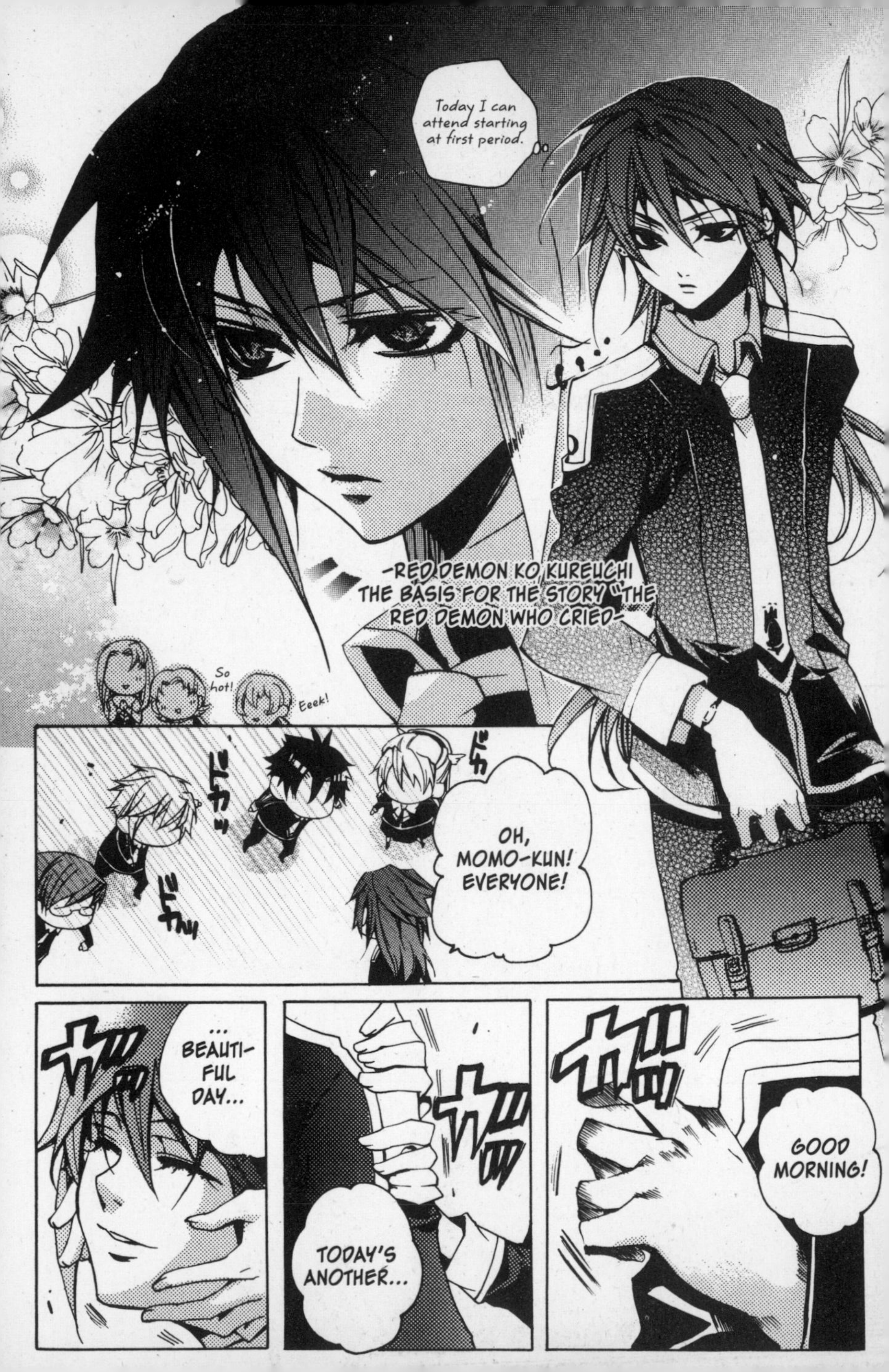
Today I can attend starting at first period.
-RED DEMON KO KUREUCHI
THE BASIS FOR THE STORY "THE RED DEMON WHO CRIED-
So hot!
Eeek!
OH, MOMO-KUN! EVERYONE!
GOOD MORNING!
TODAY'S ANOTHER...
... BEAUTI-FUL DAY...

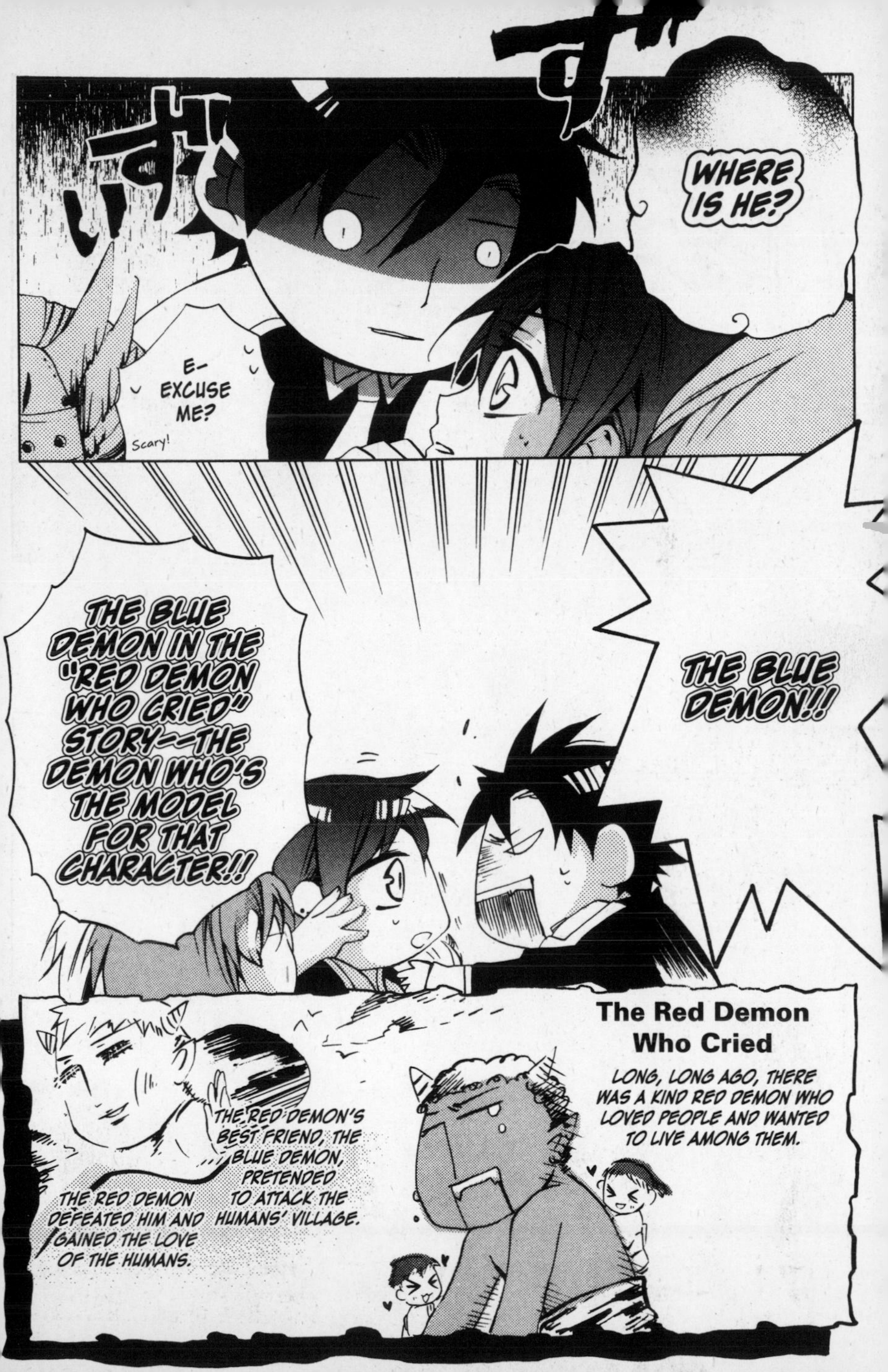
ず
ずい
WHERE IS HE?
E- EXCUSE ME?
Scary!
THE BLUE DEMON!!
THE BLUE DEMON IN THE "RED DEMON WHO CRIED" STORY--THE DEMON WHO'S THE MODEL FOR THAT CHARACTER!!
The Red Demon Who Cried
LONG, LONG AGO, THERE WAS A KIND RED DEMON WHO LOVED PEOPLE AND WANTED TO LIVE AMONG THEM.
THE RED DEMON'S BEST FRIEND, THE BLUE DEMON, PRETENDED TO ATTACK THE HUMANS' VILLAGE.
THE RED DEMON DEFEATED HIM AND GAINED THE LOVE OF THE HUMANS.

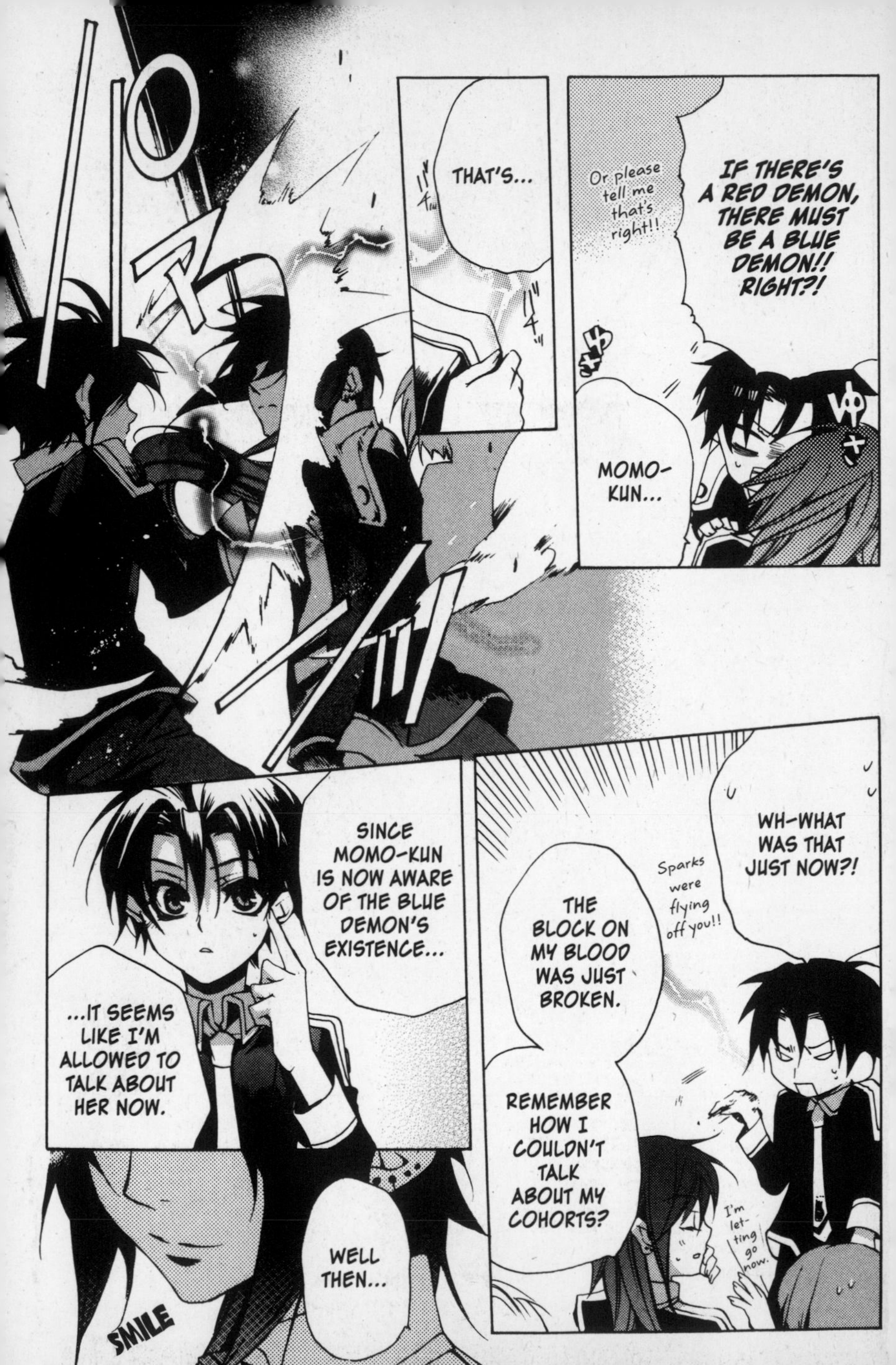
IF THERE'S A RED DEMON, THERE MUST BE A BLUE DEMON!! RIGHT?!
Or please tell me that's right!!
MOMO-KUN...
THAT'S...
WH-WHAT WAS THAT JUST NOW?!
Sparks were flying off you!!
THE BLOCK ON MY BLOOD WAS JUST BROKEN.
REMEMBER HOW I COULDN'T TALK ABOUT MY COHORTS?
I'm let-ting go now.
SINCE MOMO-KUN IS NOW AWARE OF THE BLUE DEMON'S EXISTENCE...
...IT SEEMS LIKE I'M ALLOWED TO TALK ABOUT HER NOW.
WELL THEN...
SMILE

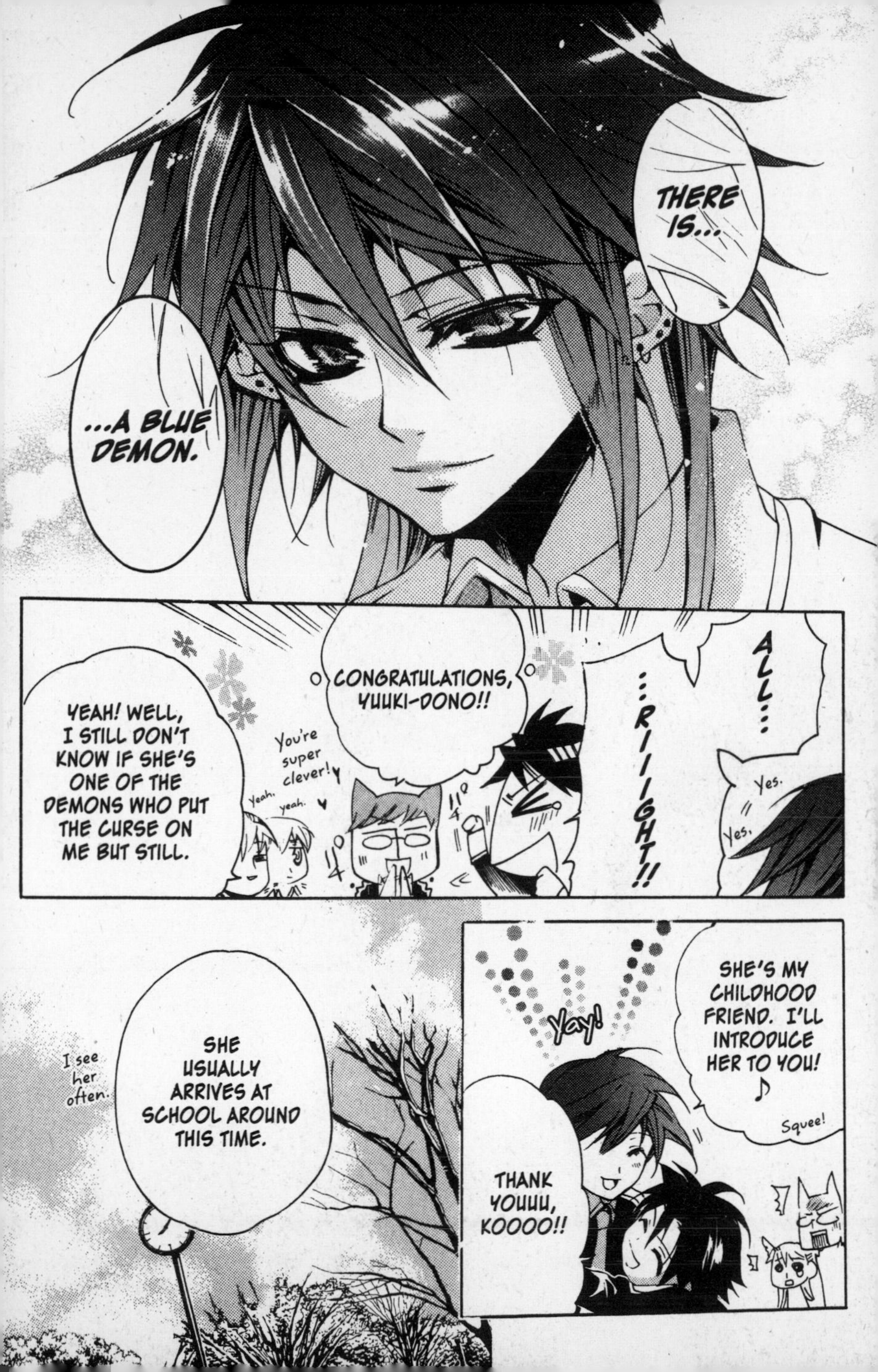
THERE IS...
...A BLUE DEMON.
...ALL...RIIIGHT!!
Yes.
Yes.
CONGRATULATIONS, YUUKI-DONO!!
You're super clever!
Yeah, yeah.
YEAH! WELL, I STILL DON'T KNOW IF SHE'S ONE OF THE DEMONS WHO PUT THE CURSE ON ME BUT STILL.
SHE'S MY CHILDHOOD FRIEND. I'LL INTRODUCE HER TO YOU! ♪
Yay!
Squee!
THANK YOUUU, KOOOO!!
SHE USUALLY ARRIVES AT SCHOOL AROUND THIS TIME.
I see her often.

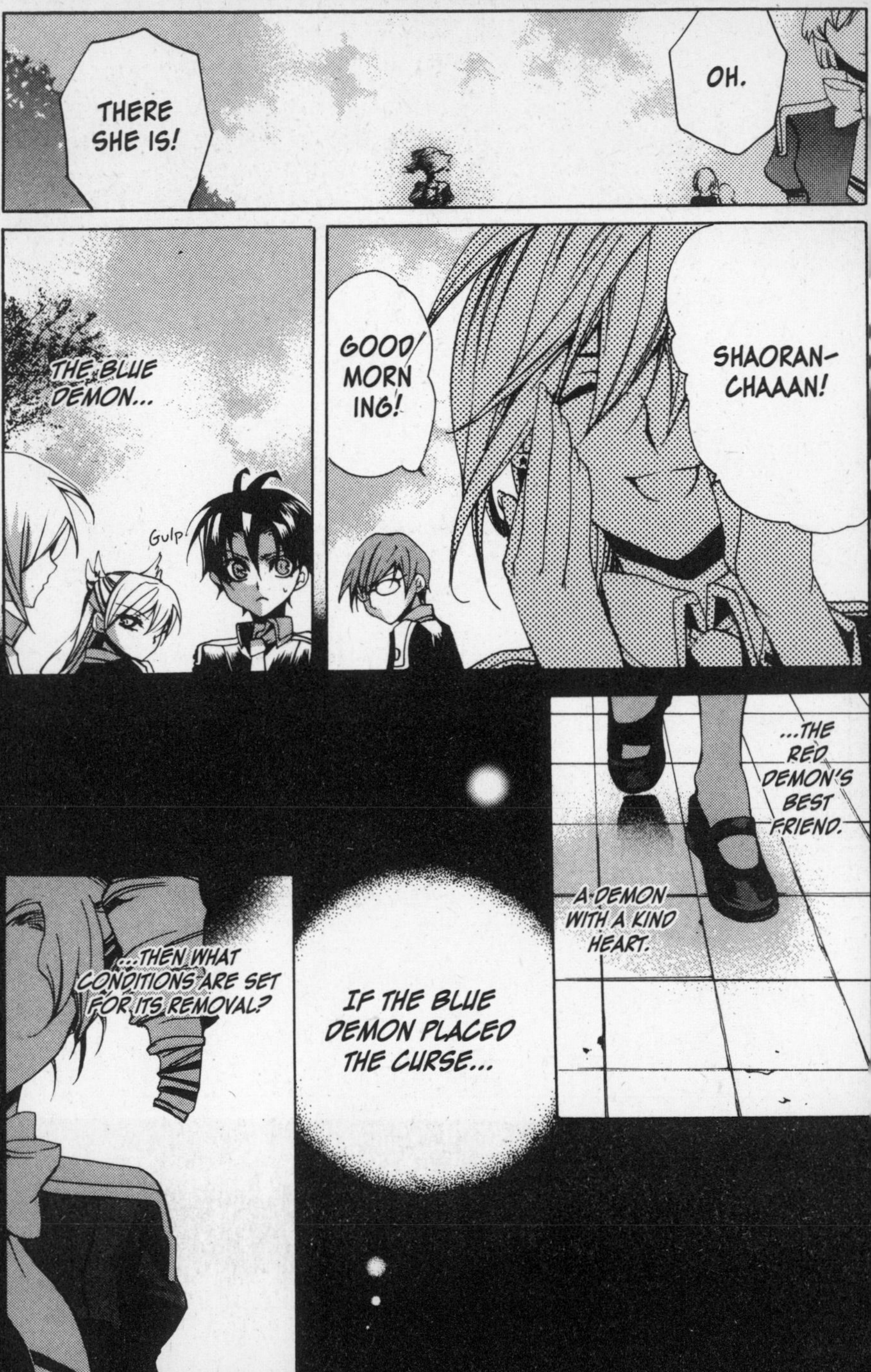
OH.
THERE SHE IS!
SHAORAN-CHAAAN!
GOOD MORNING!
THE BLUE DEMON...
Gulp
...THE RED DEMON'S BEST FRIEND.
A DEMON WITH A KIND HEART.
IF THE BLUE DEMON PLACED THE CURSE...
...THEN WHAT CONDITIONS ARE SET FOR ITS REMOVAL?

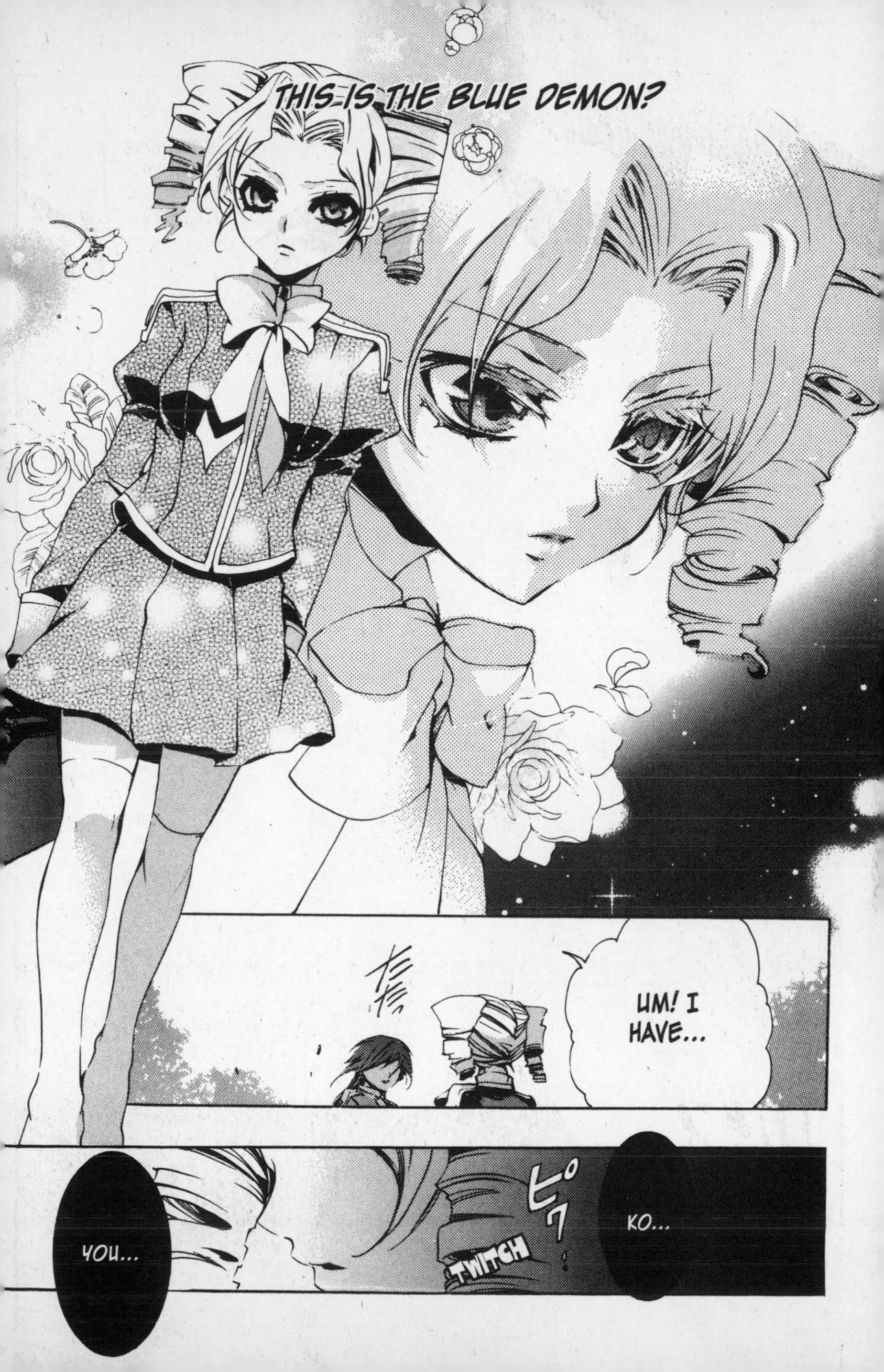
THIS IS THE BLUE DEMON?
UM! I HAVE...
KO...
ピクッ
TWITCH
YOU...

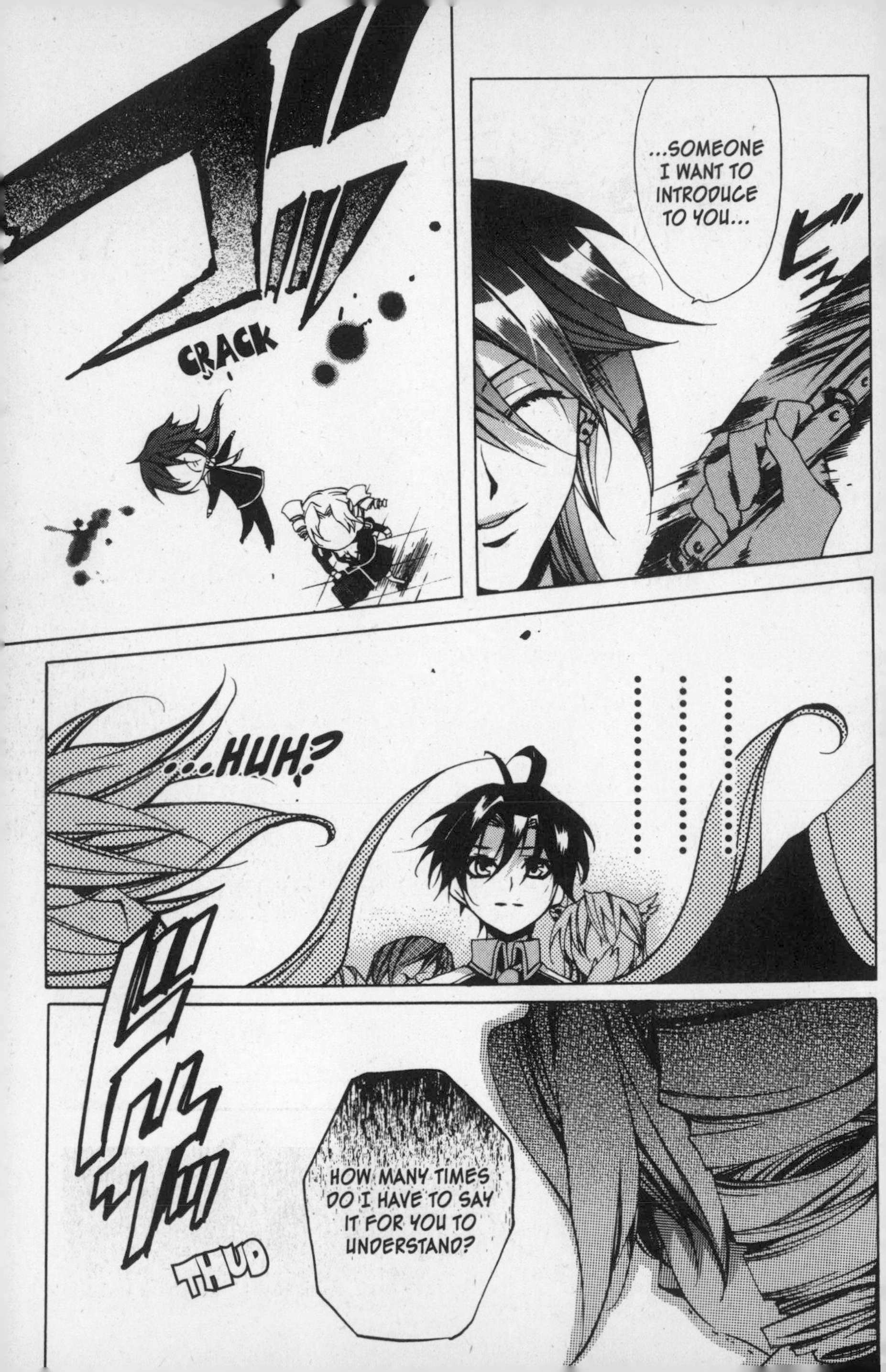
...SOMEONE I WANT TO INTRODUCE TO YOU...
CRACK
......
...HUH?
HOW MANY TIMES DO I HAVE TO SAY IT FOR YOU TO UNDERSTAND?
THUD

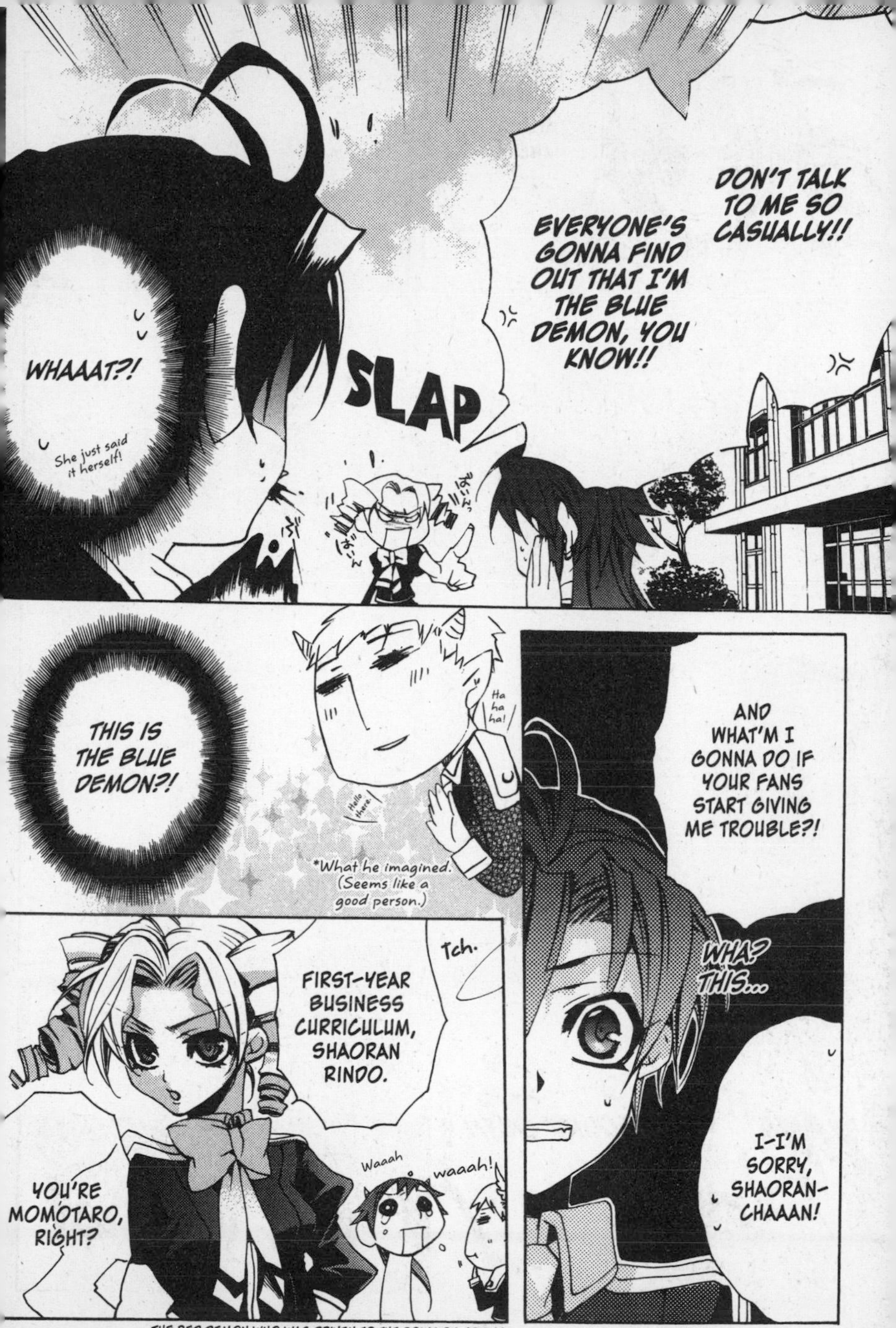
DON'T TALK TO ME SO CASUALLY!!
EVERYONE'S GONNA FIND OUT THAT I'M THE BLUE DEMON, YOU KNOW!!
SLAP
WHAAAT?!
She just said it herself!
AND WHAT'M I GONNA DO IF YOUR FANS START GIVING ME TROUBLE?!
WHA? THIS...
I-I'M SORRY, SHAORAN-CHAAAN!
THIS IS THE BLUE DEMON?!
Ha ha ha!
Hello there.
*What he imagined. (Seems like a good person.)
Tch.
FIRST-YEAR BUSINESS CURRICULUM, SHAORAN RINDO.
YOU'RE MOMOTARO, RIGHT?
Waaah waaah!

THE RED DEMON WHO WAS DRIVEN TO THE POINT OF CRYING.

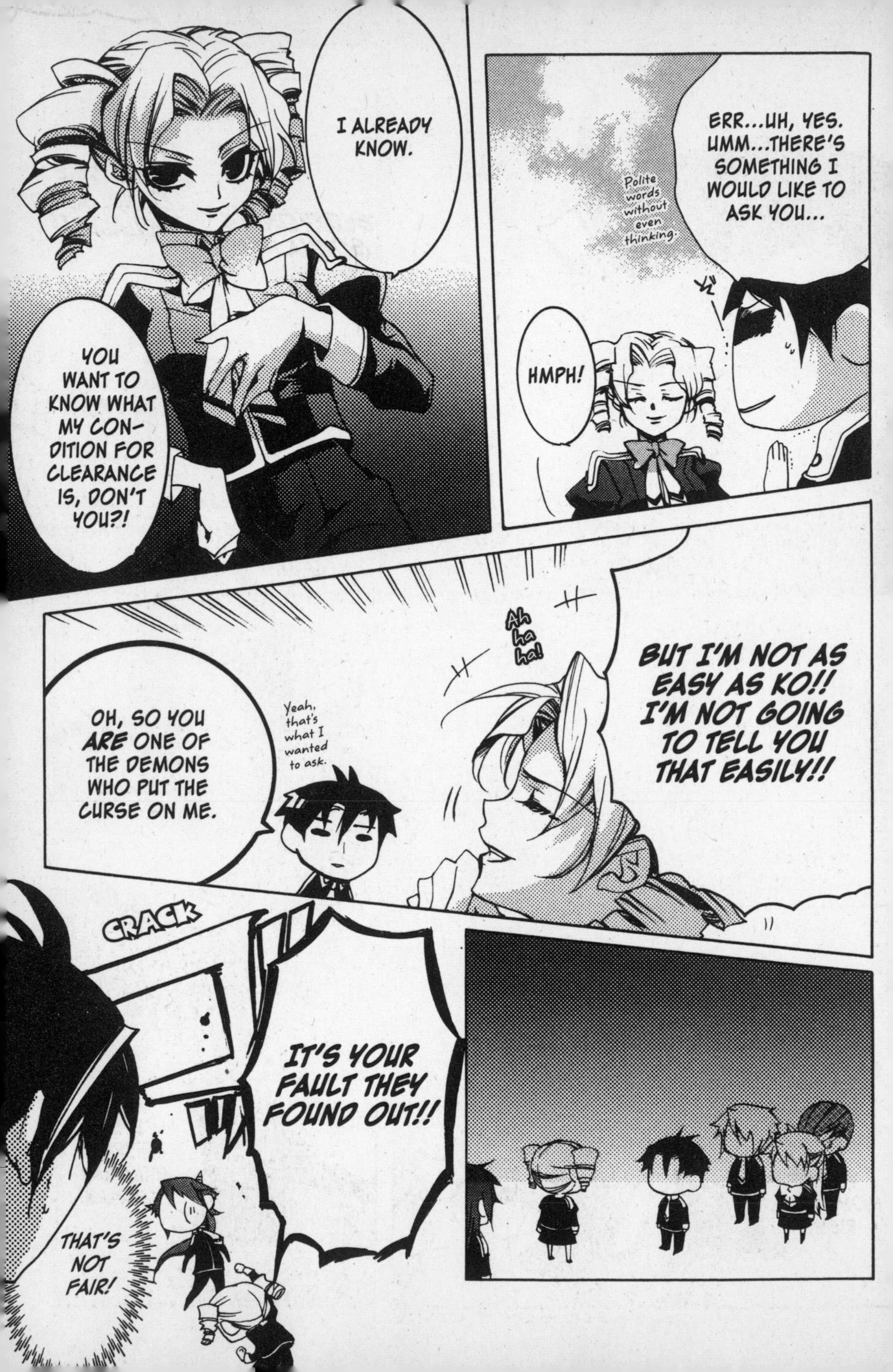
ERR...UH, YES. UMM...THERE'S SOMETHING I WOULD LIKE TO ASK YOU...
Polite words without even thinking.
HMPH!
I ALREADY KNOW.
YOU WANT TO KNOW WHAT MY CONDITION FOR CLEARANCE IS, DON'T YOU?!
BUT I'M NOT AS EASY AS KO!! I'M NOT GOING TO TELL YOU THAT EASILY!!
Ah ha ha!
Yeah, that's what I wanted to ask.
OH, SO YOU ARE ONE OF THE DEMONS WHO PUT THE CURSE ON ME.
CRACK
IT'S YOUR FAULT THEY FOUND OUT!!
THAT'S NOT FAIR!

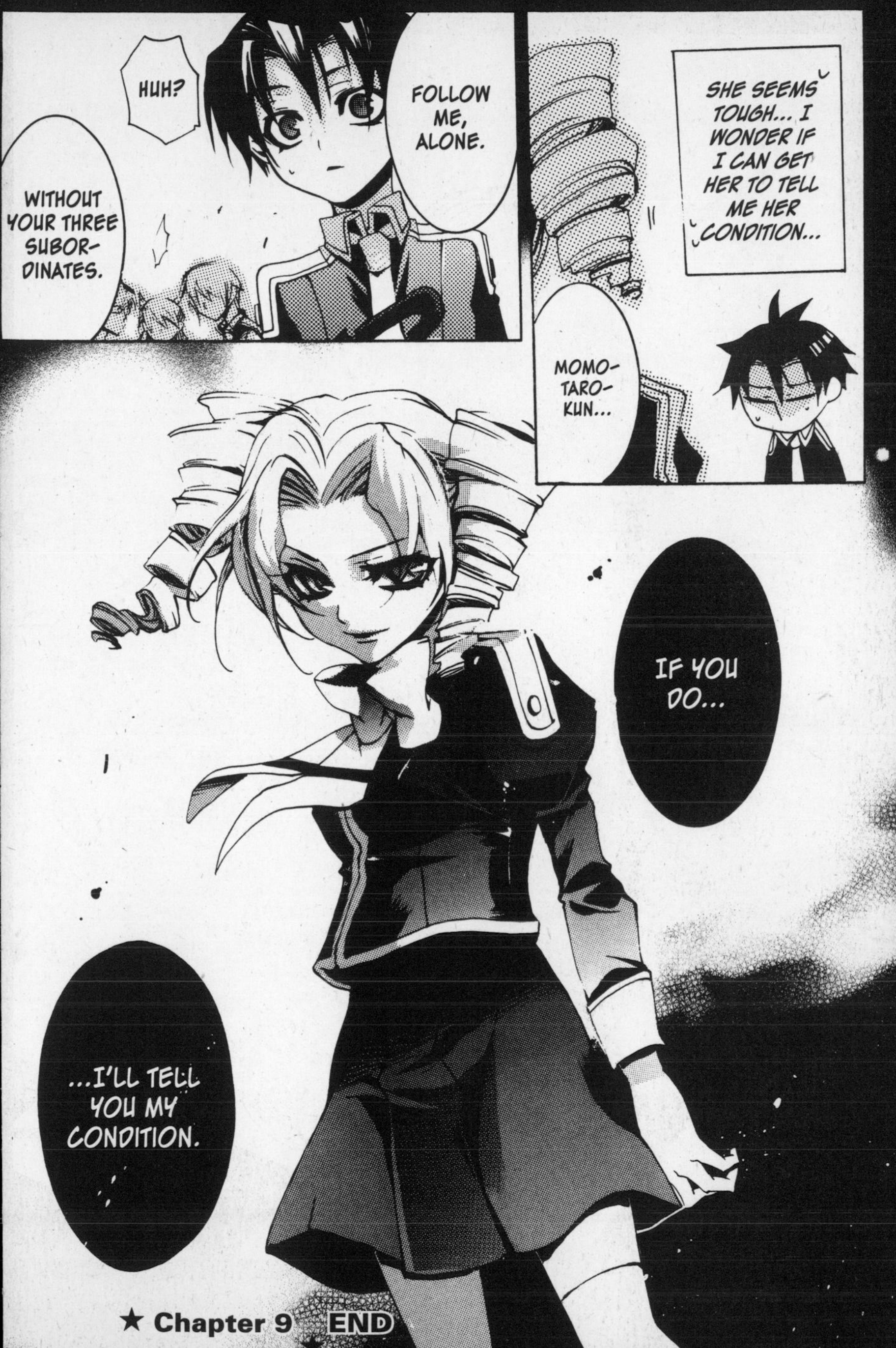
SHE SEEMS TOUGH... I WONDER IF I CAN GET HER TO TELL ME HER CONDITION...
MOMO-TARO-KUN...
FOLLOW ME, ALONE.
HUH?
WITHOUT YOUR THREE SUBOR-DINATES.
IF YOU DO...
...I'LL TELL YOU MY CONDITION.
★ Chapter 9 END ★

Chapter 10: The Contradiction in the Contract, Part 2

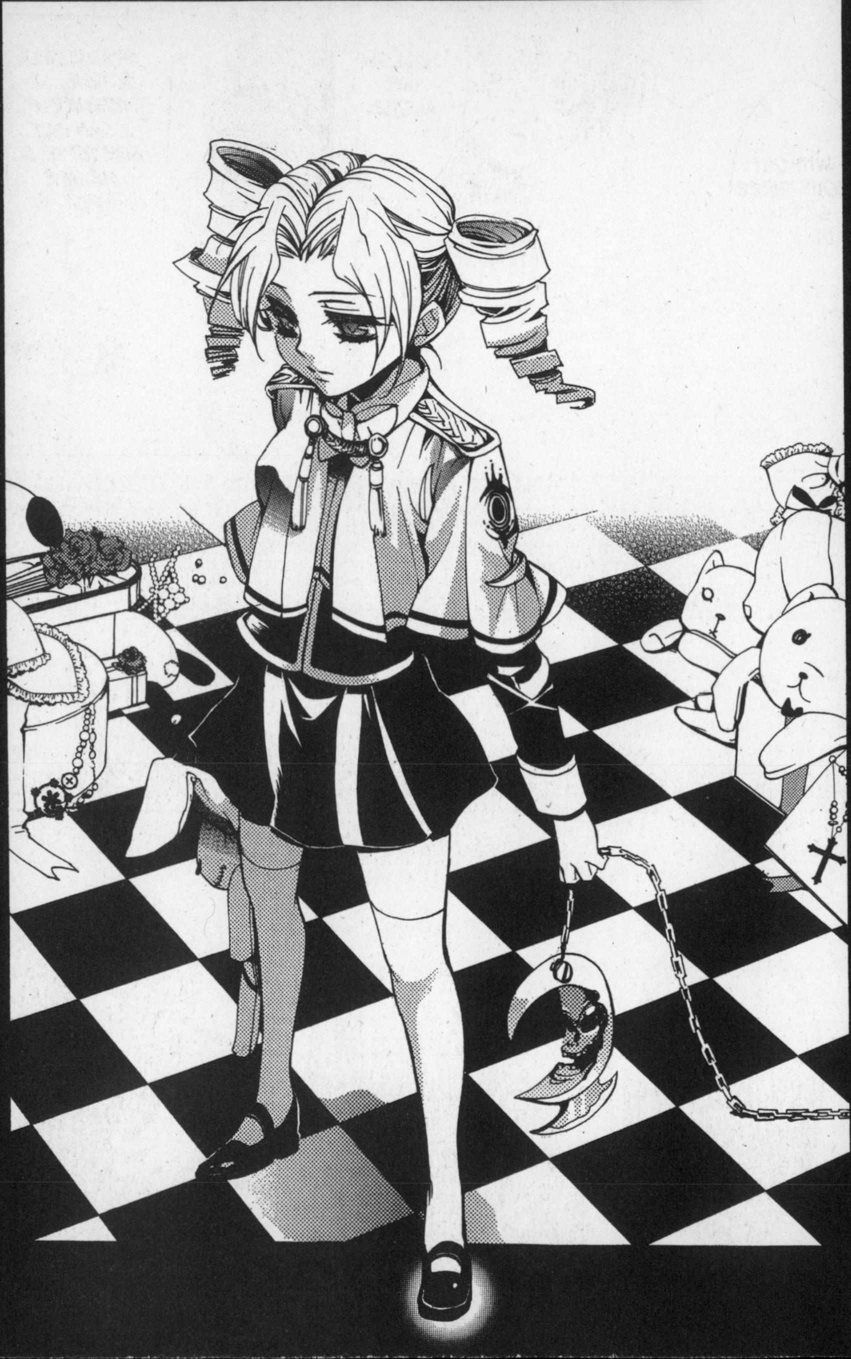

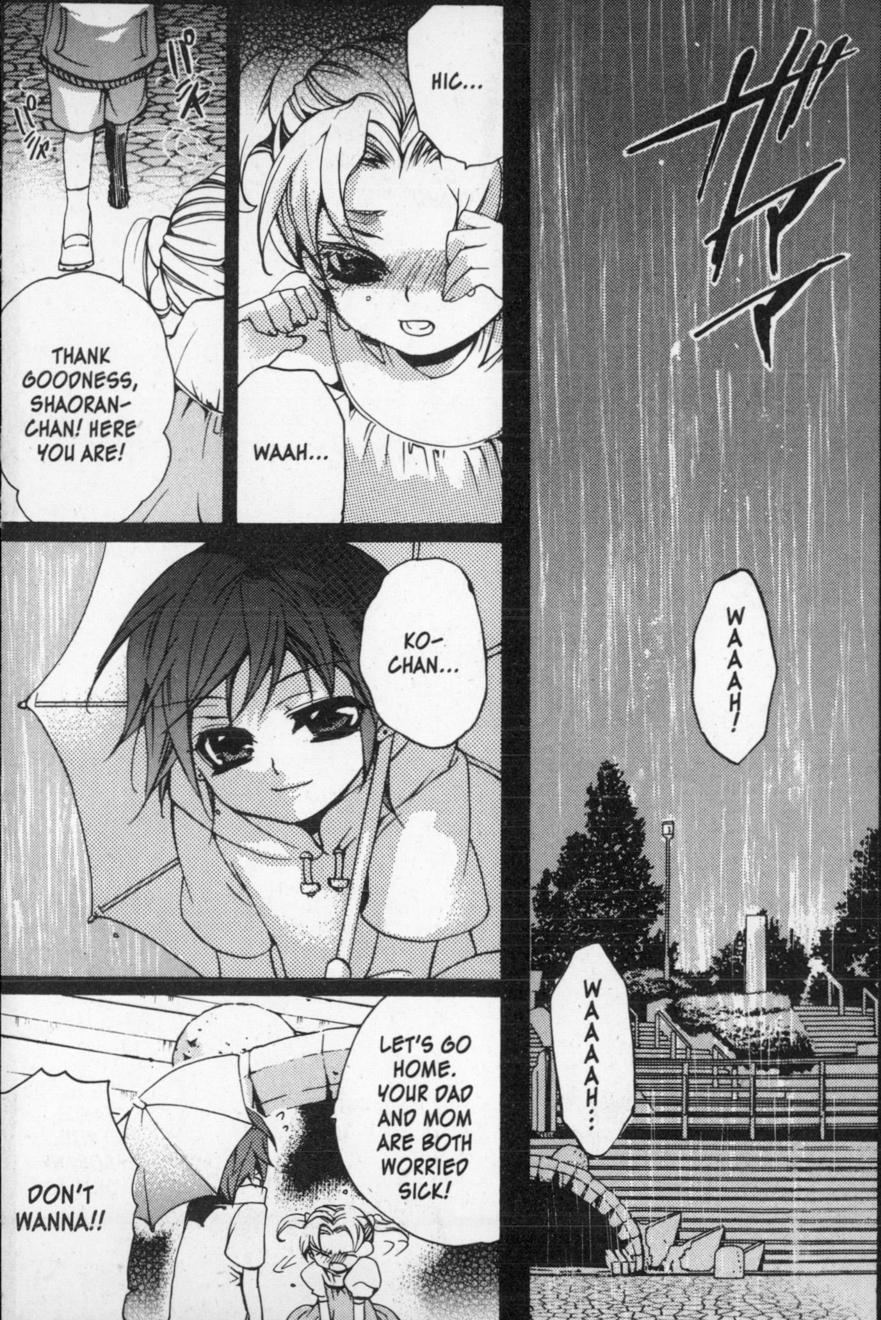
ザァァ
WAAAAH!
WAAAAAH...
HIC...
WAAH...
THANK GOODNESS, SHAORAN-CHAN! HERE YOU ARE!
KO-CHAN...
LET'S GO HOME. YOUR DAD AND MOM ARE BOTH WORRIED SICK!
DON'T WANNA!!

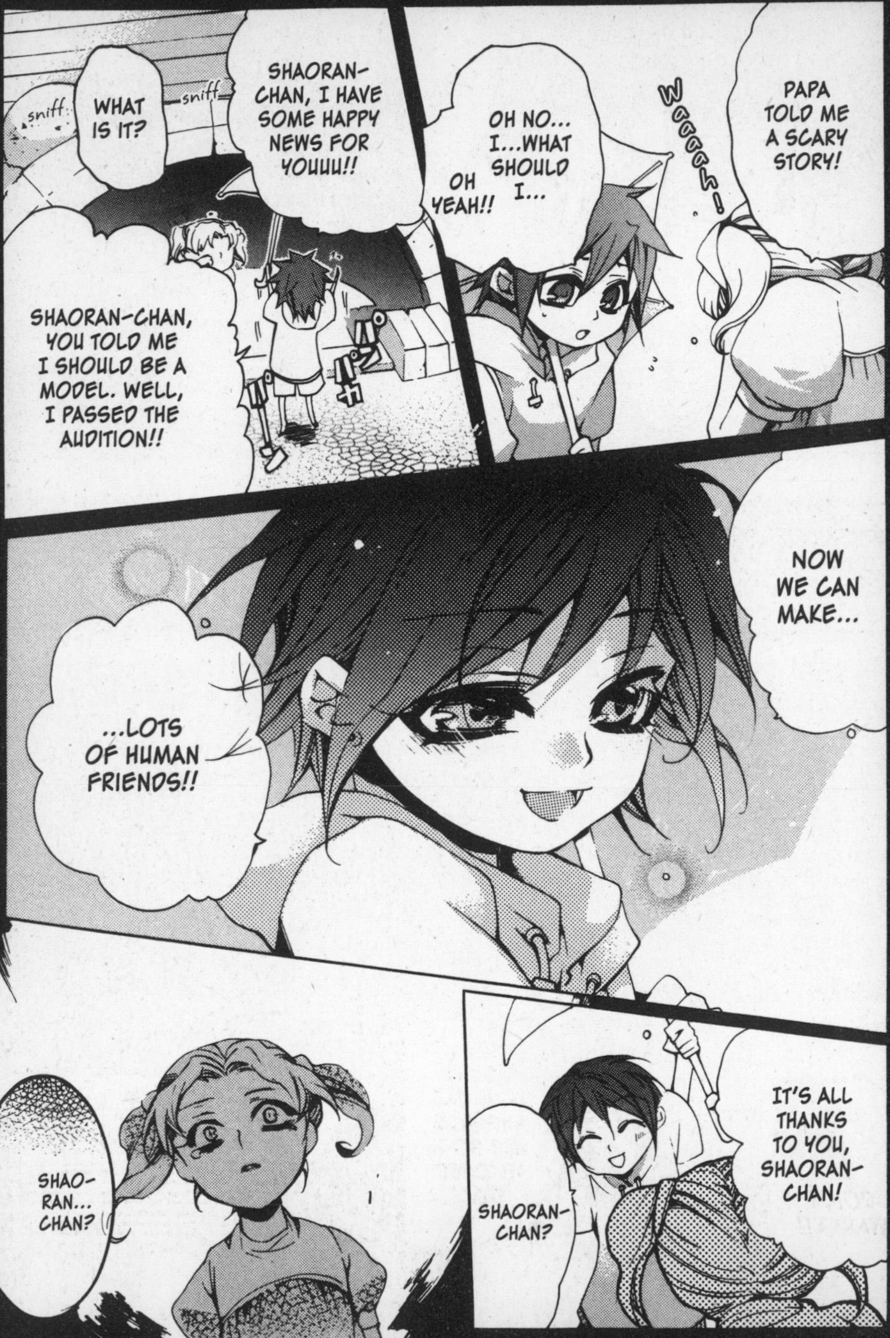
PAPA TOLD ME A SCARY STORY!
Waaaah!
OH NO... I...WHAT SHOULD I...
OH YEAH!!
SHAORAN-CHAN, I HAVE SOME HAPPY NEWS FOR YOUUU!!
sniff
WHAT IS IT?
sniff
SHAORAN-CHAN, YOU TOLD ME I SHOULD BE A MODEL. WELL, I PASSED THE AUDITION!!
NOW WE CAN MAKE...
...LOTS OF HUMAN FRIENDS!!
IT'S ALL THANKS TO YOU, SHAORAN-CHAN!
SHAORAN-CHAN?
SHAO-RAN... CHAN?

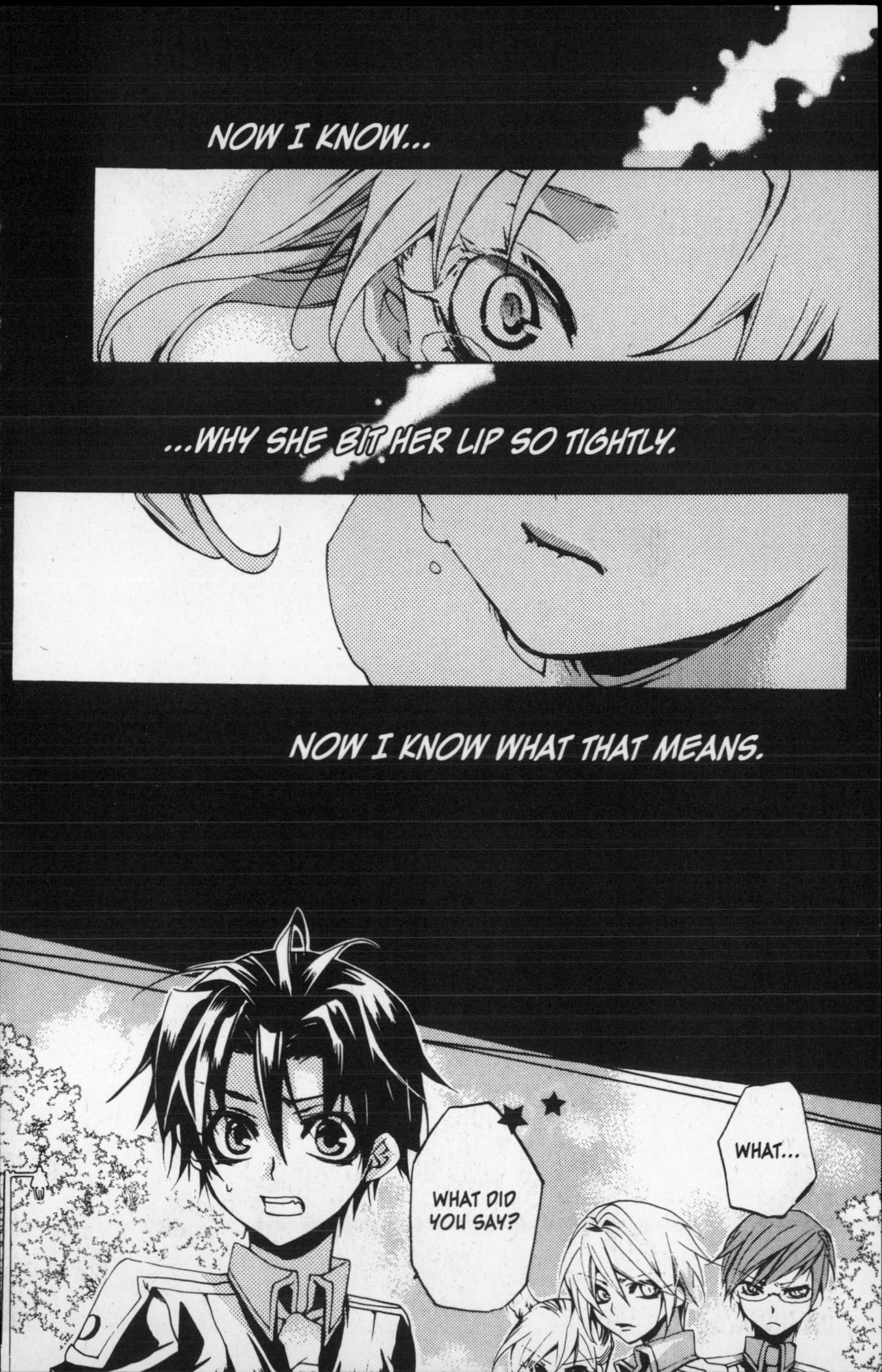
NOW I KNOW...
...WHY SHE BIT HER LIP SO TIGHTLY.
NOW I KNOW WHAT THAT MEANS.
WHAT...
WHAT DID YOU SAY?

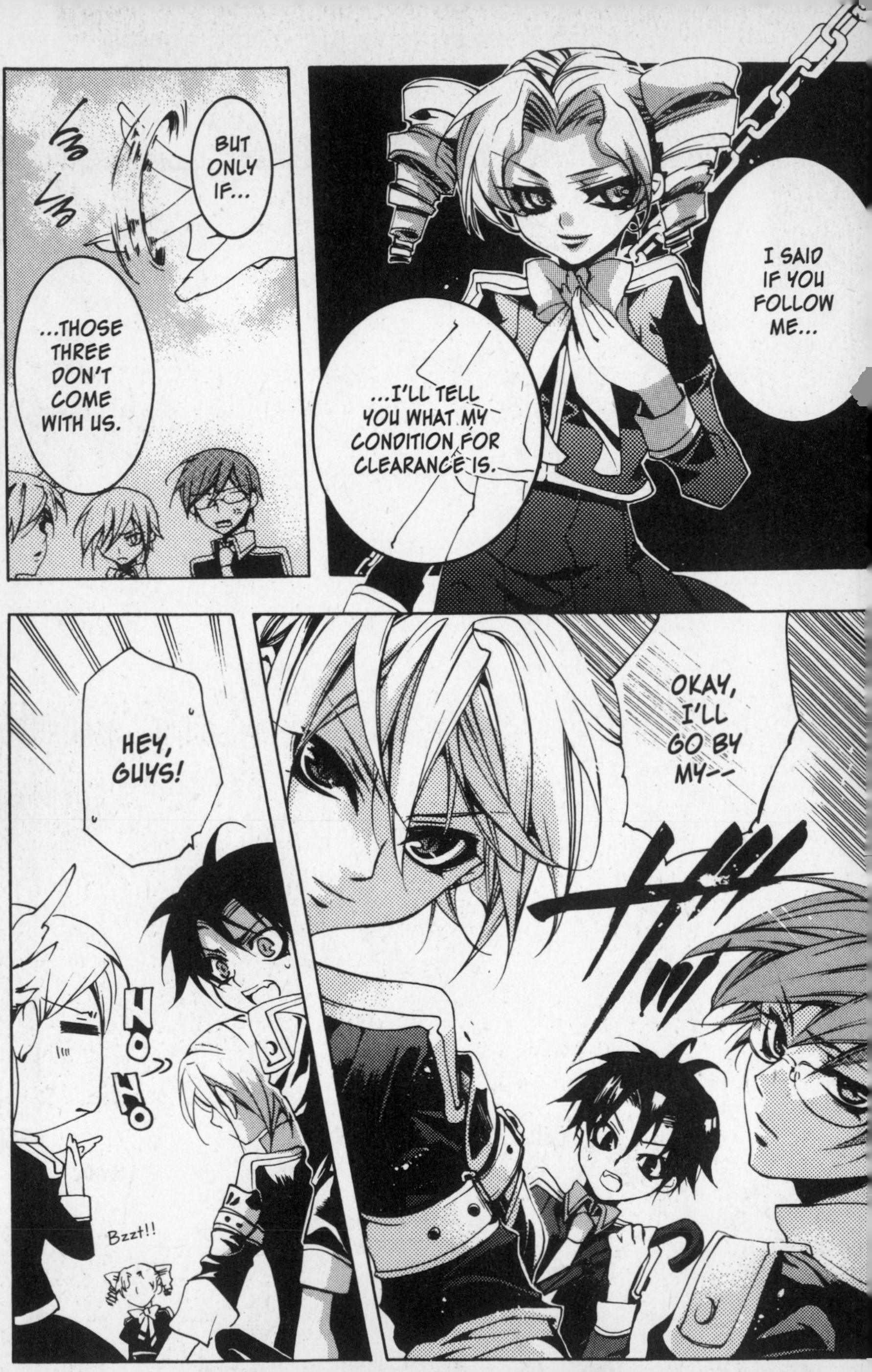
I SAID IF YOU FOLLOW ME...
...I'LL TELL YOU WHAT MY CONDITION FOR CLEARANCE IS.
BUT ONLY IF...
...THOSE THREE DON'T COME WITH US.
OKAY, I'LL GO BY MY--
HEY, GUYS!
NO NO
Bzzt!!

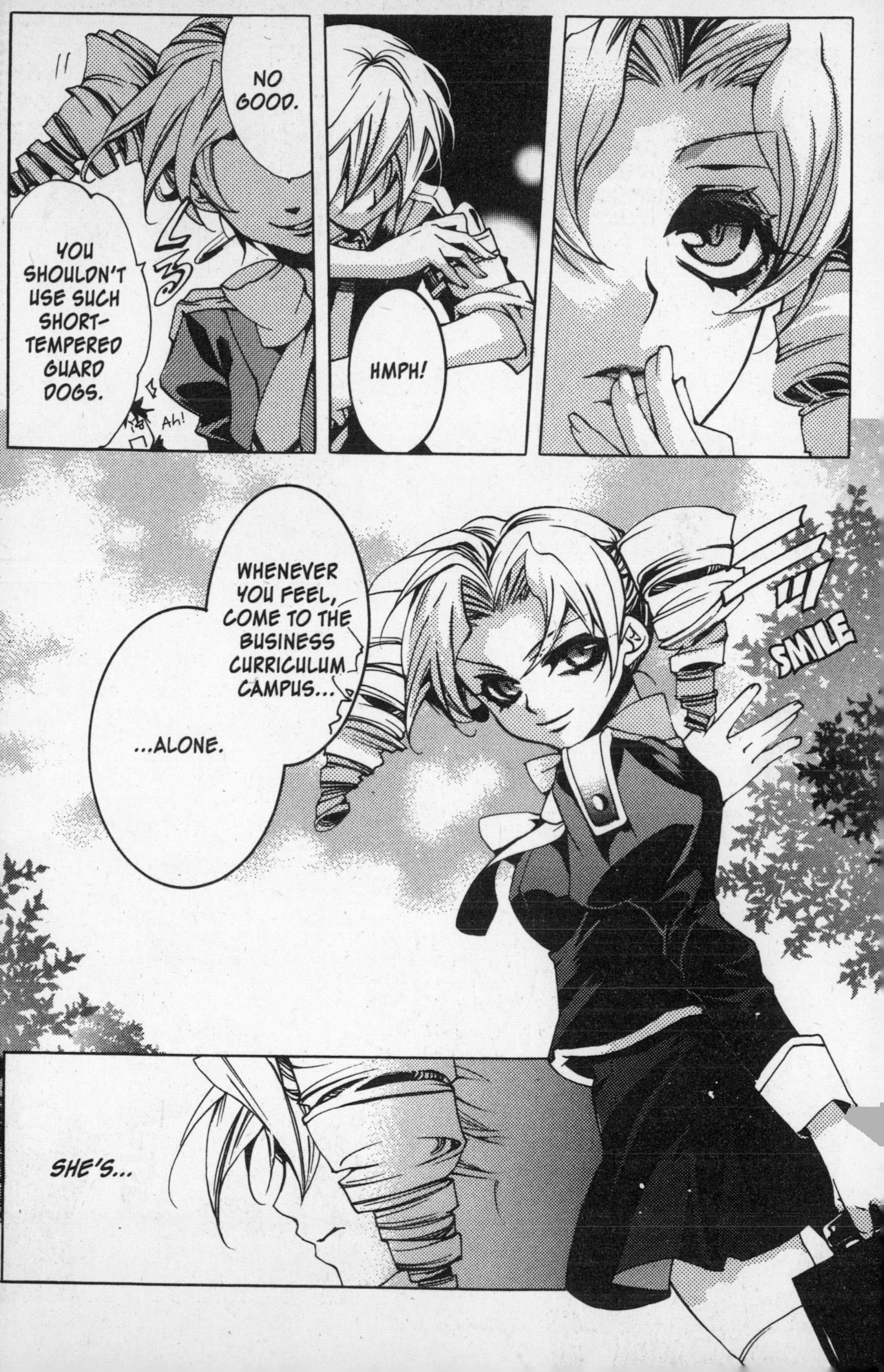
HMPH!
NO GOOD.
YOU SHOULDN'T USE SUCH SHORT-TEMPERED GUARD DOGS.
Ah!
SMILE
WHENEVER YOU FEEL, COME TO THE BUSINESS CURRICULUM CAMPUS...
...ALONE.
SHE'S...

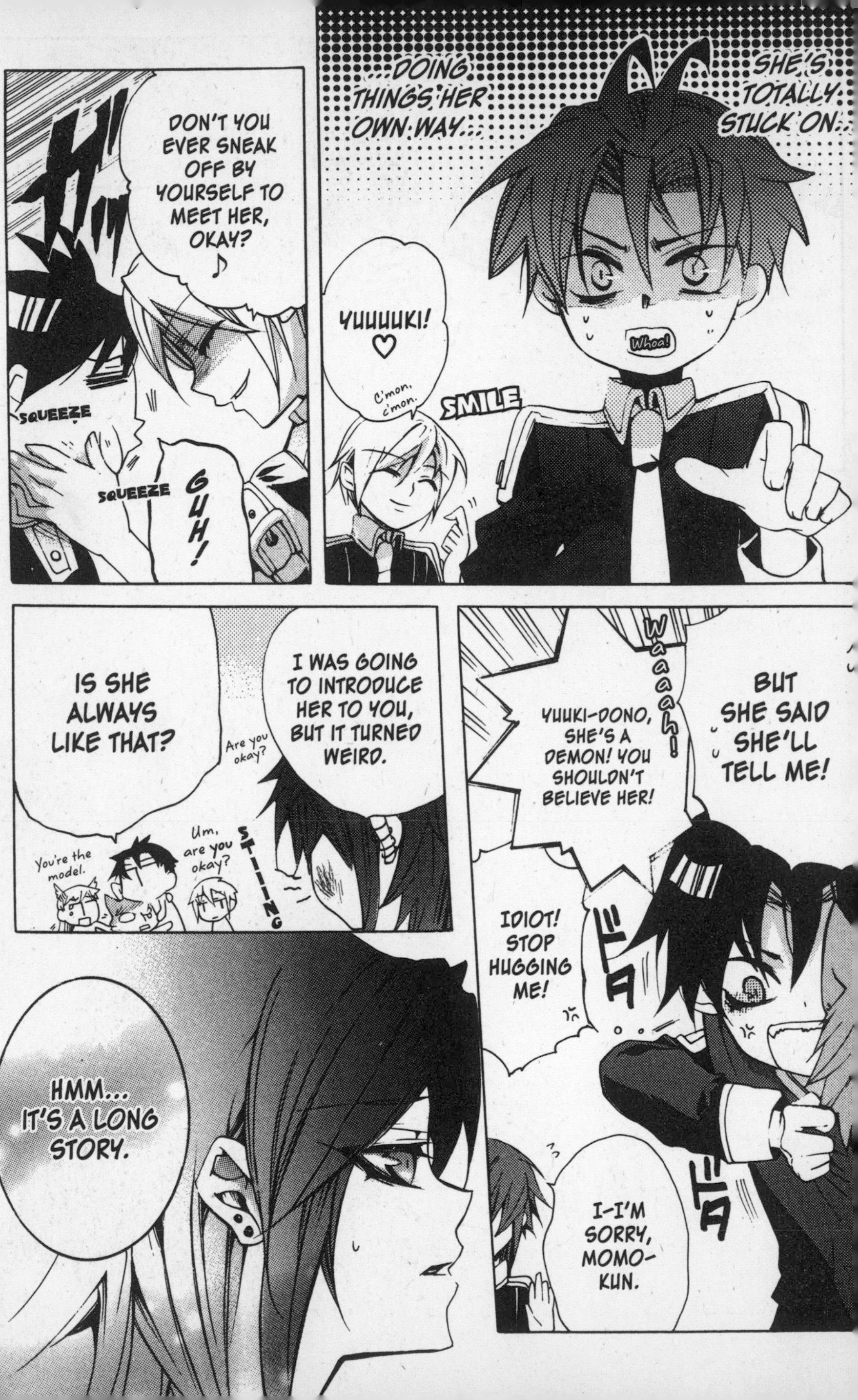
SHE'S TOTALLY STUCK ON...
...DOING THINGS HER OWN WAY...
Whoa!
YUUUUKI! ♥
C'mon, c'mon.
SMILE
DON'T YOU EVER SNEAK OFF BY YOURSELF TO MEET HER, OKAY? ♪
SQUEEZE
SQUEEZE
GUH!
Waaaah!
BUT SHE SAID SHE'LL TELL ME!
YUUKI-DONO, SHE'S A DEMON! YOU SHOULDN'T BELIEVE HER!
IDIOT! STOP HUGGING ME!
ドタ
ドタ
I-I'M SORRY, MOMO-KUN.
I WAS GOING TO INTRODUCE HER TO YOU, BUT IT TURNED WEIRD.
Are you okay?
IS SHE ALWAYS LIKE THAT?
STIIING
Um, are you okay?
You're the model.
HMM... IT'S A LONG STORY.

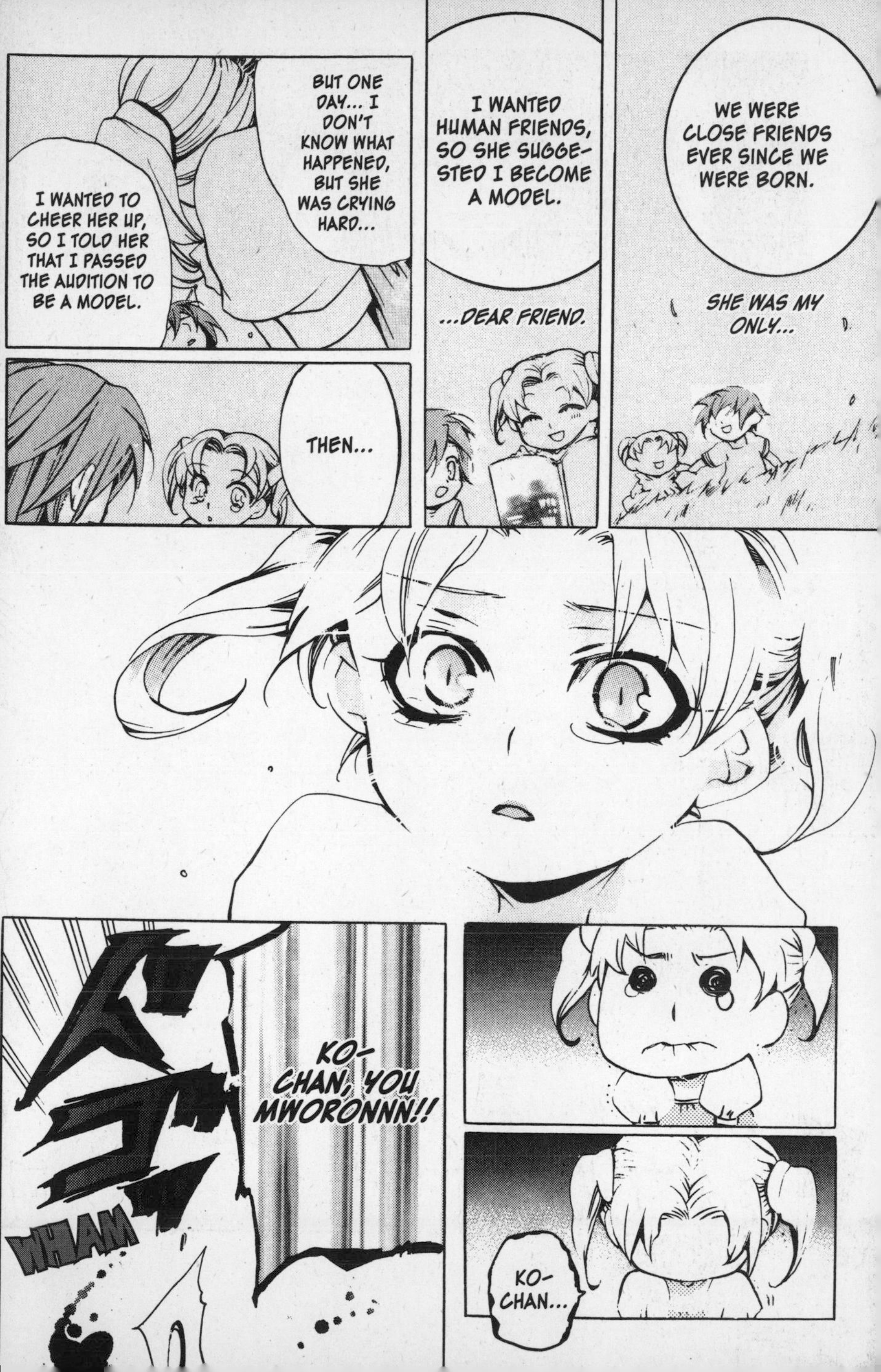
WE WERE CLOSE FRIENDS EVER SINCE WE WERE BORN.
SHE WAS MY ONLY...
I WANTED HUMAN FRIENDS, SO SHE SUGGESTED I BECOME A MODEL.
...DEAR FRIEND.
BUT ONE DAY... I DON'T KNOW WHAT HAPPENED, BUT SHE WAS CRYING HARD...
I WANTED TO CHEER HER UP, SO I TOLD HER THAT I PASSED THE AUDITION TO BE A MODEL.
THEN...
KO-CHAN...
KO-CHAN, YOU MWORONNN!!
WHAM

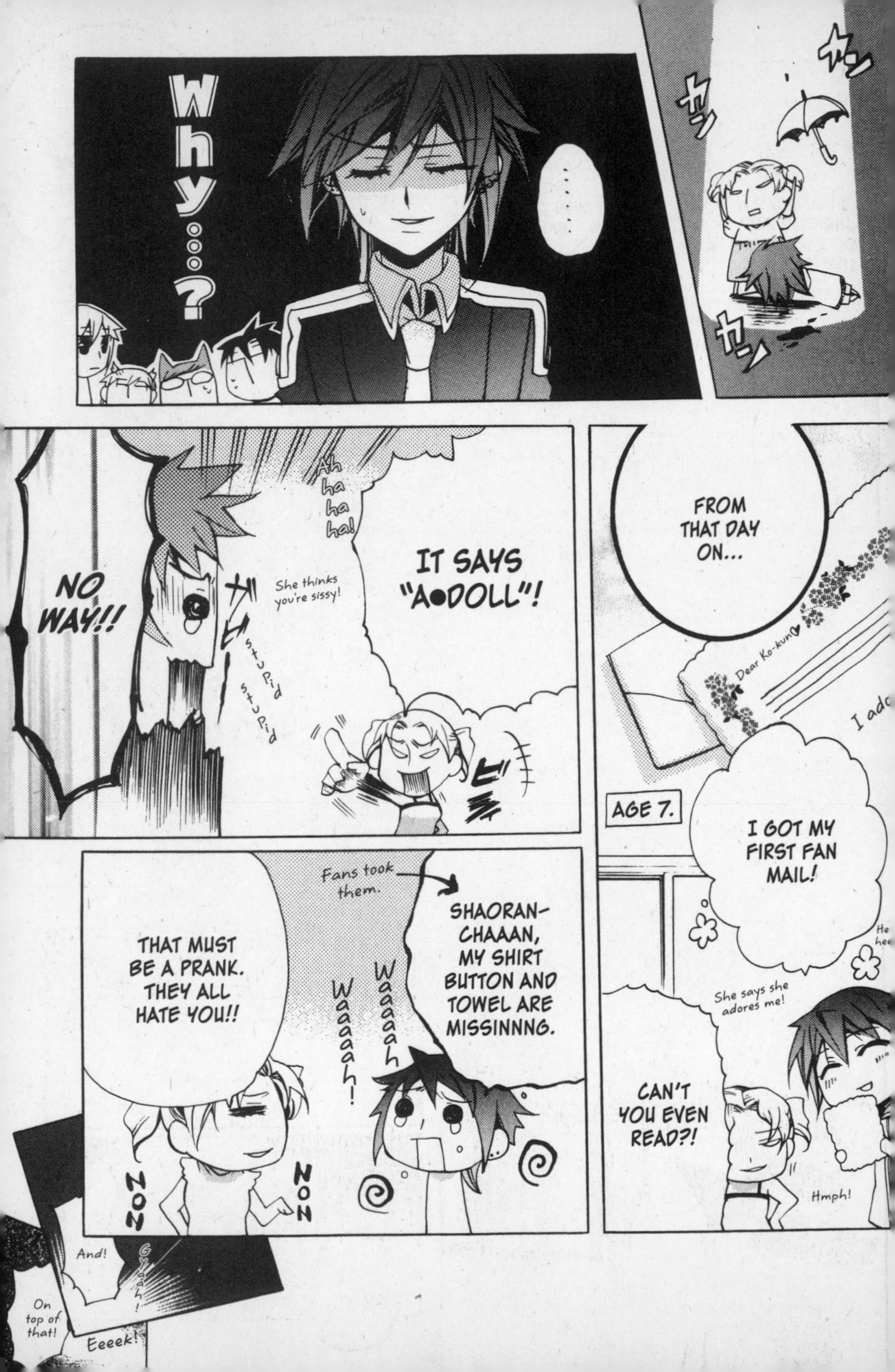

カーン
カン
カーン
Why...?
......
FROM THAT DAY ON...
Dear Ko-kun♥
Ah ha ha ha!
IT SAYS "A●DOLL"!
She thinks you're sissy!
NO WAY!!
stupid stupid
AGE 7.
I GOT MY FIRST FAN MAIL!
She says she adores me!
CAN'T YOU EVEN READ?!
Hmph!
Fans took them.
SHAORAN-CHAAAN, MY SHIRT BUTTON AND TOWEL ARE MISSINNNG.
Waaaaah Waaaaah!
THAT MUST BE A PRANK. THEY ALL HATE YOU!!
NON NON
And!
Gyaah!
On top of that!
Eeeek!

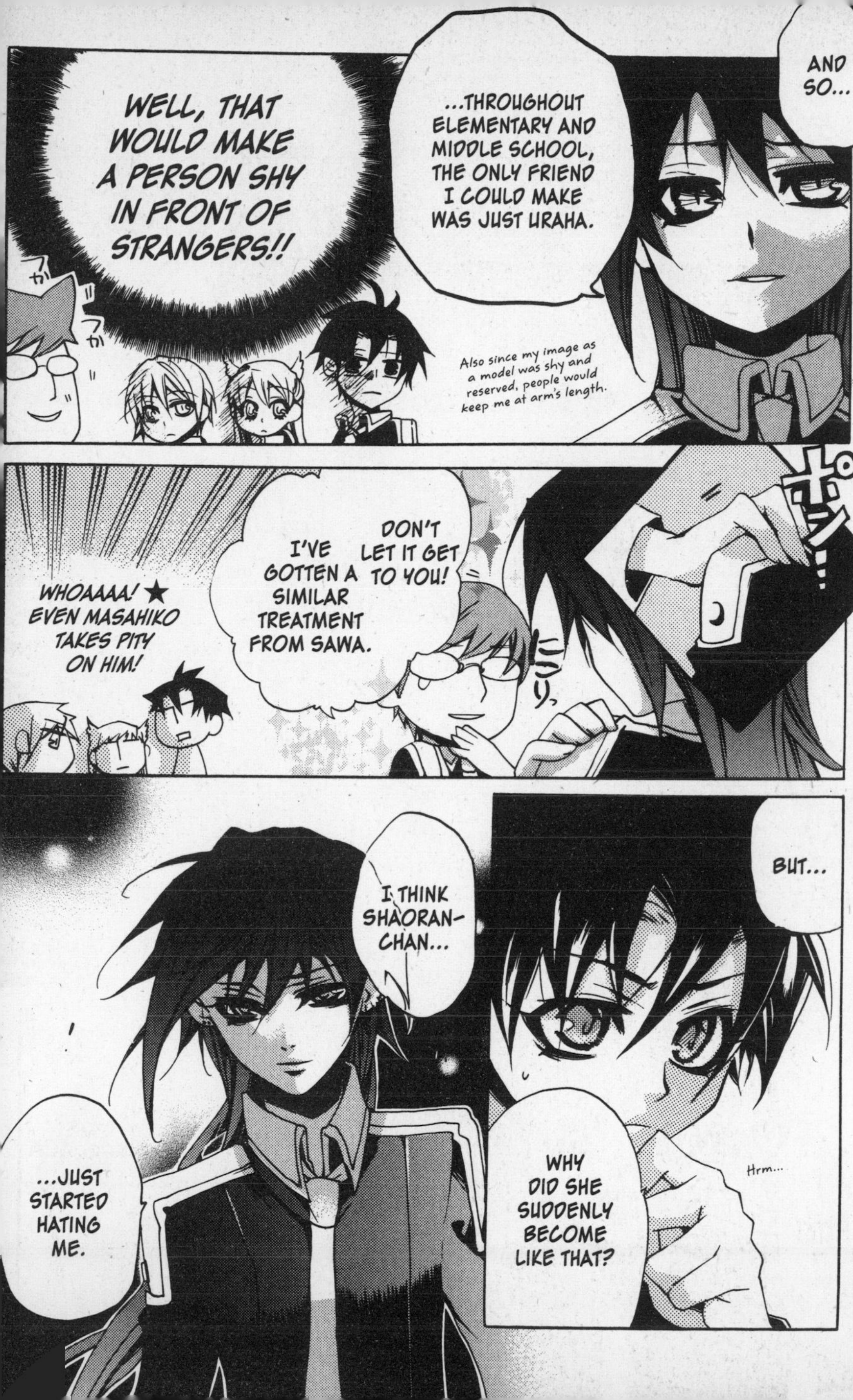
AND SO...
...THROUGHOUT ELEMENTARY AND MIDDLE SCHOOL, THE ONLY FRIEND I COULD MAKE WAS JUST URAHA.
WELL, THAT WOULD MAKE A PERSON SHY IN FRONT OF STRANGERS!!
Also since my image as a model was shy and reserved, people would keep me at arm's length.
DON'T LET IT GET TO YOU!
I'VE GOTTEN A SIMILAR TREATMENT FROM SAWA.
WHOAAAA! ★ EVEN MASAHIKO TAKES PITY ON HIM!
BUT...
WHY DID SHE SUDDENLY BECOME LIKE THAT?
Hrm...
I THINK SHAORAN-CHAN...
...JUST STARTED HATING ME.

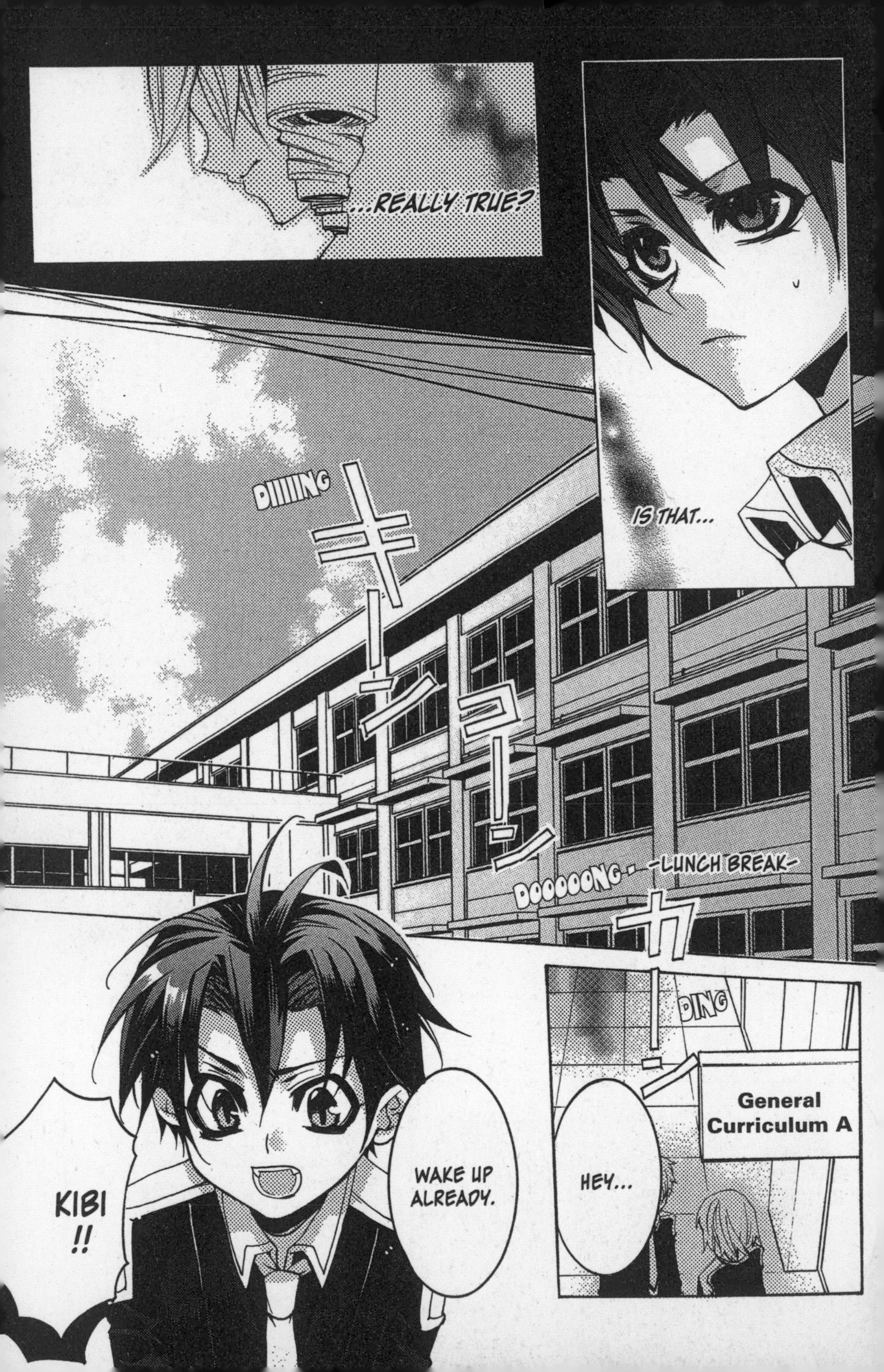
IS THAT...
...REALLY TRUE?
DIIIING
キーンコーン
DOOOOONG
-LUNCH BREAK-
カーン
DING
General Curriculum A
HEY...
WAKE UP ALREADY.
KIBI !!

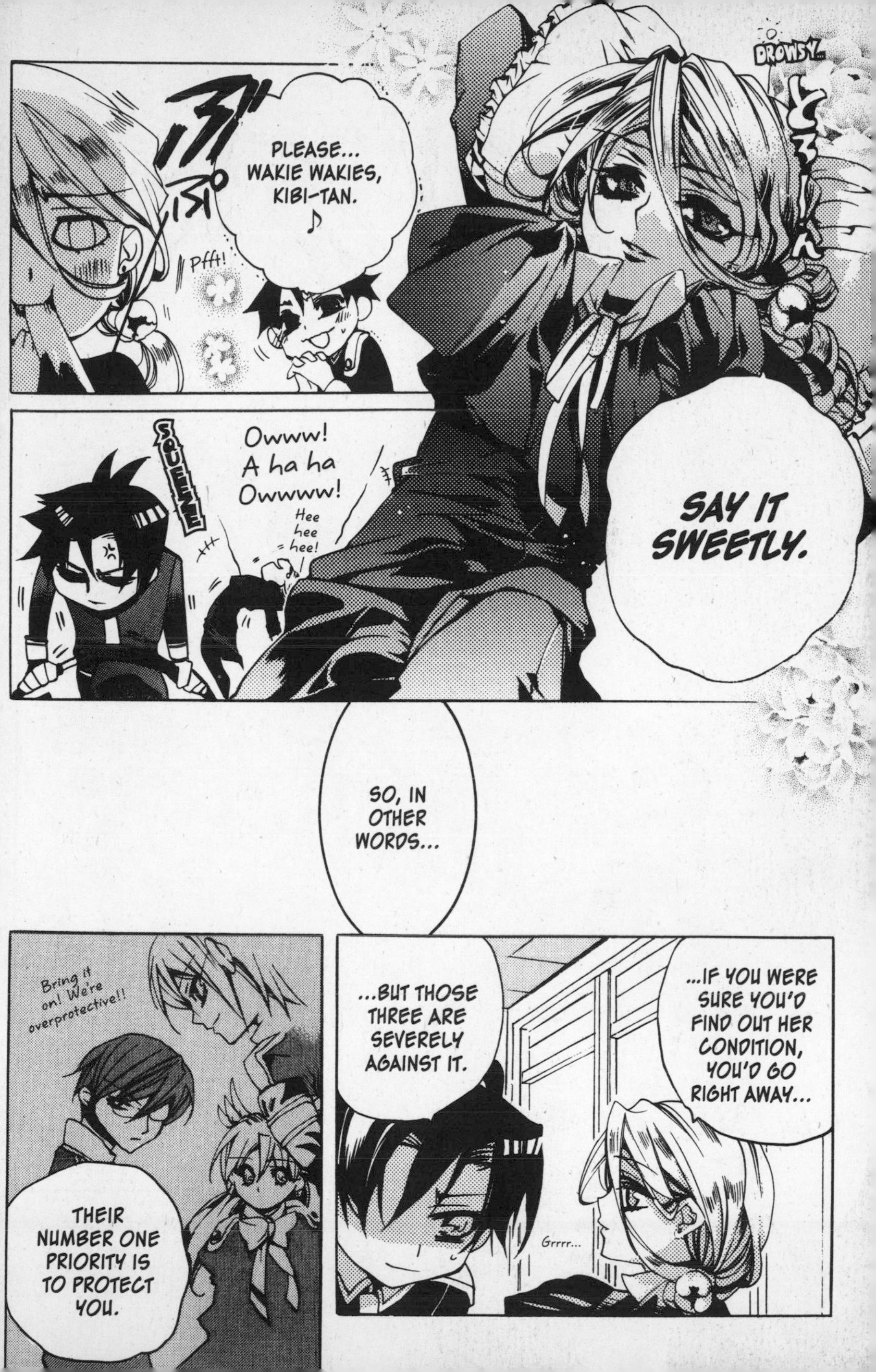
DROWSY...
SAY IT SWEETLY.
PLEASE... WAKIE WAKIES, KIBI-TAN. ♪
Pfft!
SQUEEZE
Owww! A ha ha Owwww!
Hee hee hee!
SO, IN OTHER WORDS...
...IF YOU WERE SURE YOU'D FIND OUT HER CONDITION, YOU'D GO RIGHT AWAY...
...BUT THOSE THREE ARE SEVERELY AGAINST IT.
Grrrr...
Bring it on! We're overprotective!!
THEIR NUMBER ONE PRIORITY IS TO PROTECT YOU.

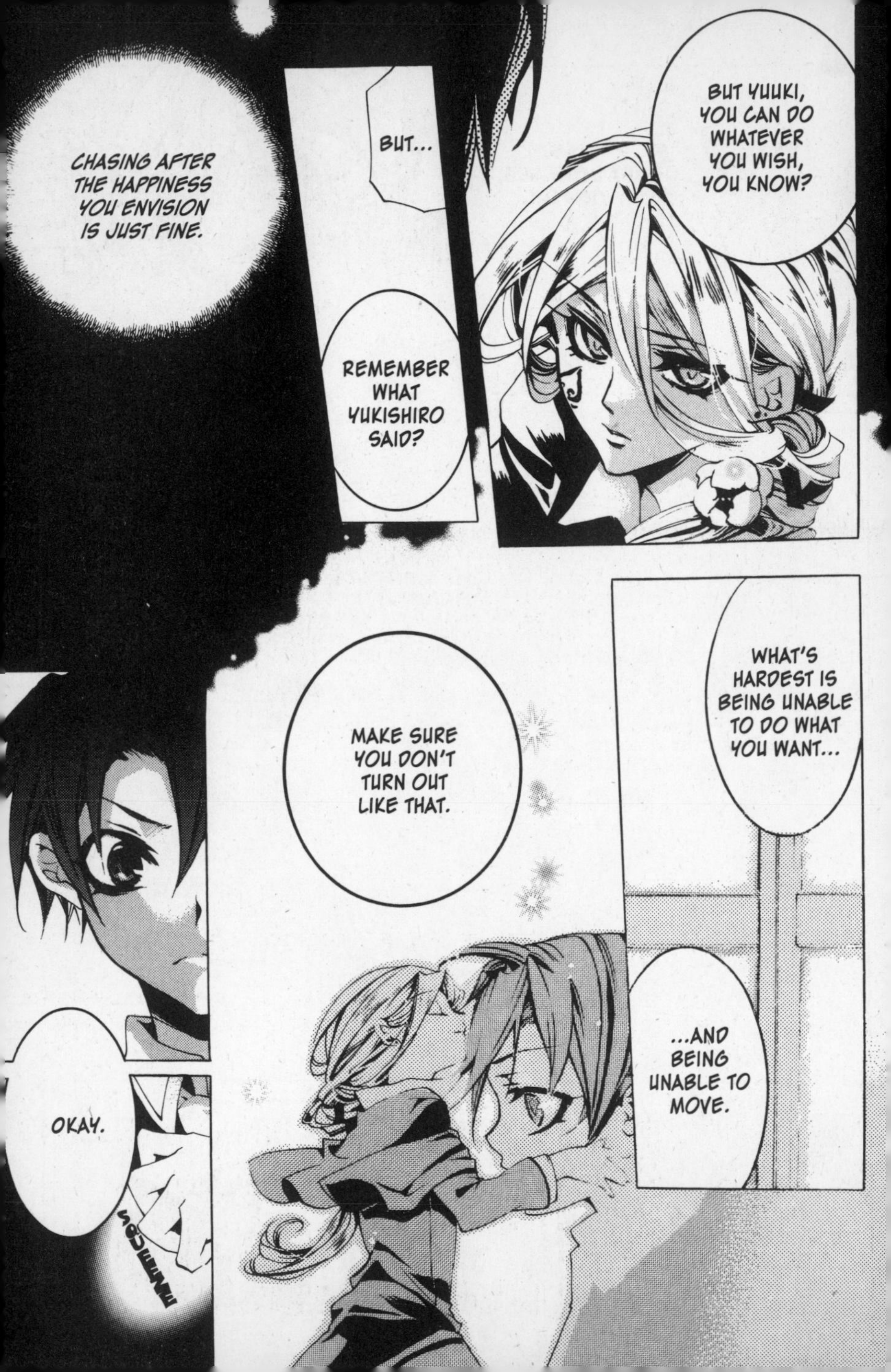
BUT YUUKI, YOU CAN DO WHATEVER YOU WISH, YOU KNOW?
BUT...
REMEMBER WHAT YUKISHIRO SAID?
CHASING AFTER THE HAPPINESS YOU ENVISION IS JUST FINE.
WHAT'S HARDEST IS BEING UNABLE TO DO WHAT YOU WANT...
...AND BEING UNABLE TO MOVE.
MAKE SURE YOU DON'T TURN OUT LIKE THAT.
OKAY.
SQUEEZE

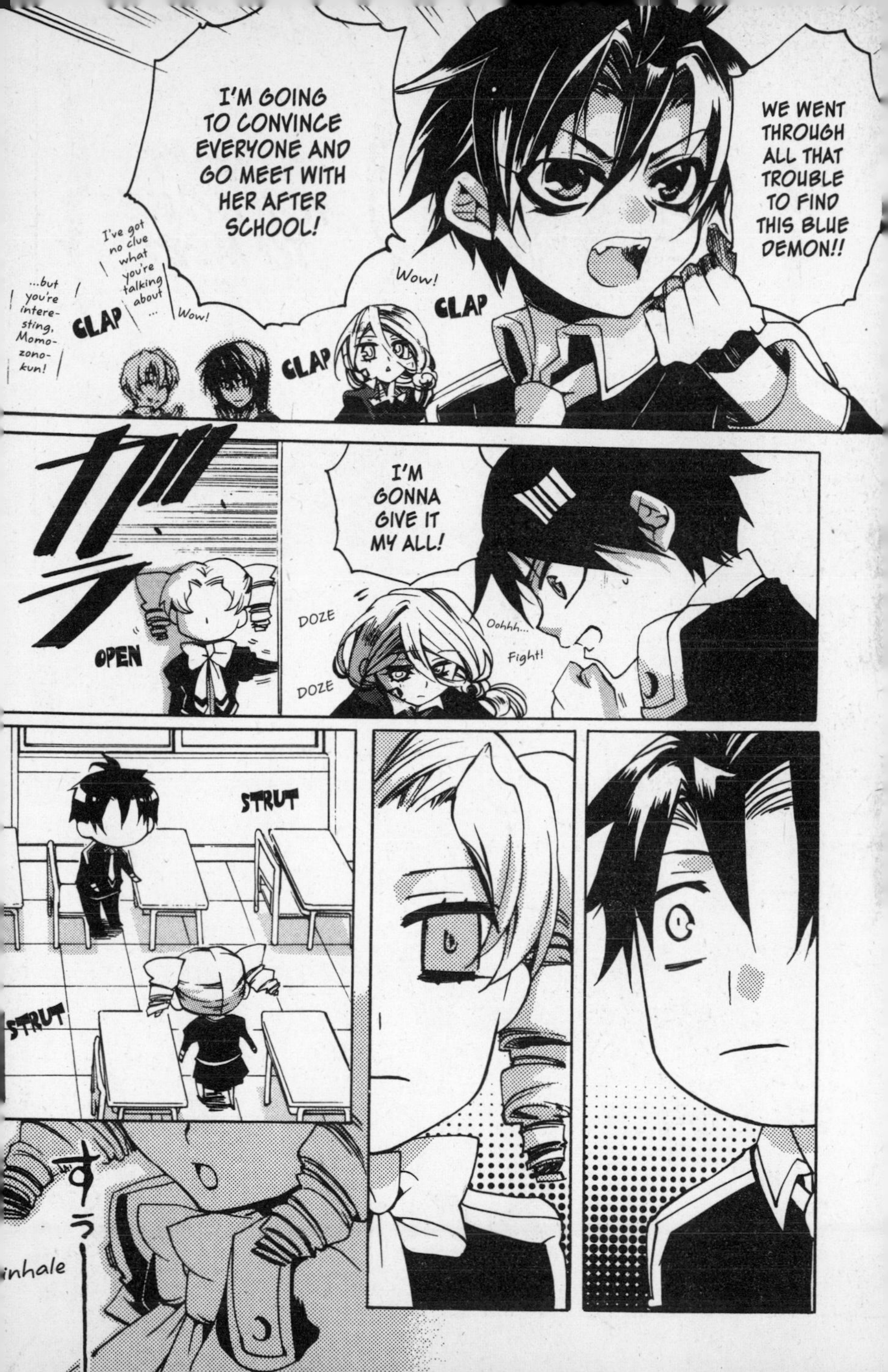
WE WENT THROUGH ALL THAT TROUBLE TO FIND THIS BLUE DEMON!!
I'M GOING TO CONVINCE EVERYONE AND GO MEET WITH HER AFTER SCHOOL!
Wow!
CLAP
CLAP
Wow!
I've got no clue what you're talking about...
...but you're interesting, Momozono-kun!
CLAP
I'M GONNA GIVE IT MY ALL!
Oohhh...
Fight!
DOZE
DOZE
OPEN
STRUT
STRUT
すぅ
inhale

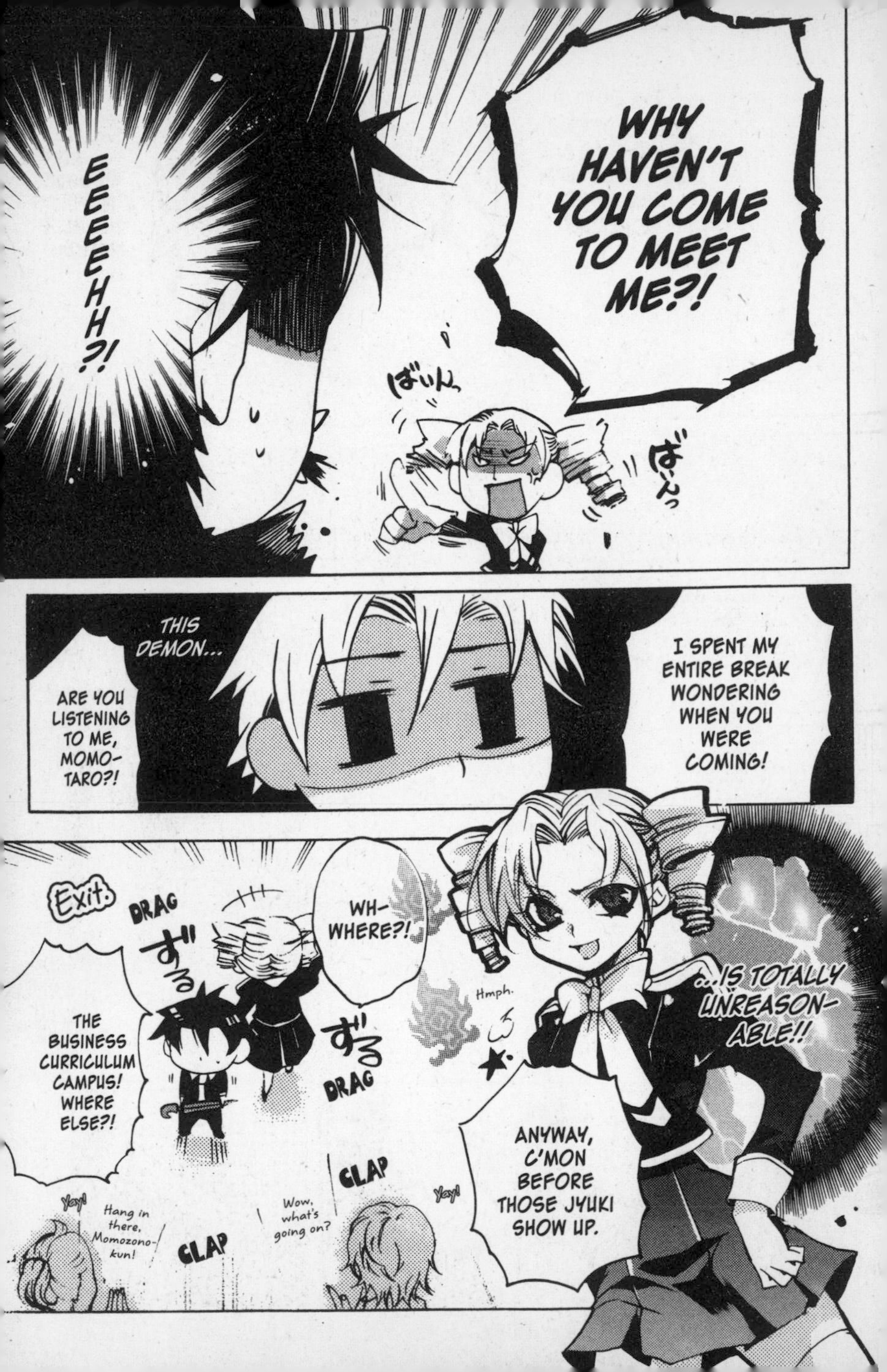
WHY HAVEN'T YOU COME TO MEET ME?!
ばいんっ
ばんっ
EEEEEHH?!
I SPENT MY ENTIRE BREAK WONDERING WHEN YOU WERE COMING!
THIS DEMON...
ARE YOU LISTENING TO ME, MOMOTARO?!
...IS TOTALLY UNREASON-ABLE!!
Hmph.
ANYWAY, C'MON BEFORE THOSE JYUKI SHOW UP.
Yay!
WH- WHERE?!
ずる
DRAG
DRAG
ずる
Exit.
THE BUSINESS CURRICULUM CAMPUS! WHERE ELSE?!
CLAP
Wow, what's going on?
CLAP
Hang in there, Momozono-kun!
Yay!

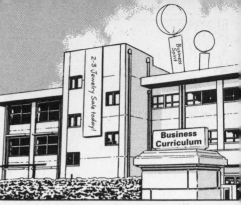

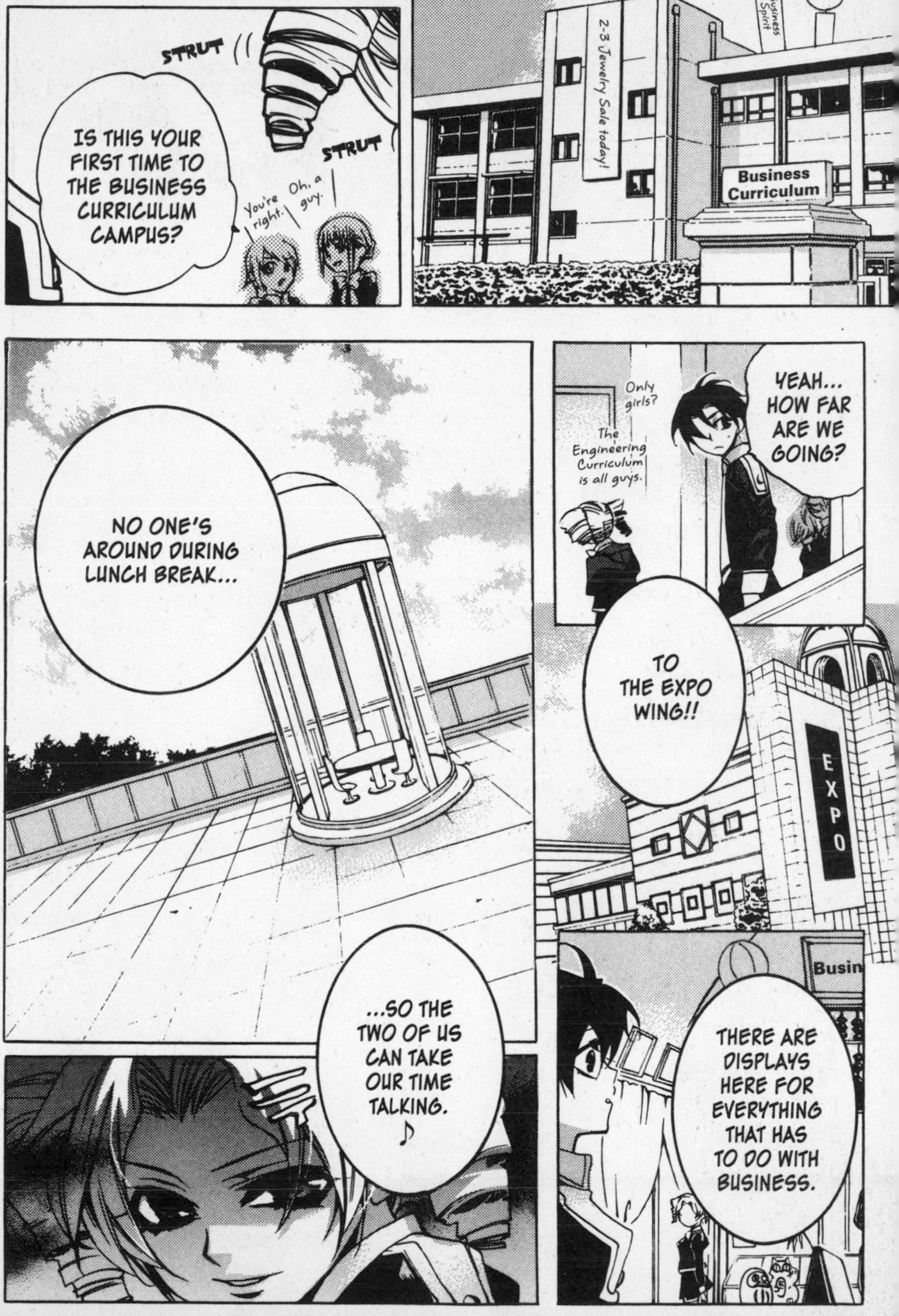
2-3 Jewelry Sale today!
Business Spirit
Business Curriculum
STRUT
IS THIS YOUR FIRST TIME TO THE BUSINESS CURRICULUM CAMPUS?
STRUT
Oh, a guy.
You're right.
YEAH... HOW FAR ARE WE GOING?
Only girls?
The Engineering Curriculum is all guys.
TO THE EXPO WING!!
EXPO
THERE ARE DISPLAYS HERE FOR EVERYTHING THAT HAS TO DO WITH BUSINESS.
NO ONE'S AROUND DURING LUNCH BREAK...
...SO THE TWO OF US CAN TAKE OUR TIME TALKING. ♪

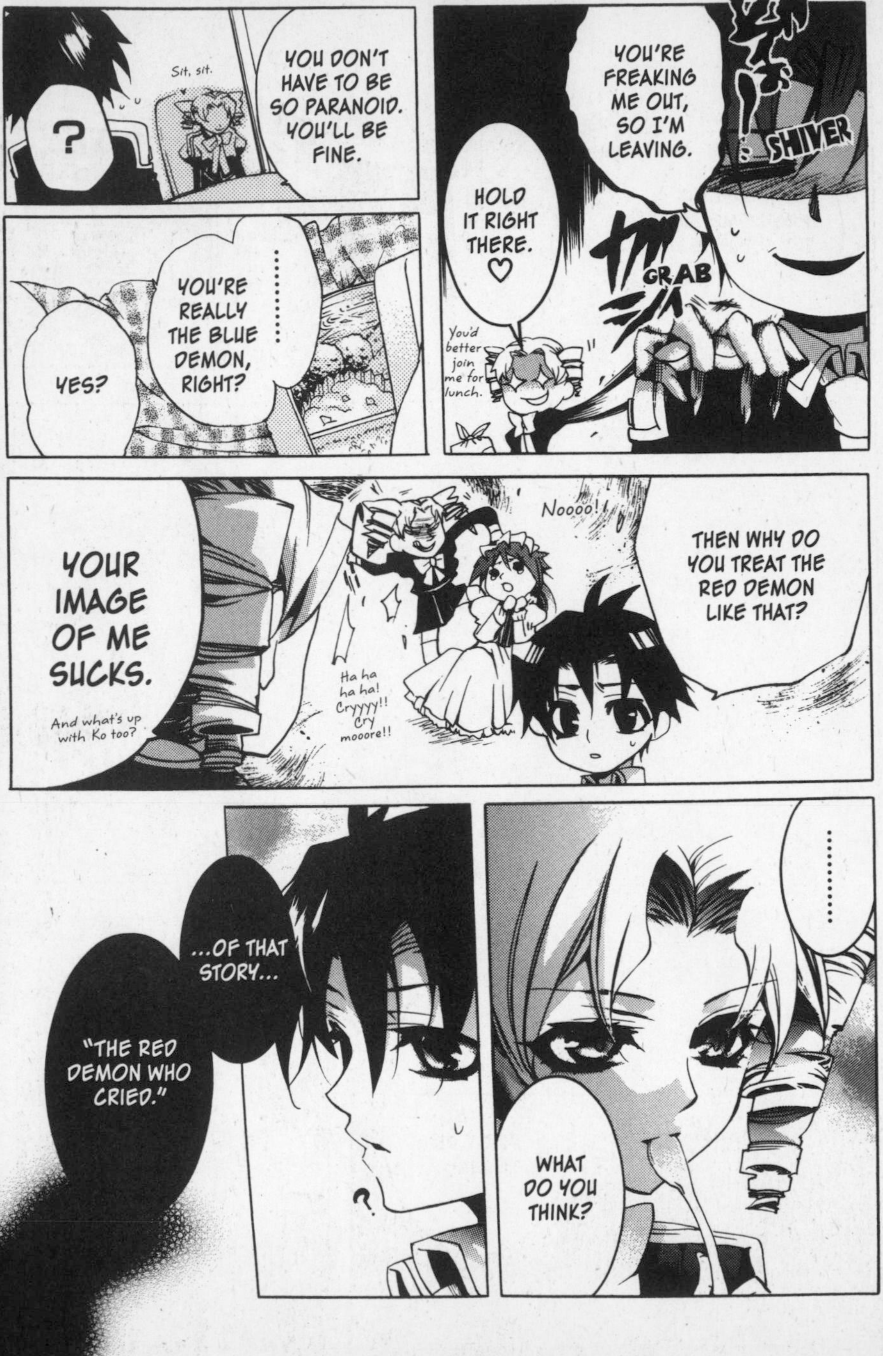
YOU'RE FREAKING ME OUT, SO I'M LEAVING.
SHIVER
HOLD IT RIGHT THERE. ♡
GRAB
You'd better join me for lunch.
YOU DON'T HAVE TO BE SO PARANOID. YOU'LL BE FINE.
Sit, sit.
?
......
YOU'RE REALLY THE BLUE DEMON, RIGHT?
YES?
THEN WHY DO YOU TREAT THE RED DEMON LIKE THAT?
Noooo!!
Ha ha ha ha! Cryyyy!! Cry mooore!!
YOUR IMAGE OF ME SUCKS.
And what's up with Ko too?
......
WHAT DO YOU THINK?
...OF THAT STORY...
"THE RED DEMON WHO CRIED."
?

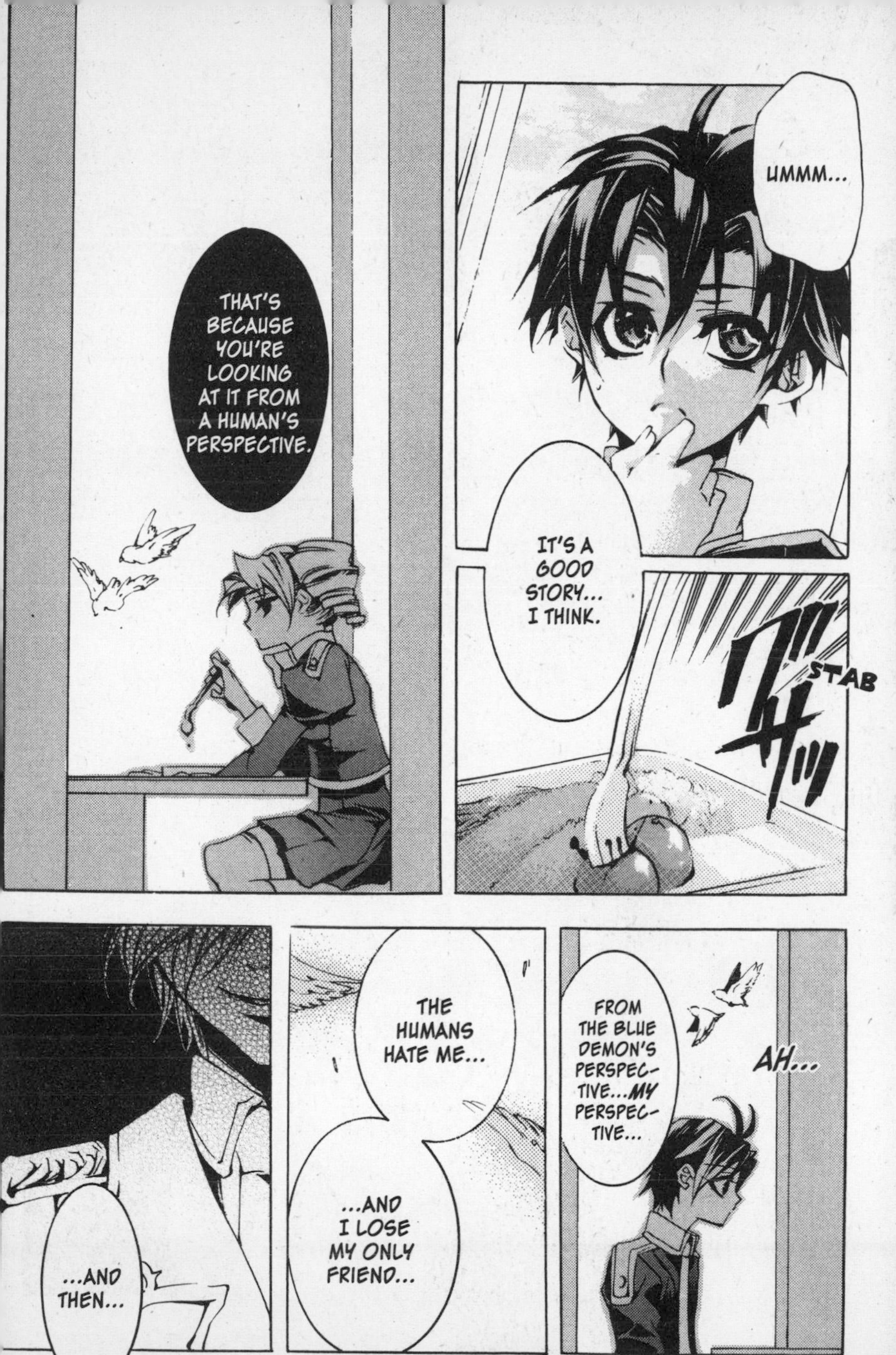
UMMM...
IT'S A GOOD STORY... I THINK.
STAB
THAT'S BECAUSE YOU'RE LOOKING AT IT FROM A HUMAN'S PERSPECTIVE.
AH...
FROM THE BLUE DEMON'S PERSPECTIVE...MY PERSPECTIVE...
THE HUMANS HATE ME...
...AND I LOSE MY ONLY FRIEND...
...AND THEN...

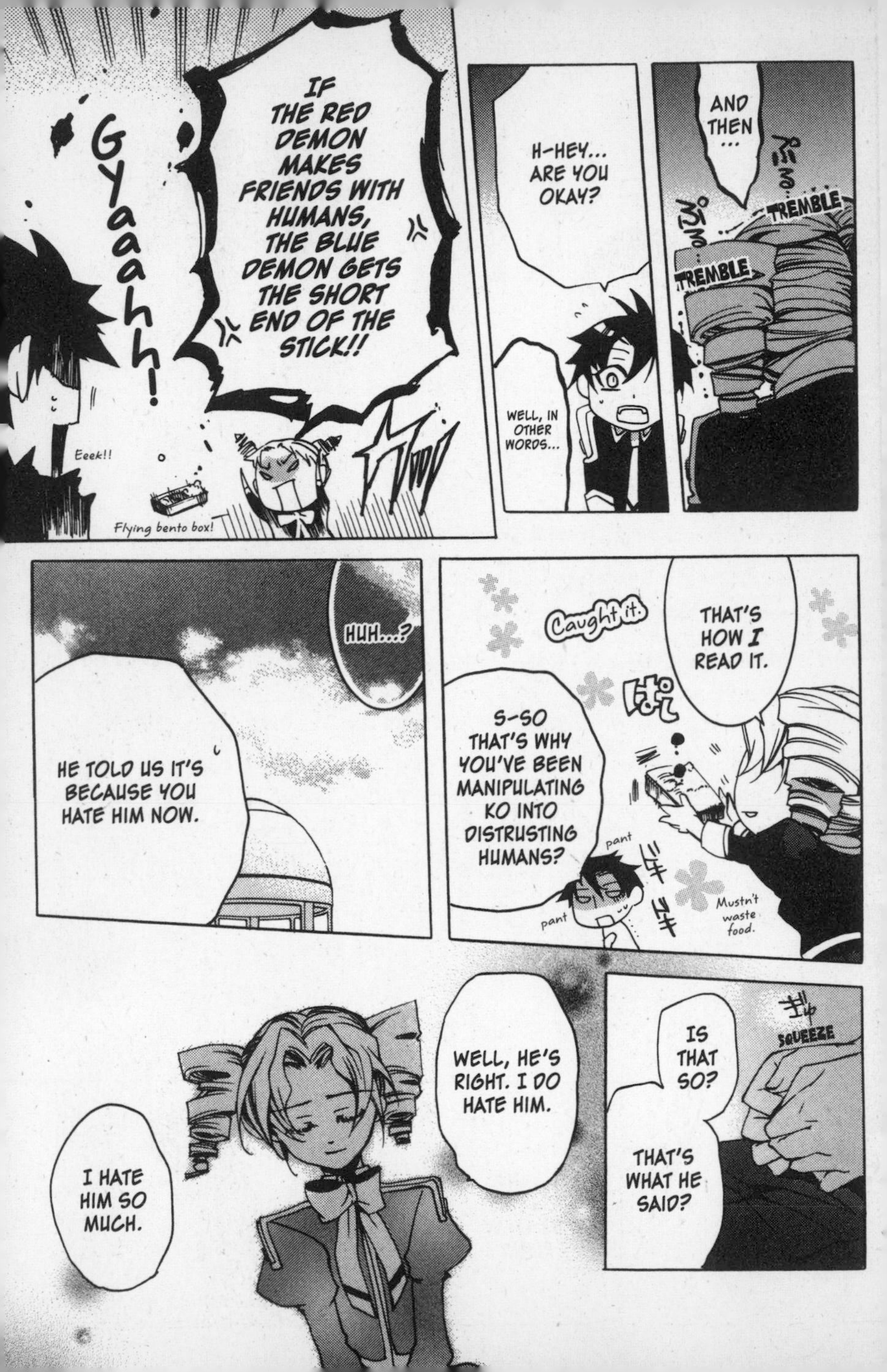
AND THEN ...
TREMBLE
TREMBLE
H-HEY... ARE YOU OKAY?
WELL, IN OTHER WORDS...
IF THE RED DEMON MAKES FRIENDS WITH HUMANS, THE BLUE DEMON GETS THE SHORT END OF THE STICK!!
Gyaaahh!
Eeek!!
Flying bento box!
THAT'S HOW I READ IT.
Caught it.
S-SO THAT'S WHY YOU'VE BEEN MANIPULATING KO INTO DISTRUSTING HUMANS?
pant
pant
Mustn't waste food.
HUH...?
HE TOLD US IT'S BECAUSE YOU HATE HIM NOW.
IS THAT SO?
SQUEEZE
THAT'S WHAT HE SAID?
WELL, HE'S RIGHT. I DO HATE HIM.
I HATE HIM SO MUCH.

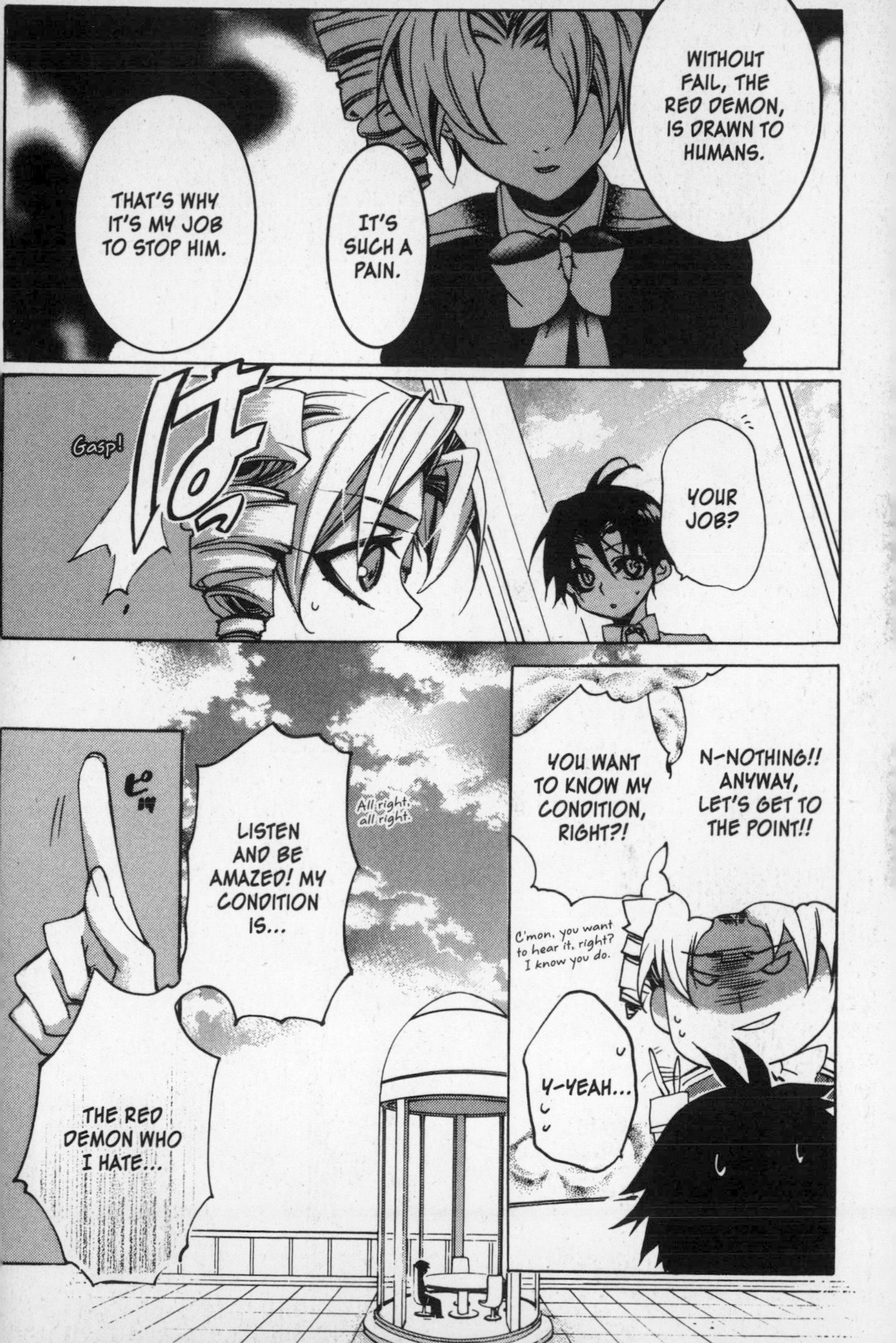
WITHOUT FAIL, THE RED DEMON, IS DRAWN TO HUMANS.
IT'S SUCH A PAIN.
THAT'S WHY IT'S MY JOB TO STOP HIM.
YOUR JOB?
Gasp!
N-NOTHING!! ANYWAY, LET'S GET TO THE POINT!!
YOU WANT TO KNOW MY CONDITION, RIGHT?!
C'mon, you want to hear it, right? I know you do.
Y-YEAH...
All right, all right.
LISTEN AND BE AMAZED! MY CONDITION IS...
THE RED DEMON WHO I HATE...

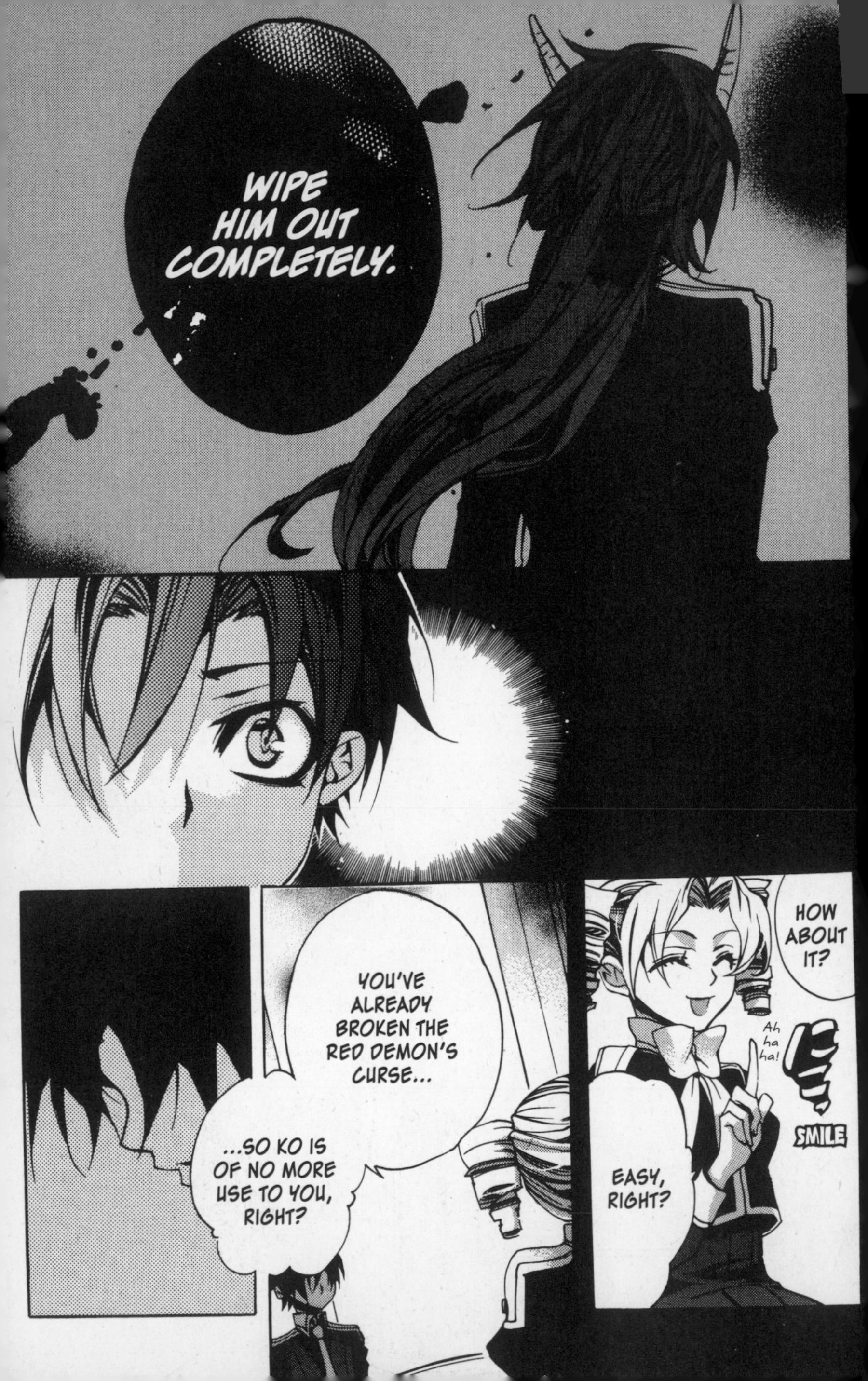
WIPE HIM OUT COMPLETELY.
HOW ABOUT IT?
Ah ha ha!
SMILE
EASY, RIGHT?
YOU'VE ALREADY BROKEN THE RED DEMON'S CURSE...
...SO KO IS OF NO MORE USE TO YOU, RIGHT?

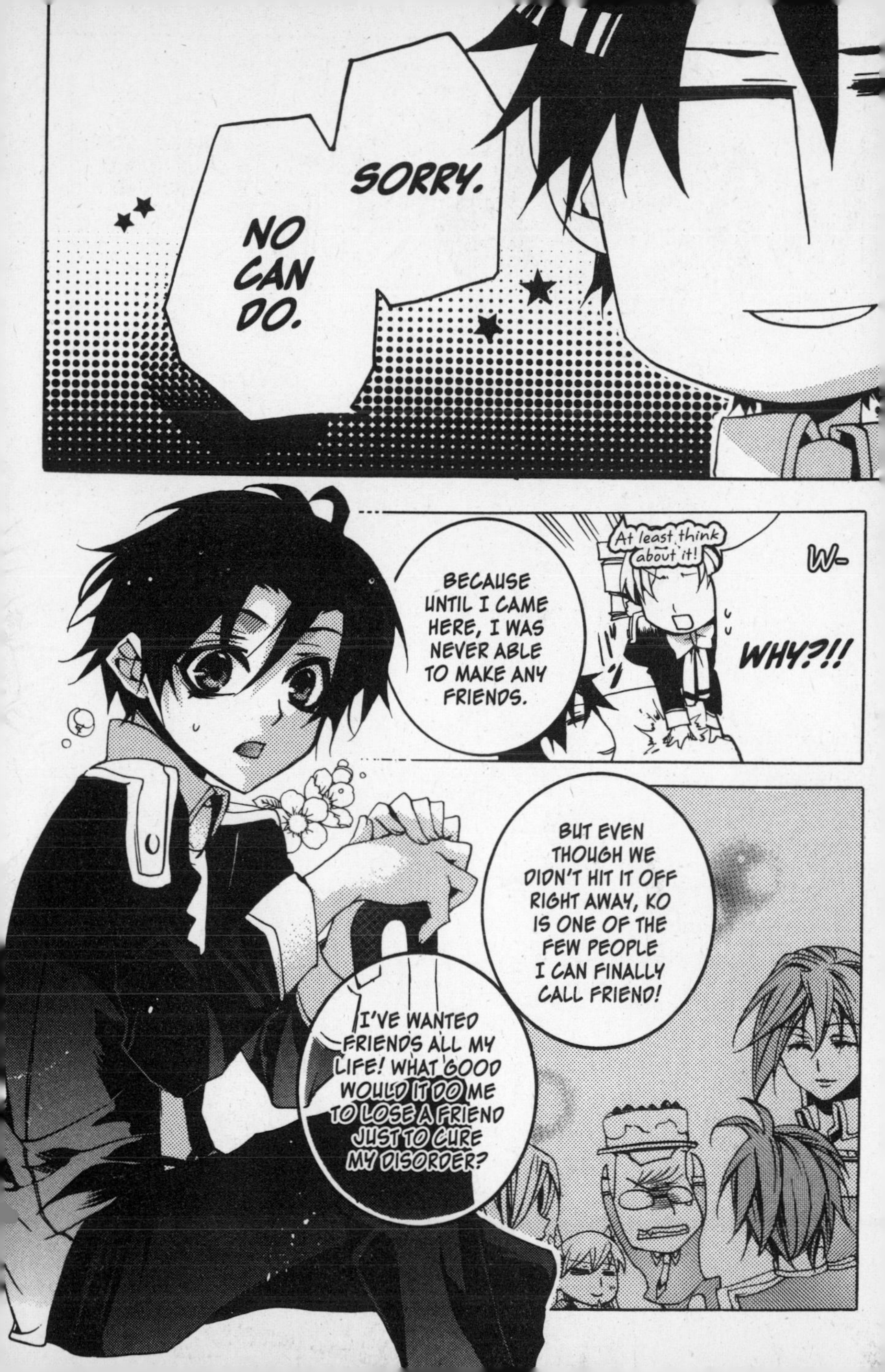
SORRY.
NO CAN DO.
W-
WHY?!!
At least think about it!
BECAUSE UNTIL I CAME HERE, I WAS NEVER ABLE TO MAKE ANY FRIENDS.
BUT EVEN THOUGH WE DIDN'T HIT IT OFF RIGHT AWAY, KO IS ONE OF THE FEW PEOPLE I CAN FINALLY CALL FRIEND!
I'VE WANTED FRIENDS ALL MY LIFE! WHAT GOOD WOULD IT DO ME TO LOSE A FRIEND JUST TO CURE MY DISORDER?

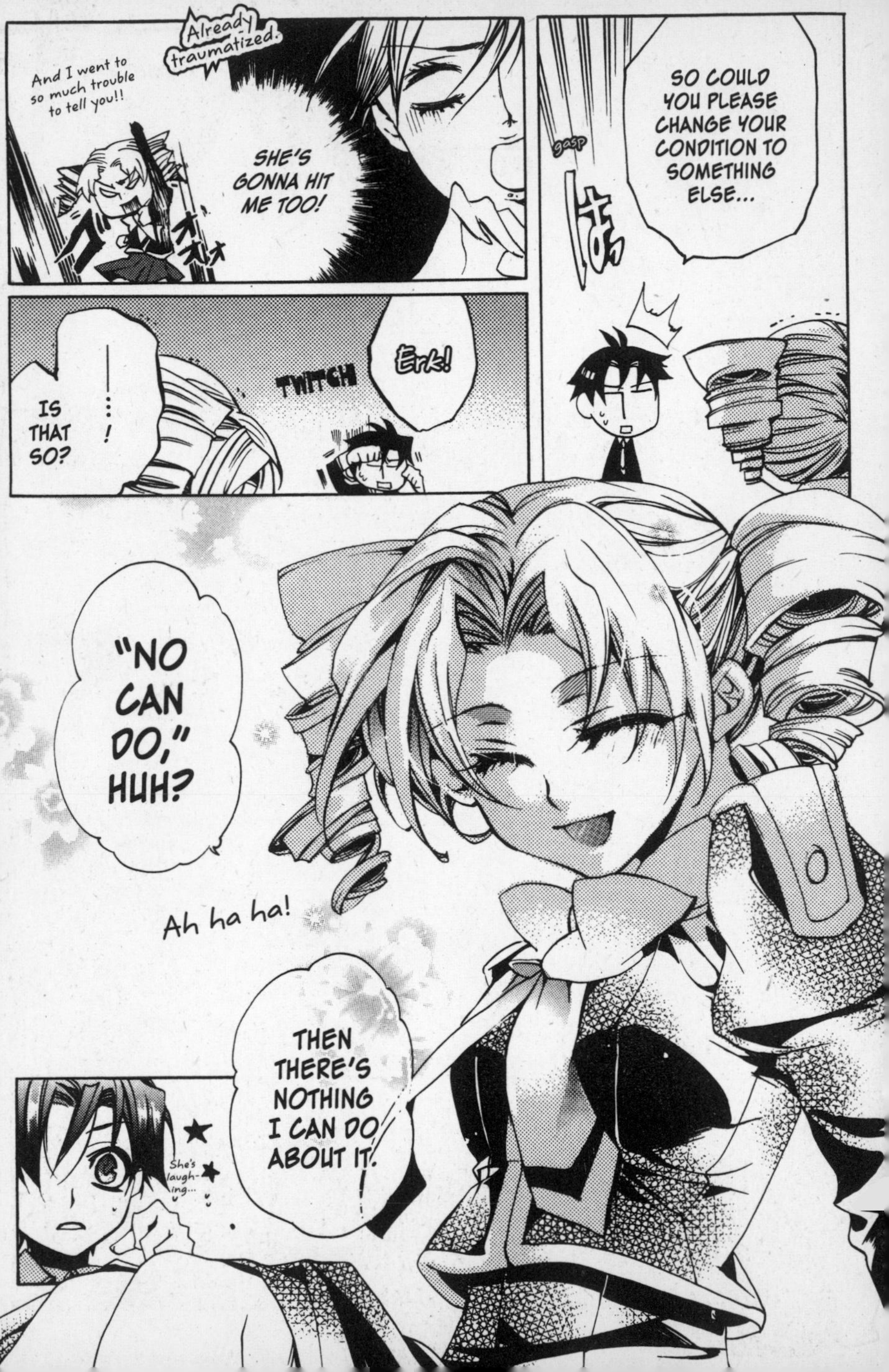
SO COULD YOU PLEASE CHANGE YOUR CONDITION TO SOMETHING ELSE...
gasp
Already traumatized.
SHE'S GONNA HIT ME TOO!
And I went to so much trouble to tell you!!
Erk!
TWITCH
......!
IS THAT SO?
"NO CAN DO," HUH?
Ah ha ha!
THEN THERE'S NOTHING I CAN DO ABOUT IT.
She's laugh-ing...

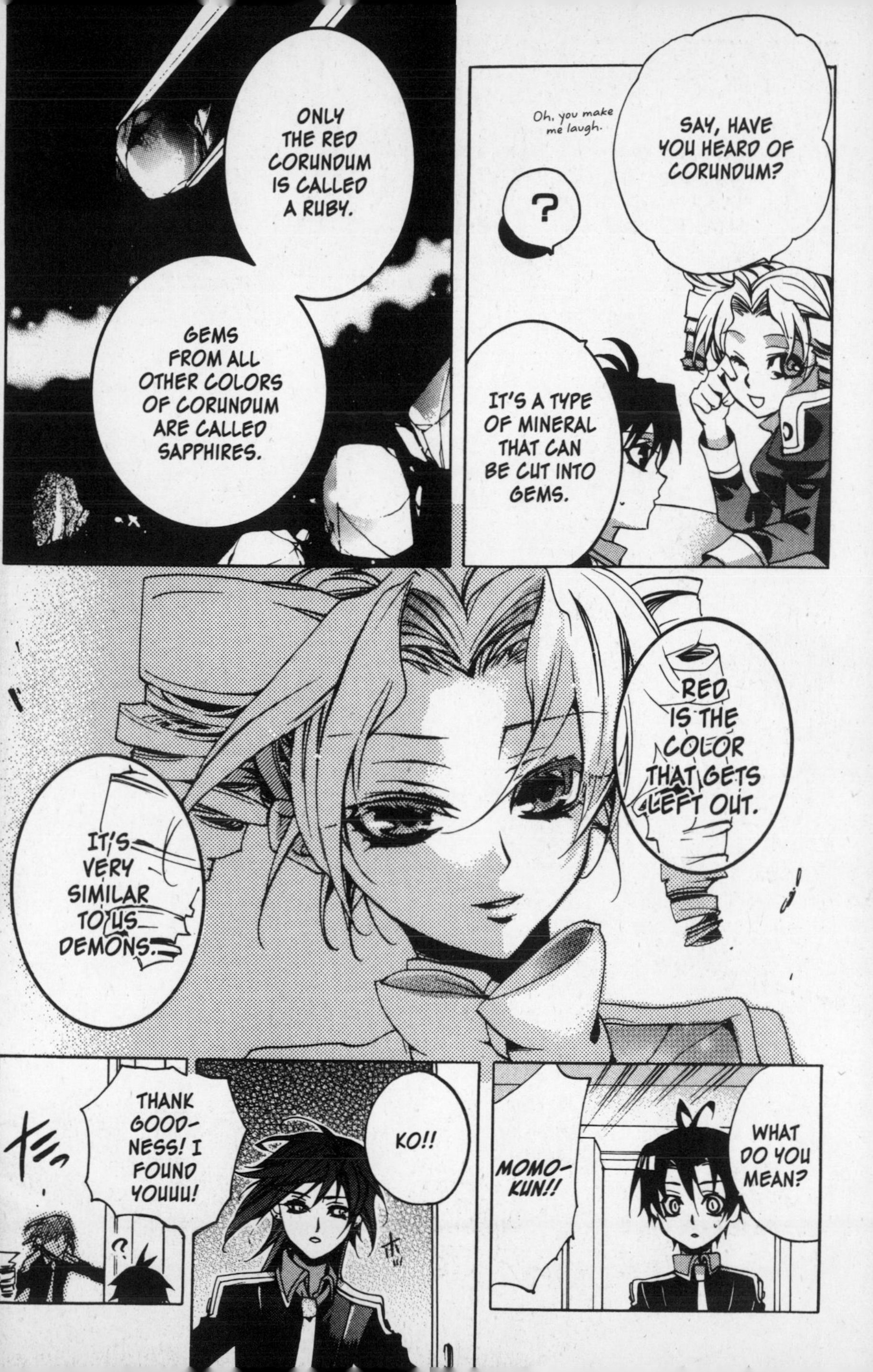
SAY, HAVE YOU HEARD OF CORUNDUM?
Oh, you make me laugh.
?
IT'S A TYPE OF MINERAL THAT CAN BE CUT INTO GEMS.
ONLY THE RED CORUNDUM IS CALLED A RUBY.
GEMS FROM ALL OTHER COLORS OF CORUNDUM ARE CALLED SAPPHIRES.
RED IS THE COLOR THAT GETS LEFT OUT.
IT'S VERY SIMILAR TO US DEMONS.
WHAT DO YOU MEAN?
MOMO-KUN!!
KO!!
THANK GOODNESS! I FOUND YOUUU!

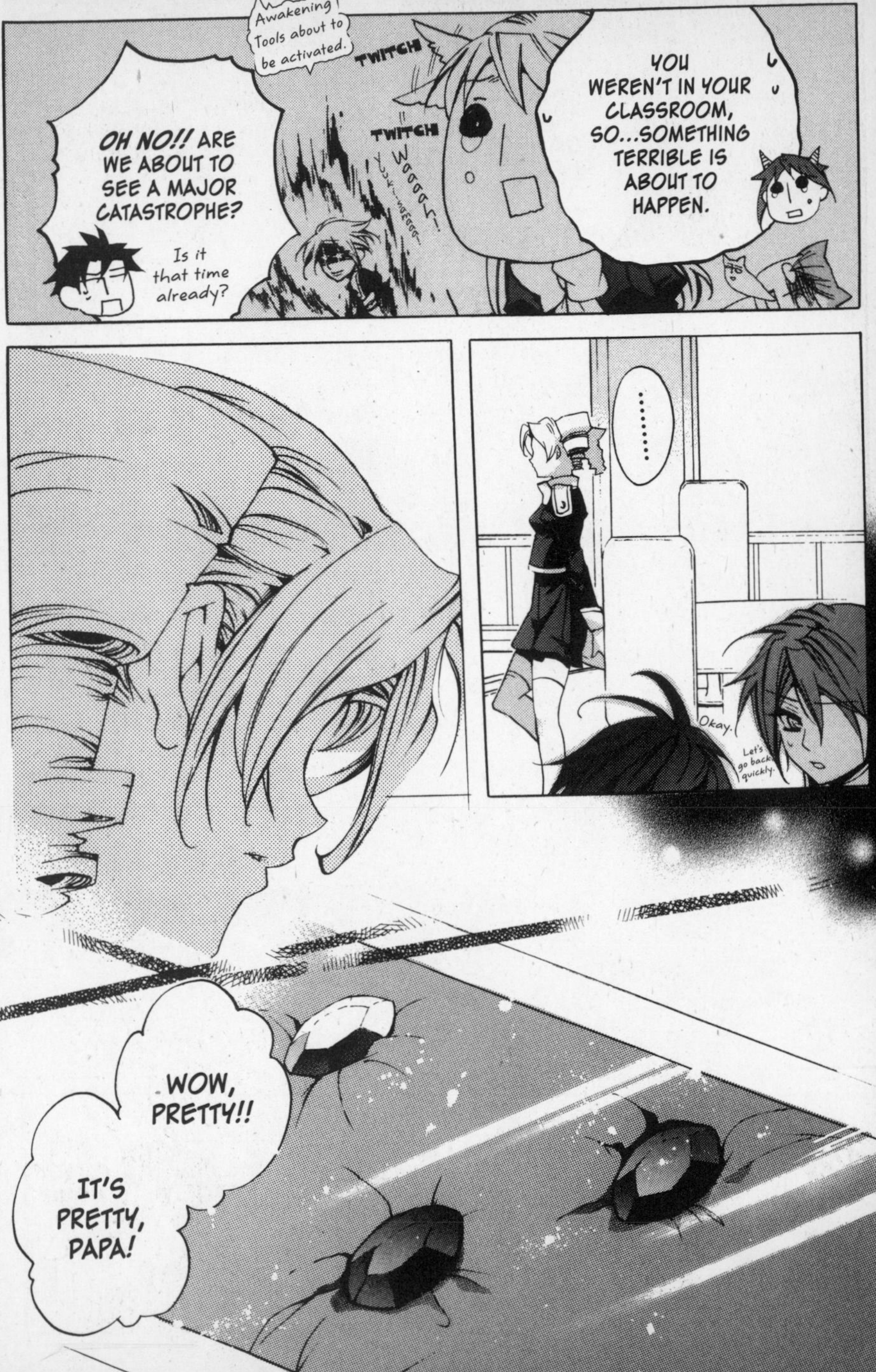
YOU WEREN'T IN YOUR CLASSROOM, SO...SOMETHING TERRIBLE IS ABOUT TO HAPPEN.
TWITCH
Awakening Tools about to be activated.
TWITCH
Waaaah!
Yuuki-saaaan!
OH NO!! ARE WE ABOUT TO SEE A MAJOR CATASTROPHE?
Is it that time already?
......
Okay.
Let's go back quickly.
WOW, PRETTY!!
IT'S PRETTY, PAPA!

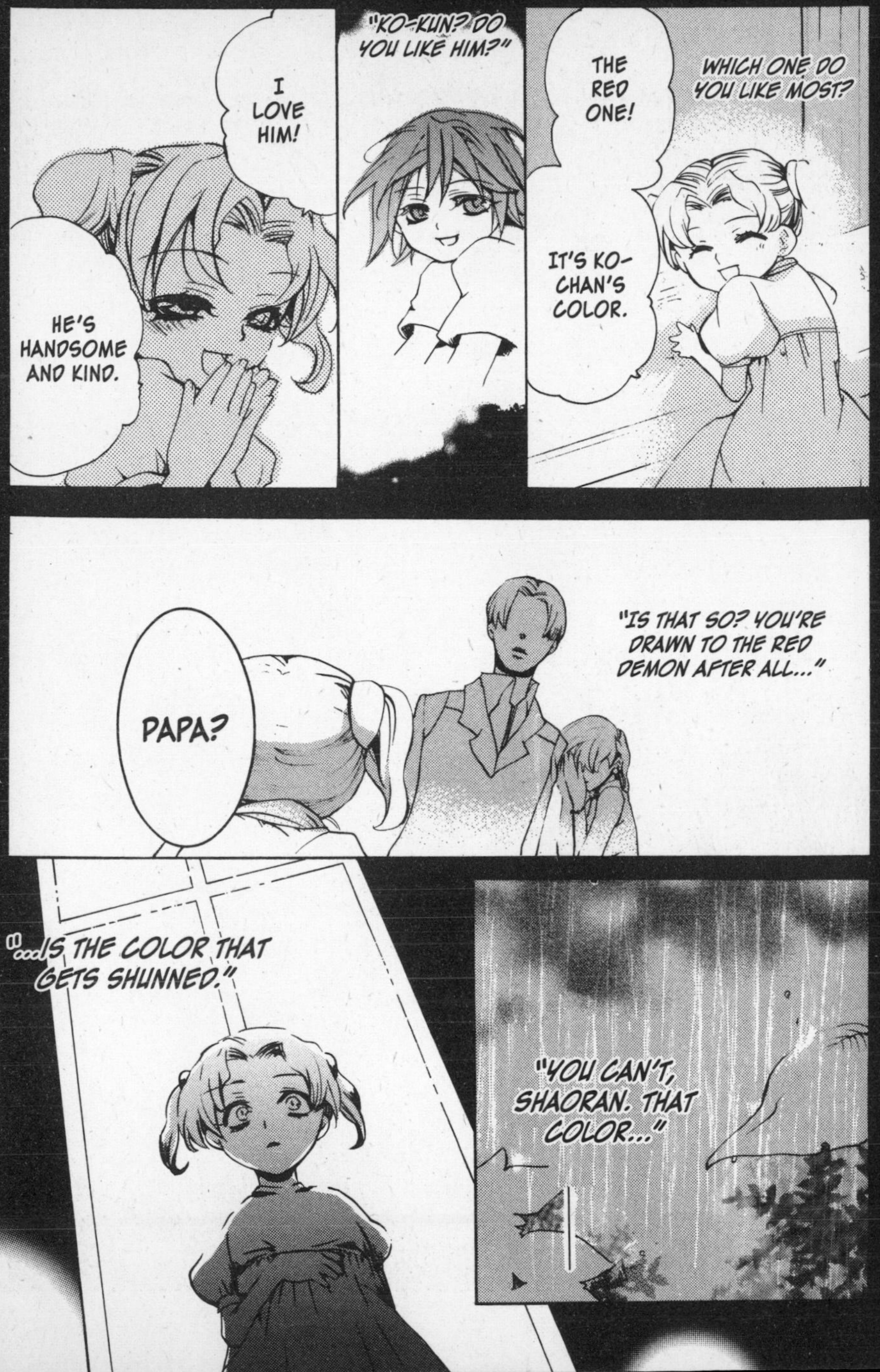
WHICH ONE DO YOU LIKE MOST?
THE RED ONE!
IT'S KO-CHAN'S COLOR.
"KO-KUN? DO YOU LIKE HIM?"
I LOVE HIM!
HE'S HANDSOME AND KIND.
"IS THAT SO? YOU'RE DRAWN TO THE RED DEMON AFTER ALL..."
PAPA?
"YOU CAN'T, SHAORAN. THAT COLOR..."
"...IS THE COLOR THAT GETS SHUNNED."

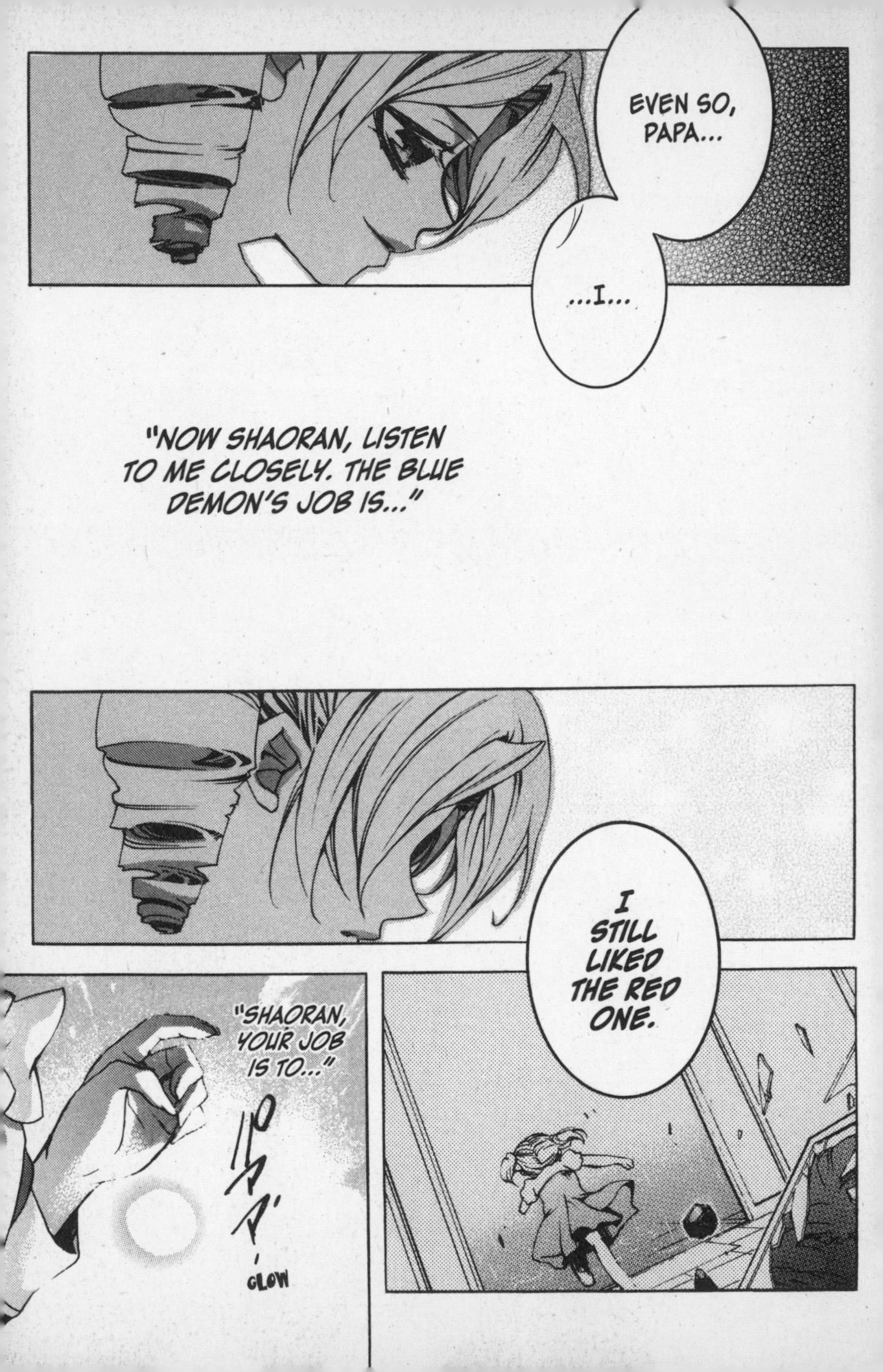
EVEN SO, PAPA...
...I...
"NOW SHAORAN, LISTEN TO ME CLOSELY. THE BLUE DEMON'S JOB IS..."
I STILL LIKED THE RED ONE.
"SHAORAN, YOUR JOB IS TO..."
GLOW

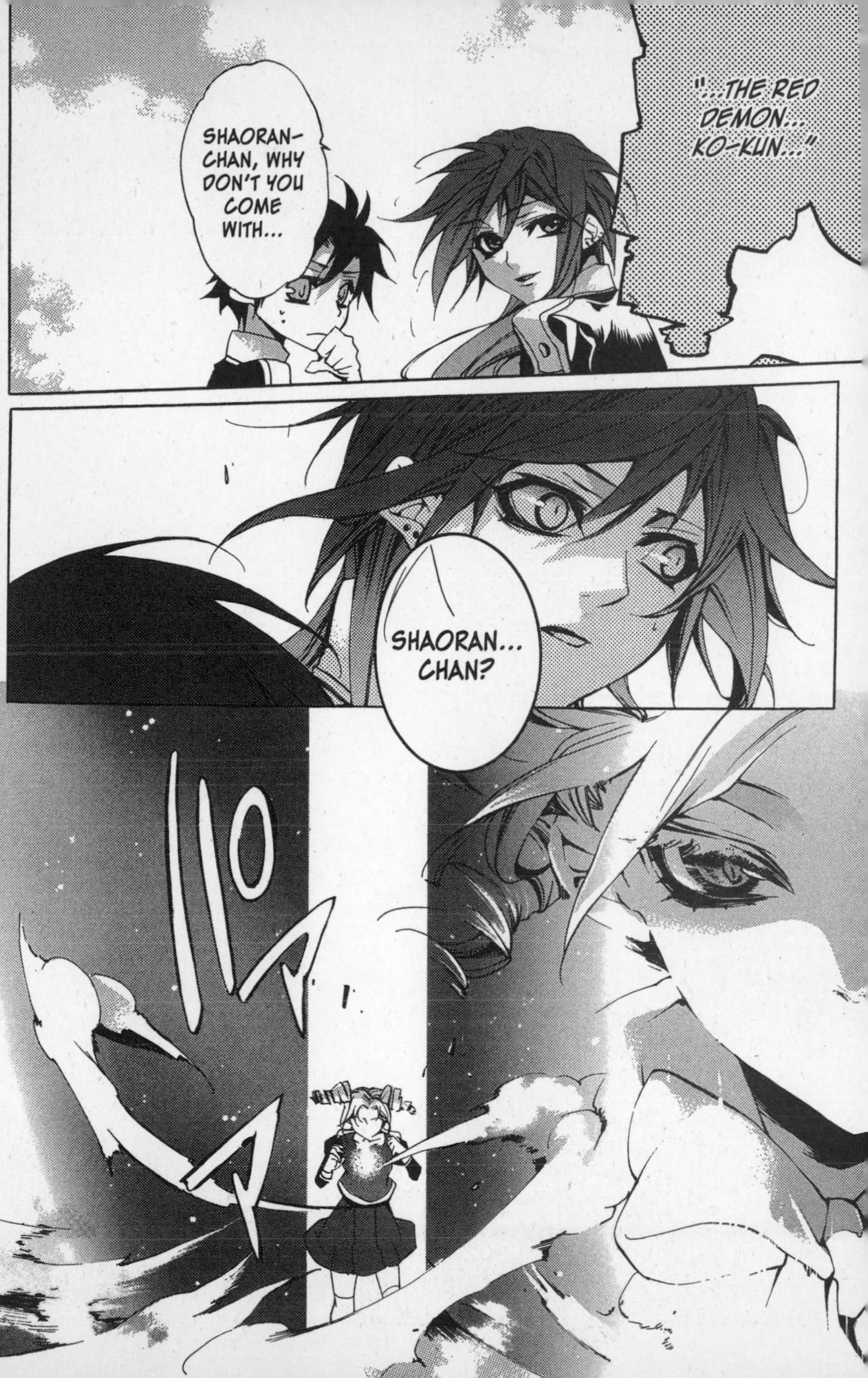
"...THE RED DEMON... KO-KUN..."
SHAORAN-CHAN, WHY DON'T YOU COME WITH...
SHAORAN... CHAN?

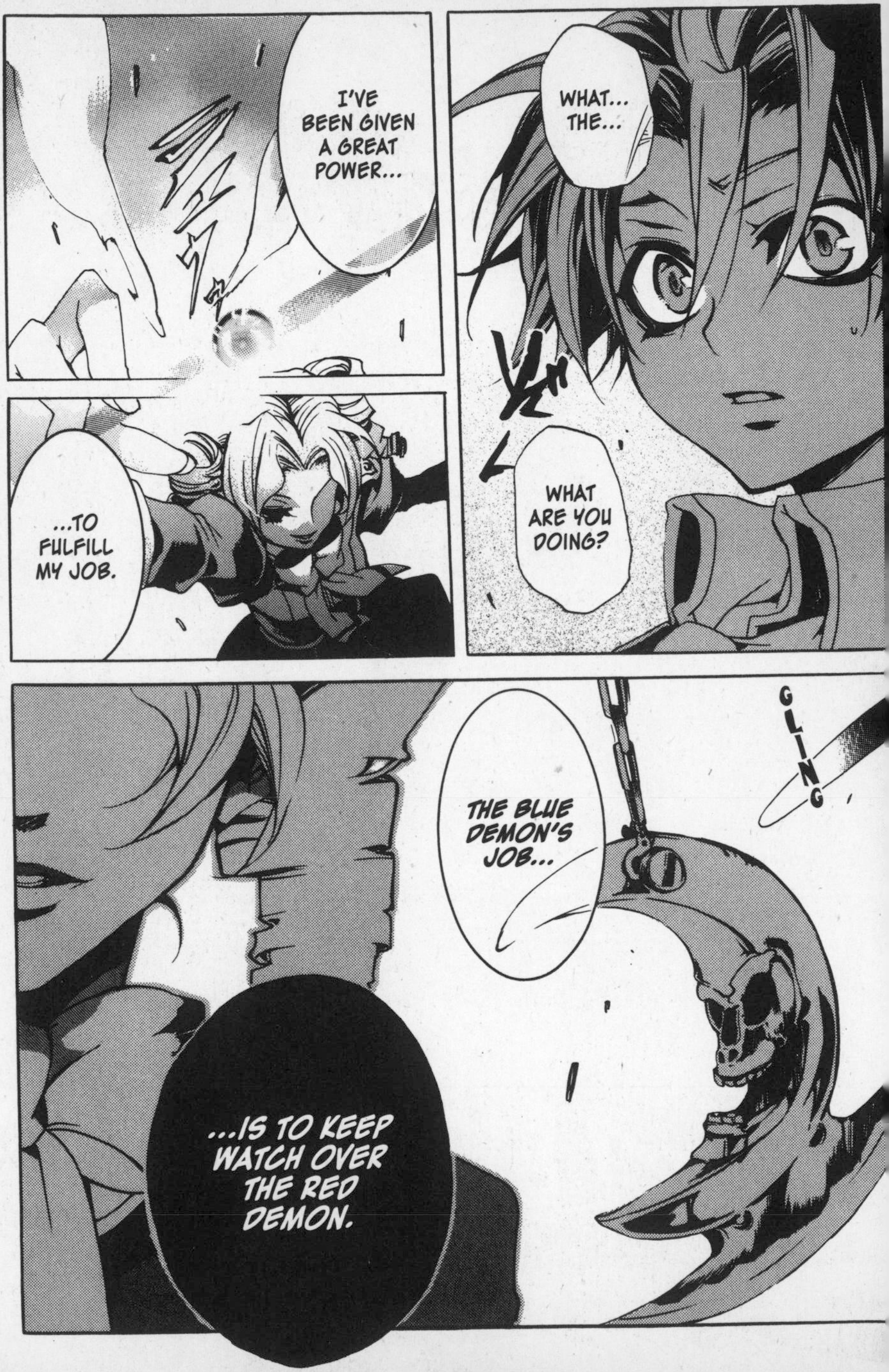
WHAT... THE...
WHAT ARE YOU DOING?
I'VE BEEN GIVEN A GREAT POWER...
...TO FULFILL MY JOB.
GLING
THE BLUE DEMON'S JOB...
...IS TO KEEP WATCH OVER THE RED DEMON.

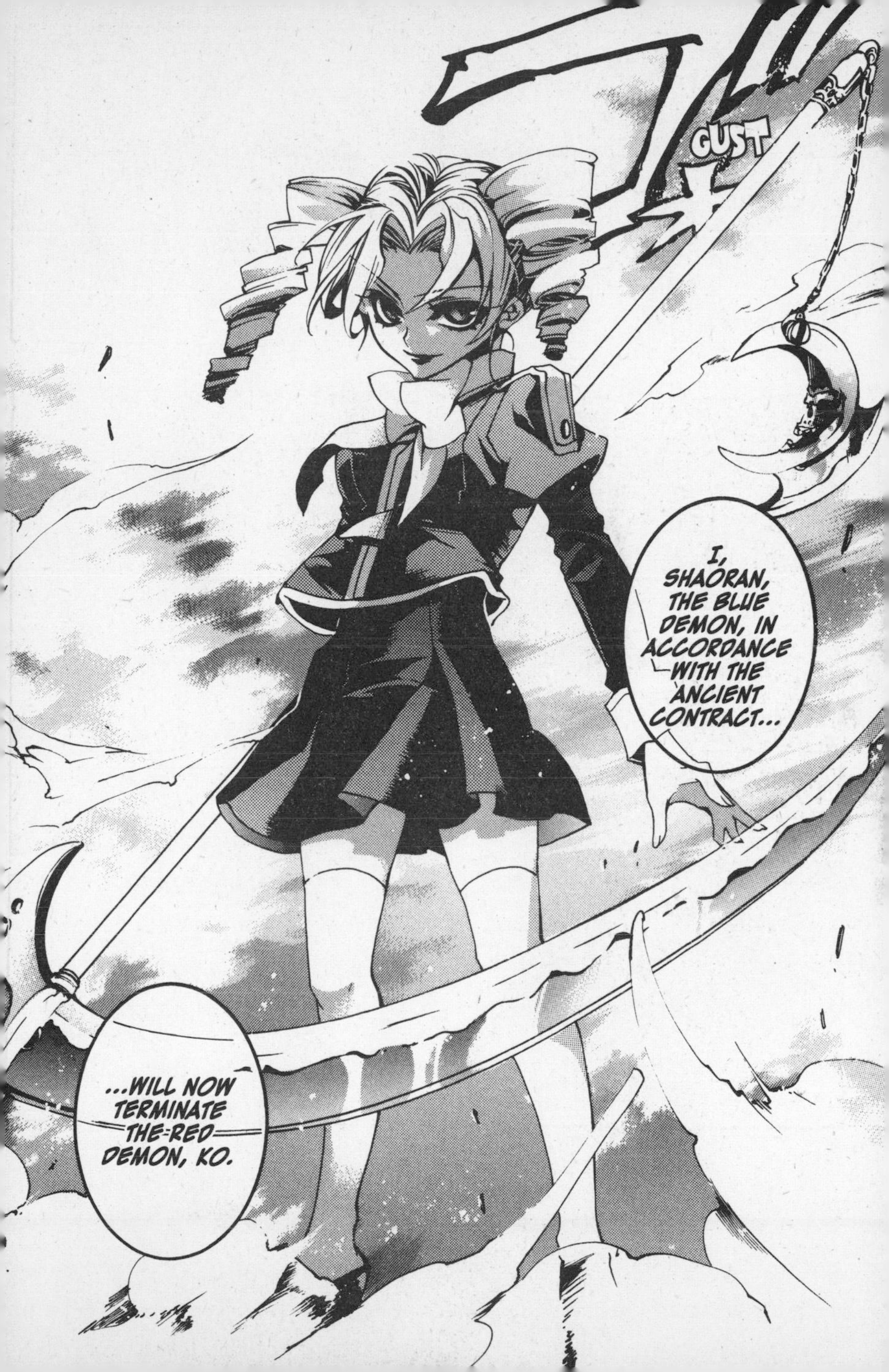
GUST
I, SHAORAN, THE BLUE DEMON, IN ACCORDANCE WITH THE ANCIENT CONTRACT...
...WILL NOW TERMINATE THE RED DEMON, KO.

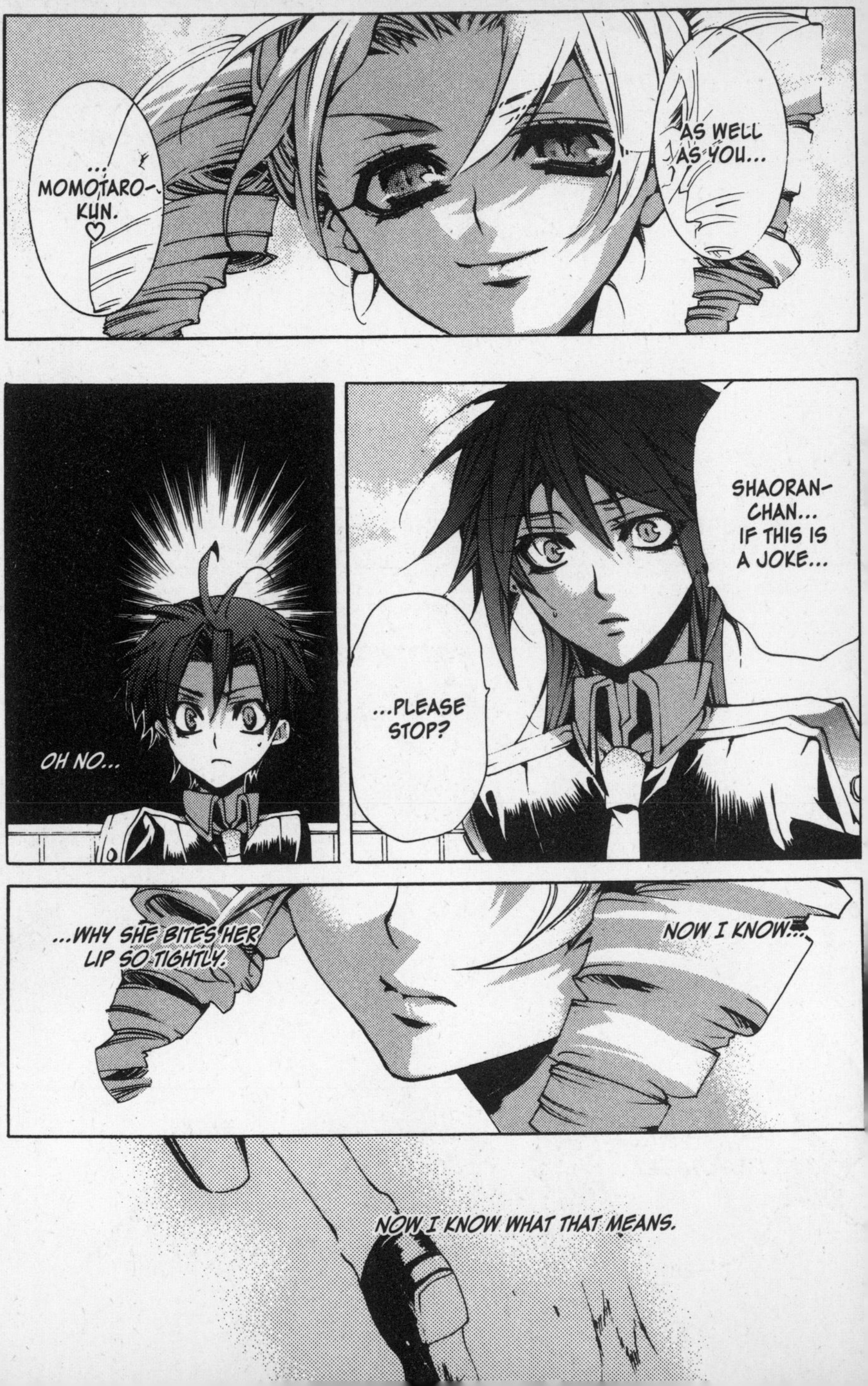
AS WELL AS YOU...
...MOMOTARO-KUN. ♡
SHAORAN-CHAN... IF THIS IS A JOKE...
...PLEASE STOP?
OH NO...
NOW I KNOW...
...WHY SHE BITES HER LIP SO TIGHTLY.
NOW I KNOW WHAT THAT MEANS.

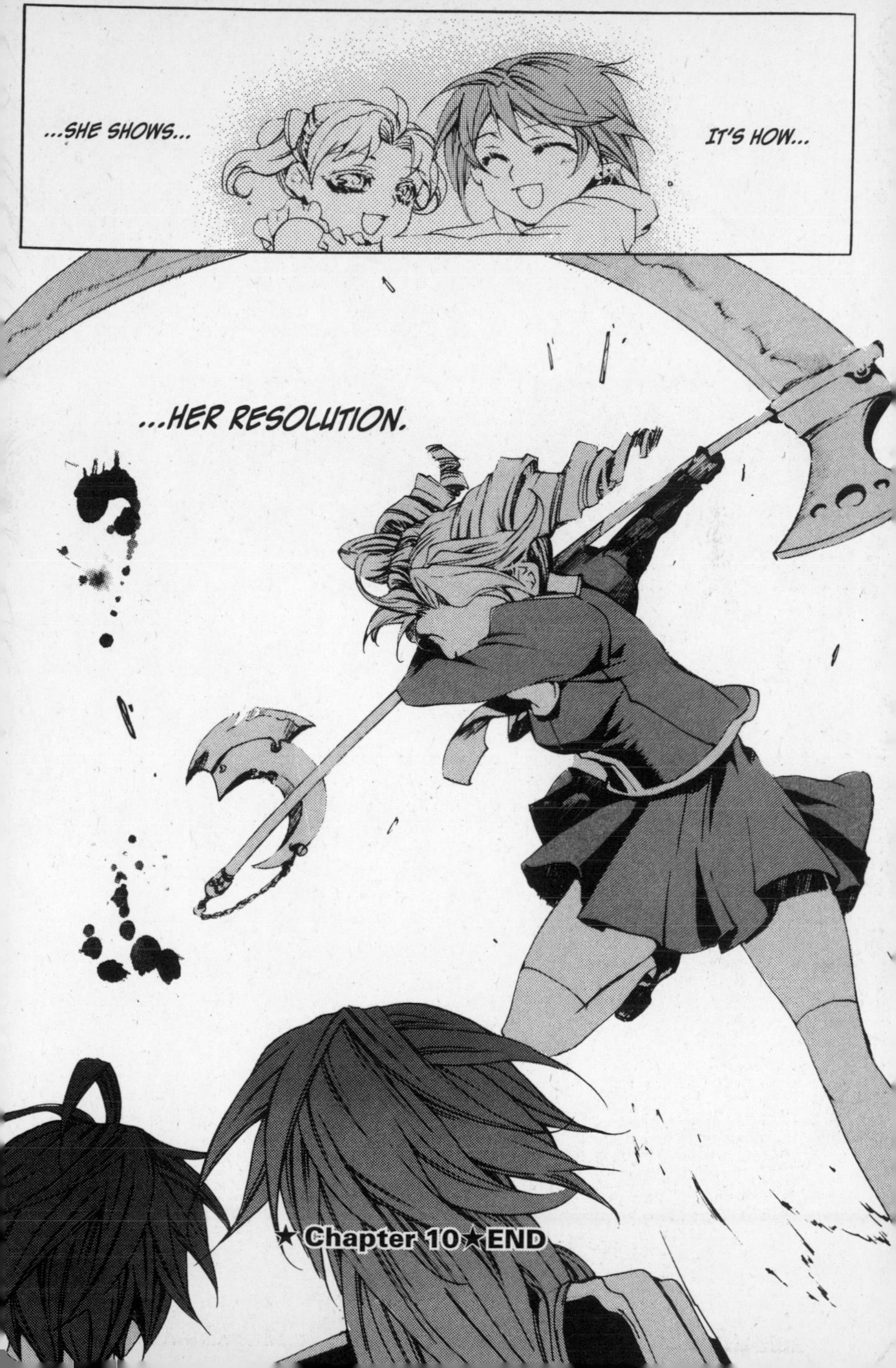
IT'S HOW...
...SHE SHOWS...
...HER RESOLUTION.
★ Chapter 10★END

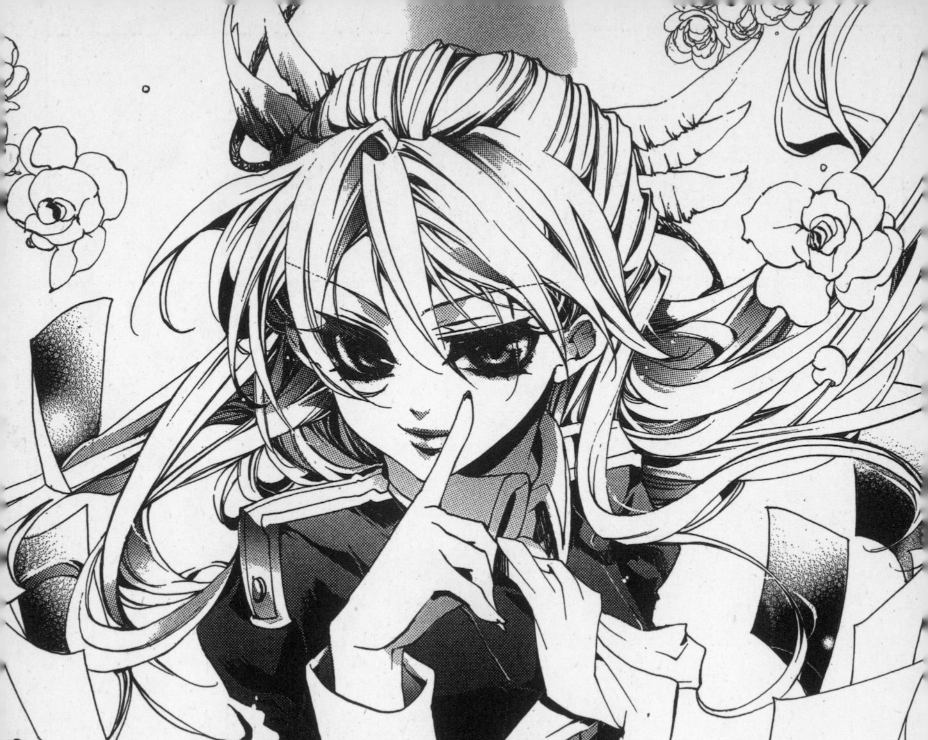

Bonus Chapter: The Hunting Zone of the Imaginative Girl

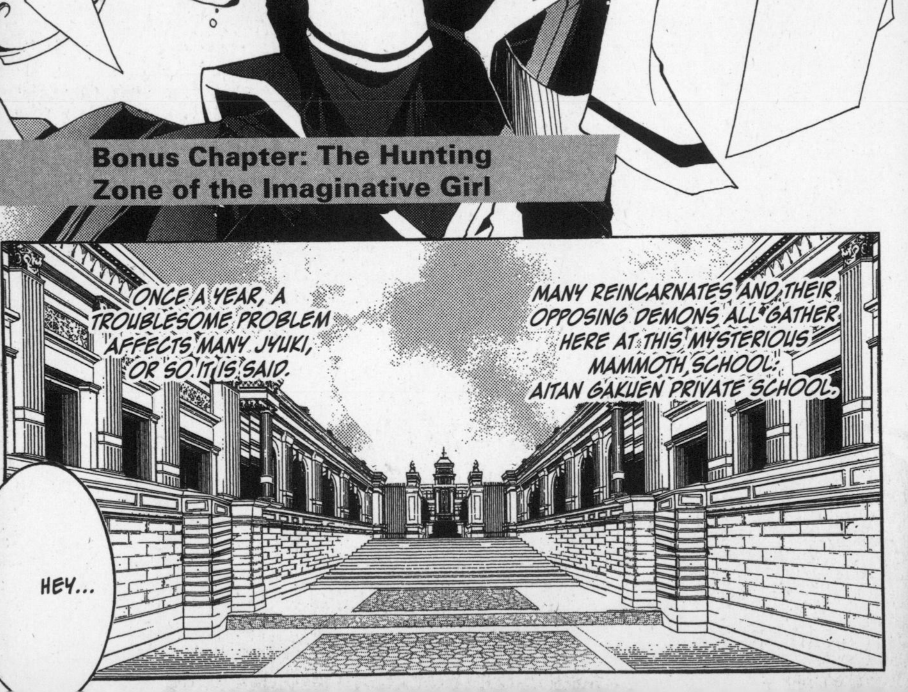
MANY REINCARNATES AND THEIR OPPOSING DEMONS ALL GATHER HERE AT THIS MYSTERIOUS MAMMOTH SCHOOL: AITAN GAKUEN PRIVATE SCHOOL.
ONCE A YEAR, A TROUBLESOME PROBLEM AFFECTS MANY JYUKI, OR SO IT IS SAID.
HEY...

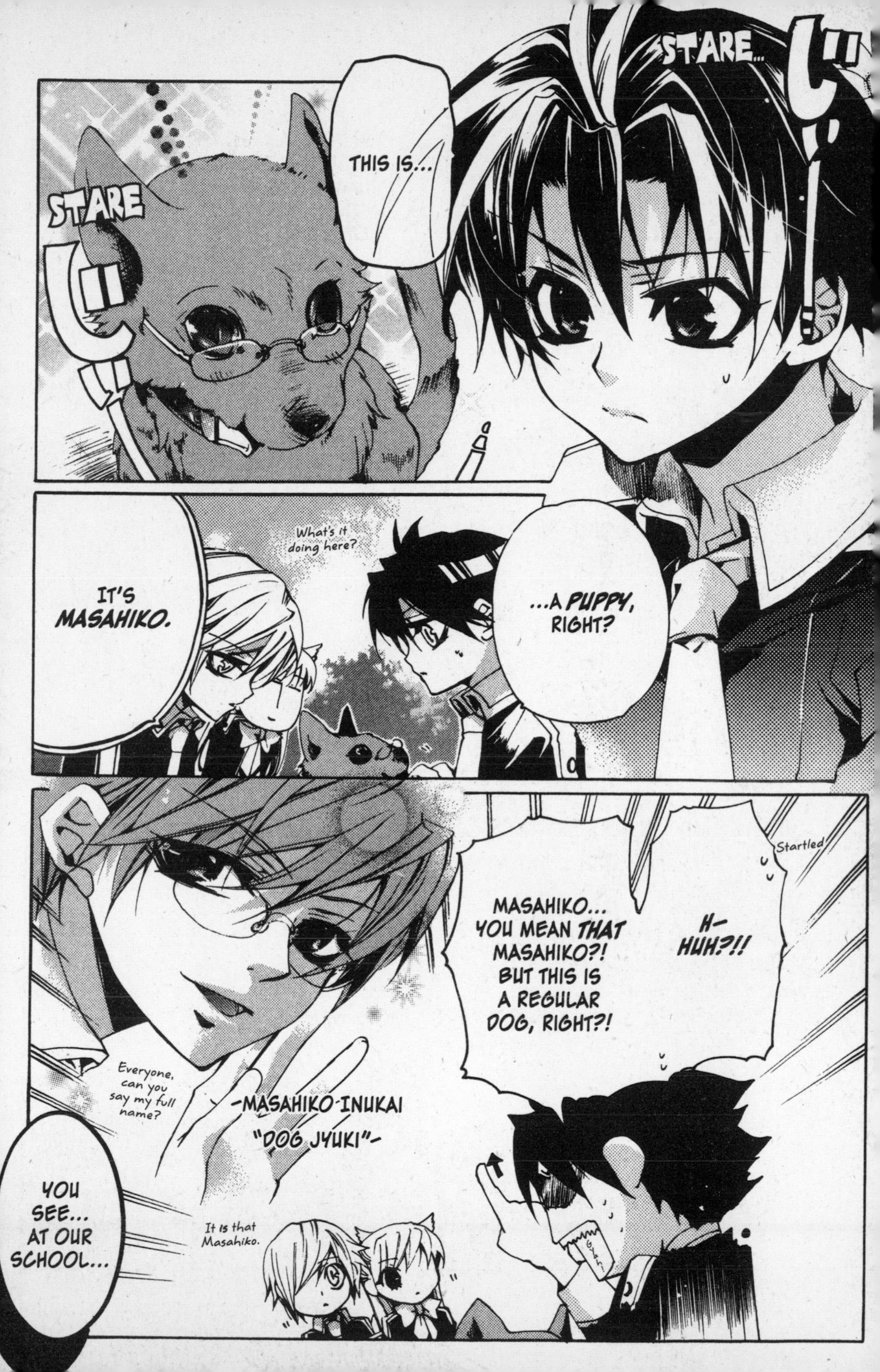

STARE...
THIS IS...
STARE
...A PUPPY, RIGHT?
What's it doing here?
IT'S MASAHIKO.
Startled
H-HUH?!!
MASAHIKO... YOU MEAN THAT MASAHIKO?! BUT THIS IS A REGULAR DOG, RIGHT?!
Everyone, can you say my full name?
-MASAHIKO INUKAI "DOG JYUKI"-
It is that Masahiko.
YOU SEE... AT OUR SCHOOL...

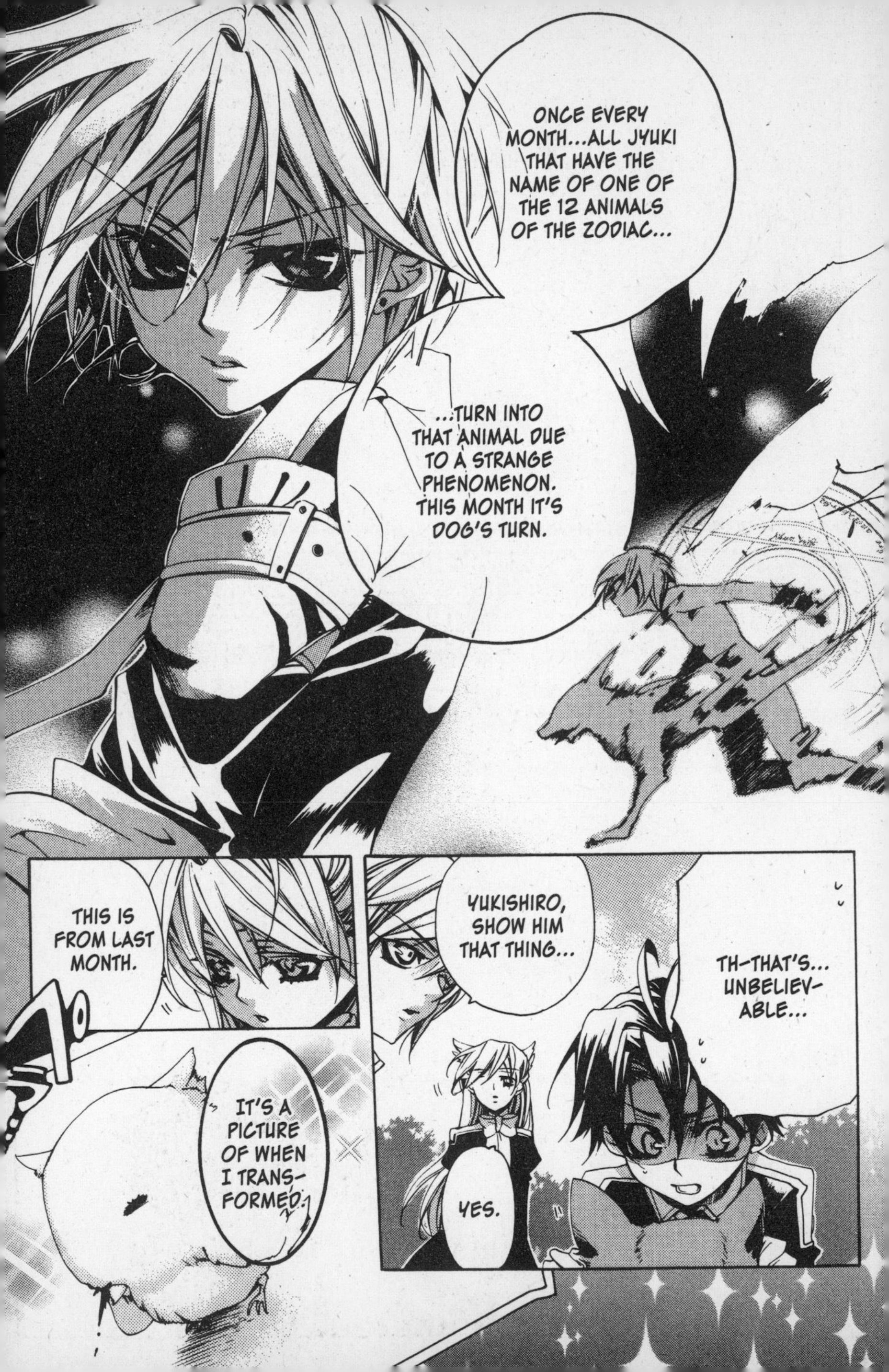

ONCE EVERY MONTH...ALL JYUKI THAT HAVE THE NAME OF ONE OF THE 12 ANIMALS OF THE ZODIAC...
...TURN INTO THAT ANIMAL DUE TO A STRANGE PHENOMENON. THIS MONTH IT'S DOG'S TURN.
TH-THAT'S... UNBELIEV-ABLE...
YUKISHIRO, SHOW HIM THAT THING...
YES.
THIS IS FROM LAST MONTH.
IT'S A PICTURE OF WHEN I TRANS-FORMED.

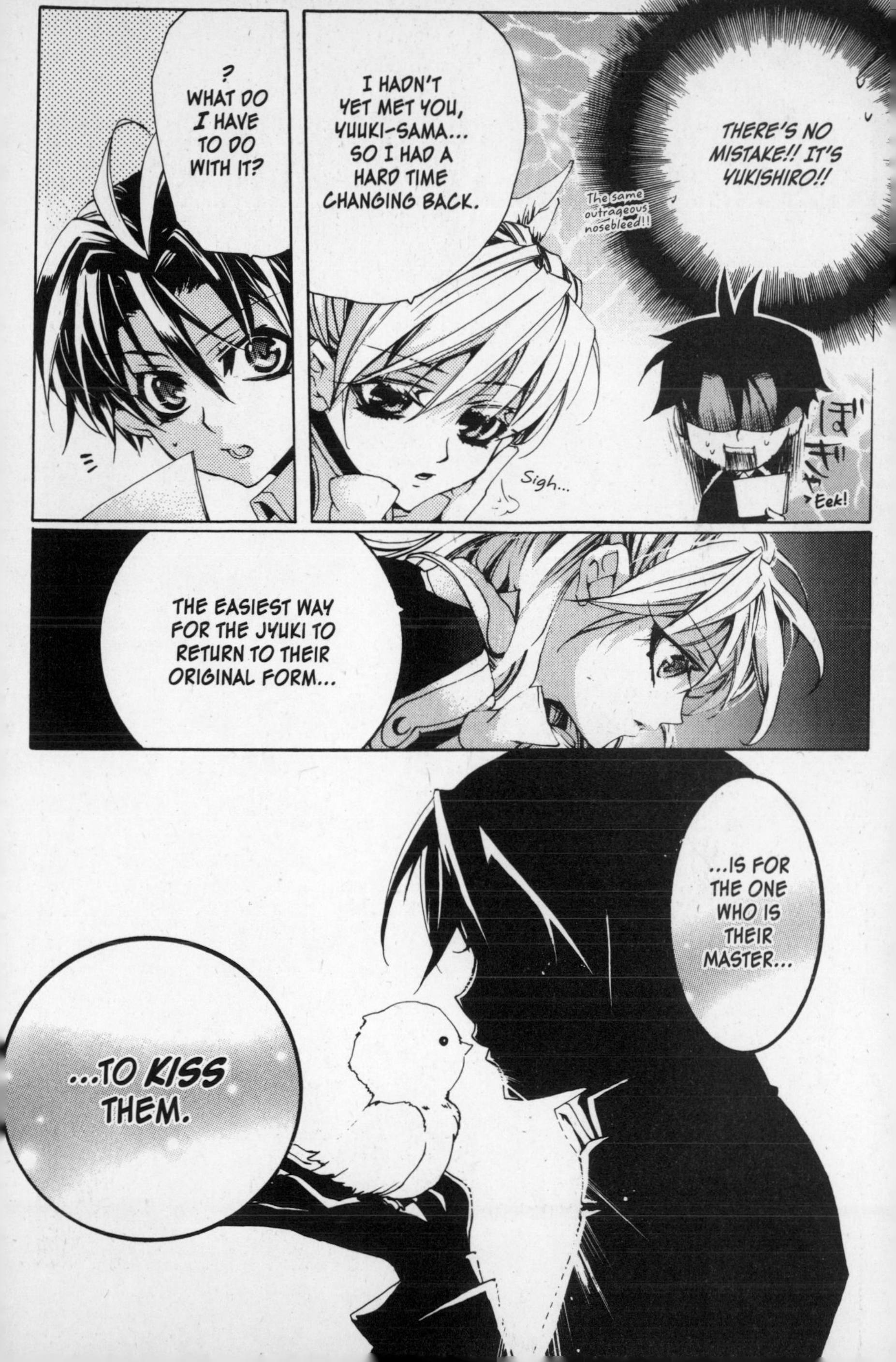

THERE'S NO MISTAKE!! IT'S YUKISHIRO!!
I HADN'T YET MET YOU, YUUKI-SAMA... SO I HAD A HARD TIME CHANGING BACK.
The same outrageous nosebleed!!
ぼぎゃ
Eek!
Sigh...
? WHAT DO I HAVE TO DO WITH IT?
THE EASIEST WAY FOR THE JYUKI TO RETURN TO THEIR ORIGINAL FORM...
...IS FOR THE ONE WHO IS THEIR MASTER...
...TO KISS THEM.

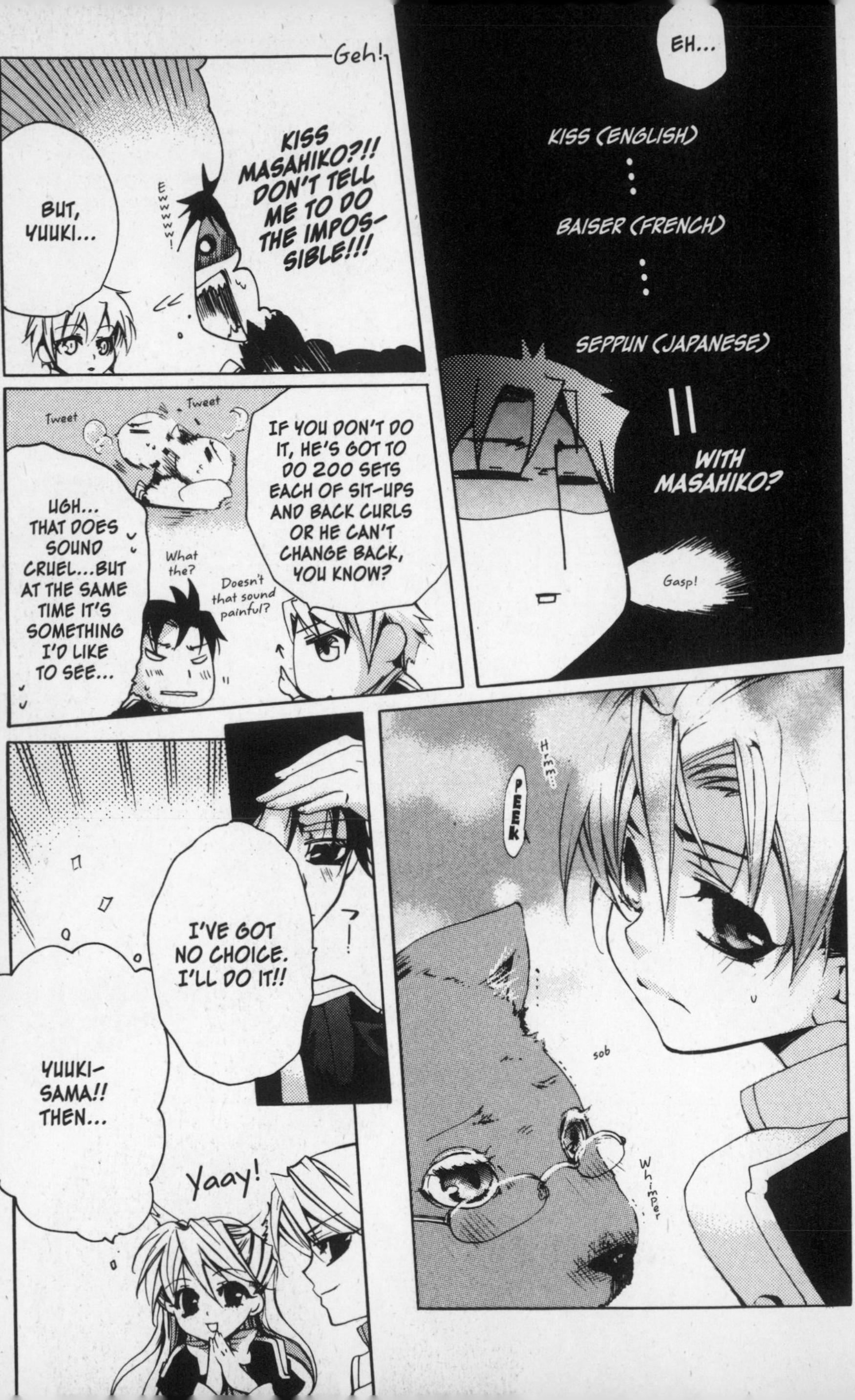
EH...
KISS (ENGLISH)
...
BAISER (FRENCH)
...
SEPPUN (JAPANESE)
=
WITH MASAHIKO?
Gasp!
Geh!
KISS MASAHIKO?!! DON'T TELL ME TO DO THE IMPOSSIBLE!!!
Ewwwww!
BUT, YUUKI...
Tweet
Tweet
IF YOU DON'T DO IT, HE'S GOT TO DO 200 SETS EACH OF SIT-UPS AND BACK CURLS OR HE CAN'T CHANGE BACK, YOU KNOW?
Doesn't that sound painful?
What the?
UGH... THAT DOES SOUND CRUEL...BUT AT THE SAME TIME IT'S SOMETHING I'D LIKE TO SEE...
Hrmm...
PEEK
sob
Whimper
I'VE GOT NO CHOICE. I'LL DO IT!!
YUUKI-SAMA!! THEN...
Yaay!

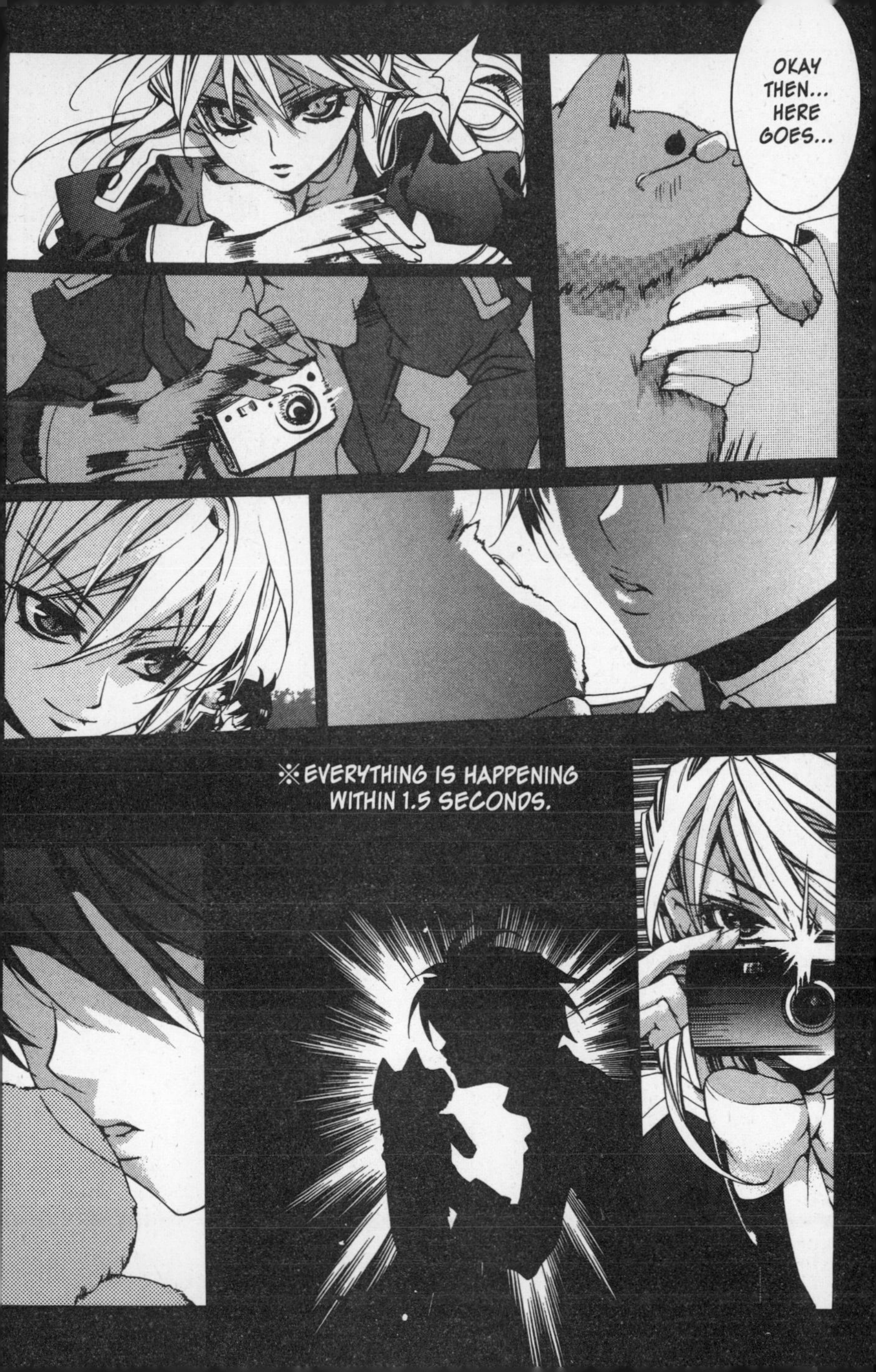
OKAY THEN... HERE GOES...
※EVERYTHING IS HAPPENING WITHIN 1.5 SECONDS.

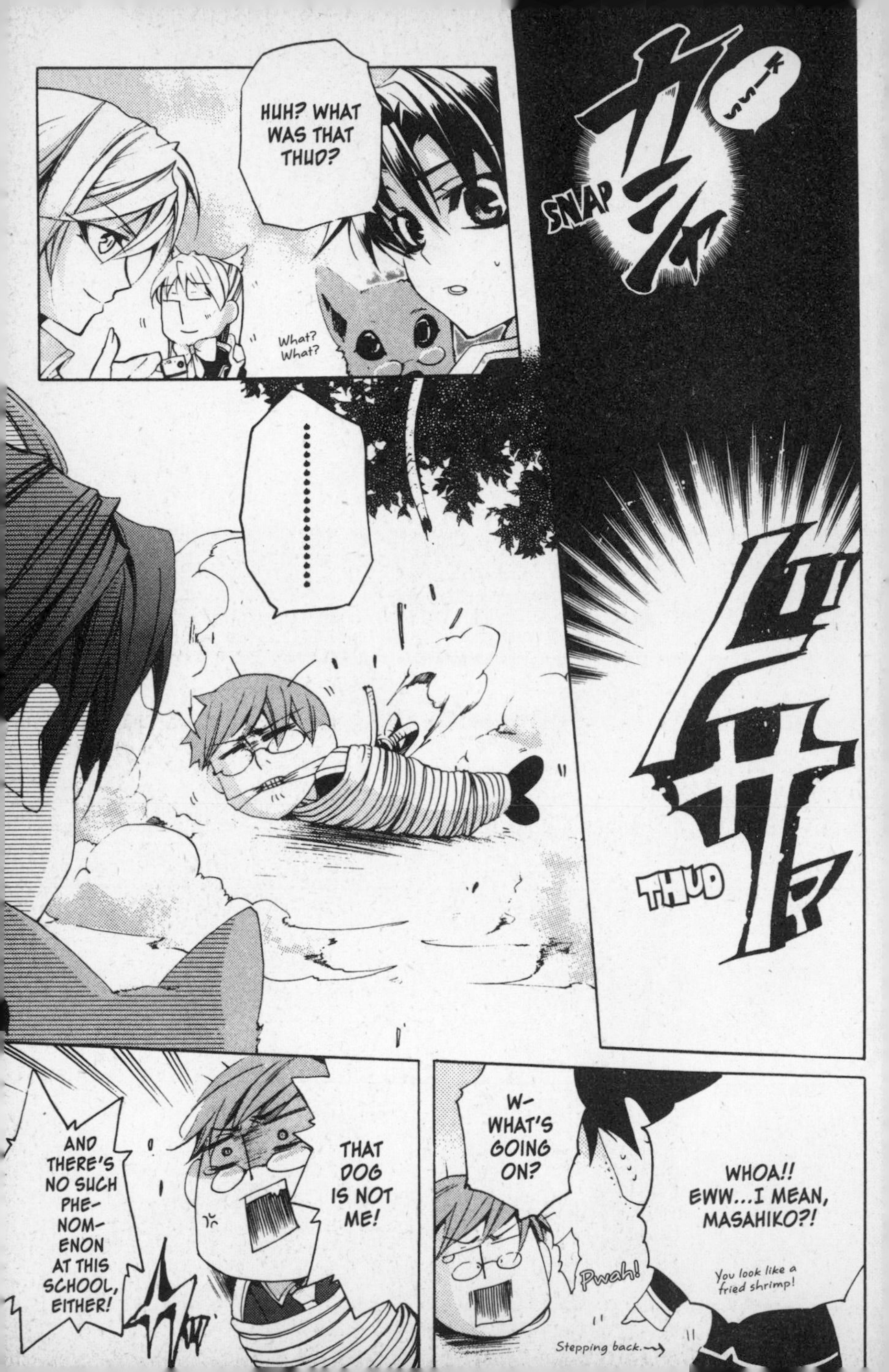
K—sss
SNAP
THUD
HUH? WHAT WAS THAT THUD?
What? What?
......
WHOA!! EWW...I MEAN, MASAHIKO?!
You look like a fried shrimp!
W-WHAT'S GOING ON?
Pwah!
Stepping back.
THAT DOG IS NOT ME!
AND THERE'S NO SUCH PHE-NOM-ENON AT THIS SCHOOL, EITHER!

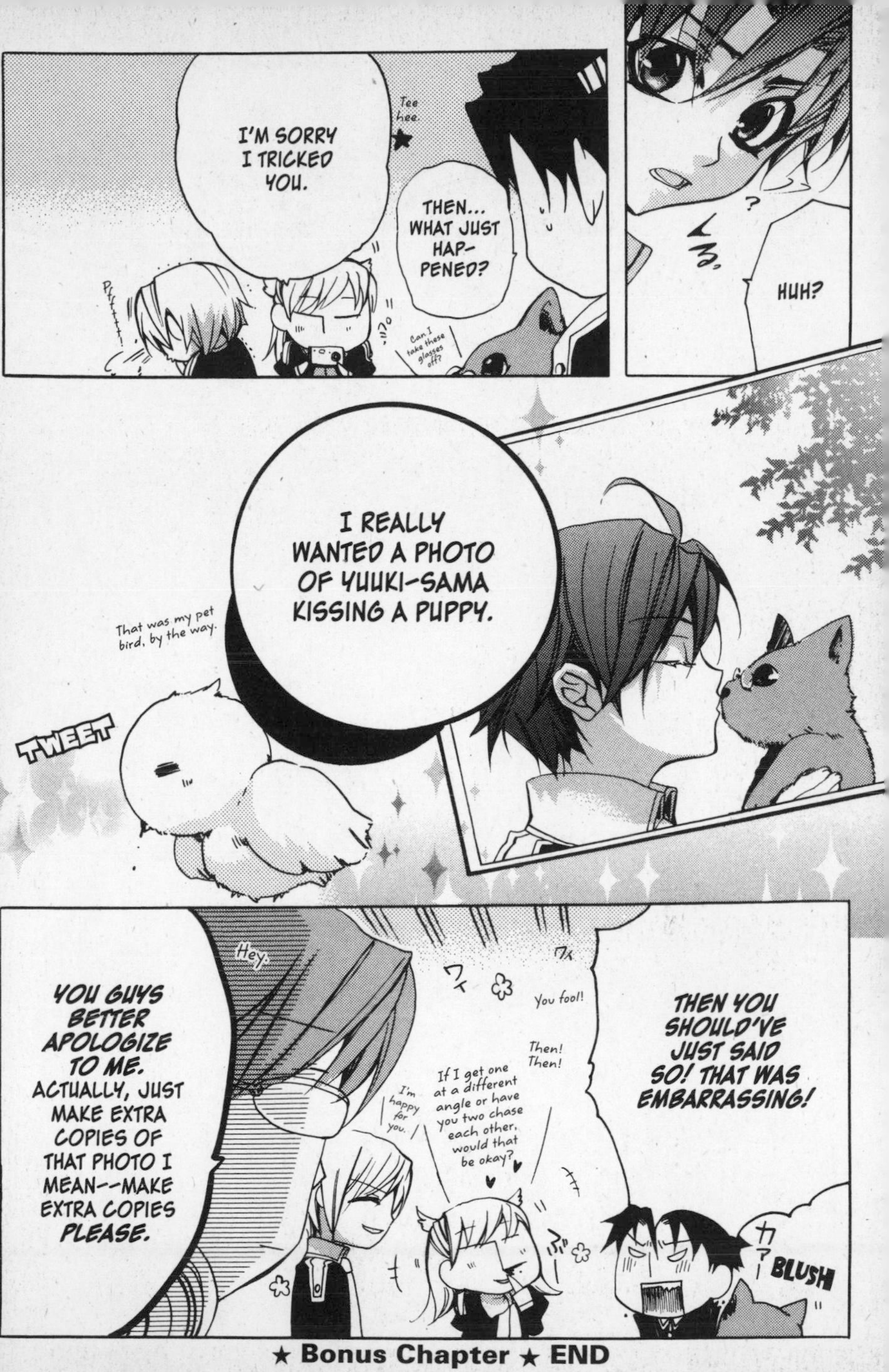
HUH?
THEN... WHAT JUST HAP-PENED?
I'M SORRY I TRICKED YOU.
Tee hee.
Can I take these glasses off?
I REALLY WANTED A PHOTO OF YUUKI-SAMA KISSING A PUPPY.
That was my pet bird, by the way.
TWEET
THEN YOU SHOULD'VE JUST SAID SO! THAT WAS EMBARRASSING!
You fool!
Then! Then!
If I get one at a different angle or have you two chase each other, would that be okay?
I'm happy for you.
Hey.
YOU GUYS BETTER APOLOGIZE TO ME. ACTUALLY, JUST MAKE EXTRA COPIES OF THAT PHOTO I MEAN--MAKE EXTRA COPIES PLEASE.
BLUSH

★ Bonus Chapter ★ END

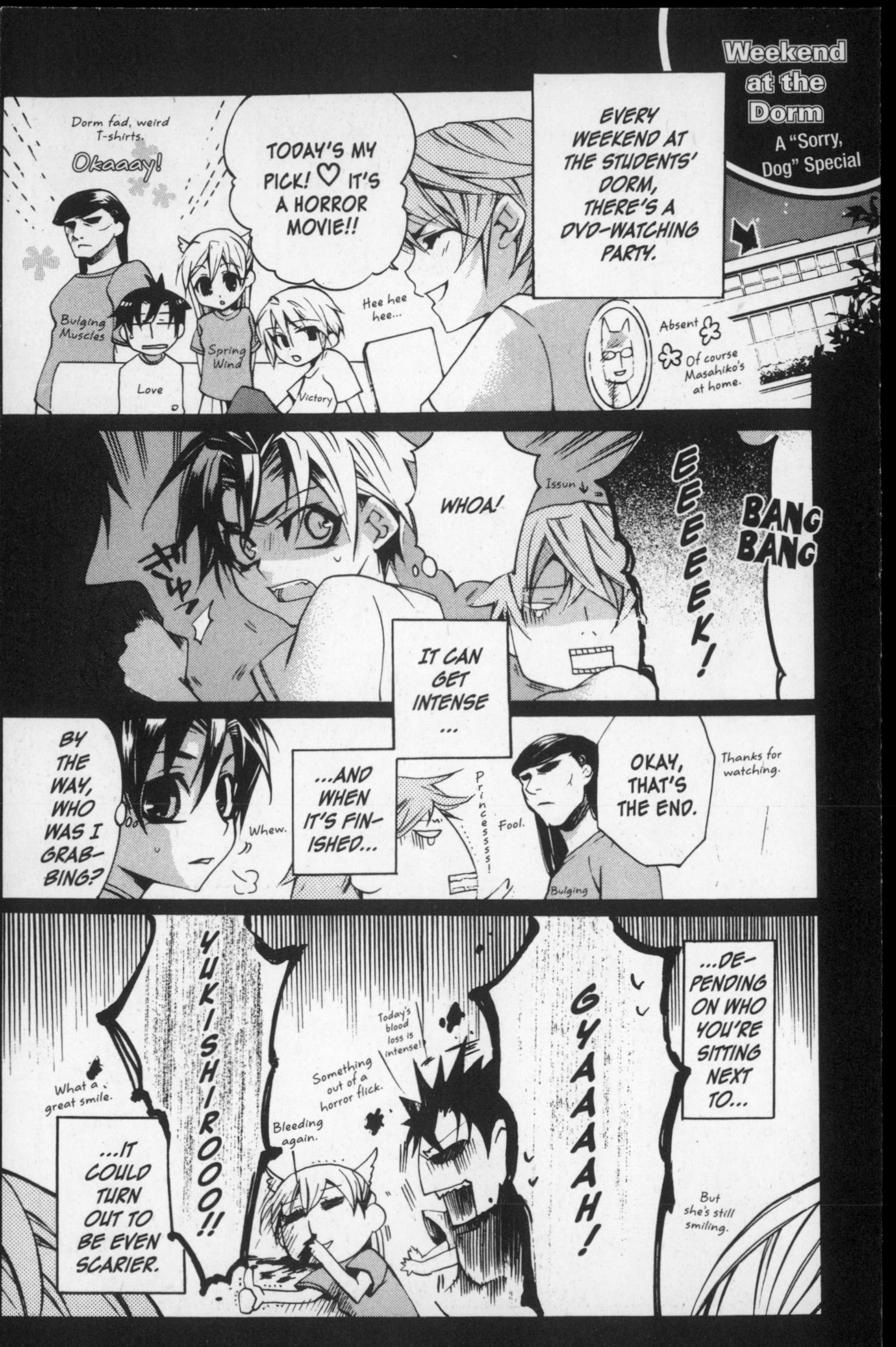
Weekend at the Dorm
A "Sorry, Dog" Special
Absent
Of course Masahiko's at home.
EVERY WEEKEND AT THE STUDENTS' DORM, THERE'S A DVD-WATCHING PARTY.
Hee hee hee...
TODAY'S MY PICK! ♡ IT'S A HORROR MOVIE!!
Dorm fad, weird T-shirts.
Okaaay!
Victory
Spring Wind
Love
Bulging Muscles
BANG BANG
EEEEEEEK!
Issun
WHOA!
IT CAN GET INTENSE...
Thanks for watching.
OKAY, THAT'S THE END.
Bulging
Fool.
Princesssss!
...AND WHEN IT'S FINISHED...
Whew.
BY THE WAY, WHO WAS I GRABBING?
...DEPENDING ON WHO YOU'RE SITTING NEXT TO...
But she's still smiling.
GYAAAAH!
Today's blood loss is intense!!
Something out of a horror flick.
Bleeding again.
YUKISHIROOOO!!
What a great smile.
...IT COULD TURN OUT TO BE EVEN SCARIER.

Postscript

•It's the second volume. This is Eri Sakondo. The characters in this volume are brought to you by blond hair and ringlets. ♥ Hee hee hee! I just can't get enough of them! ♥

•It ends on a cliffhanger at such a crucial point, but after this there should be more of a plot and all the characters' backgrounds will be weaved into the story, so please stick with it.

All right then, I pray that we can meet again in the next volume!

Eri Sakondo

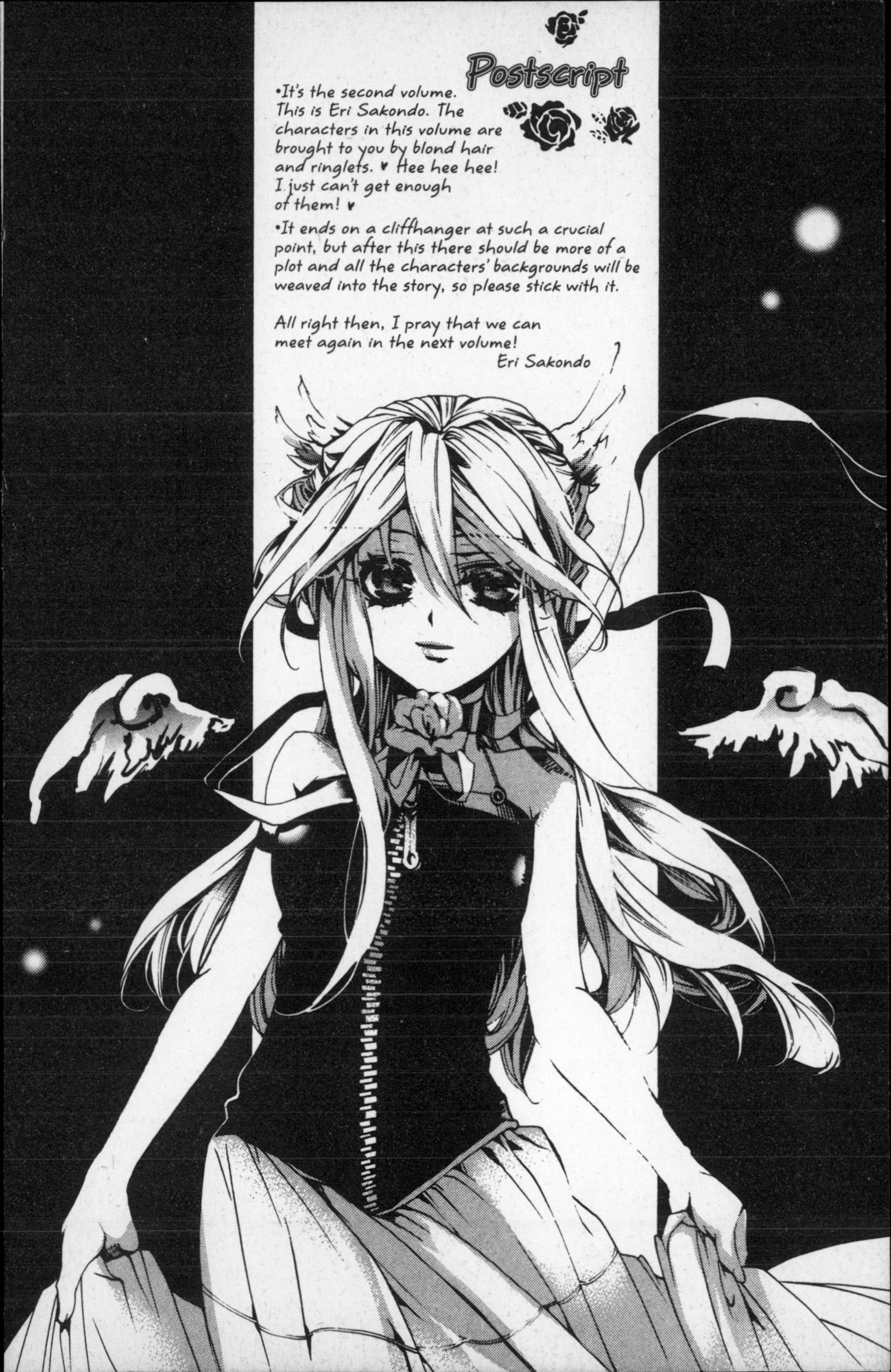

SPECIAL THANKS

- The editorial staff.
- My editor, Debi-Kita-sama.
- MR-san, G-san.
- K-san.
- My family. Kangaroo-san.
- Neko-san.

AND YOU

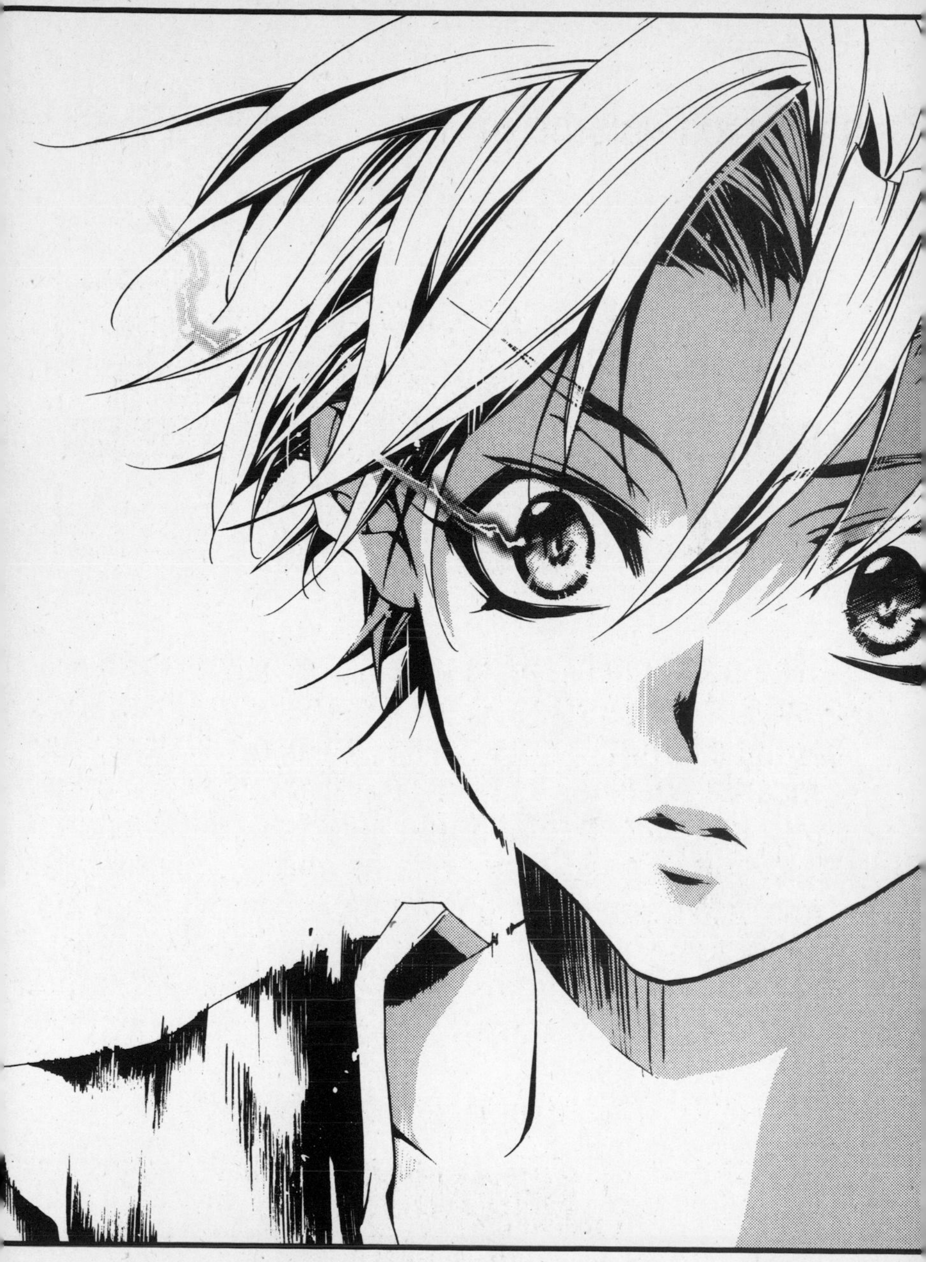

In the next volume of

MOMOGUMI PLUS SENKI

The traditional Japanese fable reveals the other side of the story as Yuuki's battle with Shaoran continues. Amidst the chaos, he discovers the true meaning behind the Red Demon's betrayal along with the history of Shaoran and Ko's relationship. Will Yuuki's good intentions be enough to create a way that makes everyone happy while breaking his curse at the same time? With friends and enemies assembling on the frontline, will the Red Demon and Blue Demon fable reach a new conclusion?!

The adventure continues in

Volume 3!

D·N·ANGEL·

The secret of the Hikari/Niwa curse is revealed!

The time has come for Satoshi to reveal to Daisuke the history behind the Hikari/Niwa curse. How will Daisuke respond when he finds out why Satoshi is destined to die so young? Meanwhile, another fight breaks out against Argentine, sending Daisuke spiraling toward death as he tries to rescue Risa...

VOLUME 13 • YUKIRU SUGISAKI

FANTASY

T TEEN AGE 13+

Happy CAFE

Enjoy VOL 1

Today's Specials

Romance, Happiness, General Wackiness

Happy
CAFE
Enjoy
VOL 1
TOKYOPOP
ART NOT FINAL
Kou Matsuzuki

Uru takes her mother's remarriage as an opportunity to work part time at the Happy Café. There, she befriends Ichirou and Shindou, two of the most unsociable guys she's ever met! To make matters worse, it turns out that Uru is not exactly meant for the waitressing world, as she's a HUGE clutz. But as this hilarious shojo tale unfolds, true happiness—and even true love—lurk just around the corner...

If you like Maid Sama! and V.B. Rose, you'll love Happy Café!

BE SURE TO VISIT WWW.TOKYOPOP.COM/SHOP FOR EVERYTHING YOU COULD EVER WANT!

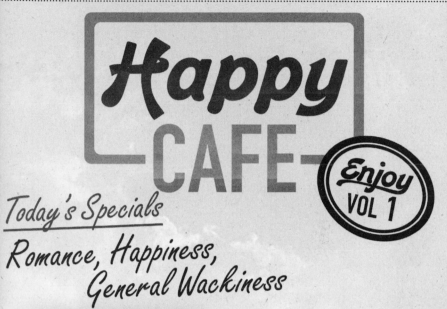

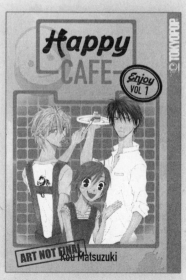

Nobody ever said
finding a soul mate
would be easy!

Maria Holic

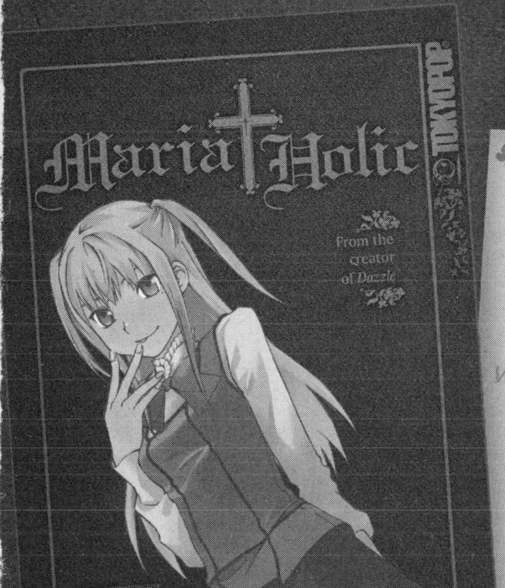
Maria Holic
TOKYOPOP
From the creator of Dazzle
Minari ENDOU
Book ONE

Because of her phobia of men, Kanako enrolls in an all-girls school to find her one true love. When she meets a captivating freshman named Mariya who fits her criteria, it turns out that her seemingly ideal mate happens to be a cross-dressing sadistic boy!

Can things get any worse?!

From Minari ENDOU, creator of the fan favorite Dazzle!

BE SURE TO VISIT WWW.TOKYOPOP.COM/SHOP FOR EVERYTHING YOU COULD EVER WANT!

STOP!

This is the back of the book.
You wouldn't want to spoil a great ending!

This book is printed "manga-style," in the authentic Japanese right-to-left format. Since none of the artwork has been flipped or altered, readers get to experience the story just as the creator intended. You've been asking for it, so TOKYOPOP® delivered: authentic, hot-off-the-press, and far more fun!

DIRECTIONS

If this is your first time reading manga-style, here's a quick guide to help you understand how it works.

It's easy... just start in the top right panel and follow the numbers. Have fun, and look for more 100% authentic manga from TOKYOPOP®!